OXFORD THEOLOGY AND RELIGION MONOGRAPHS

OXFORD THEOLOGY AND RELIGION MONOGRAPHS

Corporeal Theology

*Accommodating Theological Understanding
to Embodied Thinkers*

TOBIAS TANTON

OXFORD
UNIVERSITY PRESS

OXFORD
UNIVERSITY PRESS

Great Clarendon Street, Oxford, OX2 6DP,
United Kingdom

Oxford University Press is a department of the University of Oxford.
It furthers the University's objective of excellence in research, scholarship,
and education by publishing worldwide. Oxford is a registered trade mark of
Oxford University Press in the UK and in certain other countries

First Edition published in 2023

Impression: 1

Published in the United States of America by Oxford University Press
198 Madison Avenue, New York, NY 10016, United States of America

British Library Cataloguing in Publication Data
Data available

Library of Congress Control Number: 2022939696

ISBN 978–0–19–288458–9

DOI: 10.1093/oso/9780192884589.001.0001

Printed and bound by
CPI Group (UK) Ltd, Croydon, CR0 4YY

Contents

Acknowledgements

Cognition, if this thesis is to be believed, is *not* restricted to an isolated brain, but relies on countless interactions with the outside world and is scaffolded by invaluable environmental resources. To begin this work by acknowledging my trusty scaffolds, without whom the cognitive task of writing this thesis would not have been possible, is therefore only too fitting.

Sarah Tanton not only arduously proofread an early draft but was also a true partner in bearing the weight of writing-up stresses. Ulrich Schmiedel and Philip Fountain both devoted more time than they had to offer insightful comments on a draft. Rachel Neaum helpfully checked over eleventh-hour additions.

Graham Ward supervised both my masters and doctoral work during the five years in which this project took shape. I am grateful for his guidance and the theological community he created at the faculty. There are too many contributors to the current project in this lively Oxford community to name, but colleagues who provided solid buttresses throughout include Andrew Bowyer, Jonathan Jong, Emily Kempson, Ulrich Schmiedel, Samuel Shearn, and Simeon Zahl.

Numerous other communities constituted examples of 'cognitive coupling'. The Chapel at New College, Oxford and the Parish Church of St Mary Magdalen, Oxford provided 'laboratories' in which to participate in embodied practices; I am grateful to Erica Longfellow and Peter Groves, together with the many others who allow these communities to embody such sublime theological reflection. The Ertegun Programme has, in my estimation, lived up to its ambitions of creating an energetic interdisciplinary forum in the humanities and horizon-broadening cultural exposure. I am deeply appreciative of the ever-supportive Bryan Ward-Perkins who forged this community, Jill Walker, and all fellow Ertegunians.

A number of generous benefactors in effect provided the food and shelter upon which this body relied. I am especially grateful for the creation of the Arthur Peacocke Graduate Scholarship in Science and Theology and to Rosemary Peacocke for her kind encouragement. The Ertegun Graduate Scholarship Programme funded the MPhil project which seeded this work, and munificently continued to provide a beautiful workspace for the duration of this project; so I once again find myself indebted to the visionary philanthropy of Mica Ertegun. A St Luke's College Foundation Personal Award was helpful in making ends meet in the final year.

Tobias Tanton
The Feast of Epiphany 2022

Introduction

When the Covid-19 pandemic raced around the globe in March 2020, many
governments swiftly imposed lockdowns and other social distancing measures.
Among the numerous social practices which were disrupted was, of course, communal acts of Christian worship. Churches closed their doors, and Christians, for
a time, ceased to gather in person as had been their custom since the movement's
inception. Those with the technological know-how and requisite digital connect-
ivity (a luxury of the more affluent regions of the world) rapidly shifted their worship to gathering in online spaces.[1] Thus began a bold experiment, born out of
the necessity of avoiding a deadly contagion, in radically altering the character of
Christian worship.

One of the most pronounced features of this sudden shift was a dramatic
change in how *bodies* worshipped. The previous 'centrality of face-to-face and
intimate gatherings typically associated with nearly all religious practices and traditions'[2] was overturned. Worshippers no longer co-located their bodies in
purpose-built liturgical spaces; they no longer moved about such spaces in set
ways: kneeling, processing, singing, dancing, or performing other ritual activities;
they no longer exchanged handshakes or glances; they no longer gazed upon or
touched the material objects which fill worshipping environments; and they no
longer consumed Eucharistic bread and wine.

This is not to say that worshippers became disembodied. There were still bodies at the end of video calls and faces peering into webcams. Some attempted to
replicate or translate bodily practices in their own homes. Many struggled with
fatigue, perhaps caused in part by the particular embodiments typically associated with video calls: intensive close-up eye contact, the cognitive load of attempting to process gestures and non-verbal cues, the mirroring effect of 'self-views',
and the limitations of mobility imposed by a camera's field of vision.[3] Nevertheless,
the customary embodied interactions became severely limited by virtue of having
to be channelled through video cameras to remote locations.

These altered forms of pandemic worship brought into sharp relief the bodily
dimension of Christian worship which can all too easily be taken for granted.

---

[1] Joseph O. Baker et al., 'Religion in the Age of Social Distancing: How Covid-19 Presents New
Directions for Research', *Sociology of Religion* 81, no. 4 (2020).
[2] Ibid., 358.
[3] Jeremy N. Bailenson, 'Nonverbal Overload: A Theoretical Argument for the Causes of Zoom
Fatigue', *Technology, Mind, and Behavior* 2, no. 1 (2021).

Corporeal Theology: Accommodating Theological Understanding to Embodied Thinkers. Tobias Tanton,
Oxford University Press. © Tobias Tanton 2023. DOI: 10.1093/oso/9780192884589.003.0001

Many of the things which happen in worship could not be captured in a broadcast format or replicated in a two-dimensional remote interaction. In sacramental traditions, debates raged about the theological status of watching a Eucharist performed on screen: Were viewers participating even if they could not receive the material objects? Were these private masses? Could reviving the categories such as spiritual communion provide a timely framework for understanding what was happening? What did it mean to undertake (involuntarily) a Eucharistic fast? In traditions which emphasised sacramental worship less, the changes were no less dramatic as technologically mediated religiosity providing new limitations and opportunities. Say what you will about pandemic religion, but it simply was not the same, and the difference largely came down to changes in embodiment and materiality.

This book is not ultimately about the Covid-19 pandemic or religious adaptions to it. (It was largely prepared before the pandemic struck). However, it does deal with the embodied nature of religion and its theological import. Embodiment is easily neglected in favour other facets of religion, such as ideas, beliefs, sacred texts, etc. But when a pandemic strikes, we quickly realise that the bodily and material aspects of religion are too often taken for granted.

1 Theologising as Embodied Creatures

As with religion in general, the fact that theological understanding is the purview of *embodied* creatures is easily overlooked. Our conscious experience, interpreted through a western enlightenment paradigm, suggests that a kind of rational homunculus (a miniature person controlling the body) surveys its surroundings, formulates reasoned plans, and dispatches commands for behavioural responses.[4] This homunculus operates at arm's length from the body; the body is merely a tool to gather information and manipulate the environment; it never constrains or influences the process of rational deliberation. Recent developments in cognitive science, however, challenge such a portrait of cognition. The emerging paradigm of 'embodied cognition' suggests that cognition is profoundly shaped by the particularities of the body. Bodily postures, movements, interactions, facial expressions, and environmental factors have been shown to influence cognition, often in subtle ways which evade conscious awareness. Moreover, a greater understanding of cognitive processes has revealed ways in which they are deeply dependent on the body and its sensorimotor systems, both to represent the external world and to exploit the cognitive resources it offers.

---

[4] See, for example, Andy Clark, *Being There: Putting Brain, Body, and World Together Again* (Cambridge, MA: MIT Press, 1997), 98, 215.

This study explores the implications of this revised—or, as some claim, revolutionised—understanding of cognition for theological understanding. Accounts of religion have historically focused on cerebral phenomena, such as concepts, beliefs, and doctrines. Embodied cognition suggests that these aspects of religion cannot be conceived of independently of the body, and indeed the bodily aspects of religion, such as ritual practices, have their own cognitive import. Theological thinking has often been considered as being among the most cerebral and abstract facets of religion. However, this study will argue that theological understanding, too, is shaped by embodiment: theological concepts are grounded in our embodied experience and, conversely, the bodily practices of religion impinge on—and indeed participate in—the process of theological reflection. As a result, *theology is corporeal*.

2 Situating Corporeal Theology among Contemporary Scholarship

A confluence of developments in cognitive science, religious studies, and theology makes this study particularly timely. In particular, each of these disciplines have shown a renewed interest in the *bodily* nature of human beings. In each case, the pivot to embodiment is concomitant with a critique of older paradigms which have marginalised, or outright ignored, the role of the body. If humans are rational animals, to take Boethius' classical definition, then past approaches to the human mind have emphasised the rational at the expense of the animal.[5]

In the cognitive sciences, the past few decades have seen the rise of 'embodied cognition'. Wilson and Galonka proclaim with unbridled enthusiasm that the theory that cognition is embodied is the 'most exciting hypothesis in cognitive science'.[6] Though a relatively new research programme, its hypotheses have generated hundreds, if not thousands, of empirical studies across the cognitive sciences, including experimental psychology, neuroimaging, brain lesion studies, artificial intelligence, robotics, and animal behaviour. The data unearthed by these studies has been synthesised into larger theoretical frameworks and its claims have been subject to philosophical scrutiny.

The broad movement of embodied cognition is united by a common conviction that cognition depends on, and is shaped by, the particularities of the human body. It rejects 'traditional cognitive science' for which the details of embodiment were largely irrelevant and 'central' cognition could primarily be understood in

---

[5] Boethius, *The Consolation of Philosophy*, trans. David R. Slavitt (Cambridge, MA: Harvard University Press, 2008), 162.
[6] Andrew D. Wilson and Sabrina Golonka, 'Embodied Cognition Is Not What You Think It Is', *Frontiers in Psychology* 4, no. 58 (2013): 1.

terms of manipulating abstract symbols. Instead it proposes that the bodily tasks of perception and action are deeply implicated in cognitive processes; and these bodily interfaces with the world allow cognition to extend out into the body and its environment. As some commentators remark: 'The idea that cognition is deeply rooted in what is possible, given our bodies, our physical environment, and the relationship between perception and action, is a sea change in cognitive science.'[7] The resulting picture is one in which cognition is deeply dependent on the human body, its particular morphology, sensorimotor capacities, and means of interacting with the world.

The discipline of religious studies has also seen a pivot towards embodiment in recent decades. As Soliman, Johnson, and Song observe, most prominent theories of religion over the past two centuries—including those of Sigmund Freud, William James, Emile Durkheim, Clifford Geertz—all share 'the underlying assumption that the mind is the locus of religiousness', thereby reflecting 'a Western bias'.[8] With mind at its centre (and 'mind' understood in terms of traditional cognitive science, rather than embodied cognition's reframing of it), religious studies has focused on the 'mental' aspects of religion, such as beliefs, concepts, and doctrines. Manuel Vásquez's monumental *More than Belief: A Materialist Theory of Religion* charts the genealogy of this focus on the mind, identifying the dominance of German Protestant scholarship, with its emphasis on faith and scriptural texts, as a key driver towards this very cerebral perspective on religion.[9]

In addition to charting the long eclipse of the body, Vásquez chronicles its re-emergence in the study of religion, himself proposing a material theory of religion. Recent theories reintroduce the role of the body in religion in multiple ways: they emphasise the role of emotion and affect, which are grounded in the body, in religious experience; they attended to the way in which religion deploys the body in ritual practices; they consider how religion implicates the physical world with its rich material culture.[10] Together these trajectories rehabilitate the bodily nature of religion—long neglected in favour of doxastic accounts—a development which Fuller terms as 'religion in the flesh'.[11]

---

[7] Autumn B. Hostetter and Martha W. Alibali, 'Visible Embodiment: Gestures as Simulated Action', *Psychonomic Bulletin & Review* 15, no. 3 (2008): 497.

[8] Tamer M. Soliman, Kathryn A. Johnson, and Hyunjin Song, 'It's Not 'All in Your Head': Understanding Religion from an Embodied Cognition Perspective', *Perspectives on Psychological Science* 10, no. 6 (2015): 853.

[9] Manuel A. Vásquez, *More Than Belief: A Materialist Theory of Religion* (Oxford: Oxford University Press, 2011).

[10] E.g., Robert C. Fuller, *Spirituality in the Flesh: Bodily Sources of Religious Experience* (Oxford: Oxford University Press, 2008); Donovan O. Schaefer, *Religious Affects: Animality, Evolution, and Power* (Durham: Duke University Press, 2015).

[11] Robert C. Fuller, 'Faith of the Flesh: Bodily Sources of Spirituality', *Religious Studies Review* 31, no. 3–4 (2005): 135. This phrase gestures towards George Lakoff and Mark Johnson, *Philosophy in the Flesh: The Embodied Mind and Its Challenge to Western Thought* (New York: Basic Books, 1999).

The final discipline in the triad, theology, has likewise experienced a corporeal turn. In recent years, the first instalments of influential systematic theologies have foregrounded embodiment in their methodologies.[12] 'Contextual' theologies, which attend to concrete situations of oppression, have interrogated a wide variety of embodiments.[13] Particular theological anthropologies have sought to highlight the formative character of embodied liturgical practices.[14] The materiality of religion is likewise receiving renewed attention through treatments of ritual objects and sacred spaces.[15] Theologians are again attending to the emotional dimension of religion.[16] While theological accounts of language have typically focused on how language encodes concepts and beliefs, Rowan Williams' Gifford Lectures examine the bodily nature of language.[17] Even the philosophy of religion, which almost exclusively focused on the intellectual claims of religion, has begun to attend to bodily practices.[18]

Theology has not only returned to the theme of embodiment, but many theologians have also turned towards empirical accounts of actual bodily practices instead of relying on idealised versions of them (thereby overlapping with methodological approaches in religious studies and anthropology). This has sparked an interest in ethnography and sociological investigations among theologians and theological ethicists.[19] An interest in the particular is complemented by the emergence of contextual theologies and 'world Christianities', which highlight the insufficiencies of universalising accounts. These theologies no longer operate at an arm's length from lived religion, but engage its particularities, including how it orchestrates human bodies and material environments.

[12] Sarah Coakley, *God, Sexuality and the Self: An Essay 'on the Trinity'* (Cambridge: Cambridge University Press, 2013); Graham Ward, *How the Light Gets In: Ethical Life I* (Oxford: Oxford University Press, 2016).

[13] See Conclusion, Section 3 for numerous examples.

[14] James K. A. Smith, *Desiring the Kingdom: Worship, Worldview, and Cultural Formation* (Grand Rapids, MI: Baker Academic, 2009); James K. A. Smith, *Imagining the Kingdom: How Worship Works* (Grand Rapids MI: Baker Academic, 2013); Warren S. Brown and Brad D. Strawn, *The Physical Nature of Christian Life: Neuroscience, Psychology, and the Church* (Cambridge: Cambridge University Press, 2012).

[15] Mark Wynn, *Faith and Place: An Essay in Embodied Religious Epistemology* (Oxford: Oxford University Press, 2009); David Grumett, *Material Eucharist* (Oxford: Oxford University Press, 2016).

[16] Mark Wynn, *Emotional Experience and Religious Understanding: Integrating Perception, Conception and Feeling* (Cambridge: Cambridge University Press, 2005); Sarah Coakley, ed., *Faith, Rationality and the Passions* (Oxford: Wiley-Blackwell, 2012).

[17] Rowan Williams, *The Edge of Words: God and the Habits of Language* (London: Bloomsbury, 2014).

[18] E.g., Terence Cuneo, *Ritualized Faith: Essays on the Philosophy of Liturgy* (Oxford: Oxford University Press, 2016); Nicholas Wolterstorff, 'Knowing God Liturgically', *Journal of Analytic Theology* 4 (2016); Sarah Coakley, 'Beyond "Belief": Liturgy and the Cognitive Apprehension of God', in *The Vocation of Theology Today: A Festschrift for David Ford*, ed. Tom Greggs, Rachel Muers, and Simeon Zahl (Eugene OR: Wipf and Stock, 2013).

[19] Michael Banner, *The Ethics of Everyday Life: Moral Theology, Social Anthropology, and the Imagination of the Human* (Oxford: Oxford University Press, 2014); Coakley, *God, Sexuality and the Self*; Pete Ward, ed., *Perspectives on Ecclesiology and Ethnography* (Grand Rapids, MI: Eerdmans, 2012).

In addition to the common surge of interest in embodiment, interdisciplinary work among the triad of disciples has flourished. Cognitive science has not only taken an interest in embodiment, but it has also renewed its investigation of religion. The 'cognitive science of religion' (CSR) has become a growing subdiscipline and has attempted to isolate facets of religion which are tractable for empirical investigation. However, these research agendas have often presumed the traditional paradigms in cognitive science and religion; in keeping with a cognitivist paradigm and a doxastic-centric religion, they focus on the generation and dissemination of religious beliefs and concepts.[20] Recent articles have recognised the promise of applying embodied paradigms of cognition to religious cases, and the present project builds on these early soundings.[21]

In the converse direction, a handful of theological projects have referenced embodied cognition.[22] Two monograph-length theological works engage with 'cognitive linguistics', an early theory of embodied cognition which explored how cognitive metaphors use concrete concepts from embodied experience to structure abstract concepts.[23] However, a theological monograph which examines the full gamut of embodied cognition research, including its most recent findings and theories, is yet to appear. The present project aims to redress that lacuna by bringing Christian theology into dialogue with the embodied cognition research programme as a whole.

3 A Little Lower than the Angels

Embodiment has become somewhat of a buzzword in the humanities. Calls to adopt 'a more embodied approach' or 'to overcome Cartesian dualism' are

[20] Soliman, Johnson, and Song, 'Understanding Religion', 853. Work on the cognitive effects of ritual is an important exception to this general pattern.

[21] Matthew Day, 'Religion, Off-Line Cognition and the Extended Mind', *Journal of Cognition and Culture* 4, no. 1 (2004); Soliman, Johnson, and Song, 'Understanding Religion'; Joel Krueger, 'Extended Mind and Religious Cognition', in *Mental Religion: The Brain, Cognition, and Culture*, ed. N. Kasumi Clements (New York: Macmillan, 2016); Richard Sosis and Jordan Kiper, 'Religion Is More Than Belief: What Evolutionary Theories of Religion Tell Us About Religious Commitments', in *Challenges to Moral and Religious Belief: Disagreement and Evolution*, ed. Michael Bergmann and Patrick Kain (Oxford: Oxford University Press, 2014); Fraser Watts, 'Embodied Cognition and Religion', *Zygon* 48, no. 3 (2013).

[22] Ward, *How the Light Gets In*; Brown and Strawn, *Physical Nature of Christian Life*; Paul Scarlat, 'Embodied Cognition of Religion and Christian Orthodox Tradition', *Ortodoxia* 3 (2016). James W. Jones, *Living Religion: Embodiment, Theology, and the Possibility of a Spiritual Sense* (New York: Oxford University Press, 2019); Fraser Watts, *A Plea for Embodied Spirituality: The Role of the Body in Religion* (London: SCM, 2021). A special issue of Zygon was devoted to embodied cognition and religion; see Watts, 'Embodied Cognition and Religion'.

[23] John Sanders, *Theology in the Flesh: How Embodiment and Culture Shape the Way We Think About Truth, Morality and God* (Minneapolis: Fortress Press, 2016); Robert Masson, *Without Metaphor, No Saving God: Theology after Cognitive Linguistics* (Leuven, Belgium: Peeters, 2014). See also Erin Kidd and Jakob Karl Rinderknecht, *Putting God on the Map: Theology and Conceptual Mapping* (Lanham: Fortress Academic, 2018).

frequent. While interest in the long-neglected theme of embodiment brings a welcome realignment, the attendant risk is that theorising about the body remains vague and aloof. Engaging with embodied cognition research mitigates this risk by providing precise details of what it means to be an embodied thinker (though, as I shall observe at the end of this work, embodied cognition also has its own blinkers and limitations when it comes to discussing the body). Theological reflection on embodiment has often taken the mind–body problem—the metaphysical question about whether mind and body are one substance or two—as its point of departure.[24] However, embodied cognition research provides a far more fine-grained analysis of the role of the body. As Edelman states, 'it is not enough to say that the mind is embodied; one must say how'.[25] Embodied cognition sketches the many and varied aspects of *how* the mind is profoundly shaped by the body.

If the human mind is invariably embodied, then theological understanding is no exception. At first glance, theology appears especially abstract and seemingly detached from the cut and thrust of bodily interaction with the world. However, embodied cognition suggests that the body both furnishes the mind with its basic categories and pervasively influences even abstract reasoning. As an ever-present foundation for our cognition, it is easy to take the role of the body for granted and lose sight of the many ways in which our thinking is contingent on its situatedness within a physiological vehicle nested in a physical context. After all, we have no recourse to disembodied experience with which to contrast our bodily perspectives on the world. Theology, then, readily operates under the illusion that it is being undertaken by disembodied creatures who have access to 'pure' reasoning, rather than the idiosyncratic mind afforded by a bundle of flesh and bone, neuron and sinew, the products of a long evolutionary process.

The particular position which this study *opposes*, then, is that humans possess an *angelic theology*. By angelic theology, I do not mean angelology (theology about angels). Rather, I seek to remonstrate the view that human theological understanding is identical to that of an angel. As non-corporeal yet intellectual creatures, the way in which angels might theologise provides the ideal foil to the present project (regardless of whether one affirms their metaphysical reality or imagines them as an interesting thought experiment). Angels may well possess an angelic theology, an understanding based on 'pure' rational capacities and conveyed in angelic tongues. However, my argument is that such angelic theology is not within grasp of human beings.

---

[24] E.g., Nancey C. Murphy, *Bodies and Souls, or Spirited Bodies?* (Cambridge: Cambridge University Press, 2006).
[25] Gerald M. Edelman, *Bright Air, Brilliant Fire: On the Matter of the Mind* (London: Allen Lane, 1992), 15.

Human beings, then, have particular ways of understanding. As Clark observes, '[o]urs are not the brains of disembodied spirits conveniently glued into ambulant, corporeal shells of flesh and blood. Rather, they are essentially the brains of embodied agents capable of creating and exploiting structures in the world'.[26] Theological understanding then, if it is to be grasped by humans, must conform to these bodily ways of knowing. Hence this study will develop a recurring principle in theology which posits that God's self-communication to humanity is *accommodated* to human capacities. Insofar as embodied cognition intricately details the nature of human cognitive capacities, it deepens our understanding of the precise capacities to which revelation is accommodated.

As an exploration of theological *understanding*, this study will focus on epistemological concerns (which arise from an embodied anthropology). Epistemology provides an obvious point of contact for the cognitive sciences, which interrogate human knowledge and understanding using various empirical and theoretical tools. Although this emphasis provides a helpful focus, it also has limitations. For one, any epistemological pictures may be premised on an underlying metaphysic. Furthermore, there is more to Christian salvation that simply knowing about something.[27] These neighbouring concerns will be gestured towards at the boundaries, but ultimately lie beyond the scope of this study.

To make the case for a corporeal theology, this study is divided into three parts. Part I builds the necessary foundations by introducing both the scientific and theological dialogue partners. The principle of accommodation offers a methodology for a *theological* appropriation of embodied cognition (Chapter 1). Given both the nascent status of embodied cognition and the interdisciplinary nature of this project, care is taken to introduce the hypotheses of embodied cognition in a fashion accessible to non-specialists (Chapter 2). The remaining parts are organised around to the taxonomy of embodied cognition outlined in Chapter 2.

Part II considers the embodied nature of human concepts. It surveys and critically evaluates the empirical evidence which suggests that concepts are grounded in embodied experience (Chapter 3), and then brings these findings into dialogue with questions relating to theological concepts (Chapter 4).[28]

Part III investigates how cognitive processes stretch beyond the brain, relying on sensorimotor engagement with the world and drawing bodily states and environmental resources into a wider cognitive system. It again begins by interrogating the empirical evidence for these hypotheses (Chapter 5). Before

---

[26] Clark, *Being There*, 219.

[27] Barth, for example, has at times been criticised for transposing questions of soteriology into questions of epistemology; see, Rowan Williams, 'Barth on the Triune God', in *Wrestling with Angels: Conversations in Modern Theology*, ed. Mike Higton (London: SCM Press, 2007), 116, 126–8; John Webster, *Barth*, 2nd ed. (London: Continuum, 2004), 82.

[28] An abridged version of Chapters 3 and 4 has been published in Tobias Tanton, 'Accommodating Embodied Thinkers', *Modern Theology*, no. 37 (2021): 316–35.

jumping to theological themes, an intermediate chapter explores how embodied cognition research might apply to the specific case of embodied religious practices (Chapter 6). This renewed understanding of the cognitive import of embodied religious practices is deployed to make proposals centred on liturgical theology (Chapter 7).

A concluding chapter charts the course for a corporeal theology in dialogue with contextual theologies which have been at the forefront of attending to the body. The goal of this study, then, is to deepen our appreciation for how theological understanding is accommodated to human beings as *embodied* creatures, in all their fleshy glory and cognitive finitude.

PART I

EMBODIED COGNITION AND ITS APPLICATION TO THEOLOGY

1

Theological Prolegomenon

Accommodating Embodied Cognition

> 'what surmounts the reach
> Of human sense, I shall delineate so,
> By likening spiritual to corporal forms'
> —*John Milton*[1]

How can finite human beings with limited cognitive capacities comprehend an infinite God? Theologians have typically sought to address this vexing problem of theological epistemology by appealing to the *principle of divine accommodation* (henceforth 'accommodation'). This principle posits that God's self-disclosure condescends to present itself in a form which humans can comprehend, thereby accommodating limited human capacities. Insofar as cognitive science offers new insights into human cognitive capacities, it details (some) aspects of the human condition to which revelation must be accommodated. Thus, accommodation, I shall argue, provides a robust theological framework with which to appreciate insights from cognitive science (which are introduced in Chapter 2).

Section 1 of this chapter introduces the epistemological problem of human understanding of the divine by way of a vivid anecdote from Milton's *Paradise Lost*. Section 2 surveys early theological development of accommodation. It charts the ways in which accommodation grew from a hermeneutical tool for scriptural interpretation to a more general corollary of revelation, thereby highlighting how it solves the epistemological challenge at hand. Section 3 proposes that accommodation is a particularly well-suited framework for integrating the insights of cognitive science into theology. Finally, Section 4 pre-empts potential objections to the methodology proposed in this chapter, primarily by engaging with Barth's rejection of natural theology and a human point of contact for revelation.

---

[1] John Milton, *Paradise Lost*, ed. Stephen Orgel, Jonathan Goldberg, and Philip Pullman (Oxford: Oxford University Press, 2005), bk5, ll. 571b–3.

Corporeal Theology: Accommodating Theological Understanding to Embodied Thinkers. Tobias Tanton, Oxford University Press. © Tobias Tanton 2023. DOI: 10.1093/oso/9780192884589.003.0002

1 A Miltonian Formulation of the Problem

The fraught relationship between divine and human knowledge is hardly a new topic. Milton's epic poem *Paradise Lost* famously sets out to 'justify the ways of God to men'.[2] *En route* Milton explores the dynamics of divine revelation and human knowledge.[3] In book five, Adam asks the archangel Raphael to give him a fuller account of cosmic pre-history (which Milton has imaginatively narrated):

> But more desire to hear, if thou consent,
> The full relation, which must needs be strange,
> Worthy of sacred silence to be heard;[4]

This request presents Raphael with an epistemological challenge familiar to theologians: how can divine knowledge be made accessible to human thought and language; or conversely, how can human concepts grasp divine reality? Raphael puzzles over this difficulty:

> High matter thou enjoinest me, Oh prime of men,
> Sad task and hard: For how shall I relate
> To human sense the invisible exploits
> Of warring Spirits?[5]

The double entendre of the English 'sense' is instructive here; it refers to both the perceptual capacities of humans—as in 'the senses'—and to the act of human comprehension—as in 'to make sense'. The connection between these two senses of the word serendipitously strikes upon a connection between the bodily nature of human perception and epistemological access to the world (a connection further explored in Chapter 3). Raphael articulates his strategy to bridge the epistemological chasm between divine and human knowledge thus:

> what surmounts the reach
> Of human sense, I shall delineate so,
> By likening spiritual to corporal forms,
> As may express them best;[6]

---

[2] Ibid., bk1, l. 26.
[3] Erica Longfellow and Elisabeth Dutton, 'Paradise Lost: A Staged Reading in the Chapel of New College, Oxford', *Milton Quarterly* 49, no. 3 (2015). Cf. Amos N. Wilder, 'Mythology and the New Testament: A Review of Kerygma Und Mythos', *Journal of Biblical Literature* 69, no. 2 (1950): 122.
[4] Milton, *Paradise Lost*, bk5, ll. 555–7.   [5] Ibid., bk5, ll. 563–6a.
[6] Ibid., bk5, ll. 571b–4a.

This analogical strategy—likening spiritual to corporeal forms—is precisely the topic of this chapter.[7] It recognises that humans are corporeal creatures; and, moreover, it suggests that their *corporeality* imposes constraints on their understanding. To work within these constraints, Raphael must *translate* those spiritual forms which surpass the reach of human understanding into the more palatable corporeal forms. In order to appeal to human sense (understanding), the archangel must go via the human senses (bodily perception). Raphael's work of translation, then, is presumably a success since his analogical narration of the war in heaven is able to proceed. But before he begins, he offers a caveat:

> though what if Earth
> Be but a shadow of Heaven, and things therein
> Each to other like, more than on earth is thought?[8]

Raphael's question casts doubt on whether a perfect translation is possible. Like the images seen by those shackled in Plato's cave, perhaps the corporeal forms only ever capture but a shadow of spiritual analogues.[9] If Raphael's doubt is well-founded, then every kataphatic theological statement is accompanied by an apophatic surplus: a surplus which is not available to human comprehension. Something is, perhaps, always lost in translation.

Milton's intuitive grasp of the puzzle confronting theological epistemology is the subject of this chapter. Furthermore, his insight that 'corporal forms' are what humans require will be explored in Part II.

2 The Principle of Divine Accommodation

The 'principle of divine accommodation' observes that God, in revealing God-self to humanity, *accommodates* revelation to human understanding. There are several assumptions built into this principle that are worth unpacking. First, it recognises the *transcendence* of God. As in Milton's dialogue, this transcendence means that humans do not have unfettered direct access to God. God's 'thoughts' and 'ways' are higher than human thoughts and ways, which creates an obstacle to human comprehension of God.[10] Second, on the other side of the equation lies *human finitude*; not only is God transcendent but humans are subject to creaturely limitations, which *prima facie* pose obstacles to knowledge of divine things. It may simply be the case that there are some things humans cannot know from their

---

[7] William G. Madsen, 'Earth the Shadow of Heaven: Typological Symbolism in Paradise Lost', *PMLA* 75, no. 5 (1960): 519.

[8] Milton, *Paradise Lost*, bk5, ll. 574b–6.   [9] Madsen, 'Earth the Shadow of Heaven', 519–20.

[10] Isaiah 55:8–9; talk of God 'thinking' or having 'ways' may be understood as an anthropomorphism, itself a kind of accommodation.

bounded creaturely perspective.[11] Third, given the gap—or the gaping chasm, as Kierkegaard's infinite qualitative difference would have it—between divine transcendence and human finitude, accommodation posits the possibility of a bridge between the two.[12] God *condescends* to the level of human understanding in order to reveal God-self. (Divine condescension is a synonym for accommodation.) In order for God to communicate and commune with humans, God, transcendence notwithstanding, must reveal God-self in a way which humans can comprehend. Hence revelation must be *mediated* in a fashion which takes account of human creaturely limitations. If the constraints of human nature are not taken into account, then revelation fails as a communicative act; without accommodation to human capacities any revelation remains beyond the limits of human comprehension.

McFarland combines these three facets of accommodation when he defines it as 'the processes by which God, though utterly transcendent of and thus intrinsically inaccessible to human investigation or knowledge, works within creation to make the divine knowable to humankind'.[13] Benin offers a similar definition, but adds a diachronic perspective, noting that human understanding is constrained differently throughout history: 'Divine accommodation/condescension alleges, most simply, that divine revelation is adjusted to the disparate intellectual and spiritual level of humanity at different times in history'.[14] Accommodation thus arises from decidedly theological concerns: the transcendence of God, the finitude of human nature, the creature–creator distinction, and, ultimately, the love of God which expresses itself in the desire to be known by and commune with creatures.

The principle of accommodation appears throughout the history of theology.[15] It is a theological trope—or, more precisely, a logical manoeuvre—which has

---

[11]   For a recent discussion, see Marcus du Sautoy, *What We Cannot Know: Explorations at the Edge of Knowledge* (London: 4th Estate, 2016).

[12]   Søren Kierkegaard, *Training in Christianity, and the Edifying Discourse Which 'Accompanied' It* (London: Oxford University Press, 1941), 139.

[13]   Ian A. McFarland, 'Accommodation', in *The Cambridge Dictionary of Christian Theology*, ed. Ian A. McFarland, Iain R. Torrance, and Karen Kilby (Cambridge: Cambridge University Press, 2011), 2.

[14]   Stephen D. Benin, *The Footprints of God: Divine Accommodation in Jewish and Christian Thought* (Albany, NY: State University of New York Press, 1993), xiv.

[15]   For a survey of accommodation in both Christian and Jewish sources, see ibid. Although Benin's survey is designed to be representative rather than exhaustive, he nevertheless discusses the work of numerous important figures, including Justin Martyr, Origen, Eusebius, Pseudo-Clementine, Athanasius, Basil, Gregory of Nazianzus, Gregory of Nyssa, John Chrysostom, Theodoret of Cyrus, Aphrahat, Ephrem, Jacob of Sarug, Dionysisus bar Salibhi, Augustine, Hugh of St Victor, Anselm of Havelberg, Midrashic literature, Jacob al-Qirqisani, Sa'adia, Bahya ben Yosef ibn-Pakuda, Maimonides, William of Auvergne, Aquinas, and Calvin. See also Glenn S. Sunshine, 'Accommodation Historically Considered', in *The Enduring Authority of the Christian Scriptures*, ed. D.A. Carson (Grand Rapids MI: Eerdmans, 2016); Amos Funkenstein, *Theology and the Scientific Imagination: From the Middle Ages to the Seventeenth Century* (Princeton: Princeton University Press, 1986).

been deployed time and time again from the earliest Christian theologising. Despite its prevalence, it is often invoked without being explicitly named, let alone theorised in any detail.

2.1 Accommodation as an Exegetical Tool

Accommodation rose to prominence as an exegetical tool for interpreting scripture.[16] One of the enduring challenges faced by the early church was to situate itself in relationship to Judaism. With this inclusion of gentile converts alongside Jewish Christians, the question of which Jewish practices the gentiles would be expected to observe came to the fore, a negotiation already familiar from the New Testament texts.[17] For those who rejected the Marcionite dismissal of the Hebrew Bible, one way to account for this discrepancy was through accommodation.

For example, in his polemic against the Jewish interlocutor Trypho, Justin Martyr explains why Christians no longer follow Jewish practices: 'We, too, would observe your fleshly circumcision, your Sabbaths, and in brief, all your festivals, if we did not know why they were ordained, namely because of your sins and obduracy.'[18] For Justin, the observances legislated in the Torah were merely an accommodation to the Israelites on account of their sin. Justin goes on to cite the Israelites' creation of the golden calf as an example of a proclivity for idolatry which was accommodated in God's dealings with Israel.[19] Benin classifies this application of accommodation as 'negative', since it sees an accommodation as a punishment or a prophylactic in the face of vice.[20]

As with many early Christian texts, such polemics often adopt a hostile and condescending tone, together with a supersessionist theology. In the aftermath of the holocaust it is, of course, crucial to flag that such views have fuelled anti-Semitism. My aim here is not to endorse these particular applications of accommodation, but simply, first, to observe that the logic of accommodation is prevalent even in the early Christian thought and, second, to draw out how accommodation focuses on the way in which God's dealings are tailored to their recipients, in this case differentially throughout various periods of time.

---

[16]   McFarland, 'Accommodation', 2.   [17]   E.g., Galatians 5.
[18]   Justin Martyr, 'Dialogues Cure Trephine Judo', in *Patrologiae Cursus Completus Series Graeca*, ed. Jacques Paul Migne (Paris: Imprimerie Catholique, 1857–1912), §18. Translated in Benin, *The Footprints of God*, 4.
[19]   Justin Martyr, 'Dialogues Cure Trephine Judo', 19. Cf. Irenaeus of Lyon, *Sancti Irenaei Episcopi Lugdunensis, Libros Quinque Adversus Haereses* (1857), §4.26.21. Eusebius of Caesarea, *Proof of the Gospel*, trans. W. J. Ferrar, 2 vols. (London: 1920), §I.6. Gregory of Nazianzus, *Orationes*, ed. Jacques Paul Migne, vols. 35–6 (Paris: Imprimerie Catholique, 1857–1912), 45, 12.
[20]   Benin, *The Footprints of God*, 1.

2.2 Incarnation as Accommodation

In addition to 'negative' accommodation, which uses accommodation to dismiss past 'compromises' as no longer relevant, Benin also identifies a 'positive' accommodation.[21] This latter category identifies accommodation in the Christian narrative, notably understanding the incarnation as accommodation *par excellence*. Hence accommodation moves from a hermeneutical tool to a principle which justifies entire doctrines.

Athanasius provides an important early example of the incarnation understood in terms of accommodation. He opens *De Incarnatione* by providing two reasons for the incarnation: first, the incarnation is soteriologically necessary as a remedy for death;[22] and second, of particular interest to the present project, the incarnation is epistemologically necessary, providing humans access to knowledge of God.[23] For Athanasius, the creation of humans as rational creatures implies that God wishes humans to know God. This knowledge is mediated through images, first in humans, then in Christ:

> And why would God have made those by whom he did not wish to be known? So, lest this should happen, being good he bestowed on them of his own image, our Lord Jesus Christ, and made them according to his own image and according to the likeness, so that understanding through such grace the image, I mean the Word of the Father, they might be able to receive through him a notion of the Father, and knowing the Creator they might live the happy and truly blessed life.[24]

Initially human beings themselves, having been created in the image of God, were sufficient for knowing God.[25] However, in the postlapsarian world this image became tarnished and in need of renewal.[26] The law and the prophets are themselves an accommodation to the resulting human weakness and these were a 'sacred school of the knowledge of God and the conduct of the soul.'[27] Ultimately these measures prove insufficient to raise the gaze of human beings to the truth.

What was required, then, was a true, untarnished image of God. As the image of the Father, Christ fulfils this role.[28] In a fallen world, the incarnation of the Word therefore restores epistemological access to God: 'So, rightly wishing to help human beings, he sojourned as a human being, taking to himself a body like theirs...that...from the works done through the body we might know the Word

---

[21] Ibid., 1–2.

[22] Athanasius, *On the Incarnation*, trans. John Behr (Yonkers, NY: St Vladimir's Seminary Press, 2011), §2–10.

[23] Ibid., §11–19.   [24] Ibid., §11.

[25] Ibid., §12. Alvyn Pettersen, *Athanasius* (London: Geoffrey Chapman, 1995), 40–4.

[26] Athanasius, *On the Incarnation*, §13–14.   [27] Ibid., §12.   [28] Colossians 1:15.

of God in the body, and through him the Father.'[29] Thus, bodily knowledge of the incarnate Word mediates knowledge of the incorporeal God to humans.

Although knowledge of God via nature, 'from his providence and governance of the universe',[30] may have been sufficient in the past, Athanasius argues that this is no longer a viable alternative: 'Perhaps one might say that it was possible... to show the things concerning him through the works of creation. But this was no longer certain. Not at all! Human beings had neglected this before, and no longer were their eyes held upwards but downwards.'[31] Athanasius thus insists on the *necessity* of the incarnation for knowledge of God, at least in a postlapsarian state.

Athanasius explains the epistemological function of the incarnation in terms of divine condescension or accommodation. Adapting himself for the sake of human comprehensibility, Christ lowers himself to the human level. Condescension takes on a particular importance in the context of the Arian controversy; Christ is not a human elevated through divine adoption; on the contrary, Christ is God come down.[32] Using a common trope to illustrate the nature and necessity of accommodation, Athanasius gives the analogy of a teacher condescending to the level of a student: 'For as a good teacher who cares for his students always condescends to teach by simpler means those who are not able to benefit from more advanced things'.[33]

For Athanasius, the incarnation—the taking on of a perceptible body—is the appropriate accommodation since humans abandoned contemplation of God and instead rely on sensory perception:

> For since human beings, having rejected the contemplation of God and as though sunk in an abyss with their eyes held downwards, seeking God in creation and things perceptible, setting up for themselves mortal humans and demons as gods, for this reason the lover of human beings and the common Savior of all, takes to himself a body and dwells as human among humans and draws to himself the perceptible senses of all human beings, so that those who think that God is in things corporeal might, from what the Lord wrought through the actions of the body, know the truth and through him might consider the Father.[34]

For Athanasius, then, 'casting one's gaze downwards' and thereby focusing exclusively on material objects available to sensory perception is a symptom of human sinfulness. This at once explains the human propensity for idolatry and the necessity and epistemological efficaciousness of the incarnation: postlapsarian

---

[29] Athanasius, *On the Incarnation*, §14.   [30] Ibid.   [31] Ibid.
[32] Benin, *The Footprints of God*, 25.   [33] Athanasius, *On the Incarnation*, §15.
[34] Ibid. See also, Thomas Aquinas, *Summa Contra Gentiles* (Turnhout, Belgium: Brepols Publishers, 2010), IV, 54.54.

humans focus exclusively on material things rather than contemplation of God; they are thus driven towards idolatry; but in the incarnation God enters the world of material things, thus opening the way for humans to redirect their gaze to God:

> Once the mind of human beings descended to perceptible things, the Word himself submitted to appear through a body, so that as a human he might bring humans to himself and return their sense perception to himself, and then, by their seeing him as a human being, he might persuade them through the works he effected that he is not a man only but God and the Word of Wisdom of the true God.[35]

By taking on bodily form and becoming available to human perception God addresses—or accommodates—humans in their particular circumstances and as their capacities allow. Knowing through the senses is not intrinsic to the human condition but is an all-pervasive trait of postlapsarian humans. Hence the incarnation is the requisite for reaching a fallen humanity. In the incarnation God accommodates knowledge of the divine to creatures who are 'human and [think] all things in human terms'.[36]

2.3 Accommodation in Theological Epistemology

If the incarnation—the central act of God's revelation in Christian salvation history—can be understood in terms of accommodation, then it is only a small step further to think of accommodation as a category of theological epistemology. This further expands the scope of the application of accommodation: beyond a hermeneutical tool or a facet of a doctrine (albeit a central one), accommodation thus becomes a condition for *all* theological knowledge. The thought is relatively simple: if humans are to hear and to understand God's word, it must be mediated in a way which is comprehensible to them. Thus, all revelation must be accommodated to human beings, and accommodation applies to theological epistemology *tout court*.

In this sense accommodation is, as McFarland notes, a 'corollary of the doctrine of revelation'.[37] In other words, if revelation has occurred such that the divine has been *successfully* communicated or mediated to humans, this must have occurred in a way which humans can comprehend. Any revelation which exceeds human capacities for comprehension cannot, by definition, be communicated. In Kantian parlance, accommodation is a transcendental condition for revelation: it is a condition for the very possibility of mediation from the divine to

---

[35] Athanasius, *On the Incarnation*, §16.   [36] Ibid., §15.
[37] McFarland, 'Accommodation', 2.

the human. Hence McFarland notes that accommodation can be conceived as having a broader scope of application than merely scripture; instead it 'refers to divine condescension to creaturely capacities and includes the use of any finite reality as a vehicle of divine self-disclosure'.[38]

On this view, accommodation is not a special allowance for a specific group of people, be they the 'simpler' minds of the uneducated masses, the 'primitive' minds of past ages, or the more 'idolatrous' or 'hard-hearted' generations conditioned by Egyptian idolatry. Rather, accommodation is a requirement for divine knowledge to be revealed to *any* human being, regardless of their intellectual or moral status.

As with more specific applications of accommodation, the application of accommodation to divine interaction (*oikonomia*) with humanity *in toto* is already present in the patristic era. Gregory of Nyssa generalises accommodation to all God's activity towards humanity. God's love drives him to commune with his creation, and this requires God to condescend to a human level:

> We account for God's willingness to admit men [*sic*] to communion with Himself by His love towards mankind. But since that which is by nature finite cannot rise above its prescribed limits, or lay hold of the superior nature of the Most High, on this account, He, bringing His power, so full of love for humanity, down to the level of human weakness, so far as it was possible for us to receive it…the divine power…gives to our human nature what it is capable of receiving; and thus in the various manifestations of God to man He both adapts Himself to man and speaks in human language, and assumes wrath, and pity, and such-like emotions, so that through feelings corresponding to our own infantile life might be led as by the hand, and lay hold of the Divine nature by means of words which His foresight has given.[39]

Thus, Gregory argues that anthropomorphisms (including anthropopathisms) are a symptom of God accommodating God-self in revelation to humanity.

The application of accommodation to theological epistemology does not rule out apophaticism. If God mediates his self-revelation in ways that humans can understand, this does not imply that humans can exhaustively comprehend God. Indeed, the accommodation explicitly allows for the possibility that there are aspects of God's nature which are not communicated in revelation simply because they are beyond the capacity of finite creatures to comprehend. Both Gregory of

---

[38] Ibid.

[39] Gregory of Nyssa, *Adversus Eunomium*, ed. Jacques Paul Migne, vol. 45 (Paris: Imprimerie Catholique, 1857–1912), 1049. Cf. Origen, *Homilies Sur Jérémie*, ed. Henri de Lubac and J. Daniélou, trans. P. Husson, vol. 238 (Paris: 1977), 198–200. Translated in Benin, *The Footprints of God*, 13.

Nyssa and John Chrysostom illustrate this point with the example of a dazzling light which human capacities cannot receive unfiltered.[40]

For reasons of space, this survey has largely been restricted to the Alexandrians and Cappadocians. Accommodation, however, continues to feature regularly as a principle invoked by many influential theologians. For example, Augustine argues that religious practice and institutions are accommodated to human capacities;[41] Calvin and Aquinas both understand the human language of scripture as an accommodation;[42] and Bonaventure casts the incarnation in terms of accommodation.[43] The list could go on, but my hope is that the brief survey is sufficient to give a flavour of the way accommodation has reoccurred in Christian theology, ranging in scope from specific hermeneutical difficulties engendered by discrepancies between the Testaments, through to doctrines and theological epistemology as a whole.

3 Cognitive Science and Human Limitations

The principle of accommodation is no stranger to the dialogue between science and theology.[44] It was revived in the sixteenth and seventeenth centuries largely to deal with aspects of the biblical text which seemed at odds with emerging scientific discoveries. The heliocentric model of the solar system, which sat uneasily alongside certain biblical passages, provides an obvious example. The discrepancy between such passages and the prevailing scientific understanding was justified by arguing that the passages were an accommodation to ancient astronomical presumptions. However, the advent of cognitive science offers a new way to apply accommodation.

The examples of accommodation in Section 2 typically focus on the *content* which the principle seeks to explain. For example, first, the problem at hand might be why animal sacrifice was allowed in the Old Testament but is no longer part of early church practice; and then, second, accommodation is appealed to as a justification for this seeming discrepancy. Oftentimes very little is said about the particular aspects of human nature that necessitate accommodation. Some

[40] Gregory of Nyssa, *Adversus Eunomium*, 1049; John Chrysostom, *On the Incomprehensible Nature of God*, ed. R. J. Deferrari, trans. Paul W. Harkins, vol. 3 (Washington DC: Catholic University of America Press, 1979), 3, 722/200.

[41] Augustine, *Epistulae* (Turnhout, Belgium: Brepols Publishers, 2010), 138.131.135.

[42] Thomas Aquinas, *Summa Theologica*, Complete English ed. (Westminster MD: Christian Classics, 1981), 1–2 q.98 a.93; Jean Calvin, *Institutes of the Christian Religion*, trans. Henry Beveridge (Grand Rapids MI: Eerdmans, 1989), I.13.11. See also, Peter Bayle, 'Rimini (Gergory of)', in *The Dictionary Historical and Critical of Mr Peter Bayle* (London: J.J. Knapton and P. Knapton, 1737), 876.

[43] Bonaventure, *Breviloquium* (Turnhout, Belgium: Brepols Publishers, 2010), prologue, 4.

[44] Alister E. McGrath, *Science and Religion: An Introduction* (Oxford: Blackwell Publishers, 1999), 9.

authors point in very general terms to certain human limitations or vices which necessitate a particular accommodation, such as a simpler, uneducated, or 'primitive' mind, or a proclivity towards idolatry. However, beyond these general tendencies in human nature, little is done to explore the finitude of the human condition which requires accommodation. Insofar as human limitations constrain what can be revealed to humans, a fuller examination of these limitations explicates why revelation takes the particular shape that it does.

Given the potential fruitfulness of examining human limitations to understand how revelation is mediated, the contemporary cognitive sciences are of particular interest. The various investigative techniques which comprise the cognitive sciences—such as experimental psychology, neuro-imaging, etc.—illuminate the human cognitive profile. Moreover, they can identify the limitations of human cognition as well as the particular shape of human cognitive processes. Insofar as the cognitive sciences are able to explicate the character of human thought, they can highlight the limitations within which revelation is mediated to human beings.

It should be noted that the cognitive sciences are, of course, purely descriptive: they can only describe human thinking as it actually is, and not as it ought to be. Consequently, they cannot identify the 'correct' form of theological thinking. As Jong, Kavanagh, and Visala point out in a perceptive article, the emerging 'cognitive science of religion' could equally be dubbed the '*cognitive science of idolatry*', since it cannot adjudicate between theological correct and incorrect positions.[45] Cognitive science cannot directly prescribe theological doctrine.

The descriptive nature of cognitive science, however, is no obstacle when it is applied in the context of accommodation. Indeed, the Christian claim is precisely that God meets humanity *in its present state*; God meets humanity in its finitude, its creatureliness, its sinfulness, its noetically compromised state, its embodied nature. Hence cognitive science, along with any other disciplinary perspective which describes our present state, can be brought into dialogue with theology via accommodation. This is precisely why accommodation provides such a fruitful framework since it offers a way to configure a dialogue between a descriptive empirical science and normative theological discourse. Within accommodation, I should stress, cognitive science does not determine or prescribe the *content* of revelation, but merely describes how revelation can be mediated to human beings.

Accommodation largely retains the same logic when it is applied to limitations uncovered by cognitive science. However, this novel application also extends accommodation in two ways. First, accommodation as a hermeneutical principle was often deployed with elitist undertones; it was the more 'primitive' minds of the ancient audience of the 'simpler' minds of the masses which required

---

[45] Jonathan Jong, Christopher Kavanagh, and Aku Visala, 'Born Idolaters: The Limits of the Philosophical Implications of the Cognitive Science of Religion', in *Neue Zeitschrift für Systematische Theologie und Religionsphilosophie* (2015), 252.

accommodation.[46] Benin identifies a negative accommodation in as 'an accommodation to a rude and uneducated people who would not have understood or benefitted from a more sublime revelation'.[47] The exegetes who appealed to accommodation rarely counted themselves among its beneficiaries. Indeed, the fact that they needed to appeal to such a principle was precisely because they read the text from a vantage point of superior knowledge and understanding. By considering cognitive science within the framework of accommodation, this elitism is no longer at play. Insofar as cognitive science identifies mechanisms which are universally applicable to all human beings by virtue their common biology and environments, it exposes limitations which are pertinent to all human beings, and not only an 'inferior' class. Hence cognitive science identifies species-wide limitations, thereby 'universalising' accommodation (at least for human beings).[48]

A second, related, extension of accommodation is a shift to a transhistorical perspective. Accommodation is no longer being deployed to account for difference between revelatory dispensations at different points in history. Rather, it considers limitations common to all human beings (or *homo sapiens*) throughout history. This transhistorical perspective is possible because biblical history spans a relatively short period of evolutionary time scales; hence not much has changed in terms of the human biology over the past three thousand years. Insofar as cognitive science unearths universals about human cognition, it is equally applicable to all *homo sapiens*.

In summary, although accommodation retains its basic character, a novel application in the case of cognitive science means that accommodation is extended in a universalising fashion. Accommodation asserts that revelation is accommodated to limited human capacities, whereas cognitive science elucidates the nature of the capacities which must be accommodated.

4 Pre-empting Objections: A Dialogue with Karl Barth

The seemingly neat fit between accommodation and cognitive science is unlikely to impress neo-Orthodox theologians. In this section, I pre-empt potential objections to this methodology which arise in Barthian theology. Barth is a helpful interlocutor, not only because of his stature in modern theology but also because he deals so explicitly with theological epistemology. Insofar as Barth places revelation and knowledge of God at the centre of his theology, his thought provides a

---

[46] Alister E. McGrath, *Historical Theology: An Introduction to the History of Christian Thought*, 2nd ed. (Hoboken: John Wiley & Sons, 2012), 178–9; McGrath, *Science and Religion: An Introduction*, 10.

[47] Benin, *The Footprints of God*, xvi.

[48] The question of whether these findings are truly universal will be discussed in the Conclusion.

relevant sounding board for the scientifically informed theological epistemology I aim to develop.

Although Barth shares an interest in theological epistemology with the current project, it is by no means evident that he would approve of using cognitive science to inform theology. Barth's robust critique of the theological *status quo* of his day presents pressing questions for any theological project which engages with cognitive science: Does an appeal to a non-theological discipline import foreign methodology into theology when theology ought to establish its own methodological criteria? Does the use of a natural science imply the development of a natural theology, which Barth so vehemently rejects? Perhaps most urgently, does a focus on *human* cognition allow us to speak only of anthropology, whereas the proper subject of theology is the divine? If any of these questions are answered in the affirmative, this project will no doubt be faced with an uncompromising Barthian rebuke. This section responds to these Barthian critiques, either by demonstrating that they do not apply to the proposed methodology or by arguing against the Barthian position. My aim is not merely the negative task of anticipating and defending against potential objections but also, more positively, to sharpen the theological methodology proposed by situating it in relation to Barthian warnings.

4.1 Theological Prolegomena

In the introduction to his *Church Dogmatics*, Barth discusses the possibility of theological prolegomena, or methodological prefaces to dogmatic theology.[49] He observes that the *status quo* in systematic theology is to begin with a prolegomenon which establishes the methodology for theology to follow by borrowing from other disciplines:

> The statements...in such prolegomena present themselves...partly as borrowings from metaphysics, anthropology (ethics, according to Schleiermacher), philosophy of religion, and history of religion, partly as pure discussions on methodology. What dogmatic knowledge is, would then really be fixed *praenumerando* outside dogmatics, and would also be fixable for one who purposes taking no further trouble with dogmatics itself.[50]

Barth is highly critical of the use of extra-dogmatic disciplines for fixing the methodological parameters of dogmatics. If dogmatics is premised on revelation,

---

[49] Karl Barth, *Church Dogmatics: The Doctrine of the Word of God*, trans. G. T. Thomson, vol. 1/1 (Edinburgh: T&T Clark, 1969), 26–47.
[50] Ibid., 40.

which is solely a divine initiative, then the use of these immanent sciences has nothing to offer dogmatics.

In contrast to what he sees as the liberal *status quo*, Barth argues that any prolegomenon ought to be solely theological: 'The necessity for dogmatic prolegomena, i.e. the necessity for giving an explicit account of the special path of knowledge to be trodden by dogmatics, must, to be authoritative, be an inner necessity, grounded in the thing itself.'[51] Theology, according to Barth, must formulate its own methodology, and there is no extra-theological vantage point from which to compose a prolegomenon.

Does the present project fall foul of this Barthian prohibition against prolegomena? The appeal to cognitive science may, *prima facie*, make the present project suspect. However, I have proposed accommodation as the methodological framework for the dialogue with cognitive science. Hence the methodology proposed is decidedly *theological*. As a theological framework, accommodation ought to mollify Barthian concerns about prolegomena dictating methodologies foreign to theology: cognitive science is being brought into the discussion on theological terms.

4.2 Natural Theology

A second Barthian concern is that employing natural science to inform theology constitutes a form of natural theology. Barth, of course, famously rejects natural theology and argues that revelation ought to be the sole source of theology. He defines natural theology as 'every (positive or negative) formulation of a system which claims to be theological, i.e. to interpret divine revelation, whose subject, however, differs fundamentally from the revelation in Jesus Christ and whose method therefore differs equally from the exposition of Holy Scripture.'[52] For Barth, God cannot be discerned by examining fallen humanity or creation; instead humanity must rely solely upon God's self-revelation which stems from outside of creation.

Does deploying cognitive science, within the framework of accommodation, constitute an example of the natural theology which Barth so vehemently rejects? Appeal to any natural science may *prima facie* appear to draw on insights from the natural world (more specifically, in the case of cognitive science, insights from the nature of human cognition) as a source for theology. However, when deployed within the framework of accommodation, I contend that the case is not so clear

---

[51] Ibid., 33.
[52] Karl Barth, 'No! Answer to Emil Brunner', in *Natural Theology* (London: Centenary Press, 1946), 74–5.

cut. As outlined in Section 3, I position my theological appropriation of cognitive science in terms of the elucidation of human capacities and constraints to which revelation must be accommodated. Within such a framework, cognitive science does *not*, strictly speaking, function as a *source* for theology.

The present project does not ask what human cognition can tell us about the nature of God, as would be the case in classical natural theology. An example of such a natural theology is Augustine's psychological analogy for the Trinity, in which he uses insights into human cognition to describe the nature of God.[53] It is hardly surprising, then, that Barth found Augustine's psychological analogy (as a species of *vestigium trinitatis*) deeply problematic.[54]

The present project, however, differs markedly from Augustine's approach. Rather than relying on the *imago Dei* to draw an analogy between human persons—and human cognition in particular—and God, the claim here is more modest. Namely, it observes that since all human understanding is given a certain shape by our cognitive capacities, then this also applies to human *theological* understandings, as accommodation insists. Rather than attempting to discern the content of theology from cognitive science, the present project uses cognitive science to understand the form which this theological content must take in the minds of its human recipients.

Within the framework of accommodation, then, cognitive science applies to all theological knowledge, regardless of its source—natural or revealed (or some combination thereof). Even if one takes a strictly Barthian position, insisting that revelation is the only legitimate source of theology, it remains the case that this revealed knowledge, if it is to be communicated to humans, must be accommodated to human cognitive capacities. On this point, theologians can find allies in cognitive scientists of religion. As Pyysiäinen observes 'even if gods do exist, and reveal themselves to humans, the knowledge revealed will become known through ordinary cognitive and communicative processes which can and should be scientifically explained'.[55] Pyysiäinen's observation implicitly evokes accommodation: knowledge of God must ultimately be accommodated to human cognitive capacities.

Along these lines, Rowan Williams proposes a non-rivalrous natural theology, which offers a more nuanced account than the one which Barth pilloried.[56] Williams notes that natural theology often came to mean a theology with an alternative, even a rival source to revelation: ' "Natural theology" once meant the kind of discourse about God that you could develop without appealing to the

---

[53] Augustine, *De Trinitate*, XIII–X.   [54] Barth, *Church Dogmatics* 1/1, 383–4.
[55] Ilkka Pyysiäinen, 'Introduction: Cognition and Culture in the Construction of Religion', in *Current Approaches in the Cognitive Science of Religion*, ed. Ilkka Pyysiäinen and Veikko Anttonen (London: Continuum, 2002), 5.
[56] Williams, *Edge of Words*.

unreliable authority of claimed revelation'.[57] Furthermore, Williams acknow-ledges Barth's (and later Hauerwas') critiques of this style of theology, describing them as a 'succession of formidable assaults on a scheme that assumes the inad-missibility of revelation and the irrelevance of sacred narrative and community practice in exploring the roots of our talk about God'.[58]

In spite of this acknowledgement, Williams is unwilling to follow the Barthian line and abandon natural theology altogether. Such a position has its own dangers, according to Williams, 'suggesting, seductively, that we don't have to worry about tracing the history of this or that mode of speech...Appealing to tradition and community without some reflection on history can be a way of avoiding uncom-fortable critical questions about legitimate authority'.[59] Thus, Williams rejects both of these extremes, in favour of a middle path; or perhaps, more accurately, to reconceive them as potential allies instead of necessary rivals. He states that a '"natural" theology need not be an exercise in trying to replace revelation, to fore-stall the action of God. It may be a way of tracking that action through the impress left upon our speech and action, as upon other aspects of our world; and thus it may be...a form of 'faithful witness'.[60] Thus positioned, natural and revealed the-ology complement one another: through an exploration of natural phenomena 'we may develop an enhanced capacity to recognize at least what is being claimed in this particular discourse of revelation that is Christian theology'.[61]

This qualified, non-rivalrous mode of natural theology is reminiscent of accommodation. As Williams argues, God's action may be sovereign, not requir-ing any initiative from the natural world, but it nevertheless leaves an 'impress' on the natural order. In the same way, accommodation insists that even if the sole source of knowledge about God originates from God, this knowledge reaches the natural order in the form of human (and potentially other) recipients. Therefore, what we learn about the natural order from empirical investigation is neverthe-less relevant for an account of revelation's reception or impress; revelation does not remain trapped in a heavenly echo chamber but enters the created order.

In summary, within the framework of accommodation, cognitive science is of interest to theology regardless of the source of theology. Even if one insists upon special revelation as the sole source of theology, such revelation must neverthe-less, once it reaches its recipients, be accommodated by human understanding.

4.3 Theological Anthropology: A Human Point of Contact?

A third Barthian concern contends that investigation of human cognitive capaci-ties places undue focus on anthropology. In keeping with his insistence on

---

[57] Ibid., 1.   [58] Ibid., 2.   [59] Ibid., 5.   [60] Ibid., 180.   [61] Ibid.

revelation as the sole source of theology, Barth unremittingly insists that knowledge of God can only come through God's self-disclosure. One must therefore rely wholly on divine initiative, rather than any human capacity: 'One can *not* speak of God simply by speaking of man [*sic*] in a loud voice!',[62] Barth declares.

Barth's general concern about reducing theology to anthropology is brought into even sharper focus in the heated Barth–Brunner debate. In this debate Brunner proposed humans have certain capacities to receive and comprehend revelation which constituted a 'point of contact' (*Anknüpfungspunkt*) between revelation and its human recipients. He distinguishes between two aspects of the 'image of God': the 'material' *imago Dei* originally rendered humans righteous at creation (*justitia originalis*) but was lost at the fall through sin;[63] by contrast the 'formal' *imago Dei* distinguishes humans from other creatures—it is what makes humans human—and is retained after the fall.[64] Brunner defines the formal *imago Dei* in terms of the human capacity for words or speech (*Wortmächtigkeit*) which other creatures lack. This human capacity is, for Brunner, a point of contact and a prerequisite for human beings to receive revelation.

On the basis of his theological anthropology, Brunner is willing to countenance a revised *theologia naturalis*.[65] A doctrine of creation, he contends, means that the created order can be seen as God's handiwork: 'Wherever God does anything, he leaves the imprint of his nature upon what he does. Therefore, the creation of the world is at the same time a revelation, a communication of God.'[66] Brunner qualifies this natural theology by arguing that it only becomes accessible to humans in the wake of special revelation: 'Only the Christian, i.e. the man [*sic*] who stands within the revelation of Christ, has the true natural knowledge of God.'[67] Insofar as this limited natural theology works in concert with revelation, rather than independently of it, it resonates with Williams' non-rivalrous natural theology.

Barth, to put it mildly, was not impressed. In his famously tempestuous response, he argues that Burnner's point of contact was the first concession on a slippery slope back to the natural theology he had come to despise. For Barth, the total corruption of human nature at the fall rules out a role for any human capacity in receiving revelation. He is happy to grant Brunner's point that postlapsarian humans retain their form but argues that this point is totally irrelevant for receiving revelation: 'Even as a sinner man is man and not a tortoise. But does this mean that his reason is therefore more "suited" for defining the nature of God than anything else in the world? What is the relevance of the "capacity

---

[62] Karl Barth, *The Word of God and the Word of Man* (London: Hodder and Stoughton, 1928), 196. Emphasis original.

[63] Emil Brunner, 'Nature and Grace: A Contribution to the Discussion with Karl Barth', in *Natural Theology* (London: Centenary Press, 1946), 24.

[64] Ibid., 23.   [65] Ibid., 24–31.   [66] Ibid., 25.   [67] Ibid., 27.

for revelation" to the fact that man is man?'[68] Barth's answer to this question is unambiguously negative; human sinfulness rules out the possibility of a human point of contact.[69]

Barth is also concerned that a point of contact undermines salvation by grace alone by positing that humans contribute to their own salvation: 'The Word of God does not rely in any way upon such a capacity. To suggest such would be to posit a meeting of God by humans if not halfway, then some distance at least across the gap which separates them.'[70] Barth's overriding methodological concern is that any shift in focus away from divine initiative to human cooperation, be it in issuing forth revelation or in soteriology, ultimately opens the door to natural theology.[71]

The debate between Barth and Brunner is, I shall argue, helpfully clarified by accommodation. As established earlier, accommodation provides a general epistemological principle for theology: if humans are to comprehend revelation at all, then it must be tailored to their limited capacities. Brunner's argument for a point of contact is fundamentally compatible with accommodation. He argues that 'No one who agrees that only human subjects but not st[i]cks and stones can receive the Word of God and the Holy Spirit can deny that there is such a thing as a point of contact for the divine grace of redemption.'[72] In other words, revelation, in its accommodated form, relies upon and speaks to particular human capacities. God's ability to speak to humans depends on their capacity to 'hear'.[73] As Hart observes, without a 'point of contact' which is accommodated, revelation would fail to reach humanity:

> We must, Brunner argues, be able to speak meaningfully of a 'point of contact' for grace in nature, else we are left with a revelation and a redemption which are left floating in mid-air never actually *making* contact, and never, therefore, actually revealing anything or redeeming anybody. God's grace must *make contact* with something, and therefore there must be something with which contact can in fact *be made*, in sinful human nature.[74]

It is hardly surprising, then, that Brunner concludes his account of nature and grace with a reflection on the necessity of mediation—which can be understood as an accommodation, although he does not explicitly name it as such.

By contrast, Barth's position is difficult to reconcile with accommodation.[75] By denying a human point of contact in the form of any relevant human capacities

---

[68] Barth, 'No!', 279.   [69] Ibid., 89.

[70] Trevor A. Hart, 'A Capacity for Ambiguity: The Barth-Brunner Debate Revisited', *Tyndale Bulletin* 44, no. 2 (1993): 300.

[71] Williams, 'Barth on the Triune God', 106, 111.   [72] Brunner, 'Nature and Grace', 31.

[73] Hart, 'A Capacity for Ambiguity', 296.   [74] Ibid., 294. Original emphasis.

[75] Williams, 'Barth on the Triune God', 127.

for receiving revelation, it follows that Barth also denies the need for accommo-dation to those capacities. Barth suggests that the Word of God creates its own capacity for reception without recourse to any human capacities.[76] But if human beings must somehow be transfigured before they can receive revelation, this raises the questions of whether it is really human beings who receive revelation. As Prenter observes, such an approach results in 'a concept of revelation which, in principle, has no relation to the world'.[77] To reject a point of contact is ultimately to jeopardise the *possibility* of contact.

In an attempt to mediate the Barth–Brunner debate, Hart introduces a helpful distinction between active and passive capacities.[78] An *active* capacity would con-fer on humans the ability or aptitude to generate (or positively contribute to the generation of) revelation. By contrast, a *passive* capacity is simply the ability to receive revelation which has been independently generated: 'Such "receptivity" is not, then, a predisposition for or an innate question after the divine address: but simply the ability to hear it when it arises, however alien its substance may be, and even as it is a word of judgement which breeds resentment and rejection'.[79] Hart uses this distinction to suggest that Barth and Brunner are talking past one another: Brunner is proposing a passive capacity, but Barth's concerns about an overinflated theological anthropology or a violation of grace only apply to an active capacity. Hence if Brunner's point of contact can be clarified as a passive capacity—as is the case when it is understood within the framework of accommodation—then Barth's concerns can also be assuaged. Arguably the lan-guage of a human 'readiness' to meet God, which Barth employs later in his career, is compatible which such a view of a passive capacity.[80]

Even if one agrees with Brunner that there is a (passive) point of contact, one may wish to question his assumption that linguistic capacity is the sole relevant human capacity for receiving revelation. Brunner (together with Barth) typically equates revelation to the *text* of scripture, thereby circumscribing it to a linguistic communication.[81] In Part III of this study I argue that equating theological knowledge with linguistically mediated content is too narrow a circumscription, and religious practices also contain and convey theological content. This is not to deny a role to Brunner's 'capacity for words', but to argue that it is not the *only* relevant capacity. Other capacities, such as the capacity for bodily participation in rituals, are also salient. Thus, even though I defend (a qualified version) of

---

[76] Barth, *Church Dogmatics* 1/1, 220–1. See also Stephen Andrews, 'The Ambiguity of Capacity: A Rejoinder to Trevor Hart', *Tyndale Bulletin* 45, no. 1 (1994): 177.

[77] Regin Prenter, 'Dietrich Bonhoeffer and Karl Barth's Positivism of Revelation', in *World Come of Age*, ed. Ronald Gregor Smith (Philadelphia: Fortress Press, 1967), 97.

[78] Hart, 'A Capacity for Ambiguity', 303.   [79] Ibid., 297.

[80] Karl Barth, *Church Dogmatics: The Doctrine of God*, trans. G. T. Thomson, vol. 2/1 (Edinburgh: T&T Clark, 1980), 65. Cited in Webster, *Barth*, 80.

[81] Although Barth identifies sacrament as a form of the church's proclamation, he subordinates it to preaching: 'sacrament for the sake of preaching, and not *vice versa*'. Barth, *Church Dogmatics* 1/1, 77.

Brunner's point of contact, I shall propose broadening the suite of capacities under consideration.

In summary, accommodation provides a helpful perspective on the Barth–Brunner debate. Brunner's argument for a point of contact is consistent with the view that revelation is accommodated to human capacities, while Barth's early rejection of talk of human capacities leaves open the question of how revelation can be successfully received by human beings if it does not address them according to their condition.

5 Conclusion

The possibility of divine revelation poses a fundamental challenge for theological epistemology, namely how divine knowledge can become the purview of finite human minds. This challenge is addressed by the long-standing principle of accommodation, which asserts that God becomes accessible to humans by condescending to their capacities for comprehension. The appeal to accommodation in this chapter will provide a framework for bringing the cognitive science into dialogue with theology. Whereas accommodation asserts that God tailors revelation to human capacities, cognitive science describes the nature of (some of) these capacities, informing precisely *what revelation is accommodated to*. This is not the only possible way in which the two disciplines may interact; there may well be other frameworks for dialogue. However, by referencing empirically tractable human capacities, accommodation provides a solid theological foundation from which to engage with descriptive natural science.

The principle of accommodation asserts that theology cannot take place in isolation from anthropology.[82] If revelation reaches humans, then it becomes embroiled in the messy reality of human language, culture, history, and, indeed, human cognition. Hence, although the methodology proposed for the present project is decidedly theological, it nevertheless departs from a Barthian rejection of a point of contact for revelation in human beings. If revelation ultimately reaches human minds, then it must accommodate the shape of these minds, a shape which cognitive science can illuminate.

---

[82] Erin Kidd and Jakob Karl Rinderknecht, 'An Introduction to Conceptual Mapping', in *Putting God on the Map: Theology and Conceptual Mapping*, ed. Erin Kidd and Jakob Karl Rinderknecht (Lanham: Fortress Academic, 2018), 9.

2

Embodied Cognition

Literature, History, and Concepts

'Am I so bound up with my body and senses that I cannot exist without them?'

—*René Descartes*[1]

The principle of divine accommodation introduced in Chapter 1 proposes that
theological understanding is accommodated to human cognitive capacities. But
what are these cognitive capacities? Although the gift of revelation may be a theological assertion, the human cognitive capacities which receive and understand
this revelation are open to empirical investigation. Hence cognitive science,
which seeks to describe cognitive capacities, will be indispensable for understanding the constraints which revelation encounters in its human recipients.
Contemporary cognitive science, however, is in a state of flux. A new research
programme broadly known as 'embodied cognition' is proposing a major paradigm shift in the way human cognition is understood and simultaneously offers
an alternative portrait of human cognitive capacities. This chapter, then, introduces embodied cognition as a paradigm to provide the foundation for future
chapters, which consider how detailed findings from embodied cognition
research shape the nature of human theological understanding.

Embodied cognition is a theory in cognitive science which posits that the
human body and its interactions with its surroundings play a vital role in human
cognition. The view that cognition is embodied represents a decisive break from
so-called 'traditional cognitive science', which describes cognitive processes as
largely independent of the body and its environment, and understands the body
as merely providing inputs and outputs for the 'cognition proper' in the form of
perception and action.

In this chapter, I outline the literature, history, and key concepts of embodied
cognition. Section 1 highlights foundational texts and identifies indicators of
embodied cognition's growing influence and importance. Section 2 explores
'traditional cognitive science', the most recent historical antecedent of embodied
cognition, and one which it typically differentiates itself from. This negative

---

[1] René Descartes, *Meditations on First Philosophy: With Selections from the Objections and Replies*,
trans. Michael Moriarty (Oxford: Oxford University Press, 2008 [1641]), 18.

Corporeal Theology: Accommodating Theological Understanding to Embodied Thinkers. Tobias Tanton,
Oxford University Press. © Tobias Tanton 2023. DOI: 10.1093/oso/9780192884589.003.0003

definition of embodied cognition will lead to a positive articulation of the factors unifying diverse embodied cognition research programmes (Section 3), together with more specific claims made under its banner. Finally, the limits of embodied cognition will be explored (Section 4).

1 The Genesis of Embodied Cognition

As with many intellectual movements, the precise genesis of embodied cognition is difficult to pinpoint since various thinkers prefigure works which explicitly identify themselves as part of the movement. Many in the field acknowledge French phenomenologist Maurice Merleau-Ponty as an important influence.[2] Merleau-Ponty's magisterial *Phenomenology of Perception* argues that the body is not merely an object of our experience, but also the very seat of our subjectivity.[3] He famously investigates phenomena such as phantom limb syndrome and the blind person's cane to demonstrate the importance of bodily know-how for quotidian navigation of the world, and the importance of constant perceptual feedback for guiding action. In the discipline of psychology, Gibson's ecological theory of perception, which understands perception in terms of active engagement with one's environment, is seen as a forerunner of embodied cognition.[4]

In their survey of the field, Wilson and Foglia name three further landmark contributions.[5] First, Lakoff and Johnson's seminal work on metaphor argues that 'cognitive metaphors' use concepts rooted in bodily experience to illuminate abstract concepts.[6] Second, Varela, Thomson and Roche's programmatic *The Embodied Mind* uses theories of emergence to argue that cognition emerges from the interaction of properties of the world with details of human physiology.[7] Third, they nominate Clark's *Being There: Putting Mind, World, and Body Back Together*, which builds a case for considering cognition as a system which stretches across brain, body, and world.[8]

---

[2] E.g., see Francisco J. Varela, Eleanor Rosch, and Evan Thompson, *The Embodied Mind: Cognitive Science and Human Experience* (Cambridge, MA: MIT Press, 1991), xv–xvii; Clark, Andy. *Being There: Putting Brain, Body, and World Together Again* (Cambridge, MA: MIT Press, 1997), 171–2.

[3] Maurice Merleau-Ponty, *Phenomenology of Perception*, ed. Colin Smith (London: Routledge, 1962).

[4] James J. Gibson, *The Ecological Approach to Visual Perception* (New York: Psychology Press, 1979). E.g., see Susan L. Hurley, *Consciousness in Action* (Cambridge MA: Harvard University Press, 1998), 430–5; Lawrence A. Shapiro, *Embodied Cognition* (New York: Routledge, 2011), 29–37; Clark, *Being There*, 172.

[5] Robert A. Wilson and Lucia Foglia, *Embodied Cognition* (2015) [cited 9 December 2015]; available from http://plato.stanford.edu/archives/win2015/entries/embodied-cognition/.

[6] George Lakoff and Mark Johnson, *Metaphors We Live By* (Chicago: Chicago University Press, 1980). Cf. George Lakoff and Mark Johnson, *Philosophy in the Flesh: The Embodied Mind and Its Challenge to Western Thought* (New York: Basic Books, 1999).

[7] Varela, Rosch, and Thompson, *The Embodied Mind*. Especially chapter 8.

[8] Clark, *Being There*.

To this uncontroversial list I would add three further 'honourable mentions', which each paved the way for further empirical and theoretical work in embodied cognition. First, Clark and Chalmers' 'The Extended Mind', formulates a seminal philosophical argument that extra-somatic objects are part of the mind.[9] Second, Barsalou's empirical work illuminates the embodied nature of concepts, culminating in his theory of perceptual symbol systems.[10] Third, Damasio's neuroscientific revitalisation of the James-Lange theory of emotion, which argues that bodily states constitute emotions and thereby participate in cognition, is rarely absent from embodied cognition bibliographies. Each of these authors will be discussed in greater detail, but this cursory literature review identifies seminal works which have shaped the direction(s) of the field.

If these landmark works have charted the course for embodied cognition, many others have followed in their footsteps, resulting in a deluge of publications. Numerous monographs have developed approaches to embodied cognition, such that the field has begun to fan out into various subfields and more precise hypotheses. No fewer than eight journals have devoted special issues to the topic: *European Journal of Social Psychology*, *Italian Journal for the Philosophy of Language*, *Frontiers in Psychology*, *Phenomenology and Cognitive Science*, *Philosophical Psychology*, *The Quarterly Journal of Experimental Psychology*, and *Zygon*.[11] In a sure sign that the field is coming of age, it has passed through the rite of passage of having a handbook commissioned, more than one in fact.[12] A quick scan of the bibliography at the end of this study reveals that the majority of empirical studies cited have been published in the last decade, suggesting that the foundational contributions have grown exponentially.

As can already be sensed from this preliminary list, embodied cognition research encompasses a wide range of literature. It draws on empirical findings from various disciplines within the cognitive sciences, including experimental psychology, neuroimaging, brain lesion studies, artificial intelligence (AI),

---

[9] Andy Clark and David Chalmers, 'The Extended Mind', *Analysis* 58, no. 1 (1998).

[10] Lawrence W. Barsalou, 'Perceptual Symbol Systems', *Behavioral and Brain Sciences* 22, no. 4 (1999).

[11] The introductory articles in these special editions are: Eric Arnau et al., 'The Extended Cognition Thesis: Its Significance for the Philosophy of (Cognitive) Science', *Philosophical Psychology* 27, no. 1 (2014); Watts, Fraser. 'Embodied Cognition and Religion.' *Zygon* 48, no. 3 (2013): 745–58; Richard Menary, 'Introduction to the Special Issue on 4e Cognition', *Phenomenology and the Cognitive Sciences* 9, no. 4 (2010); Thomas W. Schubert and Gün R. Semin, 'Embodiment as a Unifying Perspective for Psychology', *European Journal of Social Psychology* 39, no. 7 (2009); Anna M. Borghi and Diane Pecher, 'Introduction to the Special Topic Embodied and Grounded Cognition', *Frontiers in Psychology* 2 (2011); Claudia Scorolli, 'Action, Perception and Language', *Rivista Italiana di Filosofia del Linguaggio* 5 (2012); Martin H. Fischer and Rolf A. Zwaan, 'Embodied Language: A Review of the Role of the Motor System in Language Comprehension', *The Quarterly Journal of Experimental Psychology* 61, no. 6 (2008); Matthew Crippen, 'Preface', *Contemporary Pragmatism* 14, no. 1 (2017).

[12] Lawrence A. Shapiro, ed., *The Routledge Handbook of Embodied Cognition* (London: Routledge, 2014); Philip Robbins and Murat Aydede, eds., *The Cambridge Handbook of Situated Cognition* (Cambridge: Cambridge University Press, 2009).

robotics, and animal behaviour. Treatments range from specific empirical studies to broader theories which synthesise these findings. At the more theoretical end, lively contributions have also been made by philosophers of cognitive science, with applications for the philosophy of mind.

Another indicator of the significance of embodied cognition is its penetration into disciplines beyond the cognitive sciences (and the directly associated philosophy). Kahneman's Nobel-prize-winning work in behavioural economics argues that economic actors often failed to behave like the rational decision makers which classical economic models had assumed.[13] He draws upon dual-process accounts of cognition which differentiate between fast, automatic cognitive processes (including many of those most closely associated with embodied cognition) and slow, deliberative ones. His research demonstrated that many economic decisions were subject to biases arising from heuristics which differ from rational solutions in predictable ways. In ethics, Haidt's influential 'social intuitionist' model of moral judgement draws upon a similar body of cognitive science.[14] He contends that embodied cognitive processes, such as emotion, often drive moral judgements, and reported reasons for making the judgement are typically developed *post hoc*. Similarly, Martha Nussbaum's influential work examines the status of moral judgements driven by emotions such as disgust and shame.[15] As noted in the Introduction, theologians have made brief forays into embodied cognition, an interdisciplinary space to which the current project seeks to make a substantial contribution.

Embodied cognition is an immensely fruitful paradigm which has generated hundreds of empirical studies and provided a unifying theoretical framework for numerous aspects of cognition, including memory, perception, emotion, judgements, conceptualisation, and others. It remains to be seen whether embodied cognition represents a revolutionary paradigm shift in cognitive science, but its early success means that it is unlikely to be considered a passing fad.

2 Traditional Cognitive Science: Inside the Cognitive Sandwich

As Mernary observes, to some extent the divergent research programmes associated with the term 'embodied cognition' are united by a common enemy.[16] That enemy is 'cognitivism' or 'traditional cognitive science'. Cognitivism itself arose as

---

[13] Daniel Kahneman, *Thinking, Fast and Slow* (London: Allen Lane, 2011).

[14] Jonathan Haidt, 'The Emotional Dog and Its Rational Tail: A Social Intuitionist Approach to Moral Judgment', *Psychological Review* 108, no. 4 (2001).

[15] Martha Craven Nussbaum, *Hiding from Humanity: Disgust, Shame, and the Law* (Princeton, NJ: Princeton University Press, 2004).

[16] Menary, 'Introduction', 459–60. Cf. Lawrence A. Shapiro, 'The Embodied Cognition Research Programme', *Philosophy Compass* 2, no. 2 (2007): 338; Wilson and Foglia, *Embodied Cognition*.

a reaction against an earlier *status quo* in psychology, namely behaviourism. It drew inspiration from one of the greatest contemporary technological achievements of its time, the computer. Taking the computer as the central metaphor for mind, cognitivism drew inferences about the computer-like architecture, content, and physical instantiation of human cognition. In this section, I briefly sketch these precursors to embodied cognition, not only to situate the movement historically but also to introduce embodied cognition, albeit negatively, in terms of the enemy it defines itself against.

2.1 From Behaviourism to Cognitivism

Behaviourism sought to make psychology a robustly empirical field by focusing on externally observable and thus measurable behaviours.[17] It criticised earlier movements in psychology that relied upon introspective methods which it argued were unreliable and difficult to measure. Instead it focused on matching environmental stimuli to behavioural responses. It took as its paradigm cases of classical conditioning, such as Ivan Pavlov's influential research on dogs.[18] Pavlov introduced unrelated stimuli (bells, metronomes, and lights) while feeding his dogs, and this learnt correlation meant that they would begin to salivate in response to these stimuli, even in the absence of food. Such responses, behaviourists argued, could be explained in terms of conditioned reflexes, without recourse to any internal mental representations.

If all human behaviour could be explained in terms of stimulus responses, then mental states were redundant. As Barsalou observes, behaviourists and ordinary language philosophers 'successfully banished mental states from consideration in much of the scientific community', and the mental images which made up these states went with them.'[19] Since only visible behaviours were considered legitimate phenomena for psychological explanation, behaviourism had the effect of doing away with the mental realm altogether: 'In a reaction against armchair introspection, behaviorism had declared that it was just as illicit to theorize about what went on in the head of the organism to generate its behavior as to theorize about what went on in its mind.'[20]

While behaviourist explanations may have been persuasive for its own paradigm cases, other cognitive tasks proved more difficult to account for in terms of

---

[17] For a classical example, see Burrhus Frederic Skinner, *Verbal Behavior* (New York: Appleton-Century-Crofts, 1957).

[18] Ēzras Asratovich Asratīan, *I.P. Pavlov: His Life and Work* (Moscow: Foreign Languages Publishing House, 1953).

[19] Barsalou, 'Perceptual Symbol Systems', 578; Lawrence W. Barsalou et al., 'Embodiment in Religious Knowledge', *Journal of Cognition and Culture* 5, no. 1–2 (2005): 21.

[20] Stevan Harnad, 'The Symbol Grounding Problem', *Physica D: Nonlinear Phenomena* 42, no. 1–3 (1990): 335.

bare stimuli and response. As a result, cognitivism emerged to challenge the methodological strictures of behaviourism. Cognitivists 'were convinced that a robust science of intelligent behaviour simply could not avoid discussing unobservable mental phenomena'.[21] Hence they reintroduced the concept of mental representations in the form of abstract symbols (see Section 2.4) as a necessary theoretical construct for explaining complex behaviour.

Cognitivism's focus on the manipulation of mental representations meant that the emphasis shifted from bodily behaviours to (supposedly) brain-bound mental processes. As Day observes, 'the modern cognitive sciences were launched by the hunch that accounting for the adaptive link between environmental stimulus and behavioural response meant explaining what was happening *inside the head*'.[22] This focus would later become one of the features of cognitivism which branches of embodied cognition would challenge.

2.2 The Mind as Computer

Aside from its rejection of behaviourism, another driver of cognitivism was a contemporary technological development. The complex and opaque nature of the human mind has meant that theorists throughout the ages have grasped for metaphors to understand it, often drawing on other scientific and technological advancements of their time: the impression of wax seals, hydraulics with its buildups of pressure and explosive releases, and complex mechanical devices with gears and cogs are all examples of fashionable technologies that have been deployed as metaphors for mind.[23] In the second half of the twentieth century a new technology took centre stage: the computer. Cognitivists readily co-opted the computer as *the* new metaphor for mind.[24] As Day observes, '[t]he conceptual breakthrough that gave birth to the cognitive research program was that if we viewed the mind as a kind of biologically realized computer, cognition could be analyzed as a species of computation'.[25] The computational theory of mind subsequently became the dominant paradigm for cognitive science.[26]

In broad terms, the computational metaphor suggests that the human mind can primarily be understood in terms of information processing. It is also applied at greater levels of detail to explain specific facets of cognition: mental

---

[21] Day, 'Religion', 102.   [22] Ibid. Emphasis original.

[23] John G. Daugman, 'Brain Metaphor and Brain Theory', in *Philosophy and the Neurosciences: A Reader*, ed. William Bechtel, Pete Mandik, and Jennifer Mundale (Oxford: Blackwell Publishers, 2001).

[24] Casting the brain in terms of a computer was pioneered by John von Neuman, see J. von Neumann, *The Computer and the Brain* (New Haven: Yale University Press, 1958).

[25] Day, 'Religion', 102.

[26] Jerry A. Fodor, *The Language of Thought* (Cambridge, MA: Harvard University Press, 1975), 27; Michael Rescorla, *The Computational Theory of Mind* (2015) [cited 2 April 2016]; available from https://plato.stanford.edu/archives/spr2017/entries/computational-mind/.

representations are understood as abstract symbols;[27] mental processes are likened to algorithms; the structure of the mind is likened to computer architecture; and the 'hardware' of the mind is thought to be largely independent of the 'software' which runs on it. In the following subsections, I tease out how the computational metaphor informs aspects of cognitivism.

2.3 The Architecture of Cognition: The Sandwich

The computational metaphor informs cognitivism's vision of the overall organisation of cognition. Computer systems typically have input (e.g., keyboards, mice) and output (e.g., monitors, printers) devices, and in between these lies a central processing unit where all the relevant computation takes place. When applied to cognition, this model considers perception as an input system which takes stimuli from the external world and 'encodes' them for subsequent processing. Furthermore, motor movement or action is characterised as an output system which is given instructions as a result of the processing. Wedged in between these input and output systems, is central cognition where cognition proper occurs. This overall architecture has been aptly described by Hurley as 'the classical sandwich'.[28]

In the sandwich model, the sensorimotor systems are thought of as separate from central cognition, and peripheral to its functioning. Under the traditional model '[p]erceptual systems pick up information from the environment and pass it on to separate systems that support various cognitive functions, such as language, memory, and thought'.[29] Likewise motor movement is distinguished from central cognition: 'actions have been considered as trivial appendages to the seemingly more sophisticated mental operations subserving "higher level" cognition, such as object identification, language comprehension, or decision making'.[30] If central cognition is 'high level', then perception and action are relegated further down the hierarchy: 'cognition (in the narrow sense) is segregated from processing in low-level systems, therefore acting like meat in a sandwich em-breaded by perception and action'.[31] Hence the stratification of perception, cognition, and action into a sandwich model relegates input and output systems to a secondary status beyond the central concerns of cognitive science.

A consequence of the sandwich model is the diminished importance of the body. It is clear both perception and action are intimately bound up in bodily capacities. To demarcate these two functions into separate systems, and to

---

[27] See Chapter 3.   [28] Hurley, *Consciousness in Action*, 1–4, 401–2.
[29] Barsalou, 'Perceptual Symbol Systems', 577.
[30] Fischer and Zwaan, 'Embodied Language', 825.
[31] Wilson and Foglia, *Embodied Cognition*. Cf. Scorolli, 'Action, Perception and Language', 1.

relegate those systems beyond the boundary of cognition proper, is therefore also to conclude that the body is largely irrelevant to cognition. As Wilson states, '[t]raditional cognitive science has certainly conceptualized central cognitive processing, what we will call cognition in the narrow sense, in abstraction from bodily mechanisms of sensory processing and motor control'.[32]

A second implication of the sandwich model is to insulate cognition from the outside world. Since central cognition relies on perception and action systems as an interface with the world, it operates at an arm's length from it. As Shapiro observes, '[b]ecause cognition begins and ends with inputs to and outputs from the nervous system, it has no need for interaction with the real world outside it'.[33] Cognition can thus process pure mental representations in splendid isolation, delegating interaction with the messy outside world to 'lower level' perception and action systems.

2.4 Cognition as Symbol Manipulation

Traditional cognitive science has not only made presumptions about the architecture of cognition but it also envisions how the central cognition, sandwiched between action and perception, functions. As Shapiro states, '[u]nifying traditional cognitive science is the idea that thinking is a process of symbol manipulation'.[34] Crucial to this understanding is what is meant by symbols. As Lakoff notes, the symbols in a computer are arbitrarily related to what they refer to (their meaning): 'As in a computer language, these symbols were meaningless in themselves, and thought was seen as the manipulation of such symbols according to formal rules that do not look at any meanings that might be attributed to the symbols'.[35] Hence the symbols thought to be manipulated in cognitive processing bear no resemblance to that which they symbolise (much like de Saussure's observation that the orthographic and phonetic forms of words typically do not resemble their referents).[36] Hence one of the functions of the perceptual system is to transduce sensory stimuli into the abstract symbols which central cognition can process.[37] This notion of symbol distinguishes the processes of central cognition from the body:

---

[32] Wilson and Foglia, *Embodied Cognition.*

[33] Shapiro, 'The Embodied Cognition Research Programme', 339.

[34] Ibid., 338. See also, Lakoff and Johnson, *Philosophy in the Flesh*, 75; Jensine Andresen, 'Introduction: Towards a Cognitive Science of Religion', in *Religion in Mind: Cognitive Perspectives on Religious Belief, Ritual and Experience*, ed. Jensine Andresen (Cambridge: Cambridge University Press, 2001), 4–5.

[35] Lakoff and Johnson, *Philosophy in the Flesh*, 76.

[36] Ferdinand de Saussure, *Course in General Linguistics*, ed. C. Bally and A. Sechehaye, trans. A. Riedlinger (New York: McGraw-Hill, 1966).

[37] See Chapter 3 for a detailed discussion.

Generally speaking, the alternative to embodied cognition is that mind is abstract and symbolic, and, as such, several encoding steps removed from sensorimotor activity. In this view, thinking is a matter of the manipulation of abstract, disembodied, symbolic information.[38]

One highly developed theory which exemplifies this approach is the language of thought hypothesis, notably developed by Fodor.[39] This hypothesis proposed that cognition takes place in a mental 'language'.[40] Though not equivalent to any spoken human language, the language of thought shares properties with such languages, such as a combinatorial syntax. Hence this language analogy provided a framework in which symbols were manipulated following a rule-based system, in line with the computational theory of mind. McGilchrist observes that this approach again largely sees the body as irrelevant to cognitive functioning:

> The belief that the structures of analytic language are hard-wired into our brains helps to perpetuate the idea that that brain is a cognitive machine, a computer that is fitted with a rule-based programme for structuring the world, rather than its being an inextricable part of an embodied, living organism that develops implicit, performative, skills through an empathic process of intelligent imitation.[41]

2.5 In the Brain but Not of the Brain

A further implication of the sandwich model is that cognition is associated exclusively with the brain. While perception and action clearly deployed various parts of the body, the obvious candidate for a central processing unit was the brain (or perhaps the central nervous system): 'The way in which central topics have been addressed deeply reflects the idea that cognitive phenomena can be accounted for locally, and that elements beyond the boundaries of the skull are of interest only insofar as they provide sensory input and allow behavioral output.'[42] If the body

---

[38] Warren S. Brown and Kevin S. Reimer, 'Embodied Cognition, Character Formation, and Virtue', *Zygon* 48, no. 3 (2013): 2013.

[39] Fodor, *The Language of Thought*.

[40] Murat Adydede, *The Language of Thought Hypothesis* (2010) [cited 28 August 2016]; available from https://plato.stanford.edu/archives/fall2015/entries/language-thought/. Cf. Masson, *Without Metaphor*, 29–30.

[41] Iain McGilchrist, *The Master and His Emissary: The Divided Brain and the Making of the Western World* (New Haven, CT: Yale University Press, 2009), 120.

[42] Wilson and Foglia, *Embodied Cognition*.

(beyond the brain) had any role to play it was solely to provide life support for the brain; the body did not directly participate in cognitive processes.[43]

Although cognition was thought to take place in the brain, the actual structure of the brain received surprisingly little attention.[44] This omission again resulted from the computer metaphor for the brain. In computer science, software can be developed largely independently of the hardware that runs it. Although all software requires some kind of hardware to be instantiated on, the physical implementations can vary. Silicon chips and vacuum tubes can both provide the electronic circuits on which computation can take place, and memory can equally be stored on magnetic hard drives, optical media, or cardboard punch cards (this is known as 'multiple realisability'). Hence as long as the two devices conform to the same *functional* standards, a software programmer need not concern themself with how those functions are physically implemented.

If the mind is like a computer, then, like software, its operation can be described in purely functional terms, and the physical details of how this computation is instantiated can be largely ignored. As Lakoff and Johnson observe, 'a consequence of the [computational] metaphor was that the hardware—or rather "wetware"—was seen as determining nothing about the nature of the program', and therefore 'it seemed natural to assume that the mind could be studied in terms of its cognitive functions, ignoring any ways in which those functions arise from the body and the brain'.[45]

Clark charts the way traditional cognitive science could simultaneously identify cognition with the brain while largely neglecting emerging discoveries about the brain:

> influential research programs in cognitive science have so often downplayed or ignored neuroscientific studies in their attempts to model or explain mental phenomena. One popular reason for such inattention was the claim, common among early workers in symbolic artificial intelligence, that the right level of description of the physical device...lay at a fair remove from descriptions of neuronal structures and processes. Instead, it was believed that some much more abstract level of description was required—for example, a description in terms of information-processing roles in a computational system. The fine detail of neuronal organization, it was thought, constituted one specific solution to the

---

[43] Chen-Bo Zhong and Julian House, 'Dirt, Pollution, and Purity: A Metaphoric Perspective on Morality', in *The Power of Metaphor: Examining Its Influence on Social Life*, ed. Mark J. Landau and Michael D. Robinson (Washington, DC: American Psychological Association, 2014), 114.

[44] Rolf A. Zwaan, 'Experiential Traces and Mental Simulations in Language Comprehension', in *Symbols and Embodiment: Debates on Meaning and Cognition*, ed. Manuel De Vega, Arthur M. Glenberg, and Arthur C. Graesser (Oxford: Oxford University Press, 2008), 177.

[45] Lakoff and Johnson, *Philosophy in the Flesh*, 75–6.

problem of how to physically construct a device that would satisfy such an abstract computational story—but that was all.[46]

In contrast, others have argued that the structure of the brain cannot be so easily abstracted from. For example, McGilchrist argues that '[t]he brain should not be thought of as an indiscriminate mass of neurones: the structure of that mass matters'.[47] This is not to say that the function of the brain could not *in theory* be described in terms of abstract information processing. Nor is it necessarily to deny the possibility that the same functionality could be implemented on a physically different (and incredibly complex) device. Rather it is to suggest that the particular physiology of the brain shapes its cognitive profile.

In summary, cognitivism reacted against behaviourism's rejection of mental representations. It did so by turning to the computational metaphor to inform its understanding of how human cognitive apparatus is structured, functions, and is best described. The resulting picture is one in which centralised processing, largely distinct from the input and output systems of perception and action, proceeds by manipulating abstract symbols in an algorithmic fashion. Although this central processing is presumably restricted to the brain, it is best described in abstraction from its physical implementation. Cognitivism provides an indispensable backdrop for understanding embodied cognition, whose research trajectories share 'a commitment to critiquing and even replacing' this traditional approach to cognition.[48] Having defined embodied cognition negatively in terms of its common enemy, I turn to a positive articulation of embodied cognition's alternative vision of the human mind.

3 The Embodied Alternative: A Cognitive Stew

Painting with broad brushstrokes, Wilson and Foglia state that '[c]ognition is embodied when it is deeply dependent upon features of the physical body of an agent, that is, when aspects of the agent's body beyond the brain play a significant causal or physically constitutive role in cognitive processing'.[49] However, this general definition remains vague and potentially fails to capture the full scope of embodied cognition research (e.g., see Section 3.3).

As Wilson and Galonka observe, '[l]ike all good ideas in cognitive science... embodiment immediately came to mean six different things'.[50] The diversity of projects has been accompanied by a proliferation of nomenclature: 'embodied cognition' functions as an umbrella term; the label '4E cognition' provides greater

---

[46] Clark, *Being There*, 129.   [47] McGilchrist, *The Master and His Emissary*, 9.
[48] Wilson and Foglia, *Embodied Cognition*.   [49] Ibid.
[50] Wilson and Golonka, 'Embodied Cognition', 1.

detail, describing cognition as 'embodied', 'embedded', 'enactive', and 'extended'; furthermore, cognition is sometimes qualified as 'situated', distributed', 'grounded', or 'scaffolded'. Some terms carve out a portion of the territory within the wider embodied cognition landscape, while others emphasise a particular approach or theory (as will be evident in Chapters 3 and 5).

Given the diversity of embodied cognition projects, it is helpful to chart its anatomy. Shapiro admirably summarises the burgeoning literature in the field by distilling its claims into three central hypotheses: 'conceptualisation', 'replacement', and 'constitution'.[51] Given the impressive scope and conceptual clarity of Shapiro's work, I shall follow his typology, introducing each hypothesis and noting how it departs from cognitivism.

3.1 Conceptualisation: Grounding Concepts with the Body

The conceptualisation hypothesis challenges the assumption that concepts (mental representations for objects, properties, states, etc.) involved in cognition are unrelated to the body. As noted earlier, the computational metaphor in cognitivism assumes that mental representations are abstract symbols akin to those used in computation or language, namely they are arbitrarily related to that which they represent. Lakoff and Johnson highlight how the sandwich model of traditional cognitive science divorces concepts from bodily sensorimotor systems: 'While perception has always been accepted as bodily in nature, just as movement is, conception—the formation and use of concepts—has traditionally been seen in purely mental and wholly separate from and independent of our abilities to perceive and move.'[52]

By contrast, the conceptualisation hypothesis proposes that the human concepts are entangled with perceptual and motor systems. By deploying sensorimotor states to partly constitute concepts, mental representations are grounded in the particularities of the body and the way it interacts with the world. As Barsalou observes, '"Grounded cognition" reflects the assumption that cognition is typically grounded in multiple ways, including simulations, situated action, and on occasion, bodily states.'[53] Unlike computational symbols, grounded concepts are intrinsically related to embodiment: 'where embodied cognition seems to depart from symbolism is in its preference for explanations of cognition that tie symbols more directly to idiosyncratic facts about organisms or interactions between organisms and their environments.'[54]

---

[51] Shapiro, *Embodied Cognition*, 4.   [52] Lakoff and Johnson, *Philosophy in the Flesh*, 37.

[53] Lawrence W. Barsalou, 'Grounded Cognition', *Annual Review of Psychology* 59 (2008): 619.

[54] Lawrence A. Shapiro, 'Symbolism, Embodied Cognition, and the Broader Debate', in *Symbols and Embodiment: Debates on Meaning and Cognition*, ed. Manuel De Vega, Arthur M. Glenberg, and Arthur C. Graesser (Oxford: Oxford University Press, 2008), 67.

3.2 Replacement: Dispensing with Internal Mental Models

If the conceptualisation hypothesis describes mental representations differently to cognitivism, the replacement hypothesis suggests that they should play a reduced role in explaining cognitive processes or be done away with altogether. Rather than cognition generating internal mental models of the world in 'central cognition', replacement suggests that many cognitive tasks simply rely on sensorimotor interactions with the world. In the to-and-fro of engaging with the world, cognitive tasks rely on action which intervenes in the world, and constant perceptual feedback. Again, contrary to the sandwich model, this interaction emphasises the role of sensorimotor systems in cognition. Cognition comes to be understood as something that happens in between the agent and its environment, rather than an insulated mind. As Clark proposes, '[i]ntelligence and understanding are rooted not in the presence and manipulation of explicit, language-like data structures, but in something more earthy: the tuning of basic responses to a real world that enables an embodied organism to sense, act, and survive'.[55]

3.3 Constitution: The Brain but Not Only the Brain

The constitution hypothesis is closely related to replacement. If cognition is understood as a process which requires interaction between brain, body, and world, then the constitution hypothesis proposes that the physical substrate on which cognition is implemented extends beyond the brain (or the central nervous system). The body states involved in emotions, or artefacts in the world such as notebooks, are proposed as constituents of a cognitive system which stretches out into the body and the world. The claim of embodied cognition is not that cognition can function independently of the brain, as though a severed appendage would in any meaningful sense continue to cognise, but rather that cognition does not, for the most part, function independently of the body and its surroundings. As Clark concludes, '[I]n light of...the apparent methodological value...of studying extended brain-body-world systems as integrated computational and dynamic wholes, I am convinced that it is valuable to (at times) treat cognitive processes as extended beyond the narrow confines of skin and skull'.[56] This contention differs from the cognitivist picture, which assumes that cognition takes place exclusively in the brain.

---

[55] Clark, *Being There*, 4.   [56] Ibid., 215.

3.4   Perception, Action, and Cognition: A Cognitive Stew

Conceptualisation, replacement, and constitution each make distinct claims about the nature of cognition. What they share in common, beyond the vague notion that cognition somehow depends on the body, is that they all challenge the cognitive sandwich model. Rather than being separate from 'cognition proper', perception and action are understood as profoundly entangled with it.[57] Moreover, both perception and action are imbricated in the tasks traditionally assumed to be the sole purview of central cognition. As Fischer and Zwaan note, 'the increasingly prevalent view today is that perceptual and action-related processes are tightly linked to each other, as well as to more abstract cognition.'[58]

The concept of *affordances*, borrowed from Gibson's ecological psychology, neatly captures how perception, action, and cognition are intertwined.[59] Affordances are the possible ways in which an organism can manipulate its environment given its particular bodily capacities. As Clark illustrates, 'to a human a chair affords sitting, but to a woodpecker it may afford something quite different.'[60] Marsh notes that the notion of an affordance 'emphasized the mutuality of individuals and the environment. Mutuality means that the perceiving and acting capabilities of an animal, such as vision and walking, will, by necessity, be complementary to surfaces and objects in the world. For example, solid surfaces in an animal's niche exist that are sufficient to support walking of creatures of that weight.'[61] Thus, the relatively simple concept of affordances captures the idea that possibilities arise for an organism on the basis of *both* the properties of its physical environment *and* the capacities of its body to interact with that environment; we do not simply perceive objects 'objectively', rather we perceive them in terms of our capacity to interact with them. The way in which cognition relies upon affordances suggest that it is fundamentally shaped by the body and the way it interacts with its environment.[62]

Clark again provides a helpful summary of how embodied cognition challenges the sandwich model, worth quoting at length:

---

[57] E.g., see Bruce Bridgeman and Merrit Hoover, 'Processing Spatial Layout by Perception and Sensorimotor Interaction', *The Quarterly Journal of Experimental Psychology* 61, no. 6 (2008): 851.

[58] Fischer and Zwaan, 'Embodied Language', 826. See also, Clark, *Being There*, 221; Anna M. Borghi and Felice Cimatti, 'Words Are Not Just Words: The Social Acquisition of Abstract Words', *Rivista Italiana di Filosofia del Linguaggio* 5 (2012): 23; Autumn B. Hostetter and Martha W. Alibali, 'Visible Embodiment: Gestures as Simulated Action', *Psychonomic Bulletin & Review* 15, no. 3 (2008): 496.

[59] Gibson, *The Ecological Approach*. See also, Anthony Chemero, 'An Outline of a Theory of Affordances', *Ecological Psychology* 15, no. 2 (2003).

[60] Clark, *Being There*, 172.

[61] Kerry L. Marsh, Michael J. Richardson, and R. C. Schmidt, 'Social Connection through Joint Action and Interpersonal Coordination', *Topics in Cognitive Science* 1, no. 2 (2009): 326.

[62] Wilson and Foglia, *Embodied Cognition*.

Perception is commonly cast as the process by which we receive information from the world. Cognition then comprises intelligent processes defined over some inner rendition of such information. Intentional action is glossed as the carrying out of the commands that constitute the output of a cogitative, central system. But real-time, real-world success is no respecter of this neat tripartite division of labor. Instead, perception is itself tangled up with specific possibilities of action—so tangled up, in fact, that the job of central cognition often ceases to exist. The internal representations the mind uses to guide actions may thus be best understood as action-and-context-specific control structures rather than as passive recapitulations of external reality. The detailed, action-neutral inner models that were to provide the domain for disembodied, centralized cogitation stand revealed as slow, expensive, hard-to-maintain luxuries—top-end purchases that cost-conscious nature will generally strive to avoid.[63]

If traditional cognitive science is premised on the cognitive sandwich, embodied cognition proposes a 'cognitive stew' instead: individual ingredients may be evidenced in higher concentrations at particular locations, but they also dissolve and mutually infuse one another. Thus, perception, action, and what was formally associated with 'central' cognition, all interpenetrate each other.

4 The Limits of Embodied Cognition

Embodied cognition researchers advocate that we break with tradition and abandon the sandwich model of cognition. Embodied cognition is proposed as a superior paradigm on a number of accounts. First, there is a substantial body of empirical evidence favouring embodied explanations of cognitive processes. Second, it offers a stronger fit with other theoretical frameworks, such as connectivism and dynamical systems theory, which are arguably better approximations of the what is understood of way the brain operates. Third, it seems more plausible in evolutionary terms, since it offers parsimonious explanations of how more complex cognitive processes bootstrap onto earlier evolutionary developments. (Examples of these species of argument can be found in Chapters 3 and 5.)

Embodied cognition not only critiques 'traditional cognitive science' but some also claim that it supersedes cognitivism altogether.[64] Others are more cautious and adopt mediating positions. For example, Clark observes that '[a] major danger attending any revolutionary proposal in the sciences is that too much of the "old view" may be discarded—that healthy babies may be carried away by floods of bathwater'.[65]

---

[63] Clark, *Being There*, 51.   [64] Wilson and Golonka, 'Embodied Cognition'.
[65] Clark, *Being There*, 22.

One recurring challenge for embodied cognition is the issue of scope. While theorists readily provide empirical support for their hypotheses, questions remain about whether these examples generalise to all cognitive processes. Although there may be compelling evidence that some concepts include sensorimotor states, does this equally apply to abstract concepts? Although particular cognitive tasks are amenable to explanations which replace mental representations with interactions, what about offline tasks which do not involve sensorimotor engagement? Although cognition relies upon non-neural resources, is this enough to say that these resources constitute cognition? These questions will be thrashed out in detail in the following chapters. However, their presence reveals a lingering question about whether compelling empirical evidence applies to cognition *in toto*.

Although the case for embodied cognition continues to garner increasing levels of empirical support, it seems far from certain that it will replace 'cognitivism' *tout court*, as bolder predictions claim. Shapiro expresses his suspicion as follows:

> Claims about the meaning of embodiment...are far from uniform in the commitments they entail. More troubling still is that the claims often step far beyond the evidence or argument made in their support.[66]

He does not wish to rule out such claims on *a priori* grounds, but merely observes that insufficient evidence has been amassed to support them. He thus argues that, at present, embodied cognition has the status of a research programme rather than a settled science.[67] Although he acknowledges the potential of embodied cognition, he also urges caution:

> Today's research program may be tomorrow's reigning theory. However, embodied cognition's status as a research program does invite special caution when considering claims that it might replace or supersede standard cognitive science.[68]

If a declaration that embodied cognition should replace 'traditional cognitive science' may be premature, Fodor's claim that the computational theory of mind is 'the only game in town' is also looking increasingly tenuous.[69] The growing body of empirical evidence clearly shows that factors beyond the brain play a role in at least *some* forms of cognition. While extant empirical data may not yet illuminate how each and every cognitive task is embodied, Wilson and Galonka argue that a conceptual transformation is required even on the basis of existing evidence; even

---

[66] Michael Kullman and Charles Taylor, 'The Pre-Objective World', *The Review of Metaphysics* 12, no. 1 (1958): 51.
[67] Shapiro, 'The Embodied Cognition Research Programme'.
[68] Shapiro, *Embodied Cognition*, 3.   [69] Fodor, *The Language of Thought*, 27.

if only some cognition demonstrably involve factors beyond the brain, they contend that a root-and-branch redefinition of cognition is required, one which 'focuses on brain-body-environment cognitive systems'.[70] Despite his tentative approach, Clark equally argues that even if embodied cognition does not vanquish cognitivism, it nevertheless represents a decisive paradigm shift:

> Cognitive science, if the embodied, embedded perspective is even halfway on target, can no longer afford the individualistic, isolationist biases that characterized its early decades. We now need a wider view—one that incorporates a multiplicity of ecological and cultural approaches as well as the traditional core of neuroscience, linguistics, and artificial intelligence.[71]

Given the nascent status of embodied cognition, and heated debate about the scope of its explanatory power, I adopt a prudent approach in the following chapters, cautiously adopting weaker versions of each of the hypotheses. In a similar vein, Hostetter and Alibali state that for their purposes 'it is not at issue whether an embodied perspective can entirely replace or should rather be integrated with more traditional views of cognition; it is sufficient that accumulating evidence indicates that much of cognition is rooted in the body'.[72] Even if embodied cognition is ultimately destined for a rapprochement with traditional cognitive science, its achievements should nevertheless be recognised.

5 Conclusion

The purpose of this chapter has been to introduce embodied cognition through its literature, history, and concepts. Embodied cognition is usefully defined by contextualising it as a critique of cognitivism. However, whether embodied cognition will overthrow or complement 'traditional cognitive science' remains to be seen. When stated positively, embodied cognition offers proposals for how cognition grounds concepts (conceptualisation), relies on sensorimotor interactions with the world (replacement), and extends to bodily and environmental resources (constitution).

The remainder of this study is structured according to this taxonomy (proposed by Shapiro). Part II considers the conceptualisation hypothesis and applies it to theological concepts. Part III interrogates the replacement and constitution hypotheses and re-evaluates the cognitive import of embodied religious practices, before teasing out implications for a liturgically informed theological anthropology.

---

[70] Wilson and Golonka, 'Embodied Cognition', 1.   [71] Clark, *Being There*, 221.
[72] Hostetter and Alibali, 'Visible Embodiment', 497.

PART II

EMBODIMENT AND THEOLOGICAL CONCEPTS

3

The Body and Human Concepts

'I see on the one side the totality of sense-experiences, and, on the other, the totality of the concepts and propositions which are laid down in books...The concepts and propositions get "meaning," viz., "content," only through their connection with sense-experiences.'

—*Albert Einstein*[1]

Chapter 2 provided a broad orientation to 'embodied cognition'. This chapter considers one of its hypotheses, namely the 'conceptualisation hypothesis'. The conceptualisation hypothesis proposes that human concepts are grounded in embodied experience. After defining the hypothesis, I turn to the 'symbol grounding problem' which motivates an account of concepts that is grounded in embodied sensorimotor experience (Section 2). The classical 'amodal' theory of concepts (Section 3)—a central tenet of the cognitivist paradigm which embodied cognition critiques—arguably fails to address the symbol grounding problem. In response, embodied cognition researchers propose that concepts are grounded in our sensorimotor modalities (Section 4). Abstract concepts, which cannot readily be linked to particular perceptions or actions, present a challenge for such a 'modal' theory of concepts, but various theories have been proposed to show how even abstract concepts might be grounded in sensorimotor states (Section 5). This broad-ranging discussion of the embodied nature of human concepts will serve as the foundation for an examination of theological concepts in Chapter 4.

1 The Conceptualisation Hypothesis

A strong version of the conceptualisation hypothesis posits that the kinds of concepts which humans can acquire are restricted by the particularity of their physiology. Lakoff and Johnson make such a claim in a thought experiment;[2] they argue that a spherically shaped being, on account of its bodily configuration, could not have concepts for 'front' and 'back': since spheres have no fronts or backs and would presumably move around their environments by rolling, the

---

[1] Albert Einstein, *Albert Einstein: Philosopher-Scientist*, trans. Paul Arthur Schilpp (New York: MJF Books, 1949), 11–13. Einstein was, of course, no stranger to abstract concepts.
[2] Lakoff and Johnson, *Philosophy in the Flesh*, 34–5.

Corporeal Theology: Accommodating Theological Understanding to Embodied Thinkers. Tobias Tanton, Oxford University Press. © Tobias Tanton 2023. DOI: 10.1093/oso/9780192884589.003.0004

concepts 'front' and 'back' would not be available to such beings. Such concepts, they contend, can only be possessed by beings whose own bodies have a front and back. This strong version of the conceptualisation hypothesis contends that bodily configuration creates a hard limit which constrains an organism's conceptual possibilities.

Shapiro is not persuaded by this argument. He asks why such a spherical being could not acquire the concepts of front and back by observing other creatures with a front and back moving about in their environment.[3] One might similarly observe that humans, despite not being spherical, can nevertheless acquire concepts related to rotational movement such as 'torque' or 'angular momentum'. These concepts may be less intuitive for humans since they do not derive from direct experience of our own bodies in motion. However, there is no absolute limit preventing humans from acquiring such concepts.

Fischer and Zwaan raise a similar objection. They note that evidence from neuroimaging studies show that the actions of others are often understood in terms of our own body's motor repertoire, but argue that this does not limit human concepts:

> the studies comparing experts and nonexperts or conspecifics and nonconspecifics…have demonstrated that motor resonance occurs when the observed actions are part of the observer's own motor repertoire. But does this mean that actions are incomprehensible to us when we do not have them in our own repertoire? This seems implausible. At some level, we do understand the action, presumably relying on perceptual processes only…For example, even though we may not show motor resonance when we see or hear a dog barking, we still understand what the dog is doing.[4]

Hence motor capacities alone do not provide an absolute limit to our understanding.

The issue at stake in the critique of Lakoff and Johnson's position is whether an organism's concepts are directly related to its body (the 'strong' conceptualisation hypothesis) or concepts are instead derived from bodily *interaction with the world* (the 'weak' conceptualisation hypothesis).[5] This weak hypothesis is not subject to Shapiro's objection; indeed, he relies on it to explain how the spherical being can acquire concepts such as 'front' and 'back', namely by using perceptual capacities to observe these features in other creatures in its environment.[6] The problem with Lakoff and Johnson's position, then, is that the body alone is the source of

---

[3] Shapiro, *Embodied Cognition*, 89–90.   [4] Fischer and Zwaan, 'Embodied Language'.
[5] This position is suggested by an analysis of the way in which colour concepts arise from both bodily perceptual capacities and properties of the outside world. Varela, Rosch, and Thompson, *The Embodied Mind*. See also, Merleau-Ponty, *Phenomenology of Perception*, 320.
[6] Shapiro, *Embodied Cognition*, 89.

concepts, and it imposes a hard limit on the kind of concepts an organism can acquire. In the weak conceptualisation hypothesis, by contrast, perceptual *experience* of the world is the source of concepts.

This weak version does not exclude the body from a role in concept acquisition, but it does complicate it. In a weak conceptualisation hypothesis the body plays an indirect rather than a direct role in shaping concepts: concepts are grounded in perceptual experience and the character of that perception is dependent on the particularity of human bodies. Hence if concepts arise from experience, then insofar as bodies shape and constrain perceptual experience they also have a bearing on concepts.

2 The Symbol Grounding Problem

The symbol grounding problem seeks to understand how symbols become meaningful. In his influential theory of 'signs' (tokens which stand in for that to which they refer), Peirce outlines three strategies by which something can become a sign by referring to entities beyond itself (though any given sign can employ any combination of these strategies).[7] *Icons* refer to objects by means of perceptual resemblance; for example, a portrait is an icon of its sitter. The meaning or referent of an icon can be easily identified by virtue of its resemblance. *Indices* refer by virtue of causal relations; for example, smoke is typically an index for fire since fire causes smoke. So long as one is familiar with the causal relationship, the meaning or referent of an index is, again, readily identifiable and is in a sense intrinsic to the sign. Finally, *symbols* refer by convention; for example, a ring is a symbol of marriage. Symbols pose a special interpretive problem since they bear an *arbitrary* relationship to their referents, and thus the form of the symbol provides no intrinsic information about its referent. One therefore relies solely on the convention which connects the symbol to its referent for reference to succeed and the symbol to be meaningful—and herein lies the symbol grounding problem: the symbols on their own are meaningless unless they are 'grounded' by a connection to a non-symbolic referent.

One way to explicate the symbol grounding problem is to consider linguistic systems of representation. As Ferdinand de Saussure points out, words in human languages bear an *arbitrary* relationship to that which they represent.[8] Both the German word '*Pferd*' and the English word 'horse' can refer to the same referent, even though they are completely different from each other. This observation

---

[7] Charles S. Peirce, *The Writings of Charles S. Peirce: A Chronological Edition*, ed. Edward C. Moore, vol. 2 (Bloomington IA: Indiana University Press, 1984), 56.

[8] Ferdinand de Saussure, *Course in General Linguistics*, ed. C. Bally and A. Sechehaye, trans. A. Riedlinger (New York: McGraw-Hill, 1966).

demonstrates that words are assigned by convention and they bear no resemblance to the object they represent, either with respect to their orthography or their phonetics (onomatopoeic words are a rare exception). Hence linguistic signs usually fall into the category of 'symbol' according to Peirce's typology.[9]

Given that linguistic signs are Peircean symbols, they fall prey to the symbol grounding problem. The problem comes into focus in Searle's famous 'Chinese room' thought experiment.[10] Searle imagines a non-Chinese speaker enclosed in a room. Chinese characters are passed into the room through a narrow slit, and the person inside then looks up the characters in a book which provides her with a response to pass back outside. From the outside, then, it appears that whoever is in the room is able to communicate in Chinese. Those who know what is happening inside the room, however, are aware that, although the person is able to manipulate the symbols with the aid of the book, she lacks any comprehension of the meaning of the symbols. As Steels observes, Searle's thought experiment provoked 'discussion about when and how symbols could be about things in the world, whether intelligence involves representations or not, what embodiment means, and under what conditions cognition is embodied'.[11]

A conclusion one might draw from Searle's hypothetical scenario is that the capacity to manipulate symbols is insufficient to grasp their meaning.[12] To understand the meaning of symbols, one must be able to connect them to lived experience. Thus, symbols only become meaningful, they only succeed as representations, if they can be related back to—or *grounded* in—our perceptual experience.[13] As McGilchrist states, 'every word, in and of itself, eventually has to lead us out of the web of language, to the lived world, ultimately to something that can only be pointed to, something that relates to our embodied existence'.[14]

One could similarly imagine a scenario in which a non-Chinese speaker is set the impossible task of learning the language with only a monolingual Chinese dictionary at their disposal.[15] When the learner looks up the meaning of one

---

[9] Arthur M. Glenberg, Manuel de Vega, and Arthur C. Graesser, 'Framing the Debate', in *Symbols and Embodiment: Debates on Meaning and Cognition*, ed. Manuel De Vega, Arthur M. Glenberg, and Arthur C. Graesser (Oxford: Oxford University Press, 2008), 2.

[10] John Searle, 'Minds, Brains and Programs', *Behavioral and Brain Sciences* 3 (1980).

[11] Luc Steels, 'The Symbol Grounding Problem Has Been Solved, So What's Next?', in *Symbols and Embodiment: Debates on Meaning and Cognition*, ed. Manuel De Vega, Arthur M. Glenberg, and Arthur C. Graesser (Oxford: Oxford University Press, 2008), 223.

[12] Friedemann Pulvermüller, 'Grounding Language in the Brain', in *Symbols and Embodiment: Debates on Meaning and Cognition*, ed. Manuel De Vega, Arthur M. Glenberg, and Arthur C. Graesser (Oxford: Oxford University Press, 2008), 102. Another conclusion is that symbol manipulation is insufficient for thought, see Shapiro, 'Symbolism', 61.

[13] Mark Johnson, *The Meaning of the Body: Aesthetics of Human Understanding* (Chicago: University of Chicago Press, 2007), 7–11; Varela, Rosch, and Thompson, *The Embodied Mind*, 8.

[14] McGilchrist, *The Master and His Emissary*, 116.

[15] Harnad, 'The Symbol Grounding Problem', 339; Michael P. Kaschak et al., 'Embodiment and Language Comprehension', in *The Routledge Handbook of Embodied Cognition*, ed. Lawrence A. Shapiro (London: Routledge, 2014), 118–20.

Chinese word, they find a definition of equally opaque Chinese words. Since (monolingual) lexicons are circular—that is, they define the words (symbols) purely in terms of other symbols—one requires an entry point (such as referential knowledge about a basic set of symbols). Glenberg and Mehta call this the 'symbol merry-go-round' argument for grounding.[16] The discovery of ancient Egyptian hieroglyphs, the symbols of a completely dead language, is analogous with the Chinese dictionary case: although hieroglyphs were grouped (perhaps even defined) with other hieroglyphs, at the time of discovery all knowledge about the meaning of these hieroglyphs had been lost. Without an entry point into the symbol system, the inscriptions remained unintelligible to Egyptologists until the discovery of the Rosetta stone, which provided a section of hieroglyphic text in parallel with translations in known languages. In the vocabulary of the symbol grounding problem, the Rosetta stone allowed researchers to connect the ungrounded hieroglyphic symbols to the grounded symbols of known languages. As Harnad explains, '[t]he only reason cryptologists of ancient languages and secret codes seem to be able to successfully accomplish something very like this is that their efforts are grounded in a first language and in real world experience and knowledge.'[17]

A similar problem arises with the symbols manipulated by computational systems. While such systems may be able to manipulate symbols with impressive speed, they are typically oblivious to what these symbols mean, that is, how they relate to entities in the world. It often takes a programmer or operator to interpret the symbols and thereby give them meaning. As Shapiro states, 'How do symbols in the head acquire their semantics? Interpreting the outputs of a calculator as numbers is one thing, but, presumably, mental symbols have their meanings independently of how anyone chooses to interpret them.'[18] Hence the ungrounded symbols of a computational system (as presupposed by the cognitivist paradigm in cognitive science) serve as a poor analogue for mental symbols.

These scenarios illustrate a fundamental issue with symbols, namely that they must be grounded by a reference to (ultimately) a non-symbolic entity for them to be meaningful. As Shapiro states, '[o]ne needs to understand (tacitly or otherwise) how symbols are connected to the world in order to know what they mean.'[19]

[16] Arthur M. Glenberg and Sarita Mehta, 'The Limits of Covariation', in *Symbols and Embodiment: Debates on Meaning and Cognition*, ed. Manuel De Vega, Arthur M. Glenberg, and Arthur C. Graesser (Oxford: Oxford University Press, 2008), 13–14.

[17] Harnad, 'The Symbol Grounding Problem', 339.

[18] Shapiro, 'The Embodied Cognition Research Programme', 339.

[19] Shapiro, 'Symbolism', 61. The causal constraint in Putnam's famous brain-in-a-vat thought experiment likewise insists that there is a causal connection between our concept tree and real trees for the concept to be able to refer to or represented trees. See Michael McKinsey, *Skepticism and Content Externalism* (2018) [cited 10 October 2021]; available from https://plato.stanford.edu/archives/win2021/entries/embodied-cognition/; Hilary Putnam, 'Brains in a Vat', in *Reason, Truth and History* (Cambridge: Cambridge University Press, 1981).

A symbol's form is, on its own, insufficient to determine its meaning; one also requires a convention which associates (at least a basic set of symbols) with experience of the world. Moreover, simply defining a symbol which lacks any intrinsic meaning in terms of yet more meaningless symbols achieves nothing.

While it is clearly possible to define *some* symbols in terms of other symbols (as occurs in human language), these definitions cannot be symbols 'all the way down'. At some point the definitions must 'bottom out' (i.e., be grounded) in a non-symbolic meaning lest the symbol system becomes self-enclosed and impenetrable. As Harnad asks, 'How can the meanings of the meaningless symbol tokens, manipulated solely on the basis of their (arbitrary) shapes, be grounded in nothing but other meaningless symbols?'[20]

In the domain of language, the symbol grounding problem challenges any account of semantics to provide an explanation for how linguistic symbols are grounded by ultimately acquiring meaning from a non-symbolic source. In light of this prerequisite, language acquisition requires more than simply learning to recognise and pronounce spoken words (and later to recognise and write written words). It also requires learning the conventions by which these linguistic symbols relate back to the world of experience, conventions which can be learnt through mechanisms such as ostentation and joint attention.[21] Although language provides a clear example of the need to ground symbol systems, the symbol grounding problem arises for any system of Peircean symbols.

Another symbol system which may be susceptible to the symbol grounding problem is the human conceptual system. Concepts are the mental representations used in cognition. As representations, concepts typically stand in for objects, events, or states of affairs in the world. Thus, these representations count as Peircean signs, but where they fit into the Peircean typology is a matter of contention.

It is important to note that the relationship between concepts used in cognition and words used in natural languages is complex.[22] Although words are often used to describe concepts (e.g., the concept 'table' or 'red'), the two should not be conflated.[23] While words are clearly associated with certain concepts, the mapping is by no means straight forward. In the case of homonyms, the same word may be associated with multiple concepts (e.g., 'bank', as in river bank or merchant bank).

---

[20] Harnad, 'The Symbol Grounding Problem', 335.

[21] E.g., accounts of joint attention include 'the idea that the joint attention triangle makes possible the development of linguistic communication. In particular, there is the idea that the existence of a common object of attention provides for something like a joint field of reference, which enable linguistic communication about it to get going and develop.' Naomi Eilan, 'Joint Attention, Communication, and Mind', in *Joint Attention: Communication and Other Minds*, ed. Naomi Eilan, et al. (Oxford: Oxford University Press, 2005), 7.

[22] For discussion, see Jesse J. Prinz, *Furnishing the Mind: Concepts and Their Perceptual Basis* (Cambridge, MA: MIT Press, 2002), 16–18.

[23] Ibid., 22.

Words in different languages may have different conceptual ranges even if they partially overlap (e.g., the English 'to know' includes concepts for which other languages use multiple words, such as *wissen* and *kennen* in German or *savoir* and *connaître* in French).[24] It is also possible to have concepts for which one has no words, as is the case of pre-linguistic infants or aphasics who can think and perform tasks requiring mental representations even though they lack language.[25] As will be discussed, part of the controversy surrounding concepts is whether they are word-like arbitrary symbols. Therefore, it is important not to conflate concepts with words so as to prejudge this matter.

Barsalou divides theories of concepts into two categories which provide the salient distinction for considering how the symbol grounding problem potentially affects concepts.[26] What is at stake in this distinction is how a concept relates to perception—in particular the specific *modes* of human perception. On the one hand, 'amodal' theories posit that concepts are abstract symbols which exist independently of perceptual states. On the other hand, 'modal' theories argue that concepts are constituted by simulations of sensorimotor states.

3 Amodal Theories of Concepts

Amodal theories assert that concepts are represented in the mind by abstract representations which are detached from the *mode(s)* of embodied perception with which they were acquired. According to amodal theories, although perception may be used to acquire concepts, once a concept is represented in the mind it becomes divorced from how it was perceived. Thus, on this view, 'representations are autonomous from perceptual systems, bodily action, and their operational details'.[27] For example, although cats may be perceived through sight, sound, smell, and touch, the concept 'cat' no longer relies on the specifics of the modes in which cats were perceived. Hence concepts used for memory, language, or thought are no longer related to the sensations from which they arise.[28] Amodal concepts are thus word-like, since their form is *arbitrarily* related to their referent.

A key aspect of amodal theories is the transduction principle.[29] Since amodal concepts are detached from their modes of perception, amodal theories assume a process which translates—or transduces—sense perception into amodal symbols

---

[24] The polysemy of the English word 'to know' is routinely observed in reflections on knowledge. E.g., see McGilchrist, *The Master and His Emissary*, 96.

[25] Lawrence W. Barsalou, 'Perceptions of Perceptual Symbols', *Behavioral and Brain Sciences* 22, no. 04 (1999): 649; Prinz, *Furnishing the Mind*, 18.

[26] Barsalou, 'Perceptual Symbol Systems', 578–82.

[27] Wilson and Foglia, *Embodied Cognition*.

[28] Barsalou et al., 'Embodiment in Religious Knowledge', 20. Cf. Antonio R. Damasio, 'Concepts in the Brain', *Mind & Language* 4, no. 1–2 (1989).

[29] Barsalou et al., 'Embodiment in Religious Knowledge', 20. Barsalou, 'Grounded Cognition', 618.

for use in conceptual processing. Hence a coherent theory of amodal concepts requires a description of the mechanisms involved in transduction to account for concepts which are learnt from perceptual experience.

Amodal theories of concepts are a natural fit for the traditional 'cognitive sandwich' model.[30] As described in Chapter 2, this model posits that a central system in which the 'real' cognition takes place is sandwiched in between perceptual 'input' systems and behaviour 'output' systems. In keeping with this model, amodal symbols are divorced from their perceptual origins (or indeed the motor representations associated with behaviour) and can operate independently of them. As Wilson states, 'on the traditional [amodal] view, not only are the internal representations employed in language, concept formation, and memory essentially distinct from those processed by the sensorimotor system, but their meaning is divorced from bodily experience'.[31] Prinz echoes this assessment:

> According to the orthodoxy, inspired by classical computing, thinking occurs in a symbolic medium, whose representations have subject-predicate structure and are manipulated by logical rules. Thoughts are more like verbal descriptions than reenactments. It is often presumed that thought must be couched in an amodal medium, carried ou[t] in a central processing system that functions independently of input systems.[32]

3.1 Examples of Amodal Theories

Barsalou observes that amodal theories were in the ascendency during the twentieth century and have become 'standard'; such '[s]tandard theories of cognition assume that knowledge resides in a semantic memory system separate from the brain's modal systems for perception (e.g., vision, audition), action (e.g., movement, proprioception), and introspection (e.g., mental states, affect)'.[33] He attributes the rise of amodal symbols to influences from developments in logic, statistics, and computer science.[34] The representational languages developed in these disciplines, including predicate calculus, probability theory, and programming languages, all employed amodal symbols, which then quickly found their way into the models of cognitive science.

One prominent example of an amodal theory of concepts is the 'language of thought' hypothesis.[35] The hypothesis asserts that 'mental representations are, in many important respects, language-like. The beliefs, desires, and other attitudes

[30] Barsalou, 'Perceptual Symbol Systems', 577.   [31] Wilson and Foglia, *Embodied Cognition.*
[32] Prinz, *Furnishing the Mind*, 151.   [33] Barsalou, 'Grounded Cognition', 618.
[34] Barsalou, 'Perceptual Symbol Systems', 578. Cf. Barsalou, 'Grounded Cognition', 619.
[35] Jerry A. Fodor, *The Language of Thought* (Cambridge, MA: Harvard University Press, 1975). Cf. Prinz, *Furnishing the Mind*, 2.

we have are relations to language-like representations'.[36] The power of combinatorial syntax in linguistics makes language an attractive model for thought. Given that the basic building blocks of language, words, are amodal symbols, this model likewise assumes that concepts used in cognition are amodal symbols. As Shapiro observers, '[c]rucially, adoption of the language of thought hypothesis seems to force a commitment to the same kind of amodal-ity of mental representations that is true of linguistic representations'.[37]

Amodal theories may also add structure to the representations: concepts might be structured as a feature list (of various features or properties, e.g., a car has wheels, windows, etc.); or into even more highly structured entities such as schemata or frames (in which concepts are assigned various types of properties, e.g., the concept 'to give' involves an agent, a patient/recipient, and an object).[38] Since feature lists and schemata define concepts in terms of other abstract concepts (their features or properties), rather than any kind of perceptual content, they too are amodal.

A specific model which construes human cognition in terms of an amodal symbol system is Landauer and Dumais' 'Latent Semantic Analysis' (LSA).[39] This theory posits that words (and their underlying concept(s)) gain their meaning by virtue of their relationship to other words, namely through statistical inferences. By performing a statistical analysis on the co-occurrence of particular words in a large corpus of texts, they relate a word to around three hundred other words on the basis of frequency of co-occurrences. Since word meaning derives from statistical relationships rather than semantic content, Kintsch notes that 'in LSA the meaning of a word is a vector of 300 numbers that are entirely vacuous by themselves'.[40]

An implicit assumption of the LSA model is that 'the vast majority of referential meaning may well be inferred from experience with words alone',[41] as opposed to non-linguistic sensorimotor experience. Hence 'the central claim of LSA…is that much of the generic referential meaning of a word W can be bootstrapped from a model that simply considers statistical properties of the family and other words that accompany word W, without having to consider the physical and social world that may accompany text'.[42] Given that in this model words (and by proxy concepts) gain their meaning solely from their relationships with other

---

[36] Shapiro, 'Symbolism', 62.   [37] Ibid.

[38] Barsalou, 'Perceptual Symbol Systems', 579.

[39] Thomas K. Landauer and Susan T. Dumais, 'A Solution to Plato's Problem: The Latent Semantic Analysis Theory of Acquisition, Induction, and Representation of Knowledge', *Psychological Review* 104, no. 2 (1997).

[40] Walter Kintsch, 'Symbol Systems and Perceptual Representations', in *Symbols and Embodiment: Debates on Meaning and Cognition*, ed. Manuel De Vega, Arthur M. Glenberg, and Arthur C. Graesser (Oxford: Oxford University Press, 2008), 146–7.

[41] Landauer and Dumais, 'A Solution to Plato's Problem', 227.

[42] Glenberg, de Vega, and Graesser, 'Framing the Debate', 4.

words, rather than by association with perceptual experience, they can clearly be classed as amodal symbols.

Landauer argues that this model of word meaning 'induces human-like meaning relations from a "senseless" stream of undefined arbitrary symbols'.[43] He points to various successes of LSA:

> LSA passes multiple choice tests at college level, scores in the adult human range on vocabulary tests, mimics categorical word sorting and semantic relationship judgements, accurately mirrors word-to-word and sentence-to-word priming, correctly reflects word synonymy, antinomy, and polysemy, induces the similarity of phrases such as 'concerned with social justice' and 'feminist,' and has been used—with no other source of data—to rank knowledge content of essays indistinguishably from expert humans.[44]

The ability to perform such tasks purely on the basis of the statistical relationships between words is impressive. At first glance, the utility of LSA provides a compelling reason to accept that the concepts underlying words may be amodal symbol systems. Amodal theories, however, have been subject to critiques on numerous fronts.

3.2 Critiques of Amodal Theories

Given that amodal theories of concepts have been dominant over the past century, and that LSA successfully models many linguistic tasks, are there compelling reasons to abandon this theory? Barsalou argues that amodal theories of concepts have numerous shortcomings which can be summarised into three central objections.[45] First, amodal symbols face a theoretical objection in that transduction from perceptual states is ill-defined, making them vulnerable to the symbol grounding problem. Second, there is a lack of direct empirical evidence that amodal concepts are implemented in human cognition. Third, even if an amodal system of concepts can describe human conceptual capacities, there are reasons to consider it a weak theory from a meta-theoretical perspective. I shall consider each of these objections in turn.

The *first* objection is theoretical, namely that amodal concepts are susceptible to the symbol grounding problem introduced earlier. If amodal concepts derive their meaning exclusively from their relationships with other amodal concepts

---

[43] Thomas K. Landauer, 'Latent Semantic Analysis (LSA), a Disembodied Learning Machine, Acquires Human Word Meaning Vicariously from Language Alone', *Behavioral and Brain Sciences* 22, no. 4 (1999): 624.
[44] Ibid.   [45] Barsalou, 'Perceptual Symbol Systems', 579–80.

(e.g., through definitions, feature lists, or schemata) rather than from intrinsic perceptual content, then one is caught on a 'symbol merry-go-round'. Amodal theories lack an account of how 'symbols become mapped back to perceptual states and entities in the world'.[46] Since such symbols ultimately lack grounding in perceptual experience, it is not clear how they establish meaning through reference to the external world.

In addition to failing to explain how symbols refer, amodal theories likewise fail to account adequately for the connection between concepts and their referents in the reverse direction: namely how objects encountered in perceptual experience become concepts during a process of acquisition. Barsalou argues that the transduction process for amodal symbols has never been adequately defined.[47] 'Transduction' seems to be merely a placeholder for the result achieved, that is, the creation of an amodal symbol. But there seem to be few details available regarding how transduction might be implemented in human cognition. What would a theoretical model of the transduction process look like? What are the mechanisms by which a perceptual state becomes transduced into an amodal symbol? If a concept is stripped of its perceptual content, what remains? The process of transduction upon which amodal theories of concepts rely remains perilously underspecified.

As an amodal symbol system, LSA is susceptible to this critique. It clearly falls prey to the symbol grounding problem: since words are defined exclusively in terms of other words, one quickly finds oneself on a 'symbol merry-go-round', in which concepts never refer to entities in the world beyond the self-enclosed symbol systems. The creators of this model themselves acknowledge the need for symbol grounding when they state that 'to be more than an abstract system like mathematics words must touch reality at least occasionally'.[48] Additionally, there seems to be little direct evidence that the human brain implements LSA.[49]

Why then is LSA so successful at performing various tasks which seemingly require an understanding of word meaning? Zwaan notes that associations among words often mirror associations in the real world; in the same way that tomatoes and lettuce, or staplers and notepads are statistically likely to occur together in the world so too are the words for these objects likely to co-occur in language.[50] Thus, LSA's success stems from the way that statistical relationships in language approximate real-world relations. However, one cannot infer from these 'second-order correlations' that the meaning of concepts (or words) is established by

---

[46] Ibid., 580.   [47] Ibid.
[48] Landauer and Dumais, 'A Solution to Plato's Problem', 227. Cf. Glenberg and Mehta, 'The Limits of Covariation', 12; Kintsch, 'Symbol Systems', 156.
[49] Barsalou, 'Perceptions of Perceptual Symbols', 639.
[50] Zwaan, 'Experiential Traces', 166.

linguistic co-occurrences.[51] Rather, symbolic representations must be grounded by a connection (i.e., reference) to real-world objects.

In addition to the theoretical problems with amodal theories, a *second* critique concerns the empirical evidence for amodal representations. Even if amodal theories can describe many human conceptual capacities, there is little direct evidence that human cognition actually implements amodal concepts.[52] Barsalou argues that the prominence of amodal concepts in modern cognitive sciences was not driven by empirical findings, but '[i]nstead, amodal symbols were adopted largely because they captured important intuitions about the symbolic character of cognition, and because they could be implemented in artificial intelligence'.[53]

The evidence which does exist for amodal symbols tends to be indirect: that is, it has been shown that they can fulfil instrumental roles in cognitive systems.[54] Hence amodal symbols are used in models which successfully perform cognitive tasks (as is the case with LSA). Such evidence is indirect since it only offers a proof of principle—that aspects of human cognition *could* be implemented according to the model—rather than direct evidence which shows that human cognition actually is implemented in such a fashion.

This observation leads to a *third* objection, namely that amodal theories of concepts are inferior on meta-theoretical criteria for evaluating theories. Drawing on philosophy of science, Barsalou observes that theories are better if they satisfy 'falsifiability, parsimony, the ability to produce provocative hypotheses that push a science forward, the existence of direct evidence for their constructs, freedom from conceptual problems in their apparatus, and integrability with theory in neighboring fields'.[55] Ironically, the power and flexibility of amodal symbols tends to make theories which employ them weaker on these criteria. It allows amodal symbols to model any computational systems and many cognitive phenomena (supplying indirect evidence), thereby providing *post hoc* explanations. Consequently, such theories lack ability to make a priori prediction and are not falsifiable. Hence Barsalou concludes that even though amodal theories of concepts model cognitive capacities, they fail to meet the criteria for good theories.

Amongst the thirty responses to the original article which outlined the case for a modal theory of concepts, Barsalou contends that none of the respondents addresses the problems inherent with amodal symbol systems.[56] Given the shortcomings of amodal symbols, typified by the language of thought hypothesis and models such as LSA, many theorists have turned to a modal theory of concepts.

---

[51] Ibid., 167.
[52] Barsalou, 'Perceptual Symbol Systems', 579; Barsalou, 'Grounded Cognition', 623.
[53] Ibid., 620.   [54] Barsalou, 'Perceptual Symbol Systems', 580.
[55] Ibid.   [56] Barsalou, 'Perceptions of Perceptual Symbols', 637.

4 Grounding Concepts with Modal Theories

How, then, can the problems with amodal representations be redressed? Harnad provides a theoretical framework for a theory of concepts which avoids the symbol grounding problem. For Harnad, the first human cognitive capacity for which a theory of concepts must account is the ability to identify objects by discriminating between different objects in the world.[57] To achieve this he posits the existence of what he calls *iconic* representations which are 'internal analog transforms of the projections of distal objects on our sensory surfaces'.[58] To unpack this rather dense description, the representations are of distal objects, that is, objects in the organism's environment. These objects create sensory impressions on the receptors of the organism's sensory modalities. Since the same object may make different impressions depending, for example, on the angle from which it is viewed, the representation needs to include potential transformations of the same object so that its various modes of presentation can be grouped together. These 'iconic' representations thus pick out objects available to sense experience. Since these representations are analogue transformations of sensory impressions, rather than mere copies which resemble them, they (somewhat confusingly) fall into the category of Peircean indices (rather than icons).

In order to *identify* objects, the objects discriminated by 'iconic' representations must be assigned to a class or category. These categories are synonymous with the names given to classes of objects (e.g., 'horse'). To identify a particular object as its appropriate category Harnad posits *categorical* representations. These representations contain the invariant features which would allow an object to be identified as belonging to a given category. By selecting the subset of relevant features of an 'iconic' representation, and matching them to a particular categorical representation, the category membership of objects can be determined.

Crucially for Harnad, neither 'iconic' nor 'categorical' representations are symbolic in the Peircean sense of bearing an arbitrary relationship to that which they represent. Instead, both types of representation resemble the sensory impressions which the objects make on an organism. Thus, the representations are a function of *both* the distal objects which function as stimuli *and* the perceptual organs which register them.

Harnad provides a *theoretical* account of how symbols can be constituted by perceptual experience, a proof principle of how symbols could in theory be grounded. This theoretical account is helpfully supplemented by Barsalou's proposal based on the findings of cognitive science, that human cognition implements a perceptual symbol system.[59] He outlines how such representations might

---

[57] Harnad, 'The Symbol Grounding Problem' , 340–1.   [58] Ibid., 342.
[59] For a detailed specification of Barsalou's proposed perceptual symbol system, see Barsalou, 'Perceptual Symbol Systems', 582–603. See also Barsalou, 'Perceptions of Perceptual Symbols'; Barsalou, 'Grounded Cognition'.

function, gestures towards underlying neural mechanisms, and gathers empirical evidence for them.

In Barsalou's account, concepts are not separated from the perceptual systems through a process of transduction. Rather, perceptual symbols 'are modal because they are represented in the same systems as the perceptual states that produced them'.[60] Hence concepts consist of the perceptual states which correspond to the various *modes* of perception in which they are acquired: visual, gustatory, olfactory, auditory, tactile, proprioceptive, and introspective perceptual states, as well as the motor movements which accompany and support them. A modal concept of a 'cat' thus includes the sights, sounds, smells, warmth, and so on one encounters when perceiving or interacting with cats. As with Harnad's iconic and categorical representations, Barsalou's modal concepts are instantiated by sensorimotor states rather than bearing an arbitrary relationship to them.

This modal theory provides a clear account of how concepts are acquired through experience. When an object is encountered for the first time, selective attention picks out a small subset of the salient perceptual features of the object, and the concept consisting of these perceptually based representations is created.[61] The perceptual states which constitute concepts on the modal view need not be a conscious 'pictorial' image, as is the case in traditional empiricist accounts of 'imagism'.[62] As Barsalou states, 'the symbol formation process selects and stores a subset of active neurons in a perceptual state'.[63] Under this account of concept acquisition an ill-defined transduction process is not required, since perceptual symbols do not require any transformation which strips them of their perceptual content.[64]

Like Harnad, Barsalou recognises the need not simply to capture snapshots of perceptual experience but also to relate multiple perceptual states to form concepts.[65] This capacity allows concepts to refer to categories of objects as well as tracking individual instances of objects (i.e., types and tokens). Similar to Harnad's categorical representations, Barsalou develops a description of 'simulators' which collect together the various perceptual states belonging to the same concept. The perceptual states, which make up the subparts of a simulator, may represent different perceptual vantage points on an object, variations among instances of the same category, different parts of an event sequence, or different modes of perception which relate to the same object or event.[66] Damasio's account

---

[60] Barsalou, 'Perceptual Symbol Systems' , 578.   [61] Ibid., 583–4.

[62] Prinz, *Furnishing the Mind*, 26; Antonio R. Damasio and Hanna Damasio, 'Brain and Language', *Scientific American* 267, no. 3 (1992): 91.

[63] Barsalou, 'Perceptual Symbol Systems', 584.

[64] Barsalou et al., 'Embodiment in Religious Knowledge', 22.

[65] Barsalou, 'Perceptual Symbol Systems', 586–7.

[66] Carmen Granito, 'Where Are Abstract Concepts From? Embodiment Beyond the Body', *Rivista Italiana di Filosofia del Linguaggio* 5 (2012): 85; Guy Dove, 'Three Symbol Ungrounding Problems: Abstract Concepts and the Future of Embodied Cognition', *Psychonomic Bulletin and Review* 23, no. 4 (2016): 1110.

of convergence zones in the brain suggests a neural mechanism by which such simulators could be implemented.[67]

Once acquired, concepts must, of course, also be deployable in 'offline' situations, when their referents are not present or immediately available to perception. In the modal account of concepts, this is achieved by *simulation*: 'Simulation is the reenactment of perceptual, motor, and introspective states acquired during experience with the world, body, and mind.'[68] Recalling a concept thereby entails partially *simulating* the perceptual states related to that concept.

Barsalou draws out the difference between the amodal and modal theories by contrasting their respective understandings of human perceptual systems. Amodal theories typically regard perception merely as a passive recording system, and 'a recording system does not interpret what each part of the recording contains—it simply creates an attenuated copy.'[69] By contrast, modal theories see perceptual systems as implementing a fully functioning conceptual system.[70] Unlike a recording, they interpret a scene by identifying their constituent parts and relations, drawing inferences, constructing new complex concepts by combining simple ones, and supporting the formulation of propositions by binding types and tokens.[71]

This contrast between perception as a recording versus a conceptual system also has implications for a broader model of cognition. Amodal theories reflect the 'sandwich' model of cognition by assuming that perceptions are 'inputs' and motor systems are 'outputs' of cognition. Since amodal representations are no longer related to perception after transduction has occurred, the central system which implements 'cognition proper' operates independently from sensorimotor systems. Modal theories of concepts overturn the 'sandwich' model of cognition by arguing that perceptual and motor systems are implicated in conceptual processing. Since, according to modal theories, conceptual representations are constituted by sensorimotor states and are activated by simulating those states, sensorimotor systems are vital for conceptual processing.

Barsalou's modal account of concepts is further developed by Prinz, who extrapolates Barsalou's insights into a fully-fledged *philosophical* theory of concepts grounded in perceptual systems.[72] He compares a perceptual account of concepts with various historical rivals, and argues that although other accounts have certain strengths, the perceptual account is ultimately superior. He begins by outlining a number of desiderata which a theory of concepts ought to satisfy.[73] An adequate theory of concepts should be able to account for different types of concepts ('scope'). In terms of contents, a concept ought to contain both reference to the extra-mental world ('intentional content') and content which can differentiate

[67] Barsalou, 'Perceptual Symbol Systems', 583.   [68] Barsalou, 'Grounded Cognition', 618.
[69] Barsalou, 'Perceptual Symbol Systems', 581.   [70] Ibid.   [71] Ibid., 581–2.
[72] Prinz, *Furnishing the Mind*.   [73] Ibid., 3–22.

between two concepts with the same reference ('cognitive content'). A theory should also explain how concepts are used to categorise objects in conceptual hierarchies ('categorisation') and combine them into more complex concepts ('compositionality'). Finally, a theory should be able to account for the way that humans acquire ('acquisition') and share ('publicity') concepts.

Having established these desiderata, Prinz sets about measuring extant theories of concepts against them.[74] He considers imagism: concepts derive from *conscious* perceptual states; definitionism: concepts are definitions composed of individually necessary and jointly sufficient conditions; 'prototype theory': category concepts are represented by a prototypical instance; exemplar theory: concepts are composed of numerous exemplars; 'theory theory': concepts function like theories in which beliefs determine categorisation judgements; and 'informational atomism': concepts are internally unstructured and obtain their identity from information in the environment. Discussing the advantages and disadvantages of each theory, he finds that although the theories often do well in some desiderata, sometimes a particular desideratum for which they were designed, they often fail in others. For example, imagism does well on acquisition and cognitive content desiderata, but falls short on desiderata such as scope, categorisation and publicity.

In contrast to existing theories which only partially fulfil the desiderata, Prinz crafts a theory of concepts which can satisfy them all. He takes inspiration from many of the other theories in an attempt to capitalise on their strengths. However, Prinz's theory develops a 'neo-empiricist' view of concepts. He agrees that older empiricist accounts, such as Locke's classical articulation, have been rendered untenable by the criticisms levelled against them. Nevertheless, he argues that empiricism can be updated in a way that overcomes these objections.[75] He subsequently argues for 'concept empiricism', a claim that '[a]ll (human) concepts are copies or combinations of copies of perceptual representations'.[76] Like Barsalou, he understands perception in a broad way which includes perceptions of the external world and one's own body: 'concept empiricism interprets perception in a fairly inclusive way. It is the view that concepts are derived from a broad class of states including emotions, motor commands, and sensations'.[77]

Prinz's theory of concepts is of particular interest since he explicitly develops it in dialogue with findings from cognitive science, taking Barsalou's work as his starting point.[78] As an empirically informed account, his desiderata for a theory of concepts include the ability to account for findings in cognitive science about the way humans use concepts.[79] For example, studies have found that humans identify some items as more typical of a given category than others.[80] Other

[74] Ibid., 25–101.   [75] Ibid., 2.   [76] Ibid., 108.
[77] Ibid., 122.   [78] Ibid., ix, 127–32.   [79] E.g., ibid., 10.
[80] Eleanor H. Rosch, 'Natural Categories', *Cognitive Psychology* 4, no. 3 (1973).

studies found that participants were faster at categorisation tasks involving mid-level categories (e.g., 'dog') rather than more specific low-level categories (e.g., 'Rottweiler') or more abstract high-level categories (e.g., 'animal').[81] Hence an adequate theory of concepts ought to be able to accommodate such findings. By including such specifics amongst his desiderata, Prinz ensures that his theory will not only accord with the broad capacities of human conceptual systems but also be more likely to reflect their actual implementation.

In summary, the modal theory of concepts, developed through the work of Harnad, Barsalou, and Prinz, attempts to overcome the shortcomings of amodal theories outlined in Section 3. Having described the modal theory, the following three subsections discuss how it addresses the problems inherent in amodal accounts: namely, it overcomes the symbol grounding problem; it enjoys the support of a wide variety of empirical evidence; and it makes for an appealing theory on meta-theoretical criteria.

4.1 Overcoming the Symbol Grounding Problem

A primary advantage of modal theories is that they overcome the symbol grounding problem; indeed, proponents of the modal theory often cite the symbol grounding problem as a motivating factor for abandoning amodal theories in favour of modal ones.[82] Modal concepts overcome the symbol grounding problem because they are not arbitrarily related to that which they represent. Rather, the content of concepts is intrinsically related to its referent. Since modal concepts are non-symbolic, one does not find oneself on a 'symbol merry-go-round' in which arbitrary, intrinsically meaningless symbols are defined purely in terms of other meaningless symbols.

Shapiro critiques the notion that amodal symbols fall foul of the symbol grounding problem.[83] He argues that amodal concepts nevertheless have a causal aetiology in relation to their referents. However, this assumes that amodal concepts are indices as opposed to symbols (according to a Peircean typology).[84] Moreover, it seems to take for granted the process of transduction which Barsalou identifies as a weakness of amodal symbols. In Barsalou's account, however, a concept which is causally related to the perceptual impressions is modal.[85] As Peircean symbols, amodal concepts are not intrinsically grounded.

---

[81] Eleanor Rosch et al., 'Basic Objects in Natural Categories', *Cognitive Psychology* 8, no. 3 (1976).

[82] Shapiro, 'Symbolism', 57; Arthur M. Glenberg and Michael P. Kaschak, 'Grounding Language in Action', *Psychonomic Bulletin & Review* 9, no. 3 (2002): 558; Shapiro, 'The Embodied Cognition Research Programme', 339.

[83] Shapiro, 'Symbolism', 58.

[84] Peirce, *The Writings of Charles S. Peirce: A Chronological Edition.*

[85] Barsalou, 'Perceptual Symbol Systems', 578, cf. 608, note 571; Barsalou, 'Perceptions of Perceptual Symbols', 638. Cf. Prinz, *Furnishing the Mind*, 31.

4.2 Empirical Evidence for Modal Concepts

In contrast to the paucity of direct empirical evidence for amodal concepts, a wide range of evidence suggests that human cognition implements modal concepts.[86] Numerous studies speak to the presence of modal concepts which are recalled via simulations in human conceptual and language processing. With respect to methodology, these studies fall into three broad categories: brain lesion studies consider cases in which a particular part of the brain has been damaged; neuroimaging studies record brain activation patterns while particular tasks are being performed; and behavioural studies measure behaviour responses (such as reaction times) as certain tasks are performed. These studies suggest that certain concepts employ simulations of motor movement, perceptual states, and emotional body states.

4.2.1 Category-Specific Deficiencies in Patients with Brain Lesions

The link between particular regions in the brain and certain conceptual categories was first discovered in brain lesion studies.[87] Surprisingly, patients who suffered certain types of localised brain lesions lost the ability to use only some conceptual categories. A study of four patients who suffered from herpes simplex encephalitis, a condition which causes damage to the temporal lobes, found that they had difficulties with identifying living things and foods, but not inanimate objects. These deficiencies affected both word comprehension and visual identification, suggesting that the deficiency was not merely linguistic but affected underlying concepts.[88] Experimenters hypothesised that the lesions to visual processing areas caused difficulties with living things because these concepts require fine visual distinctions (e.g., identification of lions, tigers, and leopards requires distinguishing between plain, striped, and spotted surfaces), whereas inanimate objects are discriminated in terms of function.[89]

Another study confirmed the hypothesis that animal and inanimate object categories rely more heavily on visual and functional information respectively.[90]

---

[86] The survey of empirical evidence in this section is not intended to be exhaustive. Instead it gives a representative selection of the main bodies of evidence in the literature. Helpful reviews of evidence can be found in Barsalou, 'Grounded Cognition'; Fischer and Zwaan, 'Embodied Language'; Florian Krause, Harold Bekkering, and Oliver Lindemann, 'A Feeling for Numbers: Shared Metric for Symbolic and Tactile Numerosities', *Frontiers in Psychology* 4, no. 7 (2013).

[87] Jenny Sheridan and Glyn W. Humphreys, 'A Verbal-Semantic Category-Specific Recognition Impairment', *Cognitive Neuropsychology* 10, no. 2 (1993); Elizabeth K. Warrington and T. Shallice, 'Category Specific Semantic Impairments', *Brain* 107 (1984); M. Caterina Silveri and G. Gainotti, 'Interaction between Vision and Language in Category-Specific Semantic Impairment', *Cognitive Neuropsychology* 5, no. 6 (1988).

[88] Warrington and Shallice, 'Category Specific Semantic Impairments', 845. For a review, see Guido Gainotti, 'The Role of Body-Related and Environmental Sources of Knowledge in the Construction of Different Conceptual Categories', *Frontiers in Psychology* 3, no. 430 (2012).

[89] Warrington and Shallice, 'Category Specific Semantic Impairments', 849.

[90] Silveri and Gainotti, 'Interaction between Vision and Language'.

Subjects were given two sets of animal definitions, one stressing visual features (e.g., 'black and white striped horse' for a zebra) and the other using non-visual information, such as metaphorical expressions, noise descriptions, or functions attributes (e.g., 'farm animal which bleats and supplies us with wool' for a sheep).[91] Identifying animals was far more successful using non-visual information, suggesting that such patients retain functional components of semantic memory whereas visual components are impaired.[92]

In other lesion cases patients suffer from precisely the opposite category identification impairment. A patient who suffered from a 'large left fronto-parietal infarct' affecting motor systems and was able to identify natural objects but had difficulty with artefactual objects and body parts.[93] Researchers noted that 'many artefacts are associated with fine hand manipulations and actions, as are body parts'.[94] Hence only semantic categories which relate to motor functions were compromised. Similar cases have been reported elsewhere.[95]

These selective deficits appear to be linked to perceptual modalities, rather than partial damage to a unified, presumably amodal, semantic system. As Warrington et al. explain:

> Such observations have usually been interpreted in terms of a unitary semantic system that has been specifically disconnected from 'lower level' modality specific perceptual systems…There are, however, a number of agnosic phenomena which are difficult to interpret in terms of a single semantic system disconnected from particular input modalities, and more easily interpreted in terms of modality specific semantic systems. Thus certain semantic memory impairments leave the patient with a stable but impoverished semantic processing ability.[96]

Lesions which cause category-specific concept deficits assist in deciding between rival theories of concepts. Given that amodal concepts are unrelated to modes of perception, one might expect them to reside in a central 'unitary semantic system'. Modal concepts, by contrast, are constituted by sensorimotor states, suggesting a role for brain regions also involved in perceptual processing. Hence the differential impairment of particular categories of concepts caused by damage to visual or motor regions of the brain provides evidence for modal concepts.

---

[91] Ibid., 692–4.   [92] Ibid., 694.

[93] Carol Sacchett and Glyn W. Humphreys, 'Calling a Squirrel a Squirrel but a Canoe a Wigwam: A Category-Specific Deficit for Artefactual Objects and Body Parts', *Cognitive Neuropsychology* 9, no. 1 (1992).

[94] Ibid., 82.

[95] Elizabeth K. Warrington and Rosaleen McCarthy, 'Category Specific Access Dysphasia', *Brain* 106, no. 4 (1983); Elizabeth K. Warrington and Rosaleen McCarthy, 'Categories of Knowledge: Further Fractionations and an Attempted Integration', *Brain* 110, no. 5 (1987).

[96] Warrington and Shallice, 'Category Specific Semantic Impairments', 830. Cf. Silveri and Gainotti, 'Interaction between Vision and Language', 679.

4.2.2 Sensorimotor Neural Activation During Conceptual Processing in Neuroimaging Studies

Category deficiencies identified in lesion studies generate a hypothesis that sensorimotor regions of the brain participate in conceptual processing in healthy patients. A number of neuroimaging studies test this hypothesis by monitoring for brain activation patterns in sensorimotor regions of the brain (which lie outside of the regions traditionally associated with language processing) during conceptual processing.[97]

One fruitful area of inquiry is the concepts at work in novel metaphors. Novel metaphors are difficult to account for on the basis of amodal theories, since the meaning which arises from a novel combination is difficult to explain based upon pre-existing definitions (or semantic relationships) of the two individual concepts which are juxtaposed. Modal representations allow for a more plausible account of novel metaphors: the sensorimotor states of which the two concepts are comprised are compared to locate the similarity in their dissimilarity. Given that the creation and (typically) intuitive comprehension of novel metaphors seems to require perceptual information which goes over and above definitional knowledge, one might expect activation in sensorimotor areas of the brain when processing novel metaphors. A neuroimaging study found precisely such an activation pattern: '[t]he novel metaphors evoked parietal activation around the intraparietal sulcus area bilaterally, suggesting that visual imagery processes were being used to instantiate and/or interpret the novel metaphors'.[98]

Beginning with a general division in language, several early neuroimaging studies looked for the difference in activation during noun and verb processing. These studies found that nouns referring to concrete objects activated visual areas of the brain whereas verbs referring to motor actions are strongly associated with motor regions.[99] Thus, in addition to classical language centres, '[c]ortical cell assemblies representing action verbs probably include additional neurons in the motor cortices, whereas cell assemblies representing concrete nouns may include additional neurons in visual cortices of both hemispheres'.[100] The associations support the notion that concepts are instantiated by sensorimotor states.

---

[97] I.e., the Broca and Wernicke areas; damage to these areas is known to cause general language deficiencies, as opposed to category-specific deficiencies Hubert Preissl et al., 'Evoked Potentials Distinguish between Nouns and Verbs', *Neuroscience Letters* 197, no. 1 (1995). Cf. Friedemann Pulvermüller, 'Brain Mechanisms Linking Language and Action', *Nature Reviews Neuroscience* 6, no. 7 (2005): 580.

[98] Marcel Adam Just, 'What Brain Imaging Can Tell Us About Embodied Meaning', in *Symbols and Embodiment: Debates on Meaning and Cognition*, ed. Manuel De Vega, Arthur M. Glenberg, and Arthur C. Graesser (Oxford: Oxford University Press, 2008), 80.

[99] Preissl et al., 'Evoked Potentials Distinguish between Nouns and Verbs', 82–3; Friedemann Pulvermüller, Werner Lutzenberger, and Hubert Preissl, 'Nouns and Verbs in the Intact Brain: Evidence from Event-Related Potentials and High-Frequency Cortical Responses', *Cerebral Cortex* 9, no. 5 (1999): 503.

[100] Pulvermüller, Lutzenberger, and Preissl, 'Nouns and Verbs', 505.

Subsequent studies have taken a more fine-grained approach to categories of words, employing the associations between animal categories and visual information, and tool categories and motor skills, found in brain lesion studies. Consistent with these associations, naming animals activated the region of the brain also involved in early stages of visual processing (the left medial occipital lobe), whereas naming tools activated the same area used to imagine hand movements (left premotor area) and an area associated with generating action words (left middle temporal gyrus).[101] Summarising the findings relating to verbs and nouns, and tools and animals, Pulvermüller states:

> Many nouns refer to visually perceivable objects and are therefore characterized by strong semantic links to visual information, whereas most verbs are action verbs and link semantically to action knowledge. Like action verbs, nouns that refer to tools are usually also rated by subjects to be semantically linked to actions, and a large number of animal names are rated to be primarily related to visual information.[102]

Even greater precision has been achieved in studies of motor cortex activation during the comprehension of action words associated with specific parts of the body. The motor cortex is 'somatotopically' arranged, meaning that specific sub-regions of the motor cortex map onto specific parts of the body.[103] This arrangement conveniently allows experimenters to test whether processing concepts related to particular parts of the body activate the relevant areas of the motor cortex. Pulvermüller articulates this hypothesis as follows: a '[c]rucial prediction of the semantic somatotopy model is that perception of spoken or written action words should activate cortical areas involved in action control and execution in a category-specific somatotopic fashion, depending on the semantics of the action words'.[104]

A study capitalised on this somatotopic arrangement by asking participants in the study to read words which refer to face, leg, and arm movements such as 'lick', 'kick', and 'pick'.[105] The activation patterns were then compared to activation patterns during the performance of motor action using the tongue, fingers, and feet. This comparison revealed a significant overlap between highly localised activation in the motor cortex during action performance and reading.[106] Another

---

[101] Alex Martin et al., 'Neural Correlates of Category-Specific Knowledge', *Nature* 379, no. 6566 (1996).

[102] Pulvermüller, 'Grounding Language', 94.

[103] Olaf Hauk and Friedemann Pulvermüller, 'Somatotopic Representation of Action Words in Human Motor and Premotor Cortex', *Neuron* 41, no. 2 (2004): 301–2.

[104] Pulvermüller, 'Grounding Language', 96.

[105] Hauk and Pulvermüller, 'Somatotopic Representation'.

[106] Ibid., 303. Cf. Friedemann Pulvermüller, Yury Shtyrov, and Risto Ilmoniemi, 'Brain Signatures of Meaning Access in Action Word Recognition', *Journal of Cognitive Neuroscience* 17, no. 6 (2005).

study found a similar somatotopic activation of the motor cortex when action words are embedded in sentences.[107] Such studies provide 'strong evidence... for the embodiment of aspects of semantics in action mechanisms'.[108]

Somatotopic activation is, on its own, insufficient to establish that the motor systems play a *constitutive* role in concepts; activation may be epiphenomenal, a by-product of the concept which is unnecessary for the conceptual processing.[109] Follow-up studies suggest that somatotopic activation is constitutive of conceptual processing on account of immediacy, automaticity, and functional relevance.[110] Activation of the motor cortex is relatively early, coming some 100–200ms after the initial stimulus, whereas post-lexical meaning-related processes typically occur around 400ms after the stimulus (immediacy).[111] Somatotopic activation occurred upon hearing face, arm, and leg action words, even when participants were focusing on a distractor task (automaticity).[112] Somatotopic activations have also been shown to be functionally relevant to language comprehension: when transcranial magnetic stimulation (TMS) was applied to specific motor cortex areas, the processing of action words relating to the relevant part of the body occurred faster.[113] In a similar study, experimenters applied TMS to either the arm or leg areas of the motor cortex and simultaneously monitored motor evoked potentials (MEPs, measurements of electrical activity in the muscles).[114] While participants listened to sentences describing arm or leg movements, the MEP in the corresponding body part decreased. Researchers interpreted this effect as interference: since the somatotopic area of the motor cortex was being used for sentence processing, the MEPs decreased.[115] The result was corroborated by a behavioural experiment: while listening to arm and leg action sentences and responding with arm and leg movements respectively, response times were slower.[116] These studies provide evidence that activation of somatotopic areas of the brain is not epiphenomenal, but plays a constitutive role in language comprehension (and hence conceptual processing).

In summary, consistent with lesion studies, numerous neuroimaging studies provide evidence that the brain's sensorimotor systems participate in conceptual

---

[107] Marco Tettamanti et al., 'Listening to Action-Related Sentences Activates Fronto-Parietal Motor Circuits', *Journal of Cognitive Neuroscience* 17, no. 2 (2005).

[108] Pulvermüller, 'Grounding Language', 97.   [109] Ibid.

[110] Ibid., 98–100; Olaf Hauk et al., 'Imagery or Meaning? Evidence for a Semantic Origin of Category-Specific Brain Activity in Metabolic Imaging', *European Journal of Neuroscience* 27, no. 7 (2008); Pulvermüller, 'Brain Mechanisms', 579.

[111] Sara C. Sereno, Keith Rayner, and Michael I. Posner, 'Establishing a Time-Line of Word Recognition: Evidence from Eye Movements and Event-Related Potentials', *Neuroreport* 9, no. 10 (1998); Pulvermüller, Shtyrov, and Ilmoniemi, 'Brain Signatures'.

[112] Pulvermüller, Shtyrov, and Ilmoniemi, 'Brain Signatures'.

[113] Friedemann Pulvermüller et al., 'Functional Links between Motor and Language Systems', *European Journal of Neuroscience* 21, no. 3 (2005).

[114] G. Buccino et al., 'Listening to Action-Related Sentences Modulates the Activity of the Motor System: A Combined TMS and Behavioral Study', *Cognitive Brain Research* 24, no. 3 (2005).

[115] Ibid., 361.   [116] Ibid.

processing. The scope of these studies is impressive, as Pulvermüller summarises: '[i]t seems that effective specific connections of language and action systems can be documented for spoken or written language, at the word and sentence levels, and for various languages (for example, English, Italian, German and Finnish) using various neuroscientific methods (fMRI, MEG, EEG and TMS)'.[117] Similarly to brain lesions studies, the activation of sensorimotor areas of the brain during concept processing challenges the view that such processing is confined to a specific centre in the brain: '[t]he picture of cortical function arising from these data is that of the cortex as a storehouse of words and their meanings bound together by distributed neuronal systems with specific topographies'.[118] Hence existing concepts are recalled through sensorimotor *simulations*, a key plank in a modal theory of concepts. Moreover, it challenges the 'sandwich' model of cognition since sensorimotor areas contribute to 'higher' cognitive processes such as conceptual processing.[119]

The crucial implication of these studies is that the activation patterns relate to the meaning of the words and concepts evoked; they show that 'the pattern of cortical activation elicited by an action word reflects the cortical representation of the action *to which the word refers*';[120] and 'cell assemblies representing words have different cortical distributions and assembly topographies *reflect semantic properties of the words*'.[121] Thus, the relationship between the meaning of the concept and its neural representation is not *arbitrary*, rather the meaning of the word is intrinsic to the representation.[122] This relationship has the capacity to establish reference without the need for an externally imposed convention.[123] Hence it demonstrates that concepts are Peircean indices rather than symbols, thereby supporting a modal theory of concepts: '[t]he fact that sensorimotor circuits get recruited, or rather, re-used for purposes, like concept formation or language processing, other than those they have been established for, such as motor and sensory information processing, strongly favors modal and embodied approaches to cognition over amodal and abstract ones'.[124]

4.2.3 Canonical and Mirror Neurons

Though scanning technologies are gradually improving, current techniques are limited by spatial and temporal resolution. Scans on live human subjects reveal activation patterns for regions in the brain but are unable to measure the activation at the neuronal level. This is a limitation of the current technology and the

---

[117] Pulvermüller, 'Brain Mechanisms', 580.
[118] Pulvermüller et al., 'Functional Links', 797.
[119] Pulvermüller, 'Grounding Language', 100.
[120] Hauk and Pulvermüller, 'Somatotopic Representation', 305. Emphasis added.
[121] Pulvermüller, Lutzenberger, and Preissl, 'Nouns and Verbs', 497. Emphasis added.
[122] Ibid., 497, 504–5; Fischer and Zwaan, 'Embodied Language', 839.
[123] Hauk and Pulvermüller, 'Somatotopic Representation', 305.
[124] Wilson and Foglia, *Embodied Cognition*. Cf. Hauk et al., 'Imagery or Meaning?', 1864.

ethical imperative to measure neural activity in live human subjects without inva-sive techniques. Although the studies outlined in the previous subsection provide good evidence for an overlap between the sensorimotor systems and conceptual systems, they are unable to illuminate how sensorimotor systems are co-opted for conceptual processing at the neuronal level. The discovery of mirror and canon-ical neurons in macaque monkeys and evidence for similar neural behaviour in humans goes some way to bridging this gap.

Researchers monitoring the activation patterns of individual neurons in live macaque monkeys discovered 'mirror neurons' that fire both when the monkey *performed* an action (e.g., grasping food) and when it *observed* a conspecific or even an experimenter performing the same action.[125] They also found 'canonical neurons', which activate both when observing an object and during motor manipulations of that same object.[126] Since monitoring individual neurons requires invasive surgery, there is no direct evidence for mirror neurons in humans; however, neurophysiological and brain-imaging studies have yielded a large amount of indirect evidence for the mirror-neuron system in humans.[127]

The discovery of mirror and canonical neurons suggests that perception and action are intricately intertwined. In the case of mirror neurons, observers under-stood the actions of others *in terms of their own motor capacity* to perform those actions.[128] The actions of others (and the intentions of those actions) are under-stood because that one has experience in performing the same action.[129] This 'indicates a neurophysiological mechanism that creates a common (parity require-ment), nonarbitrary, semantic link between communicating individuals'.[130]

Canonical neurons likewise suggest a form of bodily understanding. The con-nection between perceiving objects and actions performed on those objects, sug-gest that objects are understood, at least in part, *in terms of the bodily capacity* to manipulate them. To illustrate this point Shapiro gives the example of two other-wise identical spheres the size of a tennis ball and a ping-pong ball.[131] Although both share many of the same properties (shape, colour, etc.), they require different kinds of motor movements to be manipulated: the entire hand verses finer manipulation between the finger and thumb. Hence the two are not

[125] G. Pellegrino et al., 'Understanding Motor Events: A Neurophysiological Study', *Experimental Brain Research* 91, no. 1 (1992); Giacomo Rizzolatti and Laila Craighero, 'The Mirror-Neuron System', *Annual Review of Neuroscience* 27, no. 1 (2004): 169.

[126] Rizzolatti and Craighero, 'The Mirror-Neuron System', 170.

[127] Ibid., 174; Fischer and Zwaan, 'Embodied Language', 829; Tettamanti et al., 'Listening to Action-Related Sentences', 273.

[128] Rizzolatti and Craighero, 'The Mirror-Neuron System', 172, 179; Brown and Strawn, *Physical Nature of Christian Life*, 56–7; Brown and Reimer, 'Embodied Cognition', 842; Wilson and Foglia, *Embodied Cognition*.

[129] Barsalou, 'Grounded Cognition', 623.

[130] Rizzolatti and Craighero, 'The Mirror-Neuron System', 183. There is also evidence that mirror-neuron systems are active when humans observe a monkey or a dog performing an action which they can understand in terms of their own bodily topology, such as biting. Ibid., 179.

[131] Shapiro, *Embodied Cognition*, 110.

conceptualised as generic spheres, but as spheres which requiring certain kinds of actions. Shapiro summarises: 'how one interacts with objects in the world and which actions one can expect to accomplish, depend on the properties of one's body'.[132]

Given that mirror neurons indicate a connection between performing actions and perceiving them, while canonical neurons indicate a connection between performing an action and the affordance of an object, both suggest that humans comprehend certain objects *in terms of their own bodies*. By suggesting a body-based understanding, canonical and mirror neurons provide further evidence of the participation of motor systems in conceptualisation. Consistent with the presence of mirror neurons in humans, the somatotopic areas of the motor cortex which activate during both word comprehension and motor movement, also activate during action observation.[133] Such activation patterns support the proposition that action *concepts* are instantiated in the motor cortex, since the motor cortex is not only used for language comprehension but also to recognise and to understand perceived actions. As Barsalou states, '[t]o recognize and understand another agent's action, primates *simulate* the perceived action in their own motor system'.[134]

Although canonical and mirror neurons are only suggestive without a fuller picture of neural architecture, they offer insights into how modal concepts might be implemented at the neural level. Their presence suggests that both observed actions and objects are understood in terms of simulations of the observer's own bodily capacities.

4.2.4 Behavioural Studies on Concepts and Motor Movement
Evidence for the participation of sensorimotor brain regions during conceptual activation has also been observed in behavioural studies. If the invocation of concepts leads to sensorimotor simulations, then one might expect conceptual processing to interact with motor movement.[135] Such an interaction is borne out in a number of studies, consistent with motor simulations being used in conceptual processing.

One study found that when grasping for fixed-sized objects with the words for small and large printed on them, the word affected the grasp aperture with which the participants reached for the object.[136] Another study found the same effect

---

[132] Ibid.
[133] G. Buccino et al., 'Action Observation Activates Premotor and Parietal Areas in a Somatotopic Manner: An FMRI Study', *European Journal of Neuroscience* 13, no. 2 (2001). See also Hauk and Pulvermüller, 'Somatotopic Representation', 303; Tettamanti et al., 'Listening to Action-Related Sentences'.
[134] Barsalou, 'Grounded Cognition', 623. Emphasis added.
[135] Rolf A. Zwaan and Lawrence J. Taylor, 'Seeing, Acting, Understanding: Motor Resonance in Language Comprehension', *Journal of Experimental Psychology: General* 135, no. 1 (2006): 1–2.
[136] M. Gentilucci et al., 'Language and Motor Control', *Experimental Brain Research* 133, no. 4 (2000): 478–81.

when participants were shown words for small (e.g., 'grape') or large (e.g., 'apple') objects.[137] Yet another study found that the types of hand movement required to manipulate objects (e.g., precision vs. power grip) are activated by associated words (e.g., grape, screw vs. cucumber, hammer).[138]

Words associated with similar motor movements (e.g., playing a *piano* and typing on a *typewriter*) also prime one another.[139] As the experimenters conclude, this suggests that 'sensory/motor-based functional knowledge, namely manipulation, is a part of the lexical-semantic representation of objects and is accessed without conscious effort or explicit instructions'.[140] Again, this study suggests that we conceptualise objects in terms of the way we manipulate them with our motor movements.[141] The presence of motor representations in concepts shows that '[t]he brain does not merely represent aspects of external reality; it also records how the body explores the world and reacts to it'.[142]

Beyond individual words, priming effects have been found for larger linguistic constructions. Semantic sensibility judgements for verb–noun pairs (e.g., squeeze–tomato) were made more quickly when participants had an action-appropriate hand shape.[143] In a similar vein, another study discovered an 'action-sentence compatibility effect' in which actions compatible with given sentences were performed faster.[144] For example, participants were faster at judging the semantic sensibility of a sentence which described movement away from their body (e.g., 'you handed Liz the book') when the action to register a response also involved action way from their body (e.g., pressing a button that is further away from one's body).[145] A similar effect was found when the action involved was the manual rotation of a dial.[146]

Preparing to perform a task also activates semantic information related to the goal of the action; for example preparing to lift a magnifying glass to one's eye was faster when the word 'eye' as opposed to 'mouth' was the trigger for performing the action.[147] The experimentalists conclude, '[t]hese findings suggest that preparing for an action activates semantic information associated with the goal of

---

[137] Scott Glover et al., 'Grasping the Meaning of Words', *Experimental Brain Research* 154, no. 1 (2004).
[138] Mike Tucker and Rob Ellis, 'The Potentiation of Grasp Types During Visual Object Categorization', *Visual Cognition* 8, no. 6 (2001): 784–5.
[139] Jong-yoon Myung, Sheila E. Blumstein, and Julie C. Sedivy, 'Playing on the Typewriter, Typing on the Piano: Manipulation Knowledge of Objects', *Cognition* 98, no. 3 (2006).
[140] Ibid., 239.   [141] Zwaan and Taylor, 'Seeing, Acting, Understanding', 8.
[142] Damasio and Damasio, 'Brain and Language', 91.
[143] Roberta L. Klatzky et al., 'Can You Squeeze a Tomato? The Role of Motor Representations in Semantic Sensibility Judgments', *Journal of Memory and Language* 28, no. 1 (1989).
[144] Glenberg and Kaschak, 'Grounding Language in Action'.   [145] Ibid., 560.
[146] Zwaan and Taylor, 'Seeing, Acting, Understanding'.
[147] Oliver Lindemann et al., 'Semantic Activation in Action Planning', *Journal of Experimental Psychology: Human Perception & Performance* 32, no. 3 (2006).

the action and thereby primes access to a lexical representation associated with that goal'.[148]

The notion of 'affordances' further clarifies the connection between concepts and motor systems.[149] As Roy explains, affordances are part of the meaning of situational utterances: 'to understand the meaning of the assertion that "there is a cup on the table" includes the ability to translate this utterance into expectations of how the physical environment will look, and the sorts of things that can be done to and with the environment if the utterance is true'.[150] Consistent with the presence of canonical and mirror neurons, the notion of affordances captures the idea that objects are conceptualised in terms of bodily capacity to manipulate them. As Gibson stated, 'what we perceive when we look at objects are their affordances, not their qualities. We can discriminate the dimensions of difference if required to do so in an experiment, but what the object affords us is what we normally pay attention to'.[151]

Affordances arise from sensorimotor information about objects and environments, thereby exceeding dictionary definitions of the objects. For example, when asked to judge the semantic sensibility of a sentence such as 'hang the coat on the upright vacuum cleaner', one requires perceptual knowledge about physically manipulating the objects in question to decide whether such an action is plausible.[152] It is difficult to see how an amodal concept could perform this conceptual processing. A modal concept, by contrast, could readily be deployed to simulate the proposed action and determine whether it is feasible for the objects in question.

A study used eye-tracking technology to monitor how non-linguistic information, such as information about affordances, was combined with linguistic information.[153] For example, given the ambiguous instruction 'Pour the egg in the bowl over the flour' (where 'in the bowl' might refer to the location of the egg or its target), participants use knowledge about affordances (i.e., whether the egg was in liquid form and therefore pourable as opposed to in a shell) to disambiguate the phrase in question.[154] Hence 'the comprehender's knowledge of possible actions in a given situation is used to circumscribe linguistically relevant context'.[155] All of these studies show an interaction between motor

---

[148] Fischer and Zwaan, 'Embodied Language', 840.   [149] See Chapter 2, Section 3.4.

[150] Deb Roy, 'A Mechanistic Model of Three Facets of Meaning', in *Symbols and Embodiment: Debates on Meaning and Cognition*, ed. Manuel De Vega, Arthur M. Glenberg, and Arthur C. Graesser (Oxford: Oxford University Press, 2008), 196.

[151] Gibson, *The Ecological Approach*, 126.

[152] Glenberg and Kaschak, 'Grounding Language in Action', 559.

[153] Craig G. Chambers et al., 'Circumscribing Referential Domains During Real-Time Language Comprehension', *Journal of Memory and Language* 47, no. 1 (2002).

[154] Craig G. Chambers, Michael K. Tanenhaus, and James S. Magnuson, 'Actions and Affordances in Syntactic Ambiguity Resolution', *Journal of Experimental Psychology: Learning, Memory, & Cognition* 30, no. 3 (2004): 688–91.

[155] Ibid., 693.

movement and conceptual processing, supporting the presence of motor representations in concepts.

4.2.5 Behavioural Studies on Concepts and Perception

Behavioural studies similarly show an interaction between concepts and perception. Participants were more likely to list properties which were perceptually salient when generating properties of a particular word.[156] For example, participants were more likely to list 'seeds' as a property of 'half watermelon' than of 'watermelon'. Seeds are equally present in both variations of watermelon. An amodal theory of concepts therefore predicts that these properties would be listed at the same frequency for both variations of the objects. The preference for perceptually salient properties (i.e., 'seeds') suggests that participants perceptually simulate the relevant concepts and thus supports a modal theory of concepts.

Another study tracked participant eye movements as they listed properties for concepts such as 'bird' or 'worm'.[157] Participants' eyes, face, and hands tended to drift upward for the concept 'bird' and downward for the concept 'worm'. This again suggests perceptual simulation, as participants mirrored the *bodily movements* required for the typical perception of these animals *relative to the body*. Another eye-tracking study instructed participants to place one object into another (e.g., 'put the cube into the can').[158] As soon as the instructions reached the preposition in the sentence (i.e., 'into'), the participants eye movements were constrained to objects with the correct 'affordances'; that is, objects whose physical properties would allow them to have a cube of the given size placed inside them. The experimenters conclude that 'people comprehend language by indexing references in the environment and by considering what is possible given the affordances of the objects involved'.[159] Again, this suggests that concepts are not amodal, but rely on perceptual simulation.

4.2.6 Concept Acquisition

Developmental accounts supplement evidence that concepts are modal. For modal concepts, concept acquisition involves 'building' a concept from sensorimotor information.[160] Brown and Strawn note that shared attention is one of the important mechanisms in development. They summarise findings about joint attention mechanism as follows:

---

[156] Ling-ling Wu and Lawrence W. Barsalou, 'Perceptual Simulation in Conceptual Combination: Evidence from Property Generation', *Acta Psychologica* 132, no. 2 (2009).

[157] Barsalou et al., 'Embodiment in Religious Knowledge', 27.

[158] Chambers et al., 'Circumscribing Referential Domains'.

[159] Hostetter and Alibali, 'Visible Embodiment', 498.

[160] This sensorimotor information could derive from stimuli which a present, or from sensorimotor information stored in other concepts, see Section 5.

Sharing attention is a fundamental interpersonal process. By six months of age, infants tend to look in the direction that another person turns his or her head, and by one year they will look in the direction of another person's eye gaze. Children also readily learn to look in the direction where another person is pointing rather than at the finger doing the pointing.[161]

Not only is this tendency toward shared attention crucial for interpersonal interaction but it also assists in concept acquisition. Shared attention 'provides a common set of sensory experiences' that assist in 'grounding communications and teaching'.[162] Both adult and child experience the same modal representations simultaneously, and this allows the child to associate this stimulus with a concept. Hence shared attention provides a plausible embodied mechanism by which modal concepts can be acquired in the presence of perceptual stimuli.[163]

In summary, I have surveyed a large, though by no means exhaustive, sample of the empirical evidence concerning the nature of human concepts. The survey speaks to various levels of explanation, ranging from individual neurons (mirror and canonical), to activation in brain regions (in both intact and damaged brains), and right up to the level at which cognitive systems as a whole perform in behavioural scenarios. This evidence all converges to support a modal theory of concepts.

4.3 Addressing Meta-Theoretical Criteria

In addition to empirical evidence for modal theories of concepts, it is argued that these theories are superior on other criteria, such as capacity for prediction, parsimony, and integrability.[164] Modal theories of concepts not only accommodate existing empirical evidence but they have also been shown to have *predictive power*. Many of the studies summarised in Section 4.2 were conceived as a result of modal theories, and aimed to test the predictions arising from such theories. The capacity to make specific, empirically verifiable predictions demonstrates that modal theories have been scientifically fruitful.

The use of sensorimotor representations also makes for a more *parsimonious* theory of concepts. Rather than positing both sensorimotor representations and transduced amodal representations, modal theories propose that the former can perform the tasks necessary for a fully functional theory of concepts. Not only

---

[161] Brown and Strawn, *Physical Nature of Christian Life*, 58.   [162] Ibid., 58–9.

[163] Chen Yu, 'Linking Words to World: An Embodied Perspective', in *The Routledge Handbook of Embodied Cognition*, ed. Lawrence A. Shapiro (London: Routledge, 2014); Eilan, 'Joint Attention', 7. For more details on this mechanism, see Leonhard Schilbach et al., 'Toward a Second-Person Neuroscience', *Behavioral and Brain Sciences* 36, no. 4 (2013).

[164] Barsalou, 'Perceptual Symbol Systems'.

does this parsimony make for a more 'elegant' theory by virtue of its greater simplicity but it also has advantages within an evolutionary framework.[165] From the perspective of evolutionary theory, more economical mechanisms are favourable (*ceteris paribus*), since they require fewer resources to provide the same functionality: '[i]t is generally easier to explain how evolution puts an existing tool to new uses than to explain how new tools evolve.'[166] Moreover, it has been argued in evolutionary psychology that existing features of an organism are often co-opted to perform new functions.[167] In evolutionary terms a trait which evolved for one purpose and then is co-opted for a different function is known as 'exaptation' (as opposed to adaptation).[168] The bootstrapping of a conceptual system onto existing perceptual and motor systems is consistent with such a developmental trajectory.

The ability to marry findings from brain lesion, neuroimaging, neurophysiology, behavioural, and developmental studies with modal accounts of concepts demonstrates that modal theories of concepts can readily *integrate* with neighbouring disciplines. The capacity for known neural structures and functions to implement a modal conceptual system thus speaks in favour of modal theories.

In summary, modal theories offer responses to the key criticisms of amodal concepts. Namely, they overcome the symbol grounding problem by having concepts intrinsically linked to perception and action; avoid the under-specification of the transduction process by replacing it with simulation which accounts for concept acquisition and application; find support in a wide range of empirical evidence; and are superior in various meta-theoretical criteria. Having surveyed the various strengths of modal theories, I shall turn to a significant challenge for them: abstract concepts.

5 Building Abstract Concepts

In the preceding survey of evidence in support of modal concepts, studies typically relied on concrete concepts, such as 'bird' or 'kick'. Such concepts are readily 'imageable'; they refer to tangible objects or motor movements which are relatable to sensorimotor states. Such concepts are an obvious choice when designing a tractable experiment; it is clear which perceptual or motor states are likely associated with the concepts. However, the early focus on concrete concepts raises questions about whether it also applies to abstract concepts.[169]

---

[165] Ibid., 606–7.   [166] Prinz, *Furnishing the Mind*, 27.
[167] Stephen Jay Gould, 'Exaptation: A Crucial Tool for an Evolutionary Psychology', *Journal of Social Issues* 47, no. 3 (1991). Cf. Barsalou, 'Perceptual Symbol Systems', 589.
[168] Kintsch, 'Symbol Systems', 159.
[169] Dove, 'Three Symbol Ungrounding Problems', 1109; Prinz, *Furnishing the Mind*, 165–88. Lawrence A. Shapiro and Shannon Spaulding, *Embodied Cognition* (2021) [cited 20 October 2021]; available from https://plato.stanford.edu/archives/win2021/entries/embodied-cognition/.

Abstract concepts pose a particular challenge for modal theories. Unlike concrete concepts, they often represent things which are unobservable, intangible, or purely formal, and therefore are not readily imageable or tangible. While it is usually obvious what kind of sensorimotor content might constitute concrete concepts, it is less clear how abstract concepts such as 'democracy', 'electron', or 'truth' might be constituted by sensorimotor content.[170] Hence doubts about the sufficiency of modal accounts rest 'on the intuition that modality-specific representations are not suited for representing concepts at this level of abstraction because their referents cannot be directly experienced in perception'.[171] Some have argued that this challenge is not insurmountable. This section surveys proposals for grounding abstract concepts in sensorimotor states, before discussing whether modal theories can adequately account for abstract concepts. This analysis will lay the groundwork for Chapter 4, where I extend this discussion to perhaps the unruliest of abstract concepts, namely theological ones.

5.1 Empirical Evidence for Grounding of Abstract Concepts

A number of empirical studies have sought to gather evidence that even abstract concepts are grounded in sensorimotor states. Numbers are thought to be among the most abstract concepts, so much so that a lively debate surrounds the ontological status of numbers in philosophy. However, empirical evidence suggests that numeral representations included tactile perception associated with fingers. For example, one study found that the numerical distance effect, whereby comparisons between numbers which are semantically closer together takes longer and is more error prone, holds when participants compare symbolically represented numbers and numbers of fingers being stimulated.[172] This effect suggests that number concepts are cross-modal and include tactile representations. The researchers conclude that '[r]epresentations of sensory experiences about size and numerosity might…provide a grounding for the meaning of symbolic numbers and might therefore play a crucial role in the development of number concepts'.[173] In a similar vein, another study found that finger-counting strategies, which vary across cultures and individuals, influence the mental representation and processing of numbers.[174]

---

[170] Dove, 'Three Symbol Ungrounding Problems', 1109.
[171] Prinz, Furnishing the Mind, 167.
[172] Krause, Bekkering, and Lindemann, 'A Feeling for Numbers'.   [173] Ibid., 7.
[174] Samuel di Luca et al., 'Finger–Digit Compatibility in Arabic Numeral Processing', The Quarterly Journal of Experimental Psychology 59, no. 9 (2006). For an argument that mathematical concepts can be grounded, see George Lakoff and Rafael E. Núñez, Where Mathematics Comes From: How the Embodied Mind Brings Mathematics into Being (New York: Basic Books, 2000); Raymond W. Gibbs, Embodiment and Cognitive Science (Cambridge: Cambridge University Press, 2006), 111–14; Prinz, Furnishing the Mind, 184–7.

Gestures more generally have been suggested as a source of motor action to ground abstract concepts.[175] Researchers linked the simulation element of a modal theory of concepts with the production of gestures: 'gestures occur as the result of simulated action and perception, which are the bases of mental imagery and language production.'[176] A number of studies interrogate the way gestures relate to the content they express.[177] For example, one study found that participants retelling a cartoon they had watched gestured more than those who had simply read a description of it.[178] The researchers suggested that those who had encountered the cartoon visually had a richer spatial representation of it.

Gestures express not only concrete concepts but also abstract ones. According to a common taxonomy of gesture types, there is a 'metaphorical' class of gestures: 'Metaphoric gestures represent abstract ideas rather than concrete objects or actions, often referring not to the movements used to carry out an activity, but rather to its goal or outcome.'[179] This suggests that abstract concepts are illuminated by more concrete concepts such as spatial relations, here constituted by the motor movements related to a given gesture.[180] Beyond goals or outcomes, gestures are associated with abstract concepts such as the formal relationships in language: 'the existence of a close relationship between bodily gestures and verbal syntax implies that it is not just concrete nouns, the "thing words", but even the most apparently formal and logical elements of language, that originate in the body and emotion.'[181]

Another potential means of grounding abstract concepts is through emotions. Abstract concepts, even those not directly associated with emotions, have higher emotional content than concrete words.[182] Subsequent neuroimaging studies provide corroborating evidence, showing that areas of the brain involved in emotion processing activate when processing abstract concepts.[183] Since emotions are associated with—or even consist in—emotional body states, emotion offers a means of grounding abstract concepts in sensorimotor experience, through interoperception rather than perception of extra-somatic stimuli.[184]

---

[175] Susan Goldin-Meadow and Sian L. Beilock, 'Action's Influence on Thought: The Case of Gesture', *Perspectives on Psychological Science* 5, no. 6 (2010): 668.

[176] Hostetter and Alibali, 'Visible Embodiment', 511.

[177] For reviews, see Goldin-Meadow and Beilock, 'Action's Influence'; Hostetter and Alibali, 'Visible Embodiment'.

[178] Autumn B. Hostetter and William D. Hopkins, 'The Effect of Thought Structure on the Production of Lexical Movements', *Brain and Language* 82, no. 1 (2002).

[179] Goldin-Meadow and Beilock, 'Action's Influence', 665. See also, Hostetter and Alibali, 'Visible Embodiment', 504.

[180] This is consistent with the conceptual metaphor theory outlined in Section 5.2.

[181] McGilchrist, *The Master and His Emissary*, 119.

[182] Stavroula-Thaleia Kousta et al., 'The Representation of Abstract Words: Why Emotion Matters', *Journal of Experimental Psychology: General* 140, no. 1 (2011).

[183] Gabriella Vigliocco et al., 'The Neural Representation of Abstract Words: The Role of Emotion', *Cerebral Cortex* 24, no. 7 (2014).

[184] For the relationship between emotions and bodily states, see Chapter 5, Section 2.1.

These studies are somewhat piecemeal, since they only account for particular sets of abstract concepts or particular sensorimotor modalities. Nevertheless, they demonstrate that abstract concepts are not completely beyond the pale for modal theories. While it is not as obvious how abstract concepts relate to sensorimotor content, there are strategies by which such concepts may be grounded.

5.2 Conceptual Metaphors

Conceptual metaphor theory proposes a wide-ranging attempt to ground abstract concepts. It proposes that abstract concepts are grounded by means of 'conceptual' or 'cognitive metaphors'.[185] Lakoff and Johnson's seminal work focused on metaphors used in everyday language, rather than more rarefied novel metaphors such as those found in poetry. They argued that these metaphors were more than surface literary devices, rather they revealed something more fundamental about cognitive processes. Beneath the surface of numerous linguistic expressions lie correlations which operate at the deeper, conceptual level.

For example, the expressions 'he gave me the cold shoulder' and 'she has a warm smile' are both symptomatic of an underlying conceptual metaphor 'affection is warmth'.[186] The conceptual metaphor allows hearers of the linguistic utterances to understand the sentences as referring to affection rather than temperature. Moreover, one could easily coin a novel sentence (that did not rely on established idioms), which could be understood based on its underlying conceptual metaphor.

Conceptual metaphors do more than simply allow linguistic expressions to be generated and understood; they also illuminate concepts by structuring the way that we reason about abstract entities. Commenting on the metaphor 'love is a journey', Lakoff and Johnson argue that such a mapping 'allows forms of reasoning about travel to be used in reasoning about love'.[187] Hence various facets of what is known about a journey (that it may have a beginning, an end, face obstacles, progress over time, involve fellow 'travellers', etc.) are mapped onto love. Thus, conceptual metaphors allow inferences to be drawn about abstract concepts.

Lakoff and Johnson also account for the acquisition of conceptual metaphors through repeated exposure to regular correlations in our embodied experience.[188] By repeatedly being exposed to affection and warmth from physical contact simultaneously, the association between the two concepts becomes second nature. Similarly, the physical fact that as a container is filled its level goes up establishes a correlation between height and volume, resulting in the cognitive metaphor 'more is up'. Thus, we can talk about share prices 'rising' or 'plummeting' when

---

[185] Lakoff and Johnson, *Metaphors We Live By*; Lakoff and Johnson, *Philosophy in the Flesh*.
[186] Ibid., 50.   [187] Ibid., 65.   [188] Ibid., 47.

they do not literally do so. Hence everyday embodied experience of the world furnishes us with numerous correlations that pervade ordinary language.

Conceptual metaphors often map familiar, concrete source domains onto less familiar, abstract domains.[189] In the case of 'affection is warmth', a category which arises directly from perception, namely temperature, illuminates the less imageable, more abstract social concept of affection: 'Abstract concepts arise via metaphorical projections from more directly embodied concepts'.[190] Thus, the account does not require that abstract concepts be *directly* about sensorimotor experience. Rather it proposes the more nuanced position that sensorimotor experience furnishes us with a basic set of concepts which serve as the building blocks for more abstract concepts (through combination, metaphorical extension, etc.). Nevertheless, this mechanism allows abstract concepts to be, at bottom, constituted by sensorimotor states, and therefore grounded: 'we use concrete concepts as vehicles to structure abstract topics through metaphorical mapping; the representation of the vehicle is necessary to fully understand the topic. Since the concrete vehicles refer to sensorimotor experiences, the sensorimotor system can be used to represent abstract concepts'.[191]

A number of empirical studies provide support for conceptual metaphor theory.[192] They typically involve priming participants with concrete concepts and measuring whether this affects associated abstract concepts. One study surveyed participants who were moving through a lunch line, airport, or train station.[193] Participants were asked to interpret the ambiguous statement 'Next Wednesday's meeting has been moved forward two days', which can be conceptualised as the ego moving through time or time moving towards the participant. The study found that interpretations of the statement varied according to whether participants were arriving or departing the airport or train station, or according to their position in the lunch queue, suggesting that concepts of time are tightly bound up with spatial representations. Other studies have found a link between physical warmth and interpersonal warmth, providing evidence for the 'affection is warmth' conceptual metaphor.[194]

---

[189]   Masson, *Without Metaphor*, 13.   [190]   Lakoff and Johnson, *Philosophy in the Flesh*, 497.

[191]   Granito, 'Where Are Abstract Concepts From?', 86. Cf. Prinz, *Furnishing the Mind*, 12.

[192]   For a reviews of empirical evidence, see Gibbs, *Embodiment and Cognitive Science*, 79–122; Lakoff and Johnson, *Philosophy in the Flesh*, 81–6.

[193]   Lera Boroditsky and Michael Ramscar, 'The Roles of Body and Mind in Abstract Thought', *Psychological Science* 13, no. 2 (2002).

[194]   Lawrence E. Williams and John A. Bargh, 'Experiencing Physical Warmth Promotes Interpersonal Warmth', *Science* 322, no. 5901 (2008); Jiewen Hong and Yacheng Sun, 'Warm It up with Love: The Effect of Physical Coldness on Liking of Romance Movies', *Journal of Consumer Research* 39, no. 2 (2012); Simon Storey and Lance Workman, 'The Effects of Temperature Priming on Cooperation in the Iterated Prisoner's Dilemma', *Evolutionary Psychology* 11, no. 1 (2013); Hans Ijzerman, Angela K.-y. Leung, and Lay See Ong, 'Perceptual Symbols of Creativity: Coldness Elicits Referential, Warmth Elicits Relational Creativity', *Acta Psychologica* 148 (2014); Christine Gockel, Peter M. Kolb, and Lioba Werth, 'Murder or Not? Cold Temperature Makes Criminals Appear to Be Cold-Blooded and Warm Temperature to Be Hot-Headed', *PLOS ONE* 9, no. 4 (2014).

McGilchrist's work on the divided brain outlines a neural mechanism for cognitive metaphors.[195] He observes that the human brain is divided into two distinct hemispheres and argues that this striking physiological arrangement has important functional implications. Although crass popularisations propose spurious generalisations about hemisphere differentiation, McGilchrist marshals a wide variety of neuro-physiological, neuroimaging, and pathological studies to propose a more nuanced, evidence-based thesis for hemisphere specialisation. He argues that the hemisphere distinction turns on two modes of attention:

> the brain has to attend to the world in two completely different ways, and in so doing to bring two different worlds into being. In one, we experience—the live, complex, embodied, world of individual, always unique beings, forever in flux, a net of interdependencies, forming and reforming wholes, a world with which we are deeply connected. In the other we 'experience' our experience in a special way: a 're-presented' version of it, containing now static, separable, bounded, but essentially fragmented entities, grouped into classes, on which predictions can be based.[196]

For McGilchrist, the left hemisphere specialises in 'abstract concepts and words, along with complex syntax'.[197] By contrast, '[i]n keeping with its capacity for emotion, and its predisposition to understand mental experience within the context of the body, rather than abstracting it, the right hemisphere is deeply connected to the self as embodied'.[198] Having drawn this distinction, McGilchrist endorses conceptual metaphor theory, affirming that '[m]etaphoric thinking is fundamental to our understanding of the world because it is the only way in which understanding can reach outside the system of signs to life itself. It is what links language to life'.[199] Hence the embodied experience of the right hemisphere serves to ground the abstract representations of the left: 'the left hemisphere's most powerful tool, referential language, has its origins in the body and the right hemisphere'.[200] McGilchrist's proposal thus provides a larger neurophysiological framework in which conceptual metaphor theory might be implemented.

5.3 More than Sensorimotor States?

Evidence that abstract concepts are grounded in sensorimotor experience, either directly or by way of conceptual metaphors, is typically marshalled to extend modal theories to the most challenging cases, namely abstract concepts. However,

---

[195] McGilchrist, *The Master and His Emissary.*   [196] Ibid., 31.   [197] Ibid., 51.
[198] Ibid., 66.   [199] Ibid., 115.   [200] Ibid., 179.

the question remains as to whether this evidence is sufficient to exhaustively account for abstract concepts. Two questions of scope remain.

First, to what extent does the modal theory *exhaustively* explain any given concept? The abstract concept of affection may be illuminated by warmth, but it is equally clear that affection and warmth also differ in important ways; after all, humans have no trouble distinguishing between these two concepts.[201] One response to this issue might be to argue that affection is also illuminated by cognitive metaphors which deploy other concrete concepts, such as affection is physical proximity ('we've become really close', 'he seems distant'). If affection is comprised of a number of cognitive metaphors, then this explains why it is not reducible to any single one of them. However, the question still remains as to whether an abstract concept is simply the sum of its cognitive metaphors.

Lakoff and Johnson themselves equivocate on this point. Considering the concept of love, they argue that 'metaphors for love are significantly constitutive of our concept of love'.[202] But do they exhaust it? They come close to this claim when they say that 'Without those conventional metaphors, it would be virtually impossible to reason or talk about love.'[203] But again, this is only to claim that conceptual metaphors are ('virtually') necessary, and not that they are sufficient.

Second, is the extant evidence sufficient to account for *all* abstract concepts? While embodied cognition researchers have begun to show how some abstract concepts are grounded in sensorimotor states, it is still far from clear whether these strategies will generalise to all abstract concepts. Prinz is optimistic about the modal theory's ability to meet this scope question, asserting that '[w]ith a little creativity, we can begin to imagine how our least concrete ideas could have perceptual grounding.'[204] Although he argues that advocates for an amodal account 'have yet to produce a decisive counterexample', he readily acknowledges that his analyses 'are incomplete, and some may be refuted by empirical investigation.'[205]

Others are more sceptical about whether sensorimotor states are sufficient to account for abstract concepts.[206] In response they have proposed hybrid accounts, in which abstract concepts may include sensorimotor states, but also rely on an additional conceptual format such as internalised language: 'Some abstract concepts may rely more on metaphors while others may rely more on situations, emotions, or linguistic information.'[207] In reviewing recent literature on abstract

---

[201] Prinz, *Furnishing the Mind*, 171.

[202] Lakoff and Johnson, *Philosophy in the Flesh*, 71–2.   [203] Ibid., 72.

[204] Prinz, *Furnishing the Mind*, 169. See also, Vittorio Gallese and George Lakoff, 'The Brain's Concepts: The Role of the Sensory-Motor System in Conceptual Knowledge', *Cognitive Neuropsychology* 22, no. 3–4 (2005).

[205] Prinz, *Furnishing the Mind*, 187–8.

[206] Dove, 'Three Symbol Ungrounding Problems'.; Guy Dove, 'How to Go Beyond the Body: An Introduction', *Frontiers in Psychology* 6 (2015): 1–1.

[207] Dove, 'How to Go Beyond the Body: An Introduction', 2. This is consistent with the view that language is a cognitive tool explored in Chapter 5, Section 2.2.

concepts, Dove contends that 'there is a growing consensus that some kind of hybrid account—based on such dichotomies as modal/amodal, embodied/disembodied, and so forth—is needed'.[208]

Some of the advocates for modal theories already tacitly acknowledge this point. Insofar as McGilchrist's account of brain hemisphere distinction posits both a system for dealing with abstract representations and a system for dealing with embodied understanding, it might be classed as a hybrid account. However, McGilchrist is difficult to locate on this issue. On the one hand, he seems to assert the necessity of conceptual metaphors.[209] On the other hand, his overarching thesis is that the left hemisphere has become the 'master' and thus reasoning via symbolic representations functions increasingly independently; language 'has increasingly abstracted itself from its origins in the body and in the experiential world'.[210]

Even if hybrid accounts are ultimately necessary to explain abstraction, they nevertheless represent a significant departure from pure amodal theories. If abstract concepts were to be completely devoid of sensorimotor concepts, they would again fall foul of the symbol grounding problem. One could of course 'coin' a new, purely abstract concept, 'x'. Arguably one can have mental representations of 'x'. However, as soon as one asks what 'x' *means*, unless one can provide some grounded content (and not simply more invented purely abstract concepts) it is difficult to see how 'x' could become meaningful. Viewed this way, grounding is an essential criterion for a concept to be meaningful.[211]

In summary, it remains to be seen whether a modal theory of concepts can exhaustively account for all concepts, especially abstract ones. Nevertheless, the symbol grounding problem suggests that all *meaningful* concepts—concrete or abstract—are, at least in part, constituted by sensorimotor content. Even though some concepts seem to be able to abstract away from our bodily experience to some degree, perhaps they never truly float free, unencumbered by our fleshly nature, but remain tethered to bodily existence. This discussion of abstract concepts is crucial background for Chapter 4 which will consider abstract theological concepts.

6 Conclusion: Embodied Concepts

This chapter has outlined an embodied theory of concepts. The symbol grounding problem identifies why concepts must be grounded in sensorimotor content. Whereas amodal concepts fall prey to the symbol grounding problem, modal

---

[208] Dove, 'Three Symbol Ungrounding Problems', 1109.
[209] McGilchrist, *The Master and His Emissary*, 115.   [210] Ibid., 125.
[211] Krause, Bekkering, and Lindemann, 'A Feeling for Numbers', 7; Hostetter and Alibali, 'Visible Embodiment', 497.

concepts are constituted by sensorimotor states and ground concepts in embodied experience. In addition to satisfying this philosophical desideratum for concepts, a modal theory of concepts also finds support in a diverse range of empirical findings and meta-theoretical criteria. Abstract concepts present particular difficulties for modal theories and require further research. However, there is good reason to think that even abstract concepts are at least partially grounded in sensorimotor states, both on account of some preliminary empirical evidence and for the philosophical imperative established by the symbol grounding problem.

At the beginning of this chapter, I argued against a strong version of the conceptualisation hypothesis—that bodies place an absolute limit on an organism's conceptual repertoire. Instead I opted for a weaker version, that concepts arise from bodily interaction with the world through perception and action. The modal theory for concepts, which overcomes the symbol grounding problem by arguing that concepts are (at least in part) grounded in sensorimotor states, is consistent with this weak version of the conceptualisation hypothesis. Although our bodies may not determine our concepts, they do shape them by virtue of their perceptual modalities. The scientific and philosophical advances concerning the embodied nature of human concepts provides a new framework for old quandaries concerning theological concepts and language, which I examine in Chapter 4.

4

Grounding God? Embodying
Theological Meaning

'Come, hidden Wisdom, come, with all you bring, come to me now,
disguised as everything.'

—Malcolm Guite[1]

The difficulty of grounding abstract concepts (described in Chapter 3) poses a special challenge for *theological* concepts. Many theological concepts are not readily imageable and therefore abstract. Concepts such as sin and salvation are somewhat abstract and difficult to ground.[2] However, in this chapter I focus on perhaps the most problematic theological concept from the perspective of a modal theory, namely the human concept of God. The concept of God undoubtedly provides the ultimate test case for whether theological concepts can be accounted for by a modal theory of concepts.

I begin by describing why God-concepts are so problematic for a modal theory of concepts (Section 1). In particular I observe that the spectre of idolatry *prima facie* constitutes an obstacle for grounding God-concepts. I then consider potential strategies for grounding God-concepts which have been proposed by both cognitive scientists of religion and theologians (though theologians do not typically frame their discussions in terms of a modal theory of concepts, they are nevertheless attuned to the epistemological difficulty of limited human creatures thinking and speaking about God). First, I discuss the possibility that some form of human experience grounds God-concepts (Section 2). Second, I consider the cognitive-linguistic solution that metaphors taken from experience ground God-concepts (Section 3). A detailed exploration of anthropomorphisms highlights a special case of this wider phenomenon (Section 4). I argue that these two potential solutions both have something to offer but cannot on their own ground concepts *and* avoid idolatry. I therefore turn to a third means of grounding God, the incarnation, which I argue provides the theological solution to the problem (Section 5).

---

[1] Malcolm Guite, *Waiting on the Word: A Poem a Day for Advent, Christmas and Epiphany* (Norwich: Canterbury Press, 2015), 66.
[2] Sanders, *Theology in the Flesh*, 175.

Corporeal Theology: Accommodating Theological Understanding to Embodied Thinkers. Tobias Tanton, Oxford University Press. © Tobias Tanton 2023. DOI: 10.1093/oso/9780192884589.003.0005

1 The Problem of 'Grounding' God

As discussed in Chapter 3, abstract concepts provide a challenge to a modal theory of concepts. If abstract concepts present difficulties in general, then the concept 'God' seems to be the difficult case *par excellence*. The apparent impossibility of grounding the concept of God derives from the fact that God is not readily available in our perception. Thus, unlike the natural sciences, theology does not typically rely on an empirical methodology. These assumptions are articulated by no less a theologian than Saint Augustine. In his discussion of theological epistemology, he dismisses a mistaken methodology:

> to transfer to things incorporeal and spiritual the ideas they have formed, whether through experience of the bodily senses, or by natural human wit and diligent quickness, or by the aid of art, from things corporeal; so as to seek to measure and conceive of the former by the latter.[3]

Psychologists who study human God-concepts have likewise recognised the imperceptibility of theological concepts: 'Unlike mundane knowledge of material categories and processes, religious ideas seemingly cannot be acquired through first-hand experience, and they are not logically deduced from physics or principles of nature.'[4] The imperceptibility of God therefore raises a question about how God-concepts are represented in the human mind: 'supernatural agents and the spiritual world are often immaterial, invisible, and outside the range of human sensation and perception. That being the case, how can a person's cognitive systems integrate representations of supernatural beings into its conceptual repertoire in the first place?'[5]

This is not a new question for theologians. As Masson observes, one of the questions Aquinas addresses in his theory of analogy is '[h]ow could the medieval Christian conception of an ineffable and immaterial God be reconciled with the Aristotelian notion that all knowing is tethered to the senses?'[6] Although neither these psychologists of religion nor the theologians reference a modal theory of concepts, they describe the same challenges that modal theories face when attempting to account for abstract theological concepts. This challenge is hardly surprising given that all three share a commitment to empiricism and

---

[3] Augustine, *The Trinity* (Washington, DC: Catholic University of America Press, 1963), 3. See also, Masson, *Without Metaphor*, 15.

[4] Soliman, Johnson, and Song, 'Understanding Religion', 853. See also, Brian P. Meier et al., 'What's "Up" with God? Vertical Space as a Representation of the Divine', *Journal of Personality & Social Psychology* 93, no. 5 (2007): 699.

[5] Soliman, Johnson, and Song, 'Understanding Religion', 854.

[6] Masson, *Without Metaphor*, 15.

subsequently assume that concepts of God must be acquired through sensorimotor experience.

A modal theory, however, is not committed to the position that only concepts of directly perceptible objects can be grounded. There is no obstacle to conceptualising imaginary entities, such as unicorns, since the concept 'unicorn' is grounded in other concepts which are readily available in our embodied perceptual experience (horses and horns). Therefore, the imperceptibility of God is not, on its own, an insurmountable obstacle to conceptualising God.

There is, however, a further obstacle. In classical theism, not only is God imperceptible, but God is not an object in the world, nor the imaginative amalgamation of objects in the world (so unicorns), nor the sum total of all objects in the world (so pantheism). Thomistic accounts, for example, emphasise the otherness of God by insisting that God is not simply an object alongside others in the universe.[7] As Muis states, '[p]roperties of God cannot be known by sensory perception because God is not an object in the world'.[8] There are therefore significant disanalogies between God and unicorns; and the strategy for grounding the concept 'unicorn' fails for the concept of God.

Thus, the difficulty of grounding God is acute. It rides not only on imperceptibility, but on the ontological distinction between creator and creation. If there is an infinite qualitative difference between God and the world, as Kierkegaard and Barth contend, then the attempt to ground God in concepts taken from our experience of the world seems futile;[9] no matter how far one builds from the cliff face, an infinite chasm will never be bridged. Theologically literate psychologists of religion are in lockstep with theologians on this point; observing that Abrahamic traditions posit an ontological gap between God and creation, they pose the question 'how do we cross this ontological gap and understand God?'[10]

In addition to creating difficulties for conceptualising God, an ontological divide raises distinctly *theological* problems. In the Abrahamic faiths, there is a long tradition of identifying any attempt to associate God with perceptible objects as idolatry. This has been the case for tangible objects, visual images, and even (in a case which I discuss further later) textual imagery. According to a strict prohibition against idolatry, attempts to ground the concept 'God' are not only epistemically

---

[7] Robert Sokolowski, *The God of Faith and Reason: Foundations of Christian Theology* (Washington, DC: Catholic University of America Press, 1995); Herbert McCabe and Brian Davies, 'God and Creation', *New Blackfriars* 94, no. 1052 (2013).

[8] Jan Muis, 'Can Christian Talk About God Be Literal?', *Modern Theology* 27, no. 4 (2011): 599.

[9] Kierkegaard, *Training in Christianity, and the Edifying Discourse Which 'Accompanied' It*, 139; Karl Barth, *The Epistle to the Romans*, trans. Edwyn Clement Hoskyns (Oxford: Oxford University Press, 1968), 10, 355.

[10] Justin L. Barrett and Frank C. Keil, 'Conceptualizing a Nonnatural Entity: Anthropomorphism in God Concepts', *Cognitive Psychology* 31, no. 3 (1996): 220.

futile, but also represent the utmost theological danger. Grounding and idolatry thus form two horns of a dilemma: on the one hand, concepts which are grounded appear to be idolatrous; on the other hand, concepts which avoid idolatry by rejecting any connection to the tangible world potentially fall prey to the symbol grounding problem, and thereby lack meaning for humans (henceforth, the 'grounding-idolatry dilemma').

What is at stake is not merely the intelligibility of a single concept or a particular word in the English language; rather the difficulty here pervades all theological epistemology. As we saw in the anecdote from Milton, the very ability for humans to acquire and to possess theological knowledge depends upon a 'translation' of divine realities into a conceptual framework which embodied human beings can grasp. One cannot simply treat the concept 'God' as an exception, an aberrant concept which happens not to be grounded. Given that 'grounding' is a criterion for a concept to be meaningful (as argued in Chapter 3), to resign oneself to 'God' as an ungrounded concept is to risk rendering all God-talk meaningless. In the face of this dilemma, the following sections consider various attempts to ground the concept of God, cognisant of the twin dangers of idolatry and meaninglessness.

2 Grounding God-Concepts in Experience

One potential strategy for grounding the concept 'God' (and indeed other theological concepts and doctrines) is to associate it with experience. George Lindbeck calls this the 'experiential-expressive' account of doctrine, since it sees doctrines (and thereby concepts) as expressions of particular kinds of experience.[11] The doctrine of salvation, for example, is merely a codification of a prior experience of salvation. This approach seems appealing in light of an empiricist theory of concepts: abstract entities such as doctrines are meaningful because they are grounded by virtue of their connection to a concrete experience. The question remains, however, as to what exactly is meant by 'experience' in this context.

As discussed in Section 1, simply grounding God directly in sensorimotor experience will not suffice—such an approach risks idolatry. Sophisticated accounts of religious experience are, of course, aware of this danger. I shall briefly consider two accounts of religious experience from the perspective of the grounding problem: those of Schleiermacher and Rahner. These accounts attempt to identify an experience which corresponds to the concept of God while respecting the creator–creature ontological divide.

---

[11] George A. Lindbeck, *The Nature of Doctrine: Religion and Theology in a Postliberal Age* (London: SPCK, 1984), 31–2.

In *On Religion*, Schleiermacher presents 'intuition of the universe' as a mystical interpretation of the universe which derives from attentiveness to its interconnectedness.[12] In *Christian Faith* he offers a more formal account of the source of religion, describing 'the feeling of absolute dependence'.[13] He begins by setting out the interplay between the subject's spontaneity and receptivity in everyday experience, which are felt as partial freedom and dependence respectively. This observation, he argues, ought to be uncontroversial: '[t]o these propositions assent can be unconditionally demanded; and no one will deny them who is capable of a little introspection'.[14] Following the structure of a transcendental argument, Schleiermacher begins with this uncontroversial premise and then deduces from it the condition for the possibility of the subject he has described.[15]

In the next step of the argument, Schleiermacher invites the reader to consider the subject as a whole: 'the total self-consciousness made up of both [the feelings of freedom and dependence] together is one of *Reciprocity* between the subject and the corresponding Other'.[16] Our relation with an Other, even the world considered in its totality, is always structured by this relationship of partial freedom and partial dependence.[17] Absolute dependence cannot arise from any object given to us; we can always push back.[18] Nor is absolute freedom over objects possible; by the very fact that they are given to us in experience, they have already influenced us.[19] Only in an act of creation *ex nihilo* could a subject exercise absolute freedom.[20]

Schleiermacher subsequently uses his derivation of the feeling of absolute dependence to define God: 'the *Whence* of our receptive and active existence, as implied in this self-consciousness [of absolute dependence], is to be designated by the word "God", and that this is for us the really original signification of that word'.[21] Since Schleiermacher offers this explicit definition of the human concept of God in terms of the feeling of absolute dependence, it is no stretch to say, in the

[12] Friedrich Schleiermacher, *On Religion: Speeches to Its Cultured Despisers*, ed. Karl Ameriks and Desmond M. Clarke, trans. Richard Crouter (Cambridge: Cambridge University Press, 1996), 24.

[13] Friedrich Schleiermacher, *The Christian Faith*, ed. H. R. Mackintosh and J. S. Stewart (Edinburgh: T&T Clark, 1928), §4.

[14] Ibid., 13.

[15] Sergio Sorrentino, 'Feeling as a Key Notion in a Transcendental Conception of Religion', in *Schleiermacher, the Study of Religion, and the Future of Theology: A Transatlantic Dialogue*, ed. Brent W. Sockness and Wilhelm Gräb (Berlin: Walter De Gruyter, 2010), 102–3; Friedrich Schleiermacher, 'Selections from the First Edition of F. D. E. Schleiermacher's Christian Belief', in *Hegel, Hinrichs, and Schleiermacher on Feeling and Reason in Religion*, ed. Eric von der Luft (Lewiston: Edwin Mellen Press, 1987), 232.

[16] Schleiermacher, *Christian Faith*, 14.   [17] Ibid., 15.   [18] Ibid., 16.

[19] Ibid., 15.   [20] Ibid., 16.

[21] Ibid.; Cf. Julia A. Lamm, *The Living God: Schleiermacher's Theological Appropriation of Spinoza* (University Park, PA: Pennsylvania State University, 1996), 118.

parlance of a modal theory of concepts, that Schleiermacher seeks to *ground* the concept of God in this particular experience.

Moreover, by demarcating 'absolute' experiences from the experiences of partial freedom and dependence, Schleiermacher satisfies the axiom that God is not an object in the world. He thereby attempts to formulate an experience, the feeling of absolute dependence, which is not simply an impression caused by an interaction with the mundane world and yet nevertheless counts as a felt experience.

A similar experiential account is offered by the Roman Catholic theologian, Rahner. Like Schleiermacher, Rahner argues that knowledge of God derives from experience of the world: '[human] knowledge of God is an a posteriori knowledge from the world'.[22] He argues that this even holds true in the case of divine revelation, since the concepts it deploys are decidedly human: '[t]his is still true with verbal revelation because this too has to work with human concepts'.[23] He thereby implicitly affirms that theological concepts need to be grounded.

Like Schleiermacher, Rahner differentiates a special kind of experience from the perceptual experience of mundane objects in the world. He writes:

> For we do not have an experience of God as we have of a tree, another person and other external realities which, although they are perhaps never there before us absolutely nameless, yet they evoke their name by themselves because they simply appear within the realm of our experience at a definite point in time and space, and so by themselves they press immediately for a name.[24]

Rahner continues by describing an experience which goes beyond experience of the mundane world: 'in addition to these individual experiences of certain individual realities, there is a quite different experience, not by any means given thematic expression in the ordinary routine of our experiences: the experience of the one subject as such, that has all these experiences as its own and has to answer for them, that is itself present in its original unity and totality'.[25] This experience, according to Rahner, is universally present in humans (although it can be ignored). It arises by virtue of the structure of human subjectivity.

Rahner calls this 'transcendental experience', and defines it as follows: '[w]e shall call transcendental experience the subjective, unthematic, necessary and unfailing consciousness of the knowing subject that is co-present in every spiritual act of knowledge, and the subject's openness to the unlimited expanse of all possible reality'.[26] He aims to demonstrate that this transcendental experience

---

[22] Karl Rahner, *Foundations of Christian Faith: An Introduction to the Idea of Christianity*, ed. William V. Dych (New York: Crossroad, 1997), 52.
[23] Ibid.   [24] Ibid., 45.
[25] Karl Rahner, *God and Revelation*, vol. 18 (London: Darton, Longman and Todd, 1983), 190.
[26] Rahner, *Foundations*, 20.

contains 'an unthematic and anonymous, as it were, knowledge of God'.[27] Thus, Rahner, like Schleiermacher, seeks to identify an experience which serves to ground the concept of God.

In his explicit writings on the body, Rahner emphasises a unity of body and soul.[28] Moreover, when considering mystical experience he follows his Thomistic inheritance in acknowledging that if these experiences are to be expressed 'then inevitably it must go back to images which come from the realm of sense knowledge'.[29] In keeping with this embodied anthropology, Rahner identifies the experience which leads to theological knowledge as both embodied and transcendent.[30] Nevertheless, in his description of transcendental experience in the *Foundations* it is not clear how the unthematic experience which is the foundation for experience of God relates back to sensorimotor content.

These two brief summaries of Schleiermacher and Rahner hardly do justice to their complex concepts of experience. However, I have sought to show what their accounts have in common: first, they both identify an experience which serves to ground the concept of God, and second, in doing so they simultaneously differentiate this kind of experience from experience of everyday objects in the world. For both Rahner and Schleiermacher, God is known *through* experience of the world, even though it is not an experience of anything *in* the world.

Both Rahner and Schleiermacher set up their accounts of experience to avoid the charge of idolatry, carefully distinguishing their notions of experience of God from experience of created entities. However, it is less clear whether they are successful in grounding the concept of God. The kind of 'meta-experiences' ('absolute dependence' for Schleiermacher, 'transcendental experience' for Rahner) they identify (allegedly) arise from encounters in the world, but it is not clear that these experiences contain any sensorimotor content which would satisfy the modal theory of concepts.[31] Their attempts seem to be unable to resolve the grounding-idolatry dilemma: either the experience of which they speak is sensorimotor experience which grounds the concept of God but is thereby idolatrous, or the experience is one step removed from sensorimotor experience and thereby does not qualify as conceptual grounding.

---

[27] Ibid., 21.

[28] For Rahner's own theology of the body, see Karl Rahner, 'The Body in the Order of Salvation', in *Theological Investigations* (London: Darton, Longman and Todd, 1981). It is also noteworthy that in Rahner's discussion of the spiritual senses he notes that these are grounded in sensory perception.

[29] Karl Rahner, 'The "Spiritual Senses" According to Origen', in *Theological Investigations* (London: Darton, Longman and Todd, 1979), 81.

[30] Ellen T. Charry, 'Experience', in *The Oxford Handbook of Systematic Theology* ed. Kathryn Tanner, John Webster, and Iain Torrance (Oxford: Oxford University Press, 2007), 428.

[31] E.g., see Theodore Vial, 'Anschauung and Intuition, Again (or "We Remain Bound to the Earth")', in *Schleiermacher, the Study of Religion, and the Future of Theology: A Transatlantic Dialogue*, ed. Brent W. Sockness and Wilhelm Gräb (Berlin: Walter De Gruyter, 2010), 46.

3 Grounding God-Concepts Through Metaphors

A second strategy for grounding God-concepts is through the use of metaphors. As outlined in Chapter 3, conceptual metaphors illuminate abstract concepts by modelling them on concrete domains from our sensorimotor experience. The pervasiveness of metaphors in religious language makes them a plausible candidate for a strategy to ground God-concepts.

3.1 Metaphors in Religious Language

Metaphors are a staple of religious language. Bread, vines, light, wine, water, soap, milk, wheat, yeast, fire, warmth, brightness, height, depth, trees, sheep, houses, doors, rocks, and fortresses are but a few examples of objects or perceptual qualities which are used to illuminate more abstract theological concepts. Other metaphors use less directly perceptual concepts, such as those whose vehicle involves a social relationship or office (such as shepherding, motherhood, kingship, adoption, nuptial relations, and thieves). Although these are less obviously related to discrete perceptions, they can be grounded in our embodied, lived experience of such relations.

The necessity for metaphors in religious language has long been recognised. For instance, Aquinas's peripatetic axiom 'nothing is found in the intellect which was not first found in the senses' grounds theological knowledge in embodied experience.[32] Given this epistemological constraint, Aquinas observes that scripture describes the sacred through likeness to sensibilia, employing language which draws on the senses, including metaphor, symbol, and parable.[33] As Rikhof observes, this represents an accommodation to human capacities: 'Revelation has necessarily to be couched in metaphorical language, i.e., in similes taken from sensibilia. Without metaphorical language we would not be able to understand revelation, for our minds take their point of departure from sensibilia.'[34] Calvin echoes Aquinas' position when he grounds human knowledge of God in our experience of the world: 'God cannot reveal himself to us in any other way than

---

[32] 'Nihil est in intellectu quod non sit prius in sensu.' Thomas Aquinas, *Quaestiones Disputatae De Veritate* (Roma: Editori di san Tommaso, 1972), q. 2 a. 3 arg. 19.

[33] 'ideo oportet ut ad eorum cognitionem per sensibilium similitudines manuducatur: unde oportet modum istius scientism esse metaphoricum, sive symbolicum, vel parabolicum.' Thomas Aquinas, *Scriptum Super Libros Sententiarum Magistri Petri Lombardi Episcopi Parisiensis*, vol. 1 (Paris: P. Lethielleux, 1929), q. 1 a. 5, arg. 4. For a discussion on Aquinas' account of metaphor and analogy in relation to conceptual metaphors, see Masson, *Without Metaphor*, 131–6. See also, Sanders, *Theology in the Flesh*, 59.

[34] Herwi Rikhof, *The Concept of Church: A Methodological Inquiry into the Use of Metaphors in Ecclesiology* (London: Sheed and Ward, 1981), 173.

by a comparison with things we know.'[35] He thereby recognises the need for grounded religious language: 'Doubtless [God] accommodates himself to our ignorance when he puts on a character foreign to himself.'[36] Metaphorical language for God is repeatedly understood as a necessary accommodation, a point I return to at the end of this chapter.

Many metaphors in religious language illuminate conceptions of God. In a survey of Biblical metaphors (and similes) for God, DesCamp and Sweetser identify forty-four Old Testament and fifty New Testament metaphors.[37] They range from common metaphors such as God as 'Father' or 'King', to less well-known ones such as God as 'maggots' (Hosea 5:12). Beyond Biblical texts, metaphors are commonly deployed in theological texts. For example, Augustine deploys psychological analogies of the Trinity, and various metaphors have been proposed as models for atonement (economic, legal, Christus Victor, etc.).[38]

In addition to metaphors, religious language also contains other linguistic structures which similarly exploit concrete ideas to illuminate spiritual ones. For example, parables are often described as extended metaphors.[39] As concrete narratives, parables rely heavily on embodied knowledge:

> Rather than communicating through abstract concepts, a parable foregrounds lived experiences...Inasmuch as it draws attention to the emergence of knowledge through engagements with the sensible world, engagements that are necessarily situated and constitutive of the knower, the parable exemplifies the qualities of embodied knowledge.[40]

Narrative more generally serves as a concrete vehicle for grounding our religious cognition.[41] It typically mimics our embodied experience of the world in various ways: it is structured chronologically, involves agents performing actions, constructs settings which mirror physical worlds with material objects, and so on. All of these features make narrative amenable to representation by mental imagery

---

[35] Jean Calvin, *The Commentaries of John Calvin on the Old Testament*, 30 vols., vol. 15 (Edinburgh: Calvin Translation Society, 1843), 223.

[36] Jean Calvin, *A Commentary on the Twelve Minor Prophets*, vol. 1 (Carlisle, PA: Banner of Truth Trust, 1986), 400–1.

[37] Mary Therese DesCamp and Eve E. Sweetser, 'Metaphors for God: Why and How Do Our Choices Matter for Humans? The Application of Contemporary Cognitive Linguistics Research to the Debate on God and Metaphor', *Pastoral Psychology* 53, no. 3 (2005): 226.

[38] Thorwald Lorenzen, 'The Meaning of the Death of Jesus', *American Baptist Quarterly* 4, no. 1 (1985).

[39] E.g., Sallie McFague TeSelle, 'Parable, Metaphor, and Theology', *Journal of the American Academy of Religion* 42, no. 4 (1974): 630; Eberhard Jüngel, *God as the Mystery of the World: On the Foundation of the Theology of the Crucified One in the Dispute between Theism and Atheism*, trans. Darrell L. Guder (London: Bloomsbury, 2014), 289.

[40] Mayra Rivera, *Poetics of the Flesh* (Durham, NC: Duke University Press, 2015), 66–7. See also, Smith, *Imagining the Kingdom*, 132.

[41] I am indebted to Andrew Pinsent for the suggestion that this discussion be extended to narrative.

which deploys simulated modal concepts. Brown and Strawn observe that the sensorimotor simulations involved in offline concept activation make reading a narrative a particularly embodied experience:

> To understand the action in a story, we use our systems for controlling our own action to mentally simulate the actions described in the story, but without actually moving ourselves. So stories force us to act (implicitly) and to comprehend the consequences of the actions as told in the story. To understand the story of the Good Samaritan is to find ourselves in the roles of the various characters, mentally doing the actions that the story describes and observing their impact on other characters in the story. We also attune our emotions to those of the victim and the Samaritan.[42]

Narratives which are otherworldly nevertheless employ highly imageable concepts, even if they leave more room for the imagination. Fuller observes that the vivid imagery of apocalyptic language deploys concrete language and achieves bodily emotional effects:

> The enduring power of apocalyptic rhetoric in western religious communities thus rests—at least in part—in its ability first to evoke specific emotions and then to channel these emotions in ways that both alleviate the existential anxieties connected with these emotions and strengthen communal bonds. The repetitive nature of the plot and the frightful imagery of beasts and dragons gradually construct—and intensify—an experience of imminent threat among those in the listening audience.[43]

Given the pervasiveness linguistic devices which use concrete imagery to illuminate abstract ideas, the field is ripe for analysis via conceptual metaphor theory. Indeed, this is one area of embodied cognition research which has attracted significant interest from theologians; a number of scholars have recently applied conceptual metaphors to the case of theological concepts.[44]

These scholars contend that theological conceptual metaphors deploy the same cognitive systems as other conceptual metaphors.[45] Hence, they likewise draw upon concrete bodily experience: '[t]he vocabulary of metaphysical religion would thus appear to be traceable to a distinct set of bodily experiences'.[46] This bodily experience is used to structure abstract theological concepts, including

---

[42] Brown and Strawn, *Physical Nature of Christian Life*, 143.
[43] Fuller, *Spirituality in the Flesh*, 39.
[44] DesCamp and Sweetser, 'Metaphors for God.'; Sanders, *Theology in the Flesh*; Masson, *Without Metaphor*.
[45] Sanders, *Theology in the Flesh*, 5, 175.
[46] Fuller, *Spirituality in the Flesh*, 150. See also, Meier et al., 'What's "Up" with God?', 699.

human conceptions of God: 'Cross-domain mapping plays a foundational and inescapable role in most non-trivial conceptions and inferences. Our conceptualizations and inferences about God are no exception to this. There is no escaping the embodied mind.'[47]

The use of metaphors to describe God has led some to suggest that all theological language is metaphorical.[48] For example, DesCamp and Sweetser suggest that metaphors capture the Biblical concept of God exhaustively: 'Our working assumption was that because there is so little literal content in our target domain (God), we could learn what characteristics of God were most important to the scripture writers by examining the metaphors they chose to use to describe God.'[49]

3.2 Verticality Metaphors for God

Linguistic metaphors for God may abound in religious language, but do these metaphors probe beneath the surface of linguistic expressions to structure our cognition through conceptual metaphors? Despite the relative paucity of empirical evidence, one study investigates the association between the abstract concepts of 'God' and 'devil' with metaphors of verticality.[50] Observing that religious language presumes such associations (as in 'glory to God in the highest', 'the Devil lives down in hell'), they sought to determine 'whether these metaphors simply aid communication or implicate a deeper mode of concept representation'.[51]

The team of researchers ran a variety of different experiments to test this association, finding that: participants were faster at categorising God-related and up-related words when they were mapped to the same response button (so too devil-related and down-related words); participants were faster at categorising God-related words and pictures when they were displayed higher up on a computer screen (so too devil-related words and images when they appeared lower on the screen); and images of strangers' faces were judged to have stronger belief in God if their images appeared higher on a screen. Given that the verticality effect applied to semantic processing, visual processing of language and images, and social judgements, the experimenters concluded that their results 'are consistent with embodied theories of cognition generally and with the more specific idea that representation of divine versus profane "borrows" from the vertical domain of perception'.[52]

---

[47] Masson, *Without Metaphor*, 112. See also, Muis, 'Can Christian Talk About God Be Literal?', 593.

[48] Janet Martin Soskice, 'Can a Feminist Call God "Father"?', in *Women's Voices: Essays in Contemporary Feminist Theology*, ed. Teresa Elwes (New York: Marshall Pickering, 1992), 16; Sallie McFague, *Metaphorical Theology: Models of God in Religious Language* (Philadelphia: Fortress Press, 1982).

[49] DesCamp and Sweetser, 'Metaphors for God', 226.

[50] Meier et al., 'What's "Up" with God?'   [51] Ibid., 699.

[52] Ibid., 708.

The confirmation that 'representations of divinity borrow from quite mundane body-based perceptual processes' underlines the contingency of God-concepts.[53] Up and down are, after all, concepts which only make sense for creatures in a gravitational field. Consider a human whose experience is limited to zero-gravity environments. For such a person 'top' and 'bottom' may have the meaning to identify extremities of bodies or objects such as a head or feet. (These concepts would be similar to 'left' and 'right' for us land-dwelling humans since they designate parts of our body but are not contingent on having a gravitational field.) However, the concepts 'up' and 'down' require a gravitational field to have any referential value. Hence this way of conceptualising God seems contingent on our particular bodily situatedness. As another group of researchers observe, '[t]he supernatural, by definition, is not subject to physical constraints on space and time; however, people often represent supernatural beings as "up" or "down".[54]

Verticality is only one of many metaphorical mappings used for God. Granito points out that the up-down metaphor is insufficient for describing a concept such as divinity, since it also maps onto a number of other concepts: 'if the *up-down* schema can be mapped on several concepts like *power*, *divinity* and [emotional] *valence*, then we need further features to distinguish these concepts, features that might be provided by additional situational representations'.[55] Given the number of metaphors employed for God, the concept of divinity may be distinguished by the use of other metaphors which are not shared with power or emotion. As with the abstract concept 'affection', the question remains as to whether the concept of God is merely the sum of such metaphors. Nevertheless, the association between the concept of God and verticality demonstrates that it is, at least in part, grounded in embodied experience.

3.3 Demythologising

The presence—or necessity, as Aquinas would have it—of concrete language in human conceptions of God poses a challenge for approaches which aim to strip it away. Some approaches to demythologisation, based on Bultmann's programme to 'demythologise' the New Testament, reject concrete mythological language (though, as I shall note, this is not how Bultmann himself understands demythologisation).[56]

In defining his project, Bultmann observes that the writings of the New Testament presupposed the cosmology of its day, which he describes as a

---

[53] Ibid.
[54] Soliman, Johnson, and Song, 'Understanding Religion', 855–6.
[55] Granito, 'Where Are Abstract Concepts From?', 87.
[56] E.g., see Wilder, 'Mythology and the New Testament'.

'mythological worldview'. The first characteristic of such a worldview he identifies is that: '[t]he world is viewed as a three-storied structure, with the earth in the centre, the heaven above, and the underworld beneath. Heaven is the abode of God and of celestial beings—the angels. The underworld is hell, the place of torment'.[57] Bultmann argues that this mythological worldview is obsolete: 'it is impossible to use electric light and the wireless and to avail ourselves of modern medical and surgical discoveries, and at the same time to believe in the New Testament world of spirits and miracles'.[58] His proposal, then, is to do away with this mythological husk of religion in favour of the kerygmatic kernel it contains, which he argues should be articulated in the idiom of existential philosophy. This proposal includes exorcising the mythological worldview's three-tiered cosmology:

> What meaning, for instance, can we attach to such phrases in the creed as 'descended into hell' or 'ascended into heaven'? We no longer believe in the three-storied universe which the creed takes for granted. The only honest way of reciting the creeds is to strip the mythological framework from the truth they enshrine[59]

Bultmann's observation that our modern-day cosmology is vastly different than, and at times at odds with, a first-century Palestinian cosmology is undeniably true. However, the presence of verticality metaphors in human God-concepts reveals a problem for demythologisation, especially versions that go beyond Bultmann by rejecting (rather than simply reinterpreting) myth altogether. As noted, empirical evidence suggests that verticality is still deeply engrained in contemporary conceptions of God, conceptions presumably held by people who no longer share the cosmology of the first century. This descriptive claim poses a challenge for the normative project of demythologisation; namely, is it possible to remove verticality metaphors used for God when they not only derive from a cosmology but are also embedded in a conceptual system? Conceptual metaphor theory suggest that such concrete imagery is key to our ability to conceptualise and reason about God. Exorcising the verticality metaphor from human God-concepts, if such a development is even possible, runs the risk of altering it or leave it impoverished. Insofar as concrete language serves to ground theological discourse, removing it represents a failure to accommodate human cognitive capacities.

Tillich criticises approaches which discard mythological language. He observes that myth 'uses material from our *ordinary experience*. It puts the stories of the

[57] Rudolf Karl Bultmann, 'New Testament and Mythology', in *Kerygma and Myth: A Theological Debate*, ed. Hans Werner Bartsch (New York: Harper & Row, 1961), 1.
[58] Ibid., 5.   [59] Ibid., 4.

gods into the framework of time and space although it belongs to the nature of the ultimate to be beyond time and space.'[60] However, Tillich recognises that embracing mythology, together with its anthropomorphisms, runs the risk of straying into idolatry.[61] In light of this difficulty, he charts a middle way between the destructive demythologising and the idolatry of rampant mythology. For Tillich, demythologisation 'must be accepted and supported if it points to the necessity of recognizing a symbol as a symbol and a myth as a myth. It must be attacked and rejected if it means the removal of symbols and myths altogether.' The mythological form is not merely a husk from which the true kerygmatic content can be easily separated. Tillich's position, then, is to retain myth so long as it is recognised as such: 'All mythological elements in the Bible, and doctrine and liturgy should be recognized as mythological, but they should be maintained in their symbolic form and not replaced by scientific substitutes. For there is no substitute for the use of symbols and myths: they are the language of faith.'[62] He thus appreciates the myth's capacity to ground concepts in concrete language.

In spite of Bultmann's starker language of 'stripping the mythological framework', his own approach may be closer to Tillich's than some readings suggest. His proposal is ultimately to reinterpret mythological elements in an existential register, rather than do away with them as such.[63] He also gestures towards the power of myth to ground theological insights in concrete concepts:

> Myth speaks of the power...which man [sic] supposes he experiences as the ground and limit of his world and of his own activity and suffering. He describes these powers in terms derived from the visible world, with its tangible objects and forces, and from human life with its feelings, motives, and potentialities...He speaks of the other world in terms of this world, and of the gods in terms derived from human life.[64]

In summary, the ability for myth to ground theological concepts in concrete experience calls into questions attempts to scourge religious language of its mythological form. Myths offer yet another linguistic form which grounds theological concepts in concrete ones and thus resonates with the way humans conceptualise God by using concepts such as verticality.

---

[60] Paul Tillich, *Dynamics of Faith* (New York: Harper & Row, 1957), 56. Emphasis added.

[61] 'Faith, if it takes its symbols literally, becomes idolatrous!', ibid., 60.   [62] Ibid., 58.

[63] Rudolf Karl Bultmann, 'Neues Testament Und Mythologie: Das Problem Der Entmythologisierung Der Neutestamentlichen Verkündigung', *Kerygma und Mythos: Ein Theologisches Gespräch* 1 (1960). Ogden's English translation in Rudolf Karl Bultmann, 'New Testament and Mythology (1941)', in *New Testament and Mythology and Other Basic Writings*, ed. Schubert M. Ogden (Philadelphia: Fortress Press, 1984) opts for the more idiomatic phrase 'not picking and choosing' rather than a more literal translation of the German 'not picking and striking out (abstriche)'. This can obscure Bultmann's point that demythologising is a hermeneutical method rather than a process of elimination or subtraction.

[64] Bultmann, 'New Testament and Mythology', 10.

3.4 Evaluating Linguistic Attempts to Ground God

There is a compelling case that conceptual metaphors, together with their deploy-ment in parable, narrative, and myth, are able to ground the concept of God. The various concrete concepts associated with God provide the necessary sensori-motor representations to satisfy a modal theory of concepts. However, do concep-tual metaphors also fulfil the other horn of the grounding-idolatry dilemma?

Metaphor is often proposed as a way of avoiding the idolatry which a literal equivalent would surely commit. For example, Soskice notes that 'In any religion where God is conceived of as radically transcendent it is arguable that all lan-guage used of God will be metaphorical or at least figurative.'[65] When minding the ontological gap, metaphor arguably provides plausible deniability that one is committing an idolatrous equation of God with a thing in the world. To point out similarities and to be only partially applicable (so metaphor) is not to claim an equivalence.[66]

In contrast, Maimonides suggests that metaphors for the divine constitute a form of idolatry. He acknowledges that the language of scripture is an accommo-dation and allows 'the multitude' to understand God in terms of bodily existence:

> 'The Torah speaks according to the language of man,' that is to say, expressions, which can easily be comprehended and understood by all, are applied to the Creator. Hence the description of God by attributes implying corporeality, in order to express His existence; because the multitude of people do not easily conceive existence unless in connection with a body, and that which is not a body nor connected with a body has for them no existence.[67]

However, these corporeal metaphors for God ultimately lead readers astray, since they do not correspond to the metaphysical reality of God: 'Such is, e.g., the case with the vulgar notions with respect to the corporeality of God... It is the result of long familiarity with passages of the Bible, which they are accustomed to respect and to receive as true, and the literal sense of which implies the corporeality of God and other false notions.'[68] Metaphor, after all, uses a concrete image to illu-minate the divine (e.g., God is a rock). Are such metaphors different from a graven image in any relevant sense, since both employ something concrete, some-thing limited, something from the created order, as a placeholder for God? Even though one idol is tangible and the other is mental or linguistic, they nevertheless

---

[65] Soskice, 'Can a Feminist Call God "Father"?', 16. See also, McFague, *Metaphorical Theology*, 4–7.
[66] Elizabeth A. Johnson, *She Who Is: The Mystery of God in Feminist Theological Discourse* (Crossroad, 1993), 54.
[67] Moses Maimonides, *The Guide for the Perplexed*, trans. M. Friedländer (Skokie, IL: Varda, 2002), Pt 1, Ch 26, 35.
[68] Ibid., Pt 1, Ch 31, 41–2.

both seem to share the same strategy of relying on something concrete to stand in for God when it is ultimately incapable of doing so. Halbertal and Margalit summarise Maimonides' position as follows:

> To say 'God has a hand' is to assert a proposition, while a drawing of this hand is not a proposition. This propositional character of language can make it more dangerous than visual representations. According to this view, just as there is a ban on representations in images and pictures, so there should be a ban on linguistic representations. The war against sculpted images and paintings is thus extended to linguistic metaphors.[69]

To consider whether metaphor falls prey to the charge of idolatry, I shall consider the poignant case of anthropomorphism.

4 Anthropomorphism

Among the large number of metaphors which provide models for understanding God, anthropomorphisms are some of the most common and pervasive. Following the pattern of conceptual metaphors, they structure the abstract concept of God by using the model of a human being derived from bodily experience. This underlying conceptual metaphor can be detected in a number of linguistic expressions; as Barret and Keil observe, '[s]ometimes God-talk is blatantly anthropomorphic as in "the hand of God," and sometimes it is subtle as in "God sees" '.[70]

4.1 Anthropomorphism and Theological Incorrectness

Similarly to the study on verticality metaphors, Barrett and Keil set out to test whether anthropomorphism structures human God-concepts: 'Although this language may be considered metaphorical, it could be the case that this language actually expresses the underlying conception of God.'[71] They had participants read a short narrative about a boy in distress, which included the line 'though God was answering another prayer in another part of the world when the boy

---

[69] Moshe Halbertal and Avishai Margalit, *Idolatry*, trans. Naomi Goldblum (Cambridge MA: Harvard University Press, 1992), 54. Cf. Erin Kidd, 'The Embodied Mind and How to Pray with One', in *Putting God on the Map: Theology and Conceptual Mapping*, ed. Erin Kidd and Jakob Karl Rinderknecht (Lanham: Fortress Academic, 2018), 33.

[70] Barrett and Keil, 'Conceptualizing a Nonnatural Entity', 221.

[71] Ibid. See also Stewart Guthrie, 'Why Gods? A Cognitive Theory', in *Religion in Mind: Cognitive Perspectives on Religious Belief, Ritual and Experience*, ed. Jensine Andresen (Cambridge: Cambridge University Press, 2001), 99.

started praying, before long God responded', and participants were later asked about details of the story.[72] The experimenters reasoned that if participants used an anthropomorphic concept of God, they would infer that God finished answering one prayer before responding to another; without such an anthropomorphic conception they might equally infer that God could rescue the boy while simultaneously answering the first prayer. Moreover, this indirect method allowed them to interrogate the God-concepts which participants used in everyday reasoning rather than simply reporting 'official' theological positions.

The study revealed that participants largely deployed anthropomorphic God-concepts when making inferences about the story in spite of the fact that they held contradictory 'theologically correct' positions when explicitly surveyed about their beliefs in God, such as endorsing God's omnipresence.[73] The tendency to anthropomorphise was not restricted to God, but also applied to other abstract, mysterious entities, such as a fictional super-computer, suggesting that familiar knowledge about human beings is readily projected onto difficult-to-ground entities.

Barrett and Keil do not locate their work within an embodied cognition framework, yet it shares many affinities with the conceptualisation hypothesis. In line with conceptual metaphor theory, they suggest that we draw on experience for models to understand God: 'As natural creatures, we can only draw upon natural experiences in our attempts to characterize God.'[74] Moreover, they speculate that this form of grounding may be necessary for God-concepts: 'Perhaps conceptions of God must be anthropomorphic, even while theological beliefs maintain otherwise.'[75] As others have commented, the tendency to anthropomorphise raises the possibility that 'people use knowledge of their bodies and sensorimotor capacities and limitations to scaffold their understanding of the supernatural or divine'[76] Lakoff and Johnson's original articulation of conceptual metaphors includes a strikingly similar observation about personification. They identify personification as a pervasive ontological metaphor, which 'allows us to comprehend a wide variety of experiences with nonhuman entities in terms of human motivations, characteristics, and activities'.[77]

Barrett and Keil noted that their findings could be interpreted in two different ways. One possibility is that people have an 'official' theologically correct concept of God operative alongside an anthropomorphic one: 'people seem to possess and use more than one concept of God in real-life activities, and these parallel

---

[72] Barrett and Keil, 'Conceptualizing a Nonnatural Entity', 224.
[73] See also, D Jason Slone, *Theological Incorrectness: Why Religious People Believe What They Shouldn't* (Oxford: Oxford University Press, 2004).
[74] Barrett and Keil, 'Conceptualizing a Nonnatural Entity', 220.   [75] Ibid., 223.
[76] Soliman, Johnson, and Song, 'Understanding Religion', 854.
[77] Lakoff and Johnson, *Metaphors We Live By*, 28.

concepts have some markedly different properties'.[78] Alternatively, a stronger form of the conclusion would be that 'the vocabulary of theological correctness is employed to mask' an anthropomorphic concept of God, and hence 'the "theological" concept is actually hollow, lacking the power to facilitate meaningful representations. Perhaps the tendency to anthropomorphise God cannot be resisted because it inevitably follows from a human necessity to conceive of deity in terms of natural categories'.[79] These alternative interpretations have different consequences in theology: according to the former anthropomorphisms can be avoided, but according the latter we seemingly have no choice but to adopt them.

4.2 Acquiescing to Anthropomorphism

Theological responses to the human tendency to anthropomorphise God have varied. One approach is articulated by Sanders who closely follows cognitive metaphor theory.[80] Given his commitment to the embodiment of all concepts, Sanders argues that we simply have to swallow the pill of anthropomorphism: 'It seems to me that the "problem of anthropomorphism" is misplaced since we have no alternative, but to use the only cognitive apparatus available to us to think about God'.[81]

Sanders recognises that theology has traditionally construed anthropomorphisms as idolatry. However, given that our concepts are inextricably embodied, we simply have to use the only means available to us to conceptualise God: 'It is often said that we must not use human categories and concepts to understand God. However . . . we have no other choice than to use the mental tools available to us to think about God. Our human conceptual structures are all we have to understand anything, including God'.[82] The only alternative would be to give up conceptualising God altogether, since we do not have access to a disembodied perspective on God:

> If anthropomorphism means ascribing any human ideas to God and this is considered illegitimate, then we are consigned to the abyss of agnosticism because even concepts such as infinite, pure act, omnipotence, love, and Being Itself will have to be excluded since they make use of concepts drawn from our embodied experience.[83]

Sanders again seems to be caught on one of the grounding-idolatry dilemma. He eagerly embraces anthropomorphism because it can ground a

---

[78] Barrett and Keil, 'Conceptualizing a Nonnatural Entity', 241.   [79] Ibid.
[80] Sanders, *Theology in the Flesh*, 17–77.   [81] Ibid., 249.
[82] Ibid., 3.   [83] Ibid., 261.

concept of God in embodied experience. However, this gain comes at the expense of virtually conceding idolatry, at least in the form of anthropomorphism. Sanders' position will inevitably attract the ire of those who denounce anthropomorphism, such as Gordon Kaufmann who critiques 'the contention that the originative and ultimate reality behind everything (God) is to be understood largely in terms of images and metaphors derived from and peculiar to human existence':

> indeed, male human existence: God is pictured as lord, king, creator, judge, father, and so on. The defining model on the basis of which the conception of God is built up is that of an agent, and actor, a notion which gains its distinctive meaning almost entirely in and through human exemplifications.[84]

4.3 Cognitive Science of Idolatry

If Sanders' response to anthropomorphism is simply to acquiesce, then Jong, Kavanagh, and Visala take precisely the opposite route.[85] They argue that the kind of anthropomorphic agents found in Barrett's studies (among other aspects of religion interrogated in the cognitive science of religion) simply do not correspond to how God is conceptualised in classical theism. Anthropomorphism is, indeed, 'theologically incorrect' and should be rejected by 'classical theists'. For example, 'the classical theist might flatly deny that God is an agent, at least in the sense that CSR uses the term'.[86] Hence they argue that projects in the cognitive science of religion, including Barrett's, simply track promiscuous religious beliefs: 'the sorts of religious beliefs CSR currently attempts to explain are—by the lights of classical theistic belief—more like idolatrous beliefs...the cognitive science of religion could equally be dubbed the cognitive science of idolatry'.[87]

Cognitive science with its empirical methodology is, after all, merely a descriptive discipline: it can only tell us how humans happen to conceptualise God and not how they ought to conceptualise God. Thus, the discovery that there is a tendency to anthropomorphise does not imply that we ought to do so; it may be a mistaken tendency. From a theological standpoint, one could equally side with Calvin in interpreting this finding when he states that 'man's nature, so to speak, is a perpetual factory of idols'.[88] Given this normative insight, the appropriate response to Barrett's findings is not to 'swallow the pill', as Sanders does. Rather

---

[84] Gordon D. Kaufman, *In Face of Mystery: A Constructive Theology* (Cambridge, MA: Harvard University Press, 1993), 76. See also, Maimonides, *Guide for the Perplexed*, Pt 1.
[85] Jong, Kavanagh, and Visala, 'Born Idolaters'.   [86] Ibid., 254.
[87] Ibid., 246.   [88] Calvin, *Institutes*, 1.11.18.

what the classical theist ought to do is to work harder to ward off their bias towards anthropomorphism. Jong, Kavanagh, and Visala conclude that '[t]he tragedy of the classical theologian is precisely that idolatry is easier on the mind than orthodoxy'.[89]

If Jong, Kavanagh, and Visala take the opposite view to Sanders, then the challenge for their position comes from the opposite horn of the grounding-idolatry dilemma. They fastidiously avoid the charge of idolatry by siding with 'classical theism', but this leaves open the question of whether the classical view allows God to be grounded in the human conceptual repertoire. Their approach implicitly sides with the weaker of Barrett's interpretations about anthropomorphic concepts, namely that we can have a parallel system of theologically correct concepts that function alongside anthropomorphic ones. If Barrett's stronger interpretation—that theologically correct concepts are merely hollow and the tendency to anthropomorphise is irresistible—is correct, then no matter how hard the Jong, Kavanagh, and Visala classical theist strives they will be unable to extricate themself from their anthropomorphisms. The challenge for this position, then, is to show that the far more abstract concepts of classical theism such as divine simplicity can be grounded in embodied experience and thereby be as meaningful to embodied cognisors as the far more tractable anthropomorphic concepts.

4.4 Conclusion

Metaphors offer a promising way to ground theological concepts. However, the question remains as to whether such grounded concepts constitute idolatry. Anthropomorphism served as a test case for whether, contra Maimonides, metaphors could pass the idolatry test. If anthropomorphism is judged to be a form of idolatry, then other metaphorical language for God may well fall by the same sword. Even if Maimonides' position that all metaphors for God are idolatrous seems too extreme, the central case of anthropomorphic representations of God brings the issue to a head: it is both a *locus classicus* of idolatry and, cognitive science has suggested, a human tendency when conceptualising God.

The findings in cognitive science do not (and cannot) provide a normative guide to what we should make of anthropomorphic God-concepts. Theologians have argued for opposing positions, on the one hand, proposing that, as an inevitable by-product of our embodied means of conceptualising, anthropomorphism is the best we can do, or, on the other hand, that anthropomorphism ought to be rejected in line with classical theism. As with the grounding-through-experience strategy, both of these alternatives still seem to fall prey to one of the horns of the

---

[89] Jong, Kavanagh, and Visala, 'Born Idolaters', 265.

grounding-idolatry dilemma: the former is open to the charge of idolatry while it is not clear whether the latter can satisfy the grounding criteria.

At this point we might simply question the very possibility that humans can conceptualise God. Perhaps human concepts, on account of their embodied nature, are simply not capable of grasping God. The only option then seems to be to opt for a strong version of apophaticism and with Wittgenstein conclude that *'Wovon man nicht sprechen kann, darüber muss man schweigen.'*[90] Indeed, Maimonides reaches such a conclusion when advocates only apophatic language be used of God.[91] However, before abandoning kataphatic utterances altogether, I turn to the final strategy for grounding concepts of God.

5 Incarnation

Thus far I have argued that attempts to ground God in experience or through metaphor are, on their own, theologically insufficient, since they remain caught on the horns of the grounding-idolatry dilemma. Admittedly many of these accounts do not explicitly set out to address the symbol grounding problem. My argument, then, is that the symbol grounding problem is a helpful tool to expose deficiencies in existing approaches. I am not claiming that experiential and meta-phorical ways of grounding God are incorrect, rather I am making the modest claim that they are, on their own, insufficient and incomplete.

What is missing from the preceding discussion is the *incarnation*.[92] The attempts to ground the concept of God in experience and metaphor that have been outlined could equally have presumed a deist conception of God, a God who remains aloof and cannot finally be known by human minds. This discussion has vigilantly policed the ontological divide so as to avoid idolatry. What this assumption fails to appreciate is that while we have no recourse to bridging the ontological gap, the Christian claim is that God has done so in the incarnation.

The incarnation provides the key to grounding God-concepts while avoiding idolatry. On the one hand, Christ is not merely a metaphor for God. Rather the classical Christological formulation of the dual natures affirms that Christ is ontologically fully God. Hence to identify Christ with God is, by definition, not a form of idolatry. On the other hand, Christ is also fully human and can therefore be conceptualised in human terms. As with anthropomorphism, this provides a

---

[90] Ludwig Wittgenstein, *Tractatus Logico-Philosophicus*, trans. David Pears and Brian McGuinness (New York: Routledge, 2003), §7.

[91] Maimonides, *Guide for the Perplexed*, Pt 1, Ch 59.

[92] Sanders does refer to the incarnation in passing when he discusses bodily relativity: 'Similar to the Christian doctrine of the incarnation, God would have to assume a human perspective in order to discuss truth with us.' Sanders, *Theology in the Flesh*, 100. However, he fails to point to the incarnation when he defends anthropomorphism.

concrete means of grounding the concept of God. In short, incarnation is anthropomorphism without the idolatry.

In the remainder of this section I explore how the incarnation grounds the concept of God in a theologically licit fashion. Crucially, this account will develop the general Christian affirmation that God is known in Christ by employing the idiom of embodied cognition.[93] This exploration begins with the historical figure of Jesus of Nazareth before considering how this focal event 'ripples' outwards. Most directly, the Word becoming flesh and dwelling among us opens the possibility of knowing God corporeally, in the body of Jesus of Nazareth.[94] This corporeal knowledge allows for concrete narrations of Jesus' life in the gospels. It also continues in other forms of God's presence through sacramentality. Having explored these dimensions of the incarnation I shall return to the overarching theological theme for this study, namely how the incarnation represents an accommodation to human cognitive capacities.

5.1 Bodily Knowledge of God in the Incarnation

At the most immediate level, the incarnation is God taking on a human body. God's entry into the material world in the incarnation makes God amenable to human perceptual capacities, allowing the concept of God to be grounded in sensorimotor states. However, the incarnation not only means that Christ is physical and perceptible but also claims that God becomes embodied in human form: the Word becomes flesh. Although it is often quipped that this makes God more 'relatable' to human beings, embodied cognition offers a thicker description of what this might mean.

By foregrounding the role of the body in human cognition, embodied cognition draws out (some of) the implications of the incarnation for human understanding. The affordances available to Jesus are those generally available to other human beings by virtue of a shared embodiment. When Jesus performed an action, his observers' mirror neurons fired; observers would have understood his actions partly on account of their own bodily ability to perform such actions. If concepts are grounded in the particularities of embodiment, then Jesus shares an anthropogenic conceptual system with the rest of humanity. These rather pedestrian observations are, of course, applicable to all human beings. But in the context of the incarnation they explicate the significance of God offering a humanly accessible revelation. The incarnation introduces a shared embodiment between Christ and humanity; and this shared embodiment provides the foundation for understanding Christ at a basic level, namely understanding of Christ in terms of

---

[93] E.g., Colossians 1:15–20.   [94] John 1:14.

our own bodies. Instead of the transfer of information in some form of platonic ideal, the bodily presence of Christ allows for an understanding of God in human categories.

Ward develops a Christology which foregrounds the bodily activity of Jesus. Engaging with Merleau-Ponty, he shifts emphasis away from 'personhood'—'his consciousness, his autonomy, his history, his mission, his embodiment of the Godhead'—which has dominated the dogmatic tradition.[95] Instead he moves the emphasis to soteriology, economy, and performance.[96] The operations that constitute messianic performance are not simply explored in terms of social, economic and political dimensions (though these are not occluded). Instead the role of bodily interactions and the way they take on meaning within larger frames of reference are analysed.[97]

Given the focus on the embodied action of Christ, for Ward the work of Merleau-Ponty becomes an exegetical tool. He reads certain Christological narratives from the gospels paying particular attention to the role of embodied interactions. Healing accounts which involve touch and the Johannine post-resurrection narratives in which Christ meets first Mary Magdalene and then Thomas make for obvious examples of tactile encounters.[98] These interactions illustrate the crucial roles that bodies in general, and touch in particular, play in the process of knowing. Merleau-Ponty's description of the pre-reflective knowledge inherent in our capacity to engage our bodies with the world demonstrates how these Christological and corporeal interchanges constitute and communicate knowledge. Far from an abstract metaphysical description, Ward uses Merleau-Ponty to examine how the body participates in messianic knowledge and how Christ communicates through bodily interactions.

This engagement with Merleau-Ponty, a forerunner of embodied cognition, underscores how Christology relies on an understanding which arises for a particular kind of body. It is Jesus' body that makes him comprehensible to other bodily creatures, and it is our bodies which allow us to understand at a fundamental level the bodily activity of Jesus. Embodied cognition fills in the picture as to why—and precisely how—understanding is tied to embodiment. If concepts are grounded in sensorimotor states, then the physical body of Christ and his bodily interaction with the world grounds our conception of God. Moreover, if concepts are shaped by embodiment, then our shared embodiment with Christ provides epistemological access to God.

---

[95] Graham Ward, *Christ and Culture* (Malden, MA: Blackwell, 2005), 60.
[96] Ibid., 1, 43–9, 65.
[97] Ibid., 60–91. Cf. Graham Ward, 'Bodies: The Displaced Body of Jesus Christ', in *Radical Orthodoxy: A New Theology*, ed. John Milbank, Catherine Pickstock, and Graham Ward (London: Routledge, 1999).
[98] Ward, *Christ and Culture*, 62, 66–7, 120–1.

5.2 Narrating the Incarnation

Embodied perceptual access to Jesus was only available to those who encountered Christ in first-century Palestine. If the ascension concludes Christ's presence in the universe in human form, then one might reason that the bodily knowledge of God made possible in the incarnation is now closed off to subsequent generations. Scripture acknowledges the post-ascension imperceptibility of Christ: Thomas, in his profoundly tactile encounter with the risen Christ, enjoys perceptual access that later followers do not: 'Jesus said to him, "Have you believed because you have seen me? Blessed are those who have not seen and yet have come to believe."'[99] Pauline theology likewise acknowledges this differentiated access in the assertion that 'now we see in a mirror, dimly, but then we will see face to face. Now I know only in part (γινώσκω ἐκ μέρους); then I will know fully (ἐπιγνώσομαι), even as I have been fully known.'[100] This passage leverages the fact that in-person (face-to-face) contact is different from other communication and explicitly draws out the epistemological implications that embodied contact offers fuller knowledge.

For those living after the ascension, one way in which Christ's life is mediated is through gospel narratives: '[t]he gospel comes to us by cultural and linguistic mediation... The Faith is saving knowledge, which comes to us through history. It was copied for most of its transit by hand, from manuscript to manuscript... Our encounter is a mediated encounter.'[101] At first glance, it may appear as though embodied, sensorimotor knowledge of God in Christ is substituted for more abstract, less embodied linguistic mediation. While linguistic mediation may be less direct (a case of 'offline' rather than 'online' cognition), it nevertheless relies on the embodied nature of our cognition to comprehend it. Narratives may be one step removed from personal encounter, but they nevertheless rely on a shared embodiment afforded by the incarnation. When they describe bodily action, comprehending these actions depends on knowledge of one's own body and its interaction with the world (e.g., affordances). The stench of decay emanating from Lazarus' tomb, the granularity of the dust in which Jesus writes, how one sinks into sand (and thus a house would too), the rubbing of saliva mixed with dirt into a blind man's eyes, the betrayer's kiss, and the piercing of Christ's side are but a few examples of how bodily knowledge is articulated in and assumed by texts. Narrative moments such as these not only rely on our bodily familiarity with the world for their comprehensibility but also grasp us at a visceral level. The emphasis on the bodily interaction in Ward's Christology relies precisely on narratives which depict motor movement (such as tactile encounters).

---

[99] John 20:29.   [100] 1 Corinthians 13:12.
[101] Andrew Davison and Alison Milbank, *For the Parish: A Critique of Fresh Expressions* (London: SCM Press, 2010), 35.

In addition to language which refers directly to bodily action, embodied cognition suggests that many concepts (and therefore the narratives which deploy them) rely on sensorimotor *simulations* which derive from human embodiment. When reading the narrative of Jesus expelling the money changers from the temple, for example, one readily generates sensorimotor simulations of the scene, the objects in it, the protagonists' actions and emotions, even if these simulations are not necessarily a conscious, vivid 'mental theatre'.[102] For this reason I argued that narratives provide concrete imagery for more abstract ideas in a similar way to conceptual metaphors (see Section 3.1). Hence narratives serve to extend the conceptual grounding benefit of the incarnation to those who lack direct physical encounter with the historical Jesus.

The capacity of narratives to ground the concept of God highlights the value of narrative approaches to theology. As I have argued, the grounding of concepts is ultimately a criterion for meaningfulness. Moreover, more concrete concepts have been found to be easier to process.[103] The benefits of concrete narratives are consistent with Brown and Strawn's observations on the importance of narratives:

> a really good story typically has more impact … than a thoroughgoing exegesis of the meaning of a scriptural passage. Modern narrative theology is based on just this idea. The stories we know and carry around in our memories are funda-mental to the way we act and think, and thus they constitute the theology that we actually live out.[104]

A good example of the use of concrete narratives in theology can be found in Robert Jenson's definition of God as 'whoever raised Jesus from the dead, having before raised Israel from Egypt'.[105] This is a thoroughly grounded understanding of God; God is understood through concrete actions which are set in a material world. Such a definition need not exclude more abstract predicates of God. However, unlike abstract predicates, this kind of definition grounds God in a par-ticular concrete narrative, event, and person.

5.3 Incarnation Writ Large

Alongside the mediation of the incarnation in narrative, theologians have proposed broader understandings of incarnation.[106] These proposals extend incarnation

---

[102] Matthew 21:12–17; John 2:13–22.
[103] Maryellen Hamilton and Suparna Rajaram, 'The Concreteness Effect in Implicit and Explicit Memory Tests', *Journal of Memory and Language* 44, no. 1 (2001).
[104] Brown and Strawn, *Physical Nature of Christian Life*, 84.
[105] Robert W. Jenson, *Systematic Theology: The Triune God*, vol. 1 (New York: Oxford University Press, 1997), 63.
[106] E.g., Grumett, *Material Eucharist*, 111–22.

beyond the life of the historical Jesus, arguing that other entities also constitute examples of the incarnate Word. Unlike narratives which simply recount the incarnation, they extend the incarnation ontologically by arguing that other entities *participate* in it. They typically argue for a broader incarnational or sacramental 'logic', whereby the divine is revealed *through* the material.

In the field of ecclesiology, the church has been proposed as an extension of the incarnation. The extended Pauline metaphor which describes the church as the 'body of Christ' suggests that the church participates in the incarnation.[107] Contemporary theologies have developed this idea by describing the church as a sacrament. For example, the Vatican 2 document *Lumen gentium* states that 'the Church is in Christ like a sacrament or as a sign and instrument both of a very closely-knit union with God and of the unity of the whole human race'.[108] In a similar vein, Davison and Milbank observe that in mediating salvation the church functions as an extension of the incarnation: 'God entrusts the message, work and legacy of salvation to the human community of the Church, to human language and to human culture. In this, God extends the logic of the Incarnation, of handing himself over to the world.'[109] The mediation provided by the church, where it acts in concert with the Spirit, does not represent a rupture with or an alternative to the incarnation, but rather a continuation of it.

Too close an association between Christ and the historic institutional manifestations of the church, however, becomes problematic given the evils which have been perpetrated within by the church at various points in history.[110] Rowan Williams acknowledges Christ is 'sometimes obscured and betrayed' by the church and therefore qualifies its sacramental nature in the following terms:

> to think of the Church as sacrament leads us not towards a static picture of the Church as a simple epiphany of the 'sacred', nor to an unreal model of it as a perfect spiritual entity (somehow detached from the compromised historical communities and traditions which bear the name of church), but to a grasp of the fact that the Church is the sign of God's realised purpose, his will to come-to-be within the universe he has made, for the fulfilment of that created life.[111]

Thus, Williams preserves some sense in which the church participates in the larger movement of God towards the world in the incarnation ('come-to-be

---

[107] 1 Cor 12:12–31.
[108] Pope Paul VI, 'Dogmatic Constitution on the Church: Lumen Gentium', (Vatican, Rome: The Holy See, 1964), §1.
[109] Davison and Milbank, *For the Parish*, 35.
[110] Stephen Pickard, *Seeking the Church: An Introduction to Ecclesiology* (London: SCM, 2012), 56–80.
[111] Rowan Williams, 'The Church as Sacrament', *International Journal for the Study of the Christian Church* 10, no. 1 (2010): 12.

within the universe'), without equating the church with straightforward revelation of God ('a simple epiphany').

A more specific proposal is that the sacraments serve as extensions of the incarnation.[112] Davison and Milbank lay out the continuation between Christ and the sacraments in the following terms:

> The benefits that Christ won for us are brought to us *through* the Church. Salvation comes to us as material, speaking and communal beings: in the matter of the sacraments, through water, bread and wine, in the deposit of the faith handed on in human words and human cultures, and through the mission of a visible people of God, the Church.[113]

The ontological status of the Eucharistic elements has, of course, been the subject of significant controversy in the history of the theology, and it is not my task to resolve it here. However, those who hold that the Eucharistic bread and wine are the real presence of Christ affirm that they are an extension of the incarnation. As physical objects they are visible, tangible, and ingestible; and thereby offer a material window onto the divine.

Davison observes that one thing sacraments have in common with the gospel narratives is that both employ concrete imagery:

> The sacraments consist of words and gestures, and in this Christ's life offers us a sacramental pattern. In the Gospels he is forever making gestures, using physical things, and aligning them with words...His teaching is full of practical imagery and local colour: the camel and the gate called the Eye of the Needle, the rubbish dump in Jerusalem called Gehenna, and rural farming images in the parables.[114]

Again, this serves to underline how sacraments, like narratives, provide concrete sensorimotor content which functions as conceptual grounding.

Another proposal is that the incarnation is extended by Christ's presence in particular human beings. Saints are recognised for their Christ-likeness. In Matthew's Gospel, Christ himself identifies with the hungry, thirsty, stranger, naked, sick, and imprisoned.[115] Liberation theologians have seized on this identification to suggest that the poor have a special sacramental status. For

---

[112] Grumett, *Material Eucharist*, 152–9. Susan A. Ross, 'God's Embodiment and Women', in *Freeing Theology: The Essentials of Theology in Feminist Perspective*, ed. Catherine Mowry LaCugna (San Francisco: Harper, 1993), 206.

[113] Davison and Milbank, *For the Parish*, 29.

[114] Andrew Davison, *Why Sacraments?* (London: SPCK, 2013), 3.

[115] Matthew 25:31–46.

example, Boff argues that God 'has privileged the poor as his sacrament of self-communication'.[116] As with proposing the church as a sacrament, the fallible nature of human beings presents a difficultly for too close an equivalence between Christ and particular humans. However, insofar as such an identification is possible, the poor and the saintly—as sacramental—again offer a (more) concrete vehicle by which the concept of God can be grounded in embodied experience.

At times theologians have sought to cast the boundaries of incarnation even wider, pointing to ways in which the whole creation functions as a sacrament.[117] Ecological theologians seeking to underscore the dignity of the natural world argue for its capacity to point towards the divine. Citing Patriarch Bartholomew, the papal encyclical on the environment gestures in this direction: 'to accept the world as a sacrament of communion, as a way of sharing with God and our neighbours on a global scale. It is our humble conviction that the divine and the human meet in the slightest detail in the seamless garment of God's creation, in the last speck of dust of our planet'.[118] In a similar vein, scholars working in science and theology have proposed that incarnation permeates the material and biological world, in the form of 'deep incarnation'.[119] If the fallibility of particular entities raises questions concerning the extent to which they participate in the incarnation, then this proposal suffers from the same weakness. Fallen creation cannot participate in the incarnation if in so doing it predicates evil of God. A sacramental view of creation in general heightens the problem of theodicy.

A detailed evaluation of proposals for extending the incarnation is beyond the scope of the present study; my task here is not to circumscribe the incarnation definitively. As I have noted, certain criticisms have been levelled against too close an identification of particular entities with Christ. However, even if these proposals hold in a more limited or restricted sense, their status as participants in the incarnation is of interest to the present argument. Namely, if these entities represent God by virtue of their participation in the incarnation (at least to some degree), then they are also material objects—accessible to our sensorimotor engagement with the world—which serve to ground the concept of God.

---

[116] Leonardo Boff, 'The Need for Political Saints: From a Spirituality of Liberation to the Practice of Liberation', Cross Currents 30, no. 4 (1980): 370.

[117] E.g., 'Embracing the doctrine of the incarnation as complete emptying of God means grounding ontology, epistemology, and ethics in the material world.' Rivera, Poetics of the Flesh, 67.

[118] Pope Francis, 'Encyclical Letter Laudato Si' of the Holy Father Francis on the Care for Our Common Home' (Vatican, Rome: The Holy See, 2015), §9.

[119] E.g., Niels Henrik Gregersen, 'Deep Incarnation: Why Evolutionary Continuity Matters in Christology', Toronto Journal of Theology 26, no. 2 (2010). See also the subsequent collection of essays in Niels Henrik Gregersen, ed., Incarnation: On the Scope and Depth of Christology (Minneapolis: Fortress Press, 2015).

5.4 Conclusion: Incarnation as Grounding

The term 'grounding' resonates with the idea of a God come to dwell on Earth. Indeed, both the incarnation and conceptual grounding deploy a verticality metaphor: in the incarnation 'God comes down' (see Section 3.2) and 'grounded' concepts do not remain aloof but are rooted in our sensorimotor experience. In this section, I have argued that this serendipitous parallel is more than mere coincidence; the incarnation provides a mechanism for grounding the human concept of God without straying into idolatry. It does so by providing perceptual access and bodily knowledge in the historical person of Christ, being retold in concrete narratives, whose implied readership is embodied and relies upon its embodiment to comprehend the narrative, and through its extension in the sacramentality of other material mediations. By joining the sacred with the corporeal, the incarnation allows us to grasp the corporeal through the material.

Rowan Williams vividly describes many of the themes traced in this section in a passage reflecting on the incarnation. He contrasts the incarnation with 'a simple model of divine utterance—an otherworldly agent providing otherwise inaccessible information', thus highlighting the significance of bodily presence.[120] He then highlights how the materiality and activity of this incarnate body constitutes revelation: 'Revelation here [in the Christian context] begins precisely with a phenomenon in the material world, a body: the body of Jesus of Nazareth, which is an active and speaking body, the a helpless and suffering body, then a dead body'.[121] But Williams does not stop at the historical life of Jesus, but shows how the incarnation extends further, to narrative and sacrament and community: 'then a body that is both significantly absent and at the same time believed to be present in very diverse modes—as the community itself, as the food the community ritually shares, as the proclaimed narrative and instruction derived from the record of the literal flesh-and-blood-body'.[122] It is this corporeality which gives bodily creatures epistemological access to God, re-presenting God to humans:

> The story of Jesus body represents the unrepresentable God by tracing a movement towards silence and motionlessness within the human world: its climax is not a triumphant theophany but a death and its complex aftermath (the resurrection is not a theophany in the sense of some sort of public manifestation of triumph). It works with the existing expectations of divine manifestation, but then fleshes them out by telling a story of how divine power and liberty are 'emptied out' in the life of this body[123]

---

[120] Williams, *Edge of Words*, 176.   [121] Ibid.
[122] Ibid.   [123] Ibid.

Embodied cognition supplements this account by explicating why such a bodily manifestation of God is necessary if God is to be grasped by corporeal creatures with an embodied conceptual system.

6 Conclusion: Accommodating Human Conceptual Capacities

By way of conclusion, I shall tie the discussion in this chapter back to the overarching theological theme of accommodation. If embodied cognition explicates the modal nature of human concepts, then the incarnation articulates how this human capacity is accommodated when conceptualising God. Moreover, returning to the earlier proposals for grounding the concept of God, experience and metaphor, I argue that these provide legitimate means of grounding God-concepts when framed within the context of the incarnation.

6.1 Incarnation as Accommodation

As noted in Chapter 1, the incarnation serves as the supreme example of accommodation and thereby underwrites theological epistemology. There is nothing new about the doctrine of the incarnation I have been working with in this chapter, nor about the insight that the incarnation constitutes a form of accommodation. However, the application of embodied cognition's insights into God-concepts brings a new appreciation of what the incarnation is an accommodation to, namely the modal concepts of embodied human beings.

Since all humans are embodied creatures, the conceptualisation hypothesis sets out universal features of human concepts to which any successful revelation must be accommodated. This claim stands in contrast to Descartes' description of accommodation in the *Meditations*:

> Everyone is familiar with the distinction between ways of speaking of God (such as are common in the holy scriptures) adapted to the understanding of ordinary people, and containing a certain kind of truth, but one relative to human beings, and other ways of speaking of him, that instead express the naked truth, not in any relation to human beings.[124]

Embodied cognition questions the latter way of speaking.

---

[124] Descartes, *Meditations*, 93.

In contrast to Descartes' 'naked truth', embodied cognition proposes that all human knowing is shaped by embodiment. In terms of concepts, this means that all concepts are ultimately grounded in embodied sensorimotor experience. Hence concepts are relative to humans by virtue of their embodiment and salient variations in embodiment lead to variations in conceptual systems (see Conclusion). This directly challenges Descartes' second mode of speaking about God, since it proposes that all human concepts are relative to human beings because they are relative to embodiment.[125]

Descartes' dichotomy between two kinds of truth also leads to a restricted or 'elitist' version of accommodation: it is only the 'ordinary people' who require special accommodation, while the elite few have no need for accommodation, since they can simply access the 'naked truth'. In contrast, using cognitive science to understand shared aspects of the human condition leads to a universal form of accommodation: all humans have cognitive processes which are shaped by their embodiment and therefore all humans require modal concepts in order to grasp God (see Chapter 1, Section 3). We are all 'ordinary people' by virtue of our embodiment.

Given the embodiment of human concepts, Sanders articulates the need for accommodation in the following terms:

> if God communicated a concept to us, the concept would have to be understood by us, which means we would use the embodied conceptual processes we have to understand the communication...The way we understand God and what God does in relation to us is anthropogenic. Any communication from God will access our species-specific cognitive capacities.[126]

As noted earlier, cognitive scientists agree on this point, stating that 'even if gods do exist, and reveal themselves to humans, the knowledge revealed will become known through ordinary cognitive and communicative processes which can and should be scientifically explained'.[127] Put simply, humans only have an embodied mind with which to comprehend God.

Although the limited, embodied nature of human cognition poses an epistemological obstacle to human comprehension of God, the incarnation—as

---

[125] This is not to deny a mind-independent reality, which Descartes may have been trying to reference by 'naked truth'. It is, however, to deny any mind-independent cognition. External realities, be they in the created order or transcendent, are all expressed and understood 'relative to human beings' insofar as they are comprehended by embodied cognisors. In philosophical terms, this approach is in fundamental sympathy with Kantian epistemology; while Kant acknowledges a mind-independent reality (the 'noumenal'), he also recognised that humans must rely on their perceptual and cognitive capacities in grasping this reality (the 'phenomenal'). Whereas Kant asserts that humans bring particular 'categories' to bear on experience by means of particular schema, embodied cognition proposes that all of the details of embodiment shape how humans grasp the world.

[126] Sanders, *Theology in the Flesh*, 98.   [127] Pyysiäinen, 'Introduction', 5.

accommodation par excellence—overcomes this obstacle. In his embrace of the conceptual metaphor theory, Masson argues that for humans '[t]here is no "stepping outside" our bodily, socially, and culturally constituted conceptual framework to gain a God's-eye view of reality'.[128] There is, however, in the incarnation, God's 'stepping into' our bodily, socially, and culturally constituted world to give us a human's-eye view onto divine reality. The incarnation thus supplies the theological resources to address the question of conceptual grounding. Conversely, the modal theory of concepts offers a new framework from which to appreciate the epistemological significance of the incarnation.

6.2 Incarnating Experience and Language

In the preceding discussion, I suggested that experiential and linguistic (especially metaphorical) strategies for grounding God are insufficient. However, having argued that the incarnation provides the key to grounding God-concepts, it is time to revisit these strategies. In particular, while I have argued that these strategies are insufficient *on their own*, the incarnation opens up the possibility of God becoming available to human experience and becoming referable by human language.

As I have argued, the incarnation provided perceptual access to those who encountered the historical Jesus. In this sense, it made possible direct experience of God. Furthermore, narratives recounting the life of Jesus provide indirect experience of God, while various proposals to extend ontologically the understanding of the incarnation broaden experiential access. For example, the notion that all of creation serves as a kind of sacrament resonates with Schleiermacher's account of experience. In *On Religion*, he implores his readers to:

> Elevate yourselves at once...to that infinite dimension of sensible intuition, to the wondrous and celebrated starry sky. The astronomical theories, which orient a thousand suns with their world systems around a common point and seek for each common point again a higher world system that could be its center, and so on into infinity, outwardly and inwardly[129]

The infinite cosmos evokes a 'sensibility and taste for the infinite', which Schleiermacher defines as religion.[130] The universe as a whole, for Schleiermacher, has a sacramental quality, a position which is sympathetic with 'deep incarnation'. Similarly, the capacity of language to ground concepts of God evades the problem of idolatry when understood within the context of the incarnation. As

---

[128] Masson, *Without Metaphor*, 27.   [129] Schleiermacher, *On Religion*, 26.
[130] Ibid., 23.

Masson suggests, 'God has created a possibility for a correspondence between human language and the divine by taking on humanity.'[131] A human God can be referred to by human concepts and language. By grounding our concept of God, the incarnation authorises human language about God.

Consider anthropomorphism, which served as the test case for metaphorical attempts to ground concepts of God in the preceding discussion. The authors of the study on anthropomorphic concepts of God expressed the notion of accommodation (without identifying it as such) when they noted that '[t]heologically, this problem may be addressed by what in Christianity is called revelation: God allows self-disclosure in terms that people can understand and appreciate.'[132] However, they did not reflect on their findings about anthropomorphism in light of accommodation. Given the need for accommodation, a human proclivity towards anthropomorphic conceptualisation of God need not necessarily be considered a vice (though it clearly can be when misapplied). In fact, it is precisely such a cognitive tendency that the incarnation accommodates by allowing humans to grasp God in human terms. Athanasius articulates this point when he argues that the incarnation, as an accommodation, exploits the same human fixation on material things which leads to idolatry.[133] In the incarnation, God becomes an *anthropos*. Hence, with reference to the incarnate Word, anthropomorphic God-concepts are not 'theologically incorrect'. In summary, the incarnation *underwrites* religious experience and language; in light of the incarnation experience and language can also serve to ground human conceptions of God.

This chapter has primarily focused on the concept of 'God' as a test case for grounding theological concepts, on account of its centrality as a theological concept and because it has been the subject of empirical investigation. However, there is no reason why similar strategies (such as experience and conceptual metaphors) cannot be applied to other central theological concepts. For example, theories of atonement are routinely articulated in terms of a series of concrete metaphors.[134] Rahner's *grundaxiom*, that the economic Trinity is the immanent Trinity (and vice versa) can be understood in terms of conceptual grounding: it suggests that we can only speak of the Trinity as it exists in itself (i.e., the immanent Trinity) in terms of our (embodied) experience of the Trinity in its interaction with the world (i.e., the economic Trinity). If accepted, it also guarantees that the economic Trinity described in revelation faithfully represents the reality of the Trinity. Hence it proposes that the concept of the Trinity is grounded in experience.

In conclusion, the conceptualisation hypothesis of embodied cognition presents a special problem for theological concepts. By suggesting that all human

---

[131] Masson, *Without Metaphor*, 152.
[132] Barrett and Keil, 'Conceptualizing a Nonnatural Entity', 220.
[133] See Chapter 1, Section 2.2.   [134] Lorenzen, 'The Meaning of the Death of Jesus'.

concepts are ultimately grounded in sensorimotor experience, it raises the question of how the human concept of God can avoid idolatry. The incarnation, I have argued, resolves this epistemological conundrum by providing both a grounded and a non-idolatrous means of conceptualising God. It thereby conveys genuine revelation (i.e., avoids idolatry) while accommodating limited human understanding.

PART III

EMBODIED RELIGIOUS PRACTICES

5

Cognition Beyond the Brain

'Mind is a leaky organ, forever escaping its "natural" confines and mingling shamelessly with the body and with the world.'

—Andy Clark[1]

Where does cognition take place? While some ancients thought that the heart was the seat of intelligence, the modern answer is invariably that cognition happens in the brain. And with good reason; although neuroscience is still in its infancy and a long way off from mapping the human brain in all its complexity, it nevertheless readily demonstrates that cognitive processes correlate with patterns of neural activation. A role for the brain in cognition is uncontroversial; but findings and theories in embodied cognition call into question where the boundaries of cognition are typically drawn. Why limit cognition to neurons in the brain or to the central nervous system? Embodied cognition proposes that understanding cognition in isolation from the bodies in which brains are situated, and the environments in which bodies operate, is a mistake. The body, it suggests, does far more than simply provide life support for the brain, in which the 'real' cognition takes place. Rather, cognition is better (or only) understood when it is seen as a process distributed across a system which includes brain, body, and world.

To motivate this claim, Clark draws an analogy between cognition and the feeding behaviour of sea sponges. Sponges reduce the amount of water they pump to feed by orienting themselves relative to ambient currents. He surmises: '[t]he trick is an obvious one, yet not until quite recently did biologists recognize it. The reason for this is revealing: Biologists have tended to focus solely on the individual organism as the locus of adaptive structure. They have treated the organism as if it could be understood *independent of its physical world*.'[2] Consequently it was tempting to consider organisms in isolation, and this often blinds us to how organisms exploit their environments to perform tasks. The same temptation is present when analysing cognitive tasks, framing them without reference to an organism's context which may provide helpful support for cognitive processes— providing 'scaffolds' as Clark puts it. Much of our cognition takes place *in situ*, and features of the environment are relevant to how those tasks are performed.

This chapter introduces the hypotheses of embodied cognition which argue that cognition ought to be considered as *situated* in particular bodies and particular

---

[1] Clark, *Being There*, 53.   [2] Ibid., 46. Emphasis original.

Corporeal Theology: Accommodating Theological Understanding to Embodied Thinkers. Tobias Tanton, Oxford University Press. © Tobias Tanton 2023. DOI: 10.1093/oso/9780192884589.003.0006

environments. Taking its cue from the remainder of Shapiro's taxonomy (see Chapter 2), it explores the 'replacement' and 'constitution' hypotheses, which respectively emphasise that the process of cognition involves interaction with the outside world, and the cognition itself is distributed across physical substrates beyond the brain.

These hypotheses share the overarching claim of embodied cognition that perception and motor movement are heavily imbricated in cognitive processes, rather than functioning merely as 'input' and 'output' systems as the classical sandwich model presupposed. They can be understood as the opposite side of the embodied cognition coin to the conceptualisation hypothesis (Part II): whereas conceptualisation considers how aspects traditionally thought to be on the *inside* of 'cognition' (concepts) are permeated by aspects traditionally thought to be *outside* (perception and action); by contrast, replacement and constitution consider the way factors traditionally thought to be on the *outside* of cognition (bodily movements, postures, perceptual stimuli, environmental resources) impinge on cognitive processes which were thought to be independent of such factors. Both sides therefore insist that the boundaries previously assumed to be hard and fast are, in fact, far blurrier.

The replacement and constitution hypotheses have not been universally accepted. Hence, in addition to defining the theories and introducing empirical findings which motivate them, I shall also note critical objections. As was the case with my discussion of the conceptual hypothesis in Chapter 3, this chapter will take a cautious approach to the more extreme claims made in embodied cognition literature. Given the nascent character of the field, in which the scope of the explanatory power of theories has yet to be empirically verified, this approach seems prudent. However, even when weaker versions of the hypotheses are adopted, they nevertheless represent a significant revision of how cognition is understood. In Chapter 6, these hypotheses will be applied to the case of embodied religious practices.

1 The Replacement Hypothesis

The 'replacement' hypothesis, a second hypothesis of embodied cognition, challenges the assumption in 'classical cognitive science' that the mind, like a computer, manipulates symbols or internal mental representations. It questions the extent of such representations, favouring explanations of cognitive processes which minimise the role of mental representations or do away with them all together. It seeks to *replace* representation-heavy explanations with accounts of how the body (including the brain) interacts with the world as a dynamic system.

As with the conceptualisation hypothesis, a wide body of evidence supports the replacement hypothesis from fields such as robotics, animal cognition, and human cognition.[3] Furthermore, advocates for the replacement hypothesis have taken cues from recent mathematical findings in the area of dynamical systems theory, which maps complex systems over time. Dynamical systems theory challenges a notion of a representation as 'an internal model capable of reproducing the external environmental structure that is used by the cognitive agent to guide its behavior in relative independence from the world'.[4] A brief examination of the outfielder problem, together with a robotic counterpart, will not only showcase empirical support for the replacement hypothesis but also offers a vivid example of what is meant by this approach.

1.1 The Outfielder Problem

Wilson and Golonka nominate the 'outfielder problem' as a case in which the replacement hypothesis provides a superior explanation to a purely representational solution.[5] The outfielder problem investigates how an outfielder in a game such as cricket positions themself to catch a ball which has been struck by a batter at some distance.

Under a representational understanding, the outfielder uses a mental representation of their environment to 'solve' this problem. First, the outfielder perceives the ball being struck and estimates the ball's initial direction and speed. With this information they construct a mental representation of the ball's trajectory, calculating the ball's path and estimating its eventual landing point, in a similar fashion to solving a physics problem on paper using diagrammatic representations. Using this mental model, the outfielder can run to the predicted landing point to catch the ball. Crucially, the problem is solved by creating a representation of the scenario inside their head and then manipulating this internal model.

One difficulty with this strategy, however, is that it is difficult to perceive the ball's initial trajectory with sufficient accuracy at great distance. In light of this difficulty, the replacement hypothesis proposes a 'non-representational' strategy. One such solution (among others) is the 'linear optical trajectory' approach. To follow this approach the outfielder runs in such a way so as to make the ball appear as though it is moving in a straight line (relative to the outfielder's moving perspective). Thus, this solution replaces the fully fledged representational models inside the outfielder's head with a more manageable heuristic. Crucially, the linear optical trajectory approach relies upon constant monitoring of the ball's position relative to the outfielder, rather than constructing an internal mental representation of the scenario.

---

[3] For a summary, see Wilson and Golonka, 'Embodied Cognition', 3–8.
[4] Wilson and Foglia, *Embodied Cognition*.   [5] Wilson and Golonka, 'Embodied Cognition'.

The reason why the outfielder problem is a helpful example is that it can be decisively adjudicated on empirical grounds. The representational model suggests that outfielders will know from their initial calculations where the ball will land. It therefore predicts that the outfielder will (optimally) run in a straight line to the predicted landing site. The non-representational model, however, predicts that the outfielder will run in a curve as they arc their running course to make the ball look as though it is moving in a straight line. The empirical evidence shows that outfielders actually run in a curved fashion and thereby favours the non-representational solution.[6]

Clark notes that one of the interesting aspects of this finding is that there is a discrepancy between the actual cognitive process used and the associated phenomenology.[7] The outfielder may feel like they are working out where the ball will land before they begin to run. Moreover, the outfielder may not be explicitly aware of employing the linear optical trajectory strategy. Nevertheless, the outfielder intuitively employs this simple heuristic even though they consciously believe that they are executing a different strategy. This observation raises the prospect that human cognition employs replacement-type strategies far more frequently than conscious experience suggests.

1.2 The New Robotics

Similar solutions have been found in robotics. Robotics implementations of cognitive tasks are particularly helpful because their creator knows precisely which cognitive strategy is adopted, instead of having to infer it (sometimes problematically) from behaviour.[8] A limitation of this approach, however, is that it does not provide evidence that a certain strategy is actually implemented in human cognition. It can, however, provide proof of principle, demonstrating that a replacement strategy is able to solve a particular cognitive problem.[9]

One class of problem facing robotics is determining the basic motor movement required to navigate an environment such as a maze. Although humans beyond infancy exert little effort determining how to navigate the physical layout of an environment, the problem poses a far greater challenge for robots. As Shapiro comments:

[c]ritics are quick to point out that the greatest success stories emerging from traditional cognitive science involve analyses of symbol driven tasks that lend themselves to easy algorithmic description, like playing chess or solving the tower of Hanoi puzzle. In contrast, building a robot that can move about a

---

[6] Ibid., 6.   [7] Clark, *Being There*, 27.   [8] Wilson and Golonka, 'Embodied Cognition', 3.
[9] For an example of replacement in human cognition, see Clark, *Being There*, 30.

cluttered environment, which seems to call for cognitive capacities far less impressive than those necessary for chess, is a terribly difficult engineering problem from the perspective of traditional cognitive science.[10]

A team at Stanford built a robot called 'Shakey', which navigates its environment using a representational solution. The robot employed a 'scan–model–plan–act' framework: it scanned its surroundings, generated an internal representation of its environment, and then planned and implemented a course of action.[11] The robot was spectacularly unsuccessful at navigating a maze, even in carefully controlled ideal conditions.

By contrast, Brooks designs robots based on a 'non-representational' strategy.[12] The perception of these robots feeds directly into action rather than creating a model which is used to make inferences.[13] For example, one robot uses external sensors to implement three hierarchical layers of behaviour: it avoids objects found in its immediate path; it wanders randomly in a different direction every ten seconds; and it explores by moving towards distant objects.[14] Using these relatively simple behaviours, this robot was far better at navigating an environment than its Stanford counterpart. The key difference was that Brooks' robot did not rely on an internal copy of the world, but instead constantly interacted with the world to 'check back'. It leveraged 'the world as its own model'.[15] Clark summarises this strategy as follows:

> Notice that such creatures do not depend on a central reservoir of data or on a central planner or reasoner. Instead, we see a 'collection of competing behaviors' orchestrated by environmental inputs. There is no clear dividing line between perception and cognition, no point at which perceptual inputs are translated into a central code to be shared by various onboard reasoning devices. This image of multiple, special-purpose problem solvers orchestrated by environmental inputs and relatively simple kinds of internal signaling is…a neuroscientifically plausible model even of more advanced brains.[16]

Brooks' robots are a good example of a replacement strategy. His robots' 'bottom-up' behaviour arises from interaction with their environment, rather than a 'top-down' centralised planning system which traditional views of cognition assume.[17]

---

[10] Shapiro, 'The Embodied Cognition Research Programme', 339.
[11] Rodney A. Brooks, 'New Approaches to Robotics', *Science* 253, no. 5025 (1991): 1227–8.
[12] Rodney A. Brooks, 'Intelligence without Representation', *Artificial Intelligence* 47 (1991).
[13] Shapiro, *Embodied Cognition*, 139.
[14] Brooks, 'Intelligence without Representation', 153–4.
[15] Rodney A. Brooks, 'Elephants Don't Play Chess', *Robotics and Autonomous Systems* 6, no. 1–2 (1990).
[16] Clark, *Being There*, 14.   [17] Wilson and Foglia, *Embodied Cognition*.

The costly nature of internal models also points to a theoretical advantage for replacement solutions. In contrast to representation-heavy solutions, replacement solutions are relatively parsimonious; hence Shapiro notes that embodied cognition 'researchers often express bemusement with the traditional assumption that organisms must produce a representation of the world around them in order to navigate its topography. Why bother with a representation of the world if the world is right there in front of you?'[18] Parsimony not only makes for an elegant solution but is also evolutionary more plausible since it requires fewer cognitive resources. Moreover, survival is not determined solely by the ability of the brain, but by that of organisms as a whole: 'Adaptive success finally accrues not to brains but to brain-body coalitions embedded in ecologically realistic environments.'[19]

In light of this advantage, one ought to have a compelling reason to retain representations. Shapiro draws a parallel between representations and other unobservables in scientific theories: 'Symbols, like atoms, forces, and other unobservables, will earn their keep insofar as they do the kind of work that these other unobservables have done.'[20] Hence if replacement explanations become ubiquitous, Ockham's razor suggests that representations will be superfluous: 'if embodied cognition researchers are able to explain cognitive behaviour without assuming the existence of amodal, computational symbols, and if traditional symbolic explanations prove themselves to be as ill-founded as, for example, explanations of life that assume the presence of an élan vital, or of heat transfer that assume the existence of phlogiston, then so much the worse for symbolism.'[21] Thus formulated, the burden of proof transfers to those who wish to defend the need for representations.

1.3 Can All Representations be Replaced?

The initial success of replacement strategies, both in explaining facets of human cognition as in the outfielder problem and in developing problem-solving strategies in robotics, is impressive. This success, however, has met with mixed responses. Some are optimistic about the prospect of revolutionising cognitive science by redescribing all human cognitive process without recourse to representations. For example, Wilson and Galonka acknowledge that while replacement-style explanations have not yet been found for all cognitive tasks, they believe that it is only a matter of time:

All that we can really conclude at this time is that replacement style embodied cognition cannot explain these problems *yet*. We believe that there is no

[18] Shapiro, 'The Embodied Cognition Research Programme', 340.   [19] Clark, *Being There*, 98.
[20] Shapiro, 'Symbolism', 70.   [21] Ibid.

principled reason why these behaviors cannot be explained with replacement style embodied solutions, given that human beings are, we think, best described as the kind of perceiving, acting, embodied, non-linear dynamical systems doing the replacing.[22]

These optimists believe that ultimately 'all of cognition will lend itself to description in computationally meagre terms, or in the language of representationally bereft dynamical systems.'[23]

Others, however, are more pessimistic about the prospect of doing away with mental representations altogether. One source of pessimism arises from whether the cases cited as examples of replacement actually eliminate representation altogether. The outfielder may not create a representation of the entire scenario akin to the student solving a physics problem. However, the outfielder may well need to represent the motion of the ball relative to their movement, or the concept of a 'ball' in order to understand the task of catching it. Likewise, although Brooks' robots do not represent their surroundings with internal maps, they arguably have an internal physical state which represents specific features of their relationship to their environment such as the distance between the robot and the wall directly in front of it.

The potential that representations persist, even in supposed paradigmatic examples of the replacement hypothesis, calls into question the ability to explain cognitive processes without recourse to representations. However, this should not detract from insights provided by the replacement hypothesis. The 'linear optical trajectory' approach to ball-catching is significantly different from the central planning and execution approach; likewise, Brooks' robots implement a very different strategy to Shakey. Clark characterises this shift in the following terms: '[w]hether symbolic, text-like encodings have any role to play in these tooth-and-claw decisions is still uncertain, but it now seem[s] clear that they do not lie at its heart.'[24] Hence the examples of replacement nevertheless mark a significant paradigm shift, in which fully fledged internal models are replaced with reliance on sensorimotor interaction with the world, perhaps in concert with pared-down representations.

A second source of pessimism concerns the scope of replacement.[25] Many of the cognitive tasks successfully explained by replacement accounts appear to be low-hanging fruit: catching a ball and navigating through a maze are both clearly tasks in which perception and motor movement are central. This is not a problem

---

[22] Wilson and Golonka, 'Embodied Cognition', 11. Emphasis original. For a similar position, see Anthony Chemero, *Radical Embodied Cognitive Science* (Cambridge, MA: MIT Press, 2009); Daniel D. Hutto, *Folk Psychological Narratives: The Sociocultural Basis of Understanding Reasons* (Cambridge MA: MIT Press, 2008).
[23] Shapiro, 'The Embodied Cognition Research Programme', 344.
[24] Clark, *Being There*, 7.   [25] Shapiro and Spaulding, *Embodied Cognition*.

in itself; it makes sense to begin with the most obvious examples, before attempting more challenging cases. It does, however, raise a question concerning the scope of the replacement hypothesis: can replacement solutions can be found for *all* cognitive tasks? Shapiro voices this scepticism as follows:

> Formulating an empirically adequate theory of intelligent behaviour without appealing to representations at all, however, faces insuperable difficulties, and the idea that it is a relatively trivial matter to scale up from existing dynamic models to explain all of cognition remains wishful thinking and subject to just the problems that motivated the shift from behaviorism to cognitive science in the first place.[26]

More concretely, Clark argues that particular classes of cognitive tasks, which he calls 'representation hungry' problems, elude replacement-style explanations. Not only do such problems currently lack replacement-style explanations but Clark argues that there are also theoretical obstacles which make it difficult to see how non-representational explanations could succeed. As he notes, some organisms 'deploy the inner codes in the total absence of their environmental features. Such creatures are the most obvious represeners of their world and are the ones able to engage in complex imaginings, off-line reflection, and counterfactual reasoning. Problems that require such capacities for their solution are representation-hungry, in that they cry out for the use of inner systemic features as stand-ins for external states of affairs.'[27] The outfielder has a moving ball before their eyes and Brooks' robots are ensconced in a maze (i.e., these are examples of 'online' cognition); hence in both of these cases the cognisors can use sensorimotor cues instead of relying on internal representations. However, as Clark notes, these external replacements are not available for all kinds of cognitive tasks. Counterfactual reason, by definition, involves reasoning about states of affairs which do not exist, and therefore cannot rely on perceptual stimuli (i.e., it is 'offline'). To take a more mundane example, recalling and drawing the layout of a house (while not physically being in the house) seems to require a mental representation of the house to stand in for the actual thing. Although representations may well be superfluous if the world is 'right there in front of you', not all cognition is about aspects of the world which are ready to hand. Humans certainly seem capable of the kind of cognitive tasks which require representations: 'The brain is a statistical, embodied, and representational device. It is our ability to represent situations offline, and to represent situations contrary to perception, that make us such amazing creatures.'[28]

---

[26] Wilson and Foglia, *Embodied Cognition*.   [27] Clark, *Being There*, 147.
[28] Barsalou, 'Perceptions of Perceptual Symbols', 644.

Indeed, in Chapter 3 I assumed the presence of representations: concepts, after all, are mental representations which stand in for objects or states of affairs in the world.[29] As Barsalou points out, the modal representations for which he advocates allow humans to reason about absent entities: 'simulations provide people with a powerful ability to reason about entities and events in their absence'.[30] This view resonates with Clark's position that representations are required where entities are absent. While Barsalou's approach may fundamentally alter our understanding of the nature representations, he nevertheless retains a role for representations in cognition, arguing that we ought not 'throw out the representational baby with the amodal bathwater'.[31] As he summarises, '[p]erceptual symbol systems attempt to maintain what is important about representation while similarly attempting to maintain what is important about connectionism and embodied cognition'.[32]

1.4 Conclusion: Representational Minimalism

In summary, I have argued that it seems unlikely that representations can be replaced altogether. On this point, Clark echoes Barsalou's talk of babies and bathwater: 'A major danger attending any revolutionary proposal in the sciences is that too much of the "old view" may be discarded—that healthy babies may be carried away by floods of bathwater. This very danger attends, I believe, the New Roboticists' rejection of internal models, maps, and representations'.[33] Enthusiasm about the success of replacement ought to be tempered by caution regarding its scope.

However, this limitation should not detract from the genuine insights that the replacement hypothesis has to offer; 'One might believe that Gibson and Brooks overstate their cases against representation, yet still believe that their work marks a significant departure from symbolic explanations of cognition'.[34] What then are the lessons to be learnt?

First, in many cases representations play a far smaller role than traditional cognitive science presupposes. The debate ought to be recast from a binary question about the existence (or not) of representations, to 'a discussion between fans of maximal, detailed, action-neutral inner world models and those...who suspect that much intelligent behavior depends on more minimal resources such as multiple, partial, personalized and/or action-oriented types of inner encoding'.[35] This position is entirely consistent with the discussion of concepts in Chapter 3,

---

[29] On the tension between conceptualisation and replacement, see Shapiro and Spaulding, *Embodied Cognition*.
[30] Barsalou, 'Perceptual Symbol Systems', 578.
[31] Barsalou, 'Perceptions of Perceptual Symbols', 644.   [32] Ibid.
[33] Clark, *Being There*, 22.   [34] Shapiro, 'Symbolism', 69.
[35] Andy Clark and Josefa Toribio, 'Doing without Representing?', *Synthese* 101, no. 3 (1994): 174.

which argued that embodiment is significant for the nature of representation: 'like Barsalou's more tempered view...an account of representation that, in virtue of embodiment, requires less or different kinds of processing than traditional symbolists have supposed'.[36]

Second, if representations play a smaller (and different) role, then the explanatory burden shifts to sensorimotor interactions with the external environment (and representations which are retained facilitate these behavioural interactions rather than being manipulated in self-enclosed systems). This fundamentally reframes the boundaries of cognition from brain-bound symbolic manipulation to (brain-guided) living bodies engaging with their surroundings: 'once we recognize the role of body and environment...in constructing both problems and solutions, it becomes clear that for certain explanatory purposes, the overall system of brain, body, and local environment can constitute a proper, unified object of study'.[37] The frame in which cognitive processes are considered ought to be expanded. In Chapter 6, I apply these lessons to the case of religion.

2 The Constitution Hypothesis

The insights of the replacement hypothesis raise the further question of where cognition takes place—what are the physical media on which it is implemented? Theorists suggest that cognition may not be limited to neural firings in the brain (or signals sent through the central nervous system) but may extend to the body and potentially some extra-somatic objects. Hence the replacement hypothesis is closely related to the *constitution* hypothesis, which proposes that physical substrates outside of the brain constitute part of the mechanism for cognition. Whereas replacement focused on the way cognitive *processes* involve bodily, sensorimotor interaction with the external environment, constitution considers the environmental resources which form part of the 'machinery' of cognition.

To highlight the fact that the brain is not the sole arbiter in cognitive processes, Marsh cites the extreme example of a sea squirt:

> The sea squirt has a brief existence as a tadpole with motion, ability to detect light, and a brain and primitive spinal cord. Once it attaches to a site and thereafter ceases moving, it no longer needs a brain, and it ingests it. In a real sense, the behavior of an organism (and so too, we believe, the coordinated behavior of multiple organisms) has primacy over the emergence of a brain to coordinate such behaviors.[38]

---

[36] Shapiro, 'Symbolism', 66.   [37] Clark, *Being There*, 154.
[38] Marsh, Richardson, and Schmidt, 'Social Connection', 321.

The human brain may not be as expendable as the sea squirt's. However, Marsh's example serves to underlie how bodily behaviour can emerge without a centralised controller. The brain may not be all there is to cognition.

Recall Clark's similarly aquatic example, the sea sponge which oriented itself to ambient currents to facilitate feeding. By analogy, constitution supposes that environmental resources are similarly exploited for cognitive ends. This view again stands in contrast to the emphasis of traditional cognitive science, which 'neglects the pervasive tendency of human agents to actively structure their environments in ways that will reduce subsequent computational loads'.[39] Emotional body states and environmental memory aids are proposed as instances where cognition extends to the body and beyond the body respectively. These cases will again provide examples of the constitution hypothesis and means of evaluating it.

2.1 Emotional Body States

Emotion was proposed as an important, early example of embodied cognition.[40] The growing recognition of the important role emotion plays in cognitive processes, together with how emotions are associated with bodily changes, has led to the proposal that emotions provide evidence supporting the constitution hypothesis. More precisely, theorists have suggested that emotional body states, such as a quickened pulse or sweaty palms, participate in emotional cognition, and hence parts of the body outside of the central nervous system constitute the physical medium on which cognition is implemented.

A connection between emotions and certain bodily changes has been noted since at least the time of Aristotle, who observed that anger is accompanied by a 'boiling of the blood'.[41] In modern times, this position was formalised by the James–Lange theory of emotion. In an oft-cited passage, James indicates the centrality of bodily changes in his understanding of emotion: 'we feel sorry because we cry, angry because we strike, afraid because we tremble, and [it is] not that we cry, strike, or tremble, because we are sorry, angry, or fearful'.[42] Given this statement, some have taken James to mean that emotions are nothing but bodily changes. Subsequently, critics have argued that the James–Lange theory provides an inadequate account of emotion, since it occludes other essential aspects of emotion such as the intentionality and appraisal.[43] Even if James' account of

---

[39] Clark, *Being There*, 150.
[40] Robert A. Wilson and Lucia Foglia, *Embodied Cognition* (2011) [cited 14 January 2014]; available from http://plato.stanford.edu/archives/fall2011/entries/embodied-cognition/; Johnson, *The Meaning of the Body*, 9.
[41] Aristotle, *De Anima*, ed. W. D. Ross (Oxford: Clarendon Press, 1961), I.1 403b.
[42] William James, 'What Is an Emotion?', *Mind* 9, no. 34 (1884): 190.
[43] E.g., John Deigh, 'Cognitivism in the Theory of Emotions', *Ethics* 104, no. 4 (1994); Martha Craven Nussbaum, *Upheavals of Thought: The Intelligence of Emotions* (Cambridge: Cambridge University

emotion misses essential aspects of the phenomenon, his insight that bodily states play a crucial role in emotions may stand. For James, bodily states do not merely *express* emotions (presumably formulated in the brain), but rather *constitute* emotions.

Damasio is the foremost proponent of an updated version of the James–Lange theory in light of modern neuroscience. His work proceeds through the study of patients with impairments.[44] Localised brain damage which leads to functional impairments sheds light on the organisation of the brain and the inner workings of cognition. Of particular interest to Damasio are a class of patients with damage to brain regions which represent body states. These patients also suffered from a lack of emotional feeling, leading Damasio to suggest that emotional experience is inexorably tied up with body states.[45]

Damasio uses this connection between emotions and the body to develop an account of the physiological mechanisms involved in emotions. He envisages a three-stage process which distinguishes between 'emotion' and 'feeling'.[46] First, an emotion can either be 'triggered' by a stimulus (e.g., a snake) or a more complex cognitive process (e.g., seeing an old friend after a long absence). Second, this then causes a corresponding change in one's body state. Like a cat arching its back and puffing up its tail in the presence of a perceived threat, so too the human emotions are implemented by body states. Third, this bodily change is registered as the brain updates the 'body maps' which monitor the state of the organism, and this feeling is combined and thus associated with the original cognitive stimulus. These positive or negative feelings are used as 'somatic markers' to evaluate the subject's stance towards an actual or hypothetical situation; lose access to these somatic markers, as happens in the case particular cases of localised brain damage, and emotional experience is impaired. Damasio argues that emotion's somatic markers are pervasive in everyday decision-making as we imagine the consequences of alternative courses of action, and hence emotion, including its instantiation in the body, is 'in the loop of reason'.[47]

2.2 Otto's Notebook as Extended Mind

Scholars who contend that cognition extends beyond the brain have sought to push the boundaries even further, proposing examples in which cognition not

Press, 2001), 27–8. Cf. J. M. Barbalet, 'William James' Theory of Emotions: Filling in the Picture', *Journal for the Theory of Social Behaviour* 29, no. 3 (1999).

[44] Antonio R. Damasio, *Descartes' Error: Emotion, Reason and the Human Brain* (London: Vintage, 1994), 52–78.

[45] Ibid., 148.

[46] Antonio R. Damasio, *Looking for Spinoza: Joy, Sorrow, and the Feeling Brain* (London: Vintage, 2004), 116; Damasio, *Descartes' Error*.

[47] Damasio, *Descartes' Error*, xvii.

only stretches beyond the skull but also, in some cases, mind extends beyond the skin and into the world. Although this area of research still falls under the umbrella term 'embodied' cognition, the term is somewhat of a misnomer here, since it proposes that cognition is not limited to the body.[48] In philosophy the hypothesis has become known as the 'extended mind', and cognitive scientists often refer to 'distributed' or 'situated' cognition to capture the notion that cognition is offloaded onto extra-somatic environmental resources.

In a seminal paper setting out an argument for the extended mind, Clark and Chalmers compare the cognitive strategies of two fictional characters.[49] Otto suffers from Alzheimer's disease and thus uses a notebook to store directions to the museum of modern art. Inga, on the other hand, simply remembers the address using her biological memory. Where Inga uses an internal cognitive resource, Otto substitutes an external one. Clark and Chalmers employ a parity argument, claiming that, for all intents and purposes, Otto's notebook fulfils precisely the same function as Inga's biological memory. Moreover, insofar as Otto's memory forms part of his beliefs, his beliefs can also be said to be contained in his notebook. In light of this functional equivalence, it would be arbitrary to classify Inga's biological memory systems as part of her cognition while excluding Otto's notebook. Hence an extra-somatic physical object can constitute part of human cognitive machinery.

Beyond the formal argument that Otto's notebook constitutes part of his cognitive processes, Clark has also made some more wide-ranging proposals about potential external constituents of cognition. Perhaps his most ambitious suggestion is that public language itself functions as a cognitive tool. Clark distinguishes this function from the communicative role of language: 'the emphasis on language as a medium of communication tends to blind us to a subtler but equally potent role: the role of language as a tool that alters the nature of the computational tasks involved in various kinds of problem solving'.[50] Clark explains how language, as an external resource, can transform cognitive tasks:

Public speech, inner rehearsal, and the use of written and on-line texts are all potent tools that reconfigure the shape of computational space. Again and again we trade culturally achieved representation against individual computation. Again and again we use words to focus, clarify, transform, offload, and control our own thinking. Thus understood, language is not the mere imperfect mirror of our intuitive knowledge. Rather, it is part and parcel of the mechanism of reason itself.[51]

---

[48] Barsalou, 'Grounded Cognition', 619.   [49] Clark and Chalmers, 'The Extended Mind'.
[50] Clark, Being There, 193. See also Terrence William Deacon, The Symbolic Species: The Co-Evolution of Language and the Brain (New York: W.W. Norton, 1997).
[51] Clark, Being There, 207.

Thus, linguistic handles provide a shorthand for complex ideas, which means that they do not need to be recreated from scratch. Among the potential benefits that extending cognition through language confers, Clark identifies, first, the introduction of 'second-order cognitive dynamics', which he defines as a 'cluster of powerful capacities involving self-evaluation, self-criticism, and finely honed remedial responses';[52] and second, the ability to build on previous cognitive achievements: 'Human learning, like learning in artificial neural networks, appears to be hostage to at least some degree of path dependence. Certain ideas can be understood only once others are in place.'[53]

Studies which test the way humans rely upon extra-bodily resources for cognitive tasks are beginning to emerge. For example, Fisher and colleagues test the way in which people use external resources to buttress their own cognition. In one set of studies they observe that participants think they have knowledge 'in their head' when actually they rely upon the internet for such knowledge.[54] In a follow-up study, participants over-estimated their own ability to perform well in a quiz when their previous performance relied on the knowledge of partners.[55] These studies suggest a blurring between internal and external resources, similar to the interchangeability of Otto's notebook and Inga's biological memory.

2.2.1 Boundaries of the Mind

If mind extends to Otto's notebook or a blind person's cane, where does it end? Does having an encyclopaedia in the basement mean that one knows everything in the encyclopaedia? Clearly this kind of extension appears to be too extravagant. This concern about the over-extension of the mind has been characterised as cognitive 'bloat' or 'ooze'.[56]

Clark and Chalmers anticipate this critique and defend the special status of Otto's notebook. Although there are circumstances where Otto's notebook may cease to fulfil its function (e.g., if it is stolen), biological memory is also prone to failure (e.g., after drunkenness). Moreover, Otto's notebook fulfils a number of crucial criteria: it is always available to him; the information in it is readily available; Otto always endorses the information he finds in it; and Otto endorsed the contents when he entered them into it.[57] By fulfilling these criteria, they argue, Otto's notebook can be counted as part of Otto's cognitive system. Likewise,

---

[52] Ibid., 208.   [53] Ibid., 205.

[54] Matthew Fisher, Mariel K. Goddu, and Frank C. Keil, 'Searching for Explanations: How the Internet Inflates Estimates of Internal Knowledge', Journal of Experimental Psychology: General 144, no. 3 (2015).

[55] Matthew Fisher and Daniel M. Oppenheimer, 'Who Knows What? Knowledge Misattribution in the Division of Cognitive Labor', Journal of Experimental Psychology: Applied 27, no. 2 (2021).

[56] Fred Adams and Ken Aizawa, 'The Bounds of Cognition', Philosophical Psychology 14, no. 1 (2001): 57.

[57] Clark and Chalmers, 'The Extended Mind', 16–18.

other artefacts which fulfil these criteria are constitutive of cognition, while the encyclopaedia in the basement is not.

Another potential criterion is 'coupling'.[58] Coupling occurs when a resource used as an 'output' then becomes an 'input'. The use of pen and paper to overcome the limitations of working memory when solving a long multiplication problem provides an example of coupling: a person performing long multiplication 'outputs' the result of the first step (e.g., multiplying the right-most digits and carrying any tens) onto the paper, and this then becomes one of the 'inputs' for subsequent steps. Thus, a feedback loop is created between the problem solver and the tool, arguably weaving the pen and paper into the process of cognition as a constituent.[59] In cases of coupling 'the relevant parts of the world', such as Otto's notebook, 'are *in the loop*, not dangling at the other end of the relevant causal chain'.[60]

In contrast, Adams and Aizawa argue that it is a 'wild idea to suppose that to use a calculator is to have one's mind bleed out of one's brain into plastic buttons and semiconductors'.[61] They propose a stricter set of criteria which mark a process out as cognitive. First, they argue that cognition must involve 'non-derived content', that is, content which does not derive its meaning from social conventions or practices.[62] Otto's notebook fails in this respect, because the symbols rely on a cognitive agent to give them meaning. Second, they argue that causal processes involved in cognition are so different from the external alternatives which perform the same function that they are different in kind.[63] Third, they contend that coupling is insufficient to achieve constitution, since processes of different kinds can be coupled.[64] Based on these stricter criteria and objections, Adams and Aizawa object that many of the proposed examples do not actually count as extended cognition and they defend the traditional position that cognition in humans happens to be intracranial.

Whether extra-somatic items constitute part of the machinery of cognition ultimately depends on the criteria used to demarcate the territory of cognition.[65] There is unlikely to be any consensus on the metaphysical question of the defining features of cognition or the extent of mind in the near future.[66] However, as with the

---

[58] Shapiro, *Embodied Cognition*, 175–8. Cf. Clark and Chalmers, 'The Extended Mind', 8–9.
[59] For a philosophical critique of the claim that causal dependence coupling is sufficient for constitution, see Frederick Adams and Kenneth Aizawa, 'The Value of Cognitivism in Thinking About Extended Cognition', *Phenomenology and the Cognitive Sciences* 9, no. 4 (2010): 589–92.
[60] Clark and Chalmers, 'The Extended Mind', 9.
[61] Adams and Aizawa, 'The Bounds of Cognition', 44.   [62] Ibid., 48–51.
[63] Ibid., 44.   [64] Adams and Aizawa, 'The Value of Cognitivism', 589–97.
[65] Shapiro and Spaulding, *Embodied Cognition*.
[66] For responses to Adams and Aizawa, see Andy Clark, 'Coupling, Constitution, and the Cognitive Kind: A Reply to Adams and Aizawa', in *The Extended Mind* (Cambridge MA: MIT Press, 2010); Michael D. Kirchhoff, 'Extended Cognition & the Causal-Constitutive Fallacy: In Search for a Diachronic and Dynamical Conception of Constitution', *Philosophy and Phenomenological Research* 90, no. 2 (2015).

contested question about whether representations can be replaced in explanations of all cognitive processes, the examples of proposed cases for constitution are nevertheless insightful. One way to explicate these insights without definitively resolving the metaphysical question is to consider how environmental resources 'scaffold' the mind.

2.3 Scaffolding

Less controversial than the extended mind hypothesis is the more general concept of 'scaffolding'. As the metaphor suggests, cognitive 'scaffolds' are environmental resources which support cognitive processes from outside the body (without the added claim that these resources constitute part of the mind). Sterelny points out that a number of theorists 'have noticed how intimately human cognition—in particular, cognition that leads to competent action in the world—depends on environmental resources'.[67] He describes this dependence as scaffolding and defines it in terms of niche construction from evolutionary models: animals adapt to fill a particular environmental niche, but they can also actively shape the environment to create their niche.[68]

Sterelny raises an insightful analogy of another human process which has been fundamentally shaped by its interaction with external resources, namely digestion. He surveys a number of ways in which 'the physiological demands on hominin jaws, teeth and guts have been transformed by cooking and more generally by food preparation and food targeting'.[69] He concludes by asking whether all the technologies surrounding food preparation therefore constitute a case of 'extended digestion':

> Our under-powered jaws, short gut, small teeth and mouth fit our niche because we eat soft, rich and easily digested food. Our digestive system is *environmentally scaffolded*. But is my soup pot, my food processor and my fine collection of choppers part of my digestive system? As far as I know, no one has defended an extended stomach hypothesis, treating routine kitchen equipment as part of an agent's digestive system[70]

Although he does not deny the existence of cases of extended mind, he argues that these are only a small subset of the larger phenomenon of scaffolding, as in the case of scaffolded digestion. Like Clark and Chalmers, he devises criteria to determine whether environmental resources count as examples of extended

---

[67] Kim Sterelny, 'Minds: Extended or Scaffolded?', *Phenomenology and the Cognitive Sciences* 9, no. 4 (2010): 465.

[68] Ibid., 466.   [69] Ibid., 467.

[70] Ibid., 468. Although Sterelny is unaware of an argument for extended digestion, Adams and Aizawa draw this this analogy in Adams and Aizawa, 'The Bounds of Cognition', 47.

mind, proposing three dimensions: the resource must, first, be trusted by the agent; second, be tailored to the individual (and the individual, through skilful familiarity, tailored to it); and third, be a resource of an individual rather than a collective. However, he argues that each of these dimensions is a spectrum rather than a binary. Examples of extended mind are the minority of cases which lie on an extreme of each dimension (resources which are highly trusted, highly individualised, and exclusively the possession of an individual). He argues that scaffolding, as a broader category, is a more helpful concept which captures a wider range of cases where human cognition relies, to various degrees, on environmental resources.

Clark likewise refers to scaffolding. Although he does not define it in terms of niche construction, he nevertheless formulates a similar definition to Sterelny's: 'we may often solve problems by "piggy-backing" on reliable environmental properties. This exploitation of external structure is what I mean by the term scaffolding.'[71] Moreover, he recognises that these tools are crucial for extending human cognitive capabilities:

> If hammers and saws allow us to construct things that we could not otherwise build with our bare hands, why can't cognitive scaffolding—including but not limited to the tools of literacy like pencils and paper—allow us to think things that we could not otherwise contemplate with our bare brains?[72]

Whether or not environmental resources constitute mind, they undeniably support many cognitive processes which could not do without them.

2.4 Conclusion

As with the replacement hypothesis, the constitution hypothesis remains controversial and there is no consensus on the scope of its explanatory power. The notion that non-neural or extra-somatic items constitute part of the mind depends on how one circumscribes the term 'cognitive'. However, even for those who find the constitution hypothesis too metaphysically extravagant, the theory nevertheless invites a re-evaluation of cognitive processes. In particular, it draws attention to how many cognitive processes not only rely on brain activity but are also scaffolded by bodily states and environmental resources.

An appreciation of the physical resources which support cognition will again have important implications for understanding religion. It invites us to attend to cognitive status of embodied religious practices and material culture. Chapter 6 explores how these aspects of religion scaffold cognition.

---

[71] Clark, *Being There*.   [72] Day, 'Religion', 112.

6

Embodied Cognition in Ecclesial Practices

'All human thought and feeling—including religious
thought and feeling—are grounded in biological processes.'

—*Robert Fuller*[1]

After surveying how our cognition relies upon interactions between brain, body, and world, Clark surmises that '[b]iological reason...often consists in a rag-bag of "quick and dirty" stratagems—stratagems only available, in part, thanks to our ability to participate in various kinds of collective or environment-exploiting problem solving'.[2] As Chapter 5 explored, scaffold accounts apply to simple motor tasks or memory, but questions remain about their scope. Clark continues, '[i]t is natural to wonder, however, just how much leverage (if any) this approach offers for understanding the most advanced and distinctive aspects of human cognition—not walking, reading, wall following, and visual searching, but voting, consumer choice, planning a two-week vacation, running a country, and so on. Do these more exotic domains at last reveal the delicate flower of logical, classical, symbol-manipulating, internal cognition?'[3] To Clark's list of 'exotic domains', we might add the cognitive tasks associated with religion: pedagogy, belief formation, and even theological reflection. It is precisely this possibility which I consider in this chapter: namely, how *religious cognition is scaffolded* by factors which lie outside of the brain.

The replacement and constitution hypotheses provide helpful frameworks for rethinking the scope of religious cognition. As I already noted, the locus of religiosity has often been confined to the ideas and beliefs of the mind.[4] This circumscription mirrors how traditional cognitive science restricted cognition to internal mental models manipulated in the brain. By challenging this view of cognition, embodied cognition also invites us to reframe religion. The replacement model, by replacing internal mental models with online sensorimotor engagement with the world, points towards how embodied religious practices rely on bodily interactions with one's environment and community. The constitution hypothesis, by pushing the boundaries of cognition beyond the brain, calls us to attend to how the religious embodiments and material culture participate in

---

[1] Fuller, *Spirituality in the Flesh*, 5.
[2] Clark and Toribio, 'Doing without Representing?', 179.   [3] Ibid.
[4] Soliman, Johnson, and Song, 'Understanding Religion', 853; Vásquez, *More Than Belief*.

Corporeal Theology: Accommodating Theological Understanding to Embodied Thinkers. Tobias Tanton,
Oxford University Press. © Tobias Tanton 2023. DOI: 10.1093/oso/9780192884589.003.0007

cognitive processes. Given the conceptualisation hypothesis' (Part II) shared interest in the role of perception and action in cognition, it too has relevance to embodied religious practices. Namely, if concepts are grounded in sensorimotor experience, this not only illuminates the embodied nature of concepts, but also suggests that activating various sensorimotor states can evoke particular concepts. This again reveals the cognitive import of embodied religious practices. In short, an embodied cognitive science reveals anew the corporeal aspects of religion.

This chapter will harness a large number of empirical studies from embodied cognition research and apply their insights to embodied religious practices. It begins by discussing some methodological issues and limitations associated with the studies (Section 1). The application of empirical findings to religion begins with a narrow focus on the individual body, considering the cognitive effects of how religious practices choreograph bodily postures and movements (Section 2). A scaffolded view of cognition suggests that such a circumscription is too narrow, and the physical environment in which religious practices take place, together with their rich material culture, likewise participates in religious cognition (Section 3). The context of religious practices is also often profoundly social, and thus the interaction with other agents also forms a crucial part of the cognitive scaffolding (Section 4). Finally, how particular embodiments or environmental factors evoke particular concepts, on account of their grounding in sensorimotor states, is considered (Section 5). This wide-ranging survey thus brings dozens of embodied mechanisms unearthed in empirical research to bear on the particular case of religious practices.

'Embodied religious practices', even within the Christian tradition, are, of course, incredibly diverse. Throughout this chapter the Eucharist, as practiced in the western (Catholic or Anglican) tradition, will be the central practice from which examples will be drawn (though, where relevant, a number of other practices are cited). The centrality of the Eucharist in major Christian traditions makes it a helpful exemplar of a religious practice. This approach is also consistent with Cuneo's assertion that 'the best way to make progress on the topic of liturgy is to speak not of liturgies in the abstract but particular liturgies, offering thick descriptions of them and drawing out their implications'.[5] However, other practices and traditions are also referenced when they exhibit particular embodied cognition mechanisms. Section 6 addresses the question of whether some traditions (and their practices) are 'less embodied' than others.

The application of embodied cognition to religious practices is ultimately a descriptive task that could comfortably be located within the discipline of religious studies. The following chapter, however, will use this scaffolded account of religion to consider its implications for theology.

---

[5] Cuneo, *Ritualized Faith*, 15.

1 The Cognitive Science of Religious Practices

Applying embodied cognition research to the case of religious practices, such as a Eucharist, has various limitations. In this section, I consider how embodied cognition relates to existing cognitive approaches to religion. I discuss various difficulties facing embodied cognition research, including replication, the representativeness of samples, and ecological validity. Finally, I point to a second helpful source of 'data' on religious practices, namely ethnographic accounts.

1.1 Cognitive Science of Religion and Embodied Cognition

The phenomenon of religion is no stranger to cognitive science research. The past decades have seen the rise of the 'cognitive science of religion' (CSR). In an attempt to make the complex and diverse phenomenon of religion more tractable to empirical investigation, experimental work in CSR has typically focused on small and isolatable facets of religion. The resulting picture has been necessarily piecemeal. A number of recent articles have pointed out that one of the potential blind spots of the nascent CSR is that it has largely assumed the classical paradigm in cognitive science.[6] Consistent with this assessment is De Cruz's observation that '[m]uch research in CSR has focused on content biases as a way to understand both intuitive and reflective religious beliefs. Content biases are biases involved in the generation and transmission of beliefs.'[7] This strong emphasis on beliefs serves to further perpetuate the assumption that religion is exclusively in the head.

De Cruz also notes a divergent tradition in CSR which argues that content biases have limited explanatory value, and contextual biases also need to be taken into account.[8] For example, Gervais and Henrich highlight the case of Zeus, who once commanded a wide-spread following but no longer does.[9] They argue that this change cannot be accounted for by content biases since the conceptual content of Zeus remains largely unchanged. Instead it is disappearance of contextual factors, such as the presence of fellow believers and ritual displays, which largely explain why belief in Zeus is no longer common.[10]

The appeal to *context* biases is far more consistent with a scaffolded view of cognition. Religion is not merely the product of particular cognitive processes which take place in the head, but must be understood as a function of a far wider

---

[6] E.g., Soliman, Johnson, and Song, 'Understanding Religion', 853; Day, 'Religion'; Krueger, 'Extended Mind'; Sosis and Kiper, 'Religion Is More Than Belief'; Watts, 'Embodied Cognition and Religion'. Work on the cognitive effects of ritual are an important exception here; see Section 3.6.

[7] Helen de Cruz, 'Cognitive Science of Religion and the Study of Theological Concepts', *Topoi* 33, no. 2 (2014): 489.

[8] Ibid.

[9] Will M. Gervais and Joseph Henrich, 'The Zeus Problem: Why Representational Content Biases Cannot Explain Faith in Gods', *Journal of Cognition and Culture* 10, no. 3 (2010).

[10] Ibid., 387–8.

system which includes social and material scaffolding in an individual's environment. Although this model introduces embodied and material explanatory factors, the emphasis nevertheless remains on how particular beliefs in the head are maintained and propagated.

Day argues that CSR's reliance on classical cognitive science means that it has tended to ignore 'the ways in which the bare biological brain is prosthetically extended and embedded in the surrounding landscape'.[11] This lacuna seems rather stark given that religious traditions often involve particularly distinctive environments, objects, and movements. As Day observes:

> The recognition that in some contexts not all of the relevant computational machinery fits inside the head suggests that we should reconsider the possible role(s) and significance of material culture in religious cognition. More specifically, the broad spectrum of rituals, music, relics, scriptures, statues and buildings typically associated with religious traditions may be more than quaint ethnographic window dressing. Rather than thin cultural wrap arounds that decorate the real cognitive processes going on underneath, these elements could represent central components of the relevant machinery of religious thought.[12]

Although the application of embodied cognition to religion remains scarce, there is virtually a consensus among cognitive scientists that religion exploits ordinary cognitive mechanisms which are also used in other domains.[13] Some studies have identified areas of the brain that relate to very specific facets of religious experience.[14] However, (crass popularisations about a 'God spot' in the brain aside) these facets can hardly be equated with religion as a whole, and other studies have found far more dispersed activation patterns.[15] If religion exploits the ordinary cognitive mechanisms, then the general mechanisms identified by embodied cognition research are also readily applicable to the case of religion.[16]

1.2 Caveat Emptor: *Replication, Small Samples, WEIRD Participants, and Ecological Validity*

Having established that embodied cognition studies are applicable to religious practices, it should be noted that many of these studies share certain limitations. Whereas the case for a modal theory of concepts (Chapter 3) relied on a large

---

[11] Day, 'Religion', 101.
[12] Ibid. See also Soliman, Johnson, and Song, 'Understanding Religion', 853.
[13] E.g., Fuller, *Spirituality in the Flesh*, 17; Guthrie, 'Why Gods?', 98.
[14] E.g., Brick Johnstone et al., 'Right Parietal Lobe-Related "Selflessness" as the Neuropsychological Basis of Spiritual Transcendence', *The International Journal for the Psychology of Religion* 22, no. 4 (2012).
[15] Mario Beauregard and Vincent Paquette, 'Neural Correlates of a Mystical Experience in Carmelite Nuns', *Neuroscience Letters* 405, no. 3 (2006).
[16] Barsalou et al., 'Embodiment in Religious Knowledge', 14, 18–19, 36.

accumulation of evidence, corroborated by different experimental techniques, findings concerning embodied mechanisms identified in this chapter are sometimes less robust.

1.2.1 Replication

Many of the studies cited in this chapter employ 'priming', 'a technique whereby the presentation of one stimulus passively and temporarily affects processing or response, often in a different domain...the individual is either unaware of the influence of the priming stimulus on its measured response, or...this influence is unintended'.[17] For example, in embodied cognition research a study may test whether a certain environmental stimulus or body posture 'primes' a particular concept or memory. Priming studies have been at the centre of the so-called 'replication crisis' which has beset experimental psychology. The crisis was sparked when a team of researchers attempted to replicate the findings of one hundred studies published in three respected psychology journals in 2008; they found that (on one standard of replication), approximately one third of the studies they recreated failed to replicate the same results.[18] Subsequently, studies into the mechanisms of embodied cognition have been among those which have recorded replication failures.[19]

Interpreting failures to replicate is a difficult task. As Earp and Trafimow note, a failure to replicate cannot be equated with falsification.[20] There are any number of plausible alternative explanations: perhaps a mistake was made in the replication experiment; perhaps the effect only occurs under specific conditions; perhaps performing the experiment properly requires some tacit knowledge that the replicator does not possess. Earp and Trafimow conclude, 'we simply do not know, and cannot know, exactly what the implications of a given replication attempt are, no matter which way the data come out. There are no critical tests of theories; and there are no objectively decisive replications'.[21] Although the

[17] Azim F. Shariff et al., 'Religious Priming: A Meta-Analysis with a Focus on Prosociality', *Personality and Social Psychology Review* 20, no. 1 (2016): 28.

[18] The Open Science Collaboration, 'Estimating the Reproducibility of Psychological Science', *Science* 349, no. 6251 (2015).

[19] E.g., Eva Ranehill et al., 'Assessing the Robustness of Power Posing', *Psychological Science* 26, no. 5 (2015); Dermot Lynott et al., 'Replication of "Experiencing Physical Warmth Promotes Interpersonal Warmth" by Williams and Bargh (2008)', *Social Psychology* 45, no. 3 (2014); E. J. Wagenmakers et al., 'Registered Replication Report: Strack, Martin, & Stepper (1988)', *Perspectives on Psychological Science* 11, no. 6 (2016); Stéphane Doyen et al., 'Behavioral Priming: It's All in the Mind, but Whose Mind?', *PLOS ONE* 7, no. 1 (2012); Brian D. Earp et al., 'Out, Damned Spot: Can the "Macbeth Effect" Be Replicated?', *Basic and Applied Social Psychology* 36, no. 1 (2014) . Some replications have not found the same effect sizes for embodied priming, but they nevertheless found that the effect could be detected on a large enough sample size. E.g., David J. Johnson, Felix Cheung, and M. Brent Donnellan, 'Does Cleanliness Influence Moral Judgments? A Direct Replication of Schnall, Benton, and Harvey (2008)', *Social Psychology* 45, no. 3 (2014).

[20] Brian D. Earp and David Trafimow, 'Replication, Falsification, and the Crisis of Confidence in Social Psychology', *Frontiers in Psychology* 6 (2015): 2.

[21] Ibid.

outcomes of replications are not decisive, Earp and Trafimow argue that they can be informative (and they suggest a Bayesian model for weighing up the evidence they provide).[22]

An example of a failure to replicate an embodied cognition study, which demonstrates the difficulties of interpretation, is the study proposing the facial feedback hypothesis (that facial expressions, such as a smile, can prime positive emotions). The effect was first established in 1988 by Strack, Martin, and Stepper.[23] However, in a large-scale replication effort, seventeen laboratories each repeated Strack, Martin, and Stepper's experiment, resulting in a combined sample size of 1,894 participants. The studies failed to replicate the original findings.[24] At first glance, this meta-study would seem to provide compelling evidence against the original findings, especially given the size of the replication effort. However, in his response to the replication Strack points out that over twenty studies published since 2010 have confirmed the evaluative effect of holding a pen in one's mouth (and thereby using the muscles used to smile).[25] Moreover, studies with other methodologies have provided corroborating evidence for the facial feedback hypothesis. For example, studies found that BOTOX injections which paralyse muscles of facial expressions can alter emotional experience.[26] Strack proposes a number of reasons why the replication may have failed (participants may now be familiar with the effect, the cartoons may be out-of-date, the replication studies pointed a camera at participants which may have altered their responses, or a statistical anomaly in the replication results).[27] The authors of the replication studies are also circumspect in their conclusions, cautioning that 'it should be stressed that the [Registered Replication Report] results do not invalidate the more general facial feedback hypothesis',[28] and speculate about why the hypothesis may be correct in spite of their findings. This case demonstrates the fraught nature of interpreting failures to replicate.

Developing rigorous methodologies which can adjudicate between failures to replicate and the original findings with which they are associated is ultimately a task for the experimental psychology guild, and a number of steps have already

[22] Ibid., 8.

[23] Fritz Strack, Leonard Martin, and Sabine Stepper, 'Inhibiting and Facilitating Conditions of the Human Smile: A Nonobtrusive Test of the Facial Feedback Hypothesis', *Journal of Personality and Social Psychology* 54, no. 5 (1988).

[24] 'Whereas [Strack et al.] reported a difference between conditions of 0.82 units on a 10-point rating scale, the random effects meta-analysis of the RRR results estimated that difference to be 0.03 with a 95% confidence interval ranging from −0.11 to 0.16.' Wagenmakers et al., 'Registered Replication Report', 924.

[25] Fritz Strack, 'Reflection on the Smiling Registered Replication Report', *Perspectives on Psychological Science* 11, no. 6 (2016).

[26] Joshua Ian Davis et al., 'The Effects of Botox Injections on Emotional Experience', *Emotion* 10, no. 3 (2010); David A. Havas et al., 'Cosmetic Use of Botulinum Toxin-a Affects Processing of Emotional Language', *Psychological Science* 21, no. 7 (2010).

[27] Strack, 'Reflection', 929–30.

[28] Wagenmakers et al., 'Registered Replication Report', 124.

been taken towards rectifying the ambiguity around replication. However, for the consumers of psychological findings, it is important to flag this ongoing issue which, at the very least, places a question mark next to findings which have failed to replicate. In this chapter, I point to a number of studies which are highly suggestive of the embodied effects of ritual participation. However, the conclusions I draw will not be contingent on any particular study standing the test of time. The conclusions are dependent on ritual participation *in general* having cognitive effects. The cumulative weight of evidence provided by hundreds, if not thousands, of studies makes the presence of a general effect (of embodied factors on cognition) secure, even if doubt surrounds individual effects.[29]

1.2.2 Small Samples
One reason why the results of a study might not be robust (and therefore fail to replicate), is that its results are statistically underpowered. Many of the priming effects of embodied cognition are quite subtle. To detect these small effect sizes with a reasonable degree of statistical certainty large samples size are required. Hence studies with small samples may be insufficient to establish the existence of a particular mechanism in the population at large to a reasonable degree of certainty. This problem can be remedied simply by using larger sample sizes, or by running meta-analyses which combine the samples from multiple studies investigating the same mechanism in order to create a larger sample size.

Some of the studies referenced in this chapter used relatively small sample sizes, and as a result they are statistically underpowered. Where possible I have referred to meta-analyses or multiple studies, but given the relative nascency of embodied cognition these resources are not always available. While the results of studies with small sample sizes are suggestive, they should be treated as preliminary results awaiting further confirmation (with the concomitant possibility of disconfirmation).

1.2.3 WEIRD Participants
Another issue facing many studies in experimental psychology is the diversity of their participant pool. Experimenters frequently rely upon the most readily available participants, namely undergraduates at their academic institution. In many cases this has led to participants in western, educated, industrialised, rich, and democratic (or 'WEIRD') societies being over-represented. An analysis found

---

[29] For some of the mechanisms I cite, large volumes of evidence have been amassed. For example, a meta-analysis of 93 studies with over 11,000 participants in total, found that results suggesting that religious priming increases prosocial behaviour in religious populations are robust. See Shariff et al., 'Religious Priming'.

that, contrary to the assumptions of many experimenters, samples of this group do not generalise well to the human population in many domains.[30] It is not difficult to imagine that this cohort is also far from representative of the global population when it comes to questions of religion. A study of WEIRD participants raises the question of whether the findings can be generalised to other populations. Many recent studies have recognised this problem, and sought to test hypotheses on more diverse participant pools, often drawn from multiple geographical locations and cultures which are carefully chosen to maximise diversity.

1.2.4 Ecological Validity

Most of the empirical studies I refer to in this chapter do not directly measure responses which take place in the context of 'live' religious rituals, either because they identify mechanisms which are not specific to religious rituals or because experiments take place in a lab. One of the primary reasons for this is, quite simply, because it is very difficult to measure the effect of individual mechanisms in the context of busy rituals, in which participants are bombarded with multisensory stimuli. This scenario not only often makes measurement practically difficult without altering the flow of the ritual, but also means that it is difficult to isolate the particular cause of any given effect. Experimental studies, by contrast, typically rely on highly controlled lab environments so that they can isolate one particular variable *ceteris paribus*. The mismatch between the context of the study and the 'live' correlate raises the question of 'ecological validity'. Given the vast difference between the lab and ritual settings, it may be results in the lab do not translate to real-life contexts. Moreover, isolating individual mechanisms leaves open the question of how multiple mechanisms interact in live settings.

Certain experimental techniques are employed in order to achieve greater ecological validity. For example, one class of priming studies employs 'contextual primes'.[31] These primes introduce a subtle contextual cue to prime religiosity (among other things). For instance, an experimenter may ensure that a Muslim call to prayer can be heard in the background or that the experiment takes place inside or in view of a religious building. Contextual primes have greater ecological validity since they occur in more naturalistic situations.[32] Experiments with higher ecological validity may sacrifice the kind of precision which can be achieved in a highly controlled lab environment. Given the relative strengths of different approaches, they helpfully supplement one another.

---

[30] Joseph Henrich, Steven J. Heine, and Ara Norenzayan, 'The Weirdest People in the World?', *Behavioral and Brain Sciences* 33, no. 2–3 (2010).
[31] Shariff et al., 'Religious Priming', 28–9.   [32] Ibid., 28.

1.3 Ethnography and Historical Reconstructions

Beyond cognitive science, another way to enhance ecological validity is to consider detailed descriptions of real-world rituals. Ethnography, historical reconstructions, and material culture studies describe religious practices to a level of detail which allows particular embodiments, and associated cognitive mechanisms, to be identified. Whereas experimental work typically attempts to identify general features of human embodiment, historical and ethnographic accounts provide concrete examples of particular religious practices.

Ethnographic accounts are particularly helpful since anthropologists regularly pay close attention to embodied practices.[33] As Cohen and Leung note, psychology is helpfully augmented by ethnographic studies: 'The anthropological emphasis on practice, ritual, and what people actually do with their bodies captures this in a way that a psychology of the head does not.'[34] Hence ethnographies can work hand-in-hand with the insights provided by embodied cognition research.

Anthropologists have long insisted on participant observation as a *sine qua non* of their disciplinary self-understanding.[35] The centrality of participant observation means that ethnographers themselves participate in the bodily practices in 'live' settings, of the communities which they are studying. Their emphasis on fieldwork assumes that an embodied presence provides a deeper understanding of the culture beginning studied, and allow for a 'thick description' which could not be achieved at a distance.[36] Orsi, for example, articulates the necessity for a corporeal understanding of religion in the following terms:

> To be present in disciplined attentiveness in all the places where human beings come face to face with their gods and with each other, living and dead, for better and for worse, with our judgment held in suspension and the engine of our theory paused, I now believe is the necessary condition for developing knowledge about religion. And not only to be there, but to help men and women carry a sick family member to the healing waters, to be evangelized or harangued, to mill around in the slow empty hours that inevitably attend a religious ritual with others also waiting...Disengagement from religious experience...produces theoretical hallucinations.[37]

---

[33] William R. LaFleur, 'Body', in *Critical Terms for Religious Studies*, ed. Mark C. Taylor (Chicago: University of Chicago Press, 1998), 36.

[34] Dov Cohen and Angela K. Y. Leung, 'The Hard Embodiment of Culture', *European Journal of Social Psychology* 39, no. 7 (2009): 1287.

[35] P. Atkinson and M. Hammersley, 'Ethnography and Participant Observation', in *Handbook of Qualitative Research*, ed. N. K. Denzin and Y. S. Lincoln (Thousand Oaks, CA: Sage Publications, 1994).

[36] Pete Ward, 'Introduction', in *Perspectives on Ecclesiology and Ethnography*, ed. Pete Ward (Grand Rapids: Eerdmans, 2012), 6–7.

[37] Robert A. Orsi, 'Roundtable on Ethnography and Religion: Doing Religious Studies with Your Whole Body', *Practical Matters* 2 (2013): 1–2.

In the remainder of this chapter, I therefore draw upon ethnographic and historical accounts to furnish the application of embodied cognition studies with concrete instances of real-world religious practices.

2 Positioning and Moving the Body

At the most basic level, rituals involve scripting of the body to perform certain movements and adopt particular postures. Embodied cognition studies have detected that gestures, postures, and movements of the body all have cognitive effects. As Brown and Strawn observe, 'actions influence thought. What we are doing with our bodies has a profound influence on what we are thinking and how we are thinking about it'.[38] Hence an obvious starting point for applying embodied cognition to ritual practices is to consider the cognitive effects of the ways in which rituals script bodily movement and positioning.

2.1 Memory

Embodied cognition studies suggest that body posture and memory interact. In one study participants were faster at recalling autobiographical memories when they adopted the same body posture in which the original experience took place.[39] In light of these findings, rituals in Christian practice employ repeated postures to facilitate memory recall of previous experiences in the same posture, reinforcing the continuity of one's religious life.

Two further studies have directly tested a link between body posture and religious associations. One found that kneeling participants were more likely to judge events as miraculous and were more likely to identify images of objects as religious.[40] In the second, participants in lower, constrained postures were more likely to agree with conventional religious beliefs than those in higher, expansive postures.[41] The authors of both these studies acknowledge that these results may arise from cultural associations with kneeling, rather than anything intrinsic about the posture.[42] Even as a learned association, these studies demonstrate that trained postures influence religious judgements.

---

[38] Brown and Strawn, *Physical Nature of Christian Life*, 80.
[39] Katinka Dijkstra, Michael P. Kaschak, and Rolf A. Zwaan, 'Body Posture Facilitates Retrieval of Autobiographical Memories', *Cognition* 102, no. 1 (2007).
[40] Michael R. Ransom and Mark D. Alicke, 'On Bended Knee: Embodiment and Religious Judgements', *Current Research in Social Psychology* 21, no. 9 (2013).
[41] Robert C. Fuller and Derek E. Montgomery, 'Body Posture and Religious Attitudes', *Archive for the Psychology of Religion* 37, no. 3 (2015).
[42] Ransom and Alicke, 'On Bended Knee', 6; Fuller and Montgomery, 'Body Posture', 235.

2.2 Emotion and Judgement

In Chapter 5, I introduced Damasio's neuroscientific revitalisation of the James-Lange theory of emotion, which posited that bodily states do not merely express emotion, but constitute part of the process of emotional cognition. This insight goes beyond merely identifying the physical substrate on which emotional cognition occurs (as both neural and bodily); it also informs *how* emotions can be stimulated or modulated. In Damasio's basic account, an external perceptual stimulus leads to changes in body states, which are then felt. However, emotional priming studies test the possibility of directly inducing an emotion through emotional body states, bypassing the need for an external stimulus.

Studies have found that decreasing one's heart rate decreases anxiety, whilst increasing heart rates has the opposite effect.[43] Facial expressions also feed back into emotions: participants who tensed the muscles used for smiling (by holding a pen between their teeth) found cartoons more amusing than those who could not exercise these muscles (because they were holding a pen between their lips).[44] A similar effect has been detected for other body postures: in one study participants felt a greater sense of pride in their achievements when they were upright rather than slumping;[45] in another study participants who were slumped developed a greater sense of helplessness.[46] These emotional priming studies provide further support for Damasio's hypothesis that bodily states constitute emotion, corroborating evidence he cites from neuroscience. Emotional priming also reveals the somewhat counter-intuitive picture of emotion, namely that—contrary to the oft-assumed understanding that bodily states and behaviours *express* emotion—bodily states can impinge on mental states. Causation operates in both directions.

Damasio's work was also seminal in calling into question the assumed dichotomy between reason and emotion. Rather than emotion accompanying or providing information for rational decision making, Damasio proposes that emotions are 'in the loop' of reason, and therefore at the heart of everyday decision making.[47]

---

[43] Mark E. McKinney et al., 'The Impact of Biofeedback-Manipulated Physiological Change on Emotional State', *Basic & Applied Social Psychology* 1, no. 1 (1980); Sarah N. Garfinkel and Hugo D. Critchley, 'Threat and the Body: How the Heart Supports Fear Processing', *Trends in Cognitive Sciences* 20, no. 1 (2015).

[44] Strack, Martin, and Stepper, 'Inhibiting and Facilitating Conditions'. Cf. Albert Flexas et al., 'Affective Priming Using Facial Expressions Modulates Liking for Abstract Art', *PLOS ONE* 8, no. 11 (2013); R. B. Zajonc, Sheila T. Murphy, and Marita Inglehart, 'Feeling and Facial Efference: Implications of the Vascular Theory of Emotion', *Psychological Review* 96, no. 3 (1989). For a discussion on replication issues associated with this study, see Section 1.2.

[45] Sabine Stepper and Fritz Strack, 'Proprioceptive Determinants of Emotional and Nonemotional Feelings', *Journal of Personality and Social Psychology* 64, no. 2 (1993).

[46] John H. Riskind and Carolyn C. Gotay, 'Physical Posture: Could It Have Regulatory or Feedback Effects on Motivation and Emotion?', *Motivation and Emotion* 6, no. 3 (1982).

[47] Damasio, *Descartes' Error*, 165–200.

Several studies have extended emotional priming to measure downstream effects on attitudes and judgements. For example, one study found that arm flexion (putting one's hands underneath a table and pushing upwards) associated with approach movements (such as hugging) led to more positive attitudes towards objects, while arm extension (pushing down on a table) associated with avoidance motions (pushing something away) resulted in negative attitudes.[48] Indeed, the bodily states which prime agreement and disagreement, namely the actions associated with approach and avoidance, are one criterion for discriminating between positive and negative emotions respectively.[49] In another study participants were more likely to agree with editorial content when they were nodding their heads vertically, as opposed to shaking them horizontally.[50]

The connection between prayer postures and emotions has been directly investigated by van Cappellen and Edwards.[51] They asked participants to manipulate mannequins into the posture they would adopt to represent particular emotions, (e.g., dominance, submission, joy, sadness, gratitude, and grief). Participants were then instructed to imagine that the mannequins were religious, and where asked to manipulate them into various prayer orientations (e.g., confession, praise, prayer, repentance, thanksgiving, worship). By comparing the two sets of mannequin postures, they found that prayer postures and emotional registers varied in predictable ways; for example the postures for confession and repentance were more constrictive and downward oriented, corresponding to the emotional registers of guilt, sadness, and submission, whilst postures for praise and thanksgiving were more expansive, and upward oriented, corresponding to emotional registers for gratitude, joy, and dominance.

It is not difficult to see the relevance of emotional priming mechanisms to religious rituals. By scripting bodily movements and postures, rituals can exploit this direct pathway from bodily states to emotion. Worshippers extend their arms and hold out open palms in a range of Christian traditions; for example, Roman Catholics when reciting the Lord's Prayer, or Pentecostals whilst singing.[52] As an approach (rather than avoidance) posture, this practice is likely to prime positive emotion and to increase participants' openness to the theological content being conveyed.

---

[48] John T. Cacioppo, Joseph R. Priester, and Gary G. Berntson, 'Rudimentary Determinants of Attitudes. II: Arm Flexion and Extension Have Differential Effects on Attitudes', *Journal of Personality & Social Psychology* 65, no. 1 (1993).

[49] Jesse J. Prinz, *Gut Reactions: A Perceptual Theory of Emotion* (Oxford: Oxford University Press, 2004), 174.

[50] Gary L. Wells and Richard E. Petty, 'The Effects of Overt Head Movements on Persuasion: Compatibility and Incompatibility of Responses', *Basic & Applied Social Psychology* 1, no. 3 (1980).

[51] Patty van Cappellen and Megan Edwards, 'Emotion Expression in Context: Full Body Postures of Christian Prayer Orientations Compared to Specific Emotions', *Journal of Nonverbal Behavior* 45, no. 4 (2021).

[52] For an extended analysis of one such example, see Section 6.

2.3 Gestures

Another class of movement which can influence thought is gestures.[53] Although gestures play an important role in communicative acts, they can also directly influence the gesturer. When study participants gestured in ways compatible with a cognitive task, their performance improved, while incompatible gestures reduced performance.[54] In another study participants simultaneously performed a memorisation and an explanation task. The study found that, '[g]esturing saves speakers cognitive resources on the explanation task, permitting them to allocate more resources to the memory task'.[55] Gestures, then, go beyond merely expressing thought: 'evidence is mounting that gesture goes well beyond reflecting our thoughts, to playing a role in shaping them'.[56] They fulfil this role because gesture 'actively brings action into a speaker's mental representations, and those mental representations then affect behavior'.[57]

A developmental study on gestures found that when children are on the cusp of learning their gestures typically change before their patterns of speech.[58] In this way gestures can outrun the knowledge which can be expressed linguistically.[59] They thereby constitute representations which are more akin to mental imagery than propositional knowledge.[60] Hence they have the capacity to reveal knowledge which is held implicitly: 'the information conveyed in gesture is often not conveyed anywhere in the speech that accompanies it. In this way, gesture reflects thoughts that speakers may not explicitly know they have'.[61] As with the bodily states which constitute emotions, the bodily movements in gestures participate in cognitive process. This makes gesturing another candidate for cognition which extends beyond the brain: cognition is not *only* taking place across neural networks, but is also constituted by gestural movements.

Gestures play a ubiquitous role in religious practices. Scripted or unscripted, they may be employed in communicative acts (e.g., a homily) or parts of ritual performances (e.g., a blessing, an elevation, etc.). One clear example can be found in an ethnographic account of the 'Toronto Blessing', where Percy describes a number of gestures made by worshippers: 'Participants sometimes dance to the music, but most make gestures with their hands or arms, either raising them high (and then keeping them still), with some also moving them in a slow

---

[53]   I have already noted that gestures may provide a bridge between concrete and abstract concepts, see Chapter 3, Section 5.1.

[54]   S. L. Beilock and S. Goldin-Meadow, 'Gesture Changes Thought by Grounding It in Action', *Psychological Science* 21, no. 11 (2010).

[55]   Susan Goldin-Meadow and Susan M. Wagner, 'How Our Hands Help Us Learn', *Trends in Cognitive Sciences* 9, no. 5 (2005): 237.

[56]   Ibid., 240.   [57]   Goldin-Meadow and Beilock, 'Action's Influence', 172.

[58]   Goldin-Meadow and Wagner, 'How Our Hands Help', 239.   [59]   Ibid., 234–6.

[60]   Hostetter and Alibali, 'Visible Embodiment', 497–500.

[61]   Goldin-Meadow and Beilock, 'Action's Influence', 664.

sweeping, encompassing or wiping fashion, as though polishing an invisible giant globe.'[62] Percy notes that the globe-like movements share a particular affinity with the global outlook of the group's prayers.[63] Embodied cognition raises the prospect that such gestures do not merely express prayers for the world, but also co-constitute such prayers. The gestures assist those praying to represent the object of their prayers.

2.4 Expertise

In addition to quotidian movements and postures, specialist long-term training in motor skills also effects cognitive processes (beyond the specific capacity to perform the specialist skill). Expertise in several activities involving motor movement, including (e.g.) sports, dancing, and piano playing, alters neural behaviour, with effects on cognitive processes such as language processing, action observation, perceptual discrimination, and auditory simulation.[64] For example, one study found that while learning to play the piano allows the brain to map the auditory stimulus of hearing piano music to the motor movements involved in playing a piano; as a result, professional piano players experience activation in motor areas of their brain when they hear piano music.[65] While it is difficult, with our existing knowledge of the brain, to make definitive connections between changes in neural activation patterns and cognitive processes, behavioural studies have found that motor training can influence cognitive processes.[66] For example, one study found that novice golfers improved their putting when less hurried, while expert golfers' performance increased when under time pressure.[67] Hence expertise in motor skills, developed through repetitive training over periods of time, shapes cognitive processes: 'individuals' previous experiences acting in the

---

[62] Martyn Percy, 'Adventure and Atrophy in a Charismatic Movement: Returning to the "Toronto Blessing"', *Journal of Contemporary Religion* 20, no. 1 (2005): 79.

[63] Personal conversation.

[64] Sian L. Beilock et al., 'Sports Experience Changes the Neural Processing of Action Language', *Proceedings of the National Academy of Sciences* 105, no. 36 (2008); Sian L. Beilock and Sara Gonso, 'Putting in the Mind Versus Putting on the Green: Expertise, Performance Time, and the Linking of Imagery and Action', *The Quarterly Journal of Experimental Psychology* 61, no. 6 (2008); B. Calvo-Merino et al., 'Action Observation and Acquired Motor Skills: An fMRI Study with Expert Dancers', *Cerebral Cortex* 15, no. 8 (2005); Marc Bangert and Eckart O. Altenmüller, 'Mapping Perception to Action in Piano Practice: A Longitudinal DC-EEG Study', *BMC Neuroscience* 4, no. 1 (2003); Jens Haueisen and Thomas R. Knösche, 'Involuntary Motor Activity in Pianists Evoked by Music Perception', *Journal of Cognitive Neuroscience* 13, no. 6 (2001); Heiko Hecht, Stefan Vogt, and Wolfgang Prinz, 'Motor Learning Enhances Perceptual Judgment: A Case for Action-Perception Transfer', *Psychological Research* 65, no. 1 (2001).

[65] Bangert and Altenmüller, 'Mapping Perception'; Haueisen and Knösche, 'Involuntary Motor Activity'.

[66] Hecht, Vogt, and Prinz, 'Motor Learning Enhances Perceptual Judgment: A Case for Action-Perception Transfer'.

[67] Beilock and Gonso, 'Putting in the Mind'.

world change how they process the information they encounter by allowing them to call upon a greater network of sensorimotor regions, even when they are merely observing or listening without intending to act'.[68]

There is, to my mind, no compelling reason why 'expertise' in ritual participation should be any different. Rituals often involve repetitive motor movements which constitute a form of training. Expertise in ritual performance is therefore likely to forge connections between the motor activity required for the ritual, the sensory perceptions associated with the ritual, emotion, and the various other facets traditionally associated with 'central cognition' (concepts, judgements, etc.). One might hypothesise, therefore, that 'experts' with a long history in ritual performance will experience motor activation when they see a ritual performed in a film, or read a literary trope with an allusion to liturgical phrase.

2.5 Ritual Behaviour

Research which focuses on 'ritual' in general is perhaps most directly relevant to religious practices. Rituals, of course, need not be specifically religious; civic life, and institutions such as schools, universities, militaries, sporting teams, and parliaments each employ their own rituals. Cognitive scientists have attempted to define ritual to circumscribe it for experimental investigation (resulting in 'thinner' definitions than the ones anthropologists or theologians might proffer).[69] What these definitions all seem to share is that rituals are a scripted set of 'symbolic' movements and activities (where symbolic is contrasted to actions which are thought to result from direct physical causation, such as a medical intervention).

Relying on such definitions of ritual, a number of studies have found that performing rituals has various cognitive effects. One study found that imbuing a game with ritual cues improved the executive function of children and, in turn, improved their ability to delay gratification.[70] Another study found that rituals alleviated grief arising from losses.[71] The study examined the loss of relationships, the death of loved ones, or simply losing a lottery devised in the lab. Crucially, the alleviation of grief was stronger when participants actually performed a bodily ritual, rather than merely knowing that people often perform rituals in response

---

[68] Goldin-Meadow and Beilock, 'Action's Influence', 666.

[69] E.g., Kathleen D. Vohs et al., 'Rituals Enhance Consumption', *Psychological Science* 24, no. 9 (2013): 1715; Veronika Rybanska et al., 'Rituals Improve Children's Ability to Delay Gratification', *Child Development* 89, no. 2 (2017) ; Patricia A. Herrmann et al., 'Stick to the Script: The Effect of Witnessing Multiple Actors on Children's Imitation', *Cognition* 129, no. 3 (2013); Michael I. Norton and Francesca Gino, 'Rituals Alleviate Grieving for Loved Ones, Lovers, and Lotteries', *Journal of Experimental Psychology: General* 143, no. 1 (2014).

[70] Rybanska et al., 'Rituals Improve Children's Ability'.

[71] Norton and Gino, 'Rituals Alleviate Grieving'.

to loss. This study gives weight to the idea that ecclesial funerary practices are efficacious in assisting participants to process grief.

Finally, an intriguing study found that participants who performed a ritual prior to consuming food rated the food as more enjoyable than those who did not, and were willing to pay more for it.[72] The increase in enjoyment was more pronounced when performing ritualised gestures (i.e., the same set of gestures repeatedly) as opposed to random gestures. Furthermore, the enjoyment was also more pronounced when the participant performed the ritual themselves rather than simply observing it, suggesting that the physical act of performing the ritual is important. The effect held for chocolate, lemonade, and 'even carrots'. The researchers suggest that rituals enhance consumption 'because they lead to greater involvement and interest'.[73] If this is correct, the engaging nature of rituals heightens a person's role from a detached observer to an active participant. These findings have implications not only for ritualised meals such as the Eucharist, but also for domestic religious practices such as 'saying grace' before meals.

In this section I have narrowly focused on the individual body. However, embodied cognition also considers how bodies interact with their environments and cognition extends out into the world. In the following sections, I move beyond a limited focus on individual bodies by examining the material and social contexts in which bodies are located during liturgical performances.

3 Scaffolding Prayers: The Cognitive Import of Material Culture

Religious rituals often take place in highly elaborate settings with a specialised material culture. The material aspects of religious practices are as rich and varied as the practices themselves; they include processional patterns, vestments, incense, bells, music, art, ritual objects, architecture, and much more. My task here, again, is not to provide an exhaustive account of religious material culture, but rather to highlight relevant findings in embodied cognition which illuminate the cognitive scaffolding provided by the material aspects of ritual.

As with body movements and postures, empirical evidence suggests that interaction with particular objects and places affects aspects of cognition such as memory, emotion, and attention. The theories of embodied cognition raise the possibility that the cognition implicated in religious practices is scaffolded by, or even offloaded onto, physical media beyond the body. These theories therefore call for a particular attentiveness to the materiality of embodied practices: be it through substances ingested, tactile objects manipulated, or places inhabited.

---

[72] Vohs et al., 'Rituals Enhance Consumption'.   [73] Ibid., 1720.

In the modern Christian West, prayer is oftentimes first and foremost associated with a linguistic address, formulated 'in one's head' and directed towards God. If this is assumed to be the paradigmatic form of prayer, then there is little room for material culture in an understanding of prayer, and objects, images, and spaces are, at best, considered extraneous and expendable. In this section, I explore examples of prayer in which materiality is anything but extraneous or expendable. If cognition is indeed scaffolded by resources beyond the skin and relies upon sensorimotor interaction with the outside world, as embodied cognition contends, then the cognition involved in prayer may also be distributed across material objects.

3.1 Praying with Objects

Perhaps the most clear-cut example of extended religious cognition is the use of a rosary (or similar technology) in prayer.[74] The rosary represents the structure of a prayer in physical form; the number of beads represents repetitions, and the shape of a bead corresponds to a particular formulation. Hence keeping track of one's stage in the prayer is deferred from the brain to the beads and the hand which thumbs through them. The rosary can be said to constitute part of the cognitive task of praying. Subsequently users free up cognitive resources otherwise devoted to tracking their progress, allowing them to devote their attention elsewhere or simply to have fewer demands on their attention.

There are, of course, many other objects with which Christians interact during prayers. Icons, relics, books, images, crucifixes, and jewellery, to name but a few, have all been implicated in prayer at various times and in various traditions. For example, Cuneo observes the myriad ways in which the Eastern Orthodox tradition manipulates icons, '[i]n both their private and corporate worship, Eastern Orthodox Christians do all sorts of things with icons: they adorn them with flowers, process with them held aloft, bless them with water, prostrate themselves before them, and touch and kiss them.'[75] Corporate rituals such as the Eucharist employ still more objects: various kinds of vessels, thuribles, fabrics, bells, lecterns, candles, and monstrances, again, to give but a few examples. Other physical objects are substances which are consumed: anointing oil, holy water, incense, and the Eucharistic elements. These objects may not involve the same degree of cognitive 'coupling' as a rosary. However, an important part of knowing how to participate in these rituals is knowing how to interact with these objects. The knowledge required to pray or worship in forms which use these objects is thus

---

[74] Barsalou et al., 'Embodiment in Religious Knowledge', 48.
[75] Cuneo, *Ritualized Faith*, 106.

more than simply knowledge about the objects or what they might symbolise; it is also the bodily knowledge required to manipulate these objects.

3.2 Pilgrimage and Parish: Cognition and Place

In addition to manipulatable objects, memory can also be offloaded onto physical places. Pilgrimage, for example, can be thought of a rosary writ large. Instead of beads representing prayers, the very landscape is used to mark points of a pilgrim's prayer. Shrines, chapels, churches, and cathedrals dotted along ancient pilgrimage routes, such as the Camino Francés leading to Santiago de Compostela, each summon a pilgrim to stop and pray.[76] Moreover, the landscape itself changes during the course of the route. Beginning at Saint-Jean-Pied-de-Port, the route begins with the verdant and mountainous Pyrenees, progresses to a long, flat, and dry plateau, and ends in the more luscious Galicia. Here each variation in the climate lends prayer a different tone, recalling the wilderness and fertile promised land typology of the Exodus. Hence the landscape and cityscapes of a particular route can be thought of as a physical instantiation of prayer shaped in a particular way.[77]

The physicality of a pilgrimage is not limited to its geography. A whole range of objects relate to pilgrimage, ranging from the practical to the symbolic. As with modern day tourists, pilgrims often acquired souvenirs. As the original French meaning of this loanword suggests, a central purpose of these objects was to offload memory. Examples of seventeenth-century pilgrim souvenirs reveal that they differed from many modern analogues; rather than simply showing the façade of an important site, pilgrims often acquired miniature models of the holy places they visited which represented the physical layout of important buildings.[78] These spatial souvenirs assisted pilgrims in recalling not only what a holy place looked like, but also how they physically interacted with the site: the locations of important shrines, how they moved through a space, and the rituals they performed within the space.

The connection between space and memory has long been recognised. In his instructions on rhetoric, Cicero recommends that rhetoricians memorise an

---

[76] Far from being the practice of a bygone era, recent years have seen a resurgence of pilgrimage in Western Europe. See Rubén C. Lois-González and Xosé M. Santos, 'Tourists and Pilgrims on Their Way to Santiago. Motives, Caminos and Final Destinations', *Journal of Tourism and Cultural Change* 13, no. 2 (2015).

[77] Rowan Williams remarks on the connection between a certain landscape and a particular mode of spirituality in Rowan Williams, *Silence and Honey Cakes: The Wisdom of the Desert* (Oxford: Lion, 2003), 17.

[78] For examples of seventeenth Century models of the Church of the Nativity in Bethlehem and the Holy Sepulchre in Jerusalem, see objects AN2009.3 & AN2009.4 (respectively) in the Ashmolean, Oxford. See also object OA.10338 at the British Museum.

oration by associating sections with adjoining rooms in a building.[79] The rhetorician can thereby exploit their spatial memory to recall the sequence of points in an argument. Empirical embodied cognition studies have confirmed this connection. One cleverly designed study had a group of divers learn a list of items either under water or above ground.[80] Participants were faster at recalling the list when they were in the same environment in which they learnt it. Hence, in the same way that adopting the same body posture in which an experience took place facilitates memory recall, so too does being in the same environment.

The experiment involving divers goes some way towards addressing achieving ecological validity; it takes place in natural environments rather than artificially constructed ones, even if the task undertaken by participants is somewhat contrived. However, other studies have gone further to test the connection between place and memory in realistic contexts. One study analysed videos of two older adults as they were about to leave their home. It found that 'ongoing activities, some partially unrelated to the activity of leaving home, coupled with the structure of the physical environment could assist the participants in remembering intentions before leaving home'.[81] Another study went even further, conducting 'sensory ethnographic engagements' with international students from Tunisia, Indonesia, and Germany. It found that for these students 'movements to and through places have yielded memorial engagements that have been manifest in multisensory evocations (olfactory, gustatory, acoustic memories), embodied practice (walking, recording, burying), and in the production of artefacts (soundscape compositions, buried objects)'.[82] These studies corroborate that the connection between place and memory persists outside of the lab.

Beyond the special experience of pilgrimage, there are many more quotidian examples of where the arrangement of particular spaces has cognitive import. As Andy Clark has observed, '[h]uman brains...excel in one crucial respect: we are masters at structuring our physical and social worlds so as to press complex coherent behaviors from these unruly resources'.[83] This insight readily extends to religion, which invests significant resources in restructuring the physical world in theologically meaningful ways.

[79] Marcus Tullius Cicero, De Oratore, trans. E. W. Sutton (Cambridge, MA: Harvard University Press, 1948), II, lxxxvi, 355.

[80] D. R. Godden and A. D. Baddeley, 'Context-Dependent Memory in Two Natural Environments: On Land and Underwater', British Journal of Psychology 66, no. 3 (1975).

[81] Mattias Kristiansson, Richard Wiik, and Erik Prytz, 'Bodily Orientations and Actions as Constituent Parts of Remembering Objects and Intentions Before Leaving Home', Sensoria: A Journal of Mind, Brain, and Culture 10, no. 1 (2014): 21.

[82] Andrew Stevenson, 'We Came Here to Remember: Using Participatory Sensory Ethnography to Explore Memory as Emplaced, Embodied Practice', Qualitative Research in Psychology 11, no. 4 (2014): 346.

[83] Clark, Being There, 180.

Perhaps the most obvious example of deliberately organised space is that of church architecture. Ecclesial buildings are typically designed for particular rituals. Subsequently, a particular space creates particular affordances, enabling some patterns of movement while restricting others. These arrangements of space can encode particular theological positions. For example, in the early church baptistries were not housed in the nave of a church building, but in an adjacent chamber.[84] New, unbaptised members of a congregation were made to leave the church during the celebration of the Eucharist or barred from services altogether. They first had to complete a period of catechesis, which prepared them for baptism. The location of the baptistry outside of the nave thus encoded a clear demarcation of one's status with regards to initiation. Moreover, the process of initiation involved a physical entry into a new space. This tradition continues, albeit less strictly, beyond the early church, insofar as baptistries are typically found at the entrance to church buildings.

Similarly, spaces have also been arranged to denote degrees of importance. It has often been remarked that the progression of height and space from the entrance of a medieval cathedral to its sanctuary and high altar encode a specific cosmic hierarchy.[85] As the researchers of one study concluded, '[p]reachers, priests, or ministers often speak to their congregations from an elevated platform known as the pulpit. This practice intentionally or unintentionally builds on the sorts of perceptual representations [of verticality] examined here, with a higher vertical position suggesting a closer relationship with God'.[86] Other traditions subvert such hierarchical visions, and have done so precisely by reorganising the space in which rituals take place.

In addition to carrying particular theological connotations, spaces can also scaffold cognition by directing attention. The high altar is typically placed in such a way that it is the focal point of the interior (when it is not obscured by a rood screen, itself a theologically significant organisation of space), and during the Eucharistic rite the priest draws attention to the host by elevating it. Williams intuitively discerns how church architecture can direct attention, when he observes that 'the way in which the architecture of an old-fashioned Catholic church leads the eye towards the tabernacle where the Sacrament is reserved (a powerful instance of a non-verbal sign) likewise works on the assumption that what I have called intelligible connection happens when the normal verbal carriers are deliberately removed'.[87]

The way in which physical organisation of the world supports our religious cognition does not end at the church door. Church buildings are often located at

---

[84] Tom Devonshire Jones, Linda Murray, and Peter Murray, 'Baptistry', in *The Oxford Dictionary of Christian Art and Architecture* (Oxford: Oxford University Press, 2013).

[85] Philip F. Sheldrake, 'A Spiritual City? Place, Memory, and City Making', in *Architecture, Ethics, and the Personhood of Place*, ed. Gregory Caicco (London: University Press of New England, 2007), 55.

[86] Meier et al., 'What's "up" with God?', 708.   [87] Williams, *Edge of Words*, 168–9.

the centre of a community and the surrounding area is also frequently arranged such that the church is a focal point in the cityscape. Many churches are located on hilltops and high points in a city's topology. At the time when they were built, church towers were often the tallest structures in a town or a city, making them visible above other buildings and notable features of the skyline. All of these features make church buildings a visible, central point in the community, which serves repeatedly to draw the attention of all community members to them. Much of this seems like utterly prosaic observations; however, within the framework of embodied cognition, these seemingly mundane facts take on a new dimension. On an extended view of cognition, architects and city planners do more than merely express theological views; instead, buildings and city layouts organise our external environment to outsource aspects of our cognition, directing attention and signalling significance.

Cathedrals are particularly noteworthy from a cognitive perspective on account of their size. Not only does their grandeur lend them great visibility, but their vast cavernous interiors are also especially adept at inducing awe. Awe has been defined as an emotional response to vast stimuli.[88] Experimenters induced awe by using stimuli such as 200-foot-tall trees, nature videos, and a full-sized replica of a Tyrannosaurus rex skeleton.[89] Cathedrals no doubt qualify as awe-inducing stimuli; indeed, a seminal paper which defined awe psychologically lists cathedrals as a prototypical awe-inducing stimulus.[90]

Awe has recently received significant attention in psychology and studies have uncovered a number of cognitive effects. In the face of vast stimuli, awe makes one feel smaller and less significant;[91] one study found that people who experienced awe perceived their own bodies as smaller.[92] Another study found that awe also altered participants' perception of time to make them feel as though they had more time available; this had various flow-on effects: participants were less impatient, more likely to volunteer, preferred experiences over material products, and reported greater life satisfaction.[93] Another study found that awe increased prosociality; participants who had experienced awe were more generous and endorsed more ethical decisions.[94] Researchers hypothesised that awe has this

---

[88] Dacher Keltner and Jonathan Haidt, 'Approaching Awe, a Moral, Spiritual, and Aesthetic Emotion', *Cognition and Emotion* 17, no. 2 (2003): 303.

[89] Paul K. Piff et al., 'Awe, the Small Self, and Prosocial Behavior', *Journal of Personality & Social Psychology* 108, no. 6 (2015): 893–5; Michelle N. Shiota, Dacher Keltner, and Amanda Mossman, 'The Nature of Awe: Elicitors, Appraisals, and Effects on Self-Concept', *Cognition and Emotion* 21, no. 5 (2007).

[90] Keltner and Haidt, 'Approaching Awe', 305, 310.

[91] Shiota, Keltner, and Mossman, 'The Nature of Awe'.

[92] Michiel van Elk et al., ' "Standing in Awe": The Effects of Awe on Body Perception and the Relation with Absorption', *Collabra* 2, no. 1 (2016).

[93] Melanie Rudd, Kathleen D. Vohs, and Jennifer Aaker, 'Awe Expands People's Perception of Time, Alters Decision Making, and Enhances Well-Being', *Psychological Science* 23, no. 10 (2012).

[94] Piff et al., 'Awe'.

effect because it makes people feel small, 'implying a relative diminishment of the concepts and concerns attached to the individual self'.[95] The shift of attention from an individual to larger entities is 'vital to the collaboration and cooperation required of social groups'.[96] Finally, a study found the participants experiencing awe had a lower need for 'cognitive closure' than those experiencing joy or pride, such that 'awe-prone individuals should be especially comfortable revising their own mental structures, or acknowledging that currently held mental structures are not adequate to the occasion'.[97] The study also found that participants were less likely to refer to themselves using individualised terms. As awe-inducing spaces, cathedrals potentially generate these cognitive effects.

A recent poll showed, somewhat surprisingly, that 13 per cent of adolescents identified a visit to a church building as one of the reasons for their conversion.[98] Psychologists would urge caution about basing any strident claim on a survey that relied upon self-reporting in the absence of any controlled experiments (the literature is replete with examples where introspection misses the mark). With this caveat in mind, it is nonetheless striking that buildings ranked so highly on the survey, especially since this finding seems so counter-intuitive for many. Intuitions of respondents may well track the power of buildings to shape the mental landscape as well as the physical one.

Numerous priming studies lend support to the religious significance of church buildings. One study surveyed pedestrians as they walked by otherwise similar religious and non-religious buildings.[99] It found that the presence of religious architecture primed religiosity and led respondents to report 'more negative attitudes toward non-Christian groups, more conservative political attitudes, and more personal religiousness and spirituality regardless of their personal belief in God'.[100] Similarly, a second study found that participants were more willing to help the homeless (but not illegal immigrants) when shown pictures of them with a church in the background.[101] A third study asked participants to make decisions about insurance claims, and found that those making decisions in a chapel awarded less money to abortion pill claims than workers' compensation claims.[102] A fourth study found that participants cooperated more in a game when it was

---

[95] Ibid., 895.   [96] Ibid., 884.

[97] Shiota, Keltner, and Mossman, 'The Nature of Awe', 958.

[98] ComRes, 'Hope: Perceptions of Jesus Research', (London: ComRes, 2017), 175.

[99] Jordan P. LaBouff et al., 'Differences in Attitudes toward Outgroups in Religious and Nonreligious Contexts in a Multinational Sample: A Situational Context Priming Study', *The International Journal for the Psychology of Religion* 22, no. 1 (2012).

[100] Ibid., 1.

[101] Isabelle Pichon and Vassilis Saroglou, 'Religion and Helping: Impact of Target Thinking Styles and Just-World Beliefs', *Archive for the Psychology of Religion* 31, no. 2 (2009).

[102] Abraham M. Rutchick, 'Deus Ex Machina: The Influence of Polling Place on Voting Behavior', *Political Psychology* 31, no. 2 (2010). Cf. Shariff et al., 'Religious Priming', 43.

played in a chapel as opposed to a lecture hall.[103] Another study replicated this finding in a Hindu Temple.[104] Religious spaces have the capacity to evoke the judgements and behaviours which people associate with religion.

Beyond a church building's placement within a town or city, church buildings are also placed within a cosmic framework; namely, they are traditionally oriented towards the East. A large number of Christian (and pre-Christian) texts counsel that prayer, and therefore church buildings, should face towards the East.[105] For example, Augustine advocates praying towards the East since it is the direction of the rising sun to symbolise an orientation towards Christ. The fact that churches all face in a (roughly) common direction has also been understood as an expression of the unity of the church.[106] The archaeoastronomical way in which 'East' was determined may have varied over time and place: East could have meant the equinoctial east, or the direction from which the sun rose on either the day in which the church was founded or the day of the church's patron saint.[107] When the patron saint's day is used, the dedication of the church is inscribed into the very orientation of the building.

3.3 Visual Culture

Church structures are traditionally not simply bare edifices, but are highly ornamented. (Some strands of the Reformation form an obvious exception here; I discuss these in Section 6). A key feature of this ornamentation is a rich visual culture, including statues, paintings, needlework, stained glass windows, and the like. Although these are sometimes thought of as purely ornamental—a superfluous decoration—theories of embodied cognition again invite us to consider whether they play a more substantial role.

---

[103] Ali Ahmed and Osvaldo Salas, 'Religious Context and Prosociality: An Experimental Study from Valparaíso, Chile', *Journal for the Scientific Study of Religion* 52, no. 3 (2013).

[104] Dimitris Xygalatas, 'Effects of Religious Setting on Cooperative Behavior: A Case Study from Mauritius', *Religion, Brain & Behavior* 3, no. 2 (2013).

[105] For a survey, see Stephen C. McCluskey, 'Orientation of Christian Churches', in *Handbook of Archaeoastronomy and Ethnoastronomy*, ed. Clive L. N. Ruggles (New York: Springer, 2015).

[106] R. I. Harper, 'The Kalendarium Regine of Guillaume De St. Cloud', (Emory University, 1966), 145–7, 241–3.

[107] McCluskey, 'Orientation of Christian Churches', 1708–1709; Eva Spinazzè, 'The Alignment of Medieval Churches in Northern-Central Italy and in the Alps and the Path of Light inside the Church on the Patron Saint's Day', *Mediterranean Archaeology and Archaeometry* 16, no. 4 (2016); Anne Sassin Allen, 'Church Orientation in the Landscape: A Perspective from Medieval Wales', *Archaeological Journal* 173, no. 1 (2016); Ian Hinton, 'Church Alignment and Patronal Saint's Days', *The Antiquaries Journal* 86 (2008); José M. Abril, 'Evidence of Churches Aligned to the Sun on the Patron Saint's Day in Southern Spain after the Twelfth Century', *Journal of Skyscape Archaeology* 3, no. 1 (2017); Peter G. Hoare, 'Orientation of English Medieval Parish Churches', in *Handbook of Archaeoastronomy and Ethnoastronomy*, ed. Clive L. N. Ruggles (New York: Springer, 2015).

I have already discussed the significance of the spatiality of pilgrimage. Pilgrimage, however, need not be literal. Rudy documents how late medieval images that depict Jerusalem as a populated cityscape functioned as a 'virtual pilgrimage'.[108] Commenting on one painting which includes a series of scenes from the Passion, she remarks: '[o]ne is meant to walk through this painting, as Christ does, not simply to look at a series of disconnected narrative images'.[109] She continues, '[t]he effect on the viewer is an almost uncontrollable urge to reconstruct the chronological narrative, to trace the path and use the vignettes to imagine the narrative unfolding, possibly filling in details where possible'.[110] Thus these images use the spatial layout of an artwork as a proxy for the spatial progression of a pilgrimage. They too can function as an externalised version of memory, guiding the viewer through the narrative.

Beyond augmenting biological memory, images can also play an important role in diverting attention. As with many depictions of Christ's passion, Rudy emphasises how this visual culture encourages, or even demands, perspective-taking; various strategies are used to bring the viewer 'into' the narrative scene.[111] For example, in one of the pieces she analyses, she observes that '[t]he miniaturist portrays several modern [i.e., fifteenth-century] pilgrims who walk along the city roads…The contemporary pilgrims stand as proxies for the viewer'.[112] This perspective-taking shapes the experience of contemplating the image: 'The devotion takes on an intense immediacy if we take up the position of the pilgrim'.[113] The ultimate goal of this strategy is to elicit empathy: '[t]hese images do not recreate a literal map of Jerusalem but are, like almost all medieval Passion narratives, constructed to allow the viewer to empathize with Christ'.[114]

A crucial part of the empathy elicited by these images is an invitation to share the emotion of the depicted figure. The facial expressions and bodily postures of the figures depicted convey an affective dimension which is crucial for appreciating the narrative. (I explore the empirical findings surrounding emotional contagion in the next section.) Analysing an intimate close-up of the figure of Christ carrying the cross, Rudy comments: 'Supplementing the physical proximity is a psychological one: Christ and one of the angels looks plaintively out of the picture. They exude grief. Such images promote the viewer's empathy'.[115] The visual culture associated with the emotional highs and lows of Holy Week is a particularly poignant example of viewers being invited to enter into Christ's betrayal and suffering, Mary's sorrow, and the fear, joy, and surprise of the resurrection. It is by

---

[108] Kathryn M. Rudy, 'Virtual Pilgrimage through the Jerusalem Cityscape', in *Visual Constructs of Jerusalem*, ed. Bianca Kühnel, Galit Noga-Banai, and Hanna Vorholt (Turnhout, Belgium: Brepols, 2014).
[109] Ibid., 384.   [110] Ibid.   [111] Ibid., 381.   [112] Ibid., 387.
[113] Ibid., 388.   [114] Ibid., 381.   [115] Ibid., 388.

no means the only context for emotion-laden imagery, as the emotive force of so many biblical narratives is conveyed in visual culture.

Beyond specific works of art, the practice of reflecting upon the passion scenes in the station of the cross during Holy Week provides a more general example of virtual pilgrimage. In this practice participants circumambulate a church building to reflect on fourteen scenes from Christ's journey to the cross. The physical aspect of this practice differentiates it from simply listening to a retelling of the passion narrative. Again, participants become onlookers to Christ's journey, and are often invited to take up the perspective of various characters in the narrative. Moreover, the practice maps the *via dolorosa*, Christ's journey to the cross, onto the space of a church building, forging associations between space, narrative, memory, and emotive responses.

These examples highlight how visual culture is far from simply decorative. The visual media are significant scaffolds for cognition: aiding memory, evoking emotion, guiding attention, structuring practices. In line with the replacement hypothesis, the cognition involved in religious practices is not simply brain-bound contemplation; rather it relies on interaction with images.

3.4 The Materiality of Texts

Christianity's rich textual tradition is one obvious way in which religious cognition can be offloaded. As mentioned, Clark proposes that language itself is more than a method of communication, but also functions as a cognitive scaffold.[116] There can be little doubt that texts provide important scaffolding for religious practices. Not only is theological thought codified in countless treatises, but much of cultic life is accompanied by textual aides: prayer books include liturgical text and rubrics for ritual instruction; books of hours provide texts for personal piety; other devotional manuals instruct practitioners. Given the variations in liturgy owing to the various feast days and seasons of the liturgical calendar, it is difficult to store all liturgical formulations required through the year in biological memory. Textual records provide an indispensable scaffold for biological memory.

As scholars of the history of the book have stressed, these codices (and other media) are far more than merely repositories for linguistic content; they are important physical objects in their own right. Their materiality can reveal a great deal about their construction, provenance, and history of usage. To return to Rudy's work, the significance of the materiality of texts can be clearly recognised in the case of medieval manuscripts. Rudy examines medieval manuscripts, not primarily for the text they contain, but for the 'dirt' and other markings they have

---

[116] Clark, *Being There*, 193. Cf. Deacon, *Symbolic Species*.

accrued that provide clues about their usage patterns. She has pioneered scientific methods of quantifying the relative amounts of dirt, which indexes usage, on various parts of a manuscript.[117]

One of the ways in which votaries interacted with their manuscripts was through kissing and rubbing. Rudy argues that form of interacting with manuscripts is related to the practice of using the *pax*, a liturgical object which the priest kissed and then displayed or circulated for others to kiss.[118] Congregants then kissed the *pax* themselves as it circulated (or viewed it on an altar) instead of directly greeting the priest with a kiss during the passing of the peace. The laity extended this practice to their personal devotion, including the kissing of manuscripts: 'The rituals of the Christian liturgy required that priests interact with objects that were figured or painted to serve as referents to things outside themselves. Congregants imitated priests in their private devotional rituals, including but not limited to kissing the pax.'[119]

Rudy documents how manuscripts show signs for wear from kissing or rubbing with the fingers.[120] These actions left tell-tale signs of wear and dirt on portions of texts or parts of images, to the extent that parts of manuscripts were 'obliterated' from repeated usage. This form of usage was so common that the construction of manuscripts was adapted to allow for it: 'Illuminators realized that priests would wear down the image with repeated use, so they painted small crosses at the bottom of the page to denote the place where the priest should aim his lips. In this example, the priest has indeed kissed the osculatory tablet, but has also slipped his lips upward and kissed the body on the cross, as well as the foot of the cross, depositing grease from his nose.'[121]

Usage pattern on manuscripts can reveal a great deal about their owners. Rudy points to examples where some figures were rubbed or kissed, but not others. In one case, she even tentatively draws conclusions about the marital life of a couple who owned a manuscript produced in the Southern Netherlands shortly after 1460:

> Neither of [the owners] kissed or touched the image of St Wilgefortis, who is shown crucified in a floor-length gown with an ermine stole and a full beard...Believers, especially women who found themselves in unhappy marriages, venerated St Wilgefortis. Thus, we might cautiously surmise that the couple who owned this particular manuscript had various anxieties and problems, but that a bad marriage

---

[117] Kathryn M. Rudy, 'Dirty Books: Quantifying Patterns of Use in Medieval Manuscripts Using a Densitometer', *Journal of Historians of Netherlandish Art* 2, no. 1–2 (2010).
[118] Kathryn M. Rudy, 'Kissing Images, Unfurling Rolls, Measuring Wounds, Sewing Badges and Carrying Talismans: Considering Some Harley Manuscripts through the Physical Rituals They Reveal', *Electronic British Library Journal* (2011): 1.
[119] Ibid., 2.   [120] Ibid., 21–30.   [121] Ibid., 21.

did not top the list. The images that are uncharacteristically undamaged can be as telling as those that are heavily rubbed.[122]

In this example, the materiality of the manuscript reveals a great deal about its owners' pattern of devotion.

Although not universal, kissing and hand-to-hand contact are common embodiments of intimacy (erotic or otherwise) in many cultures. This is not an arbitrary cultural association, but is underpinned by the biological particularities of the human body. In particular, the tongue and lips, together with hands and fingers, have among the highest nerve density of any body part, and thus a larger corresponding area in the sensorimotor cortex.[123] Given that kissing on the lips and hand holding therefore allow for the highest levels of sensory stimulation exchanged between two people, it is hardly surprising that it is a common form of expressing intimacy.

The biologically grounded intimacy of kissing and hand rubbing is also exploited by religious practices which use this bodily means of contact. I have already discussed technologies such as rosaries, which involve tactile interaction. In addition to the kissing of the *pax* and manuscripts, kissing is deployed in a number of other ecclesial practices: Eastern Orthodox Christians typically kiss icons when they enter a church and during the course of the liturgy; in the Good Friday liturgy participants kiss a crucifix; a deacon kisses the gospel text before reading it.[124] These actions signify intimacy in part because of the kinds of bodies humans have.

Rudy also points to many other ways in which people interacted with manuscripts: 'owners who treated their manuscript prayer books as objects of physical devotion often both *added* and *subtracted* material. They added small prints, curtains, pilgrims' badges, extra prayers, and notes about the family; they subtracted paint and ink in the course of using, kissing, and rubbing'.[125] The sewing of circular badges into manuscripts was an expression of Eucharistic piety.[126]

---

[122] Ibid., 30.

[123] Wilder Penfield and Edwin Boldrey, 'Somatic Motor and Sensory Representation in the Cerebral Cortex of Man as Studied by Electrical Stimulation', *Brain* 60, no. 4 (1937). The somatotopic arrangement of the motor cortex has been known for a long time, having been first discovered by early neurologists stimulating freshly severed spinal cords after the introduction of the guillotine into France after the revolution; see, comment by Pulvermüller Andreas Knoblauch, 'Symbols and Embodiment from the Perspective of a Neural Modeller', in *Symbols and Embodiment: Debates on Meaning and Cognition*, ed. Manuel De Vega, Arthur M. Glenberg, and Arthur C. Graesser (Oxford: Oxford University Press, 2008), 141.

[124] Cf. Romans 16:16; 1 Corinthians 16:20; 2 Corinthians 13:12; 1 Thessalonians 5:26; 1 Peter 5:14.

[125] Rudy, 'Kissing Images', 4.

[126] Kathryn M. Rudy, 'Sewing the Body of Christ: Eucharist Wafer Souvenirs Stitched into Fifteenth-Century Manuscripts, Primarily in the Netherlands', *Journal of Historians of Netherlandish Art* 8, no. 1 (2016).

Another means of altering a manuscript was to sew a curtain over a particular image.[127] Some extant manuscripts still have their curtains intact, while others have needle holes suggesting they once had curtains. Rudy observes that this manuscript alteration illuminates its ritual usage: 'Having to lift a curtain before contemplating the image would have added a layer of physicality and ritual to the process of reading and looking, and it would have put the votary into a specific haptic relationship with the manuscript'.[128]

Other explicit cues in manuscripts betray that they were ritual objects. For example, some texts include 'formulas littered with crosses, indicating that the reader was to cross himself repeatedly while reading them, and thus turn the act of reading into a physical ritual'.[129] This practice persists in some modern-day prayer books. The reading of these books is far more than a transfer of information; rather the books are but a facet of a broader ritual practice.

Rudy's work on manuscripts has two important implications for the present project. First, it shows that ritual objects, with their particular affordances and signs of usage, can be used to reconstruct ritual practices. As Rudy remarks, '[w]hile rituals can be difficult to reconstruct...Occasionally signs of wear on ritual objects themselves reveal how they were used. Manuscripts in particular often hold signs of wear, including dirt, fingerprints, smudges, and needle holes, which index some of the physical rituals they have witnessed'.[130] Insofar as objects such as manuscripts allow rituals to be reconstructed, embodied cognition can be applied to illuminate the cognitive effects of ritual action such as kissing.

Second, Rudy's work demonstrates that these material texts were about far more than conveying information to their owners; they were objects of profound and intimate *interaction*. The replacement hypothesis alerts us to the possibility that prayer may be far broader than merely a linguistic formulation directed towards God; for the owners of the manuscripts Rudy examines, prayer is an interactive exercise which happens *between* the votary and their manuscript. More than simply being an 'input' into a votary's prayer, one might suggest that the manuscript constituted their particular form of prayer. In the absence of the manuscripts, the kind of prayer in which these votaries engage would simply not be possible.

The significance of the materiality of texts is not restricted to Rudy's medieval Netherlandish examples, illuminating as this case study is. A survey of all extant Greek biblical texts, from late antiquity until about the end of the first millennium CE, reveals that the largest number of texts are not preserved in the form of manuscripts but amulets.[131] Early Christians took over (and adapted) early

---

[127]   Rudy, 'Kissing Images', 10–14.   [128]   Ibid., 10.   [129]   Ibid., 51.
[130]   Ibid., 1.
[131]   Correspondence with Jeremiah Coogan; see also Theodore S. de Bruyn and Jitse H. F. Dijkstra, 'Greek Amulets and Formularies from Egypt Containing Christian Elements: A Checklist of Papyri, Parchments, Ostraka, and Tablets', *The Bulletin of the American Society of Papyrologists* 48 (2011).

traditions in which 'incantations', texts entreating supernatural powers to 'heal, protect, constrain or avenge', were placed into amulets to confer benefits on its wearer.[132] Biblical texts in the early church were not merely documents to be read and studied, they were also material objects to be worn on the body or affixed to places.[133]

3.5 Multisensory Stimuli

Thus far I have focused on visual and haptic stimuli created by material culture. Religious rituals, however, are far more multisensory affairs. As Robert McCauley observes, '[s]ome religious rituals are renowned for their sensory pageantry. Rituals employ countless means of arousing participants' emotions. No sensory modality has been neglected. Religious rituals are replete with the smells of burning incense and the tastes of special foods, the sounds of chanting and the sights of ornate attire, the kinesthetic sensations of the dancer and the haptic sensations of the fully immersed'.[134] In this section I consider the cognitive effects of the other sensory stimuli, such as sound, smell, taste, and attire in ritual.

3.5.1 Music and Sound

Music is a common ingredient of ecclesial practices. It has long been intuitively held that various types of music have the capacity to elicit different emotions, with film scores being an obvious example. Most listeners will immediately recognise the affective difference between a funeral dirge and a triumphant Easter hymn. Empirical studies have borne out this connection and shown that music can modulate affective states in listeners.[135] For example, one study surveyed 800 crying episodes experienced by 331 North American adults, and found that 8 per cent of these episodes were triggered by music.[136] Beyond individual pieces of music being associated with particular emotions, a study found that particular characteristics of music modulated emotion in specific ways: '[m]ajor keys, non-harmonized melodies, and faster tempos were associated with

---

[132] Theodore S. de Bruyn, *Making Amulets Christian: Artefacts, Scribes, and Contexts* (Oxford: Oxford University Press, 2017), 2.

[133] Ibid., 167.

[134] Robert N. McCauley, 'Ritual, Memory, and Emotion: Comparing Two Cognitive Hypotheses', in *Religion in Mind: Cognitive Perspectives on Religious Belief, Ritual and Experience*, ed. Jensine Andresen (Cambridge: Cambridge University Press, 2001), 118.

[135] For a summary of available studies, see John A. Sloboda, *Exploring the Musical Mind: Cognition, Emotion, Ability, Function* (Oxford: Oxford University Press, 2005), 203–24. Cf. Baker et al., 'Religion in the Age of Social Distancing', 364.

[136] William H. Frey and Muriel Langseth, *Crying: The Mystery of Tears* (Minneapolis, MN: Winston Press, 1985).

happier responses, whereas their respective opposites were associated with sadder responses'.[137]

The emotional effect of music can lead to other flow-on effects. A study found that manipulating the mood of participants with music they found happy or sad resulted in changes in visual perception.[138] Participants were more accurate in identifying happy and sad faces among noise if the face was consistent with their mood. Hence the emotional effect of music and other emotional triggers in religious rituals have the capacity to change the way we perceive the world.

Diverging traditions of music have resulted in 'sacred' and 'secular' categorisations. Since music associated with religion is distinctive, it can be used to prime religiosity. One study found that playing instrumental religious music (as opposed to instrumental secular music or white noise) to participants decreased the rate of cheating, but only in religious participants.[139] Music can therefore function as a non-verbal cue which primes religiosity (in the initiated). Furthermore, it is an example of religious priming increasing prosocial behaviour.[140]

Beyond that which would commonly be classified as music, other aspects of the soundscape prime religiosity. Two studies have found that participants in the Middle East increased prosocial behaviour when there was an audible Islamic call to prayer in the background.[141] This finding may well extend to sounds closely associated with Christian worship, such as the tolling of church bells.

3.5.2 Olfactory Cues

Smells are yet another environmental condition which can trigger memories.[142] A study of older adults asked participants to recall autobiographical events when prompted by a word, picture, or odour.[143] It found that olfactory stimuli triggered memories from earlier in life (typically the first decade of life), whereas visual and verbal cues evoked more memories from early adulthood. Moreover, odour-triggered memories 'were associated with stronger feelings of being brought back in time and had been thought of less often than memories evoked by verbal and

---

[137] Gregory D. Webster and Catherine G. Weir, 'Emotional Responses to Music: Interactive Effects of Mode, Texture, and Tempo', *Motivation and Emotion* 29, no. 1 (2005): 19.

[138] Jacob Jolij and Maaike Meurs, 'Music Alters Visual Perception', *PLOS ONE* 6, no. 4 (2011).

[139] Martin Lang et al., 'Music as a Sacred Cue? Effects of Religious Music on Moral Behavior', *Frontiers in Psychology* 7, no. 814 (2016).

[140] For a review, including a meta-analysis of ninety-three studies, see Shariff et al., 'Religious Priming'.

[141] Erik P. Duhaime, 'Is the Call to Prayer a Call to Cooperate? A Field Experiment on the Impact of Religious Salience on Prosocial Behavior', *Judgment and Decision Making* 10, no. 6 (2015); Mark E. Aveyard, 'A Call to Honesty: Extending Religious Priming of Moral Behavior to Middle Eastern Muslims', *PLOS ONE* 9, no. 7 (2014).

[142] For a review, see Frank R. Schab, 'Odor Memory: Taking Stock', *Psychological Bulletin* 109, no. 2 (1991).

[143] Johan Willander and Maria Larsson, 'Smell Your Way Back to Childhood: Autobiographical Odor Memory', *Psychonomic Bulletin & Review* 13, no. 2 (2006).

visual information'.[144] This finding suggests that smell is able to excavate more deep-seated memories. Religious rituals exploit this connection by using distinctive odours. The smell of burning candles and incense often permeates church buildings. The connection between smell and memory suggests that this can evoke memories of attending church services that stretch back to childhood.

Incense has also been found to have psychoactive effects. A study found that burning and inhaling frankincense (*boswellia* resin) results in a feeling of warmth and a positive affective modulation.[145] The researchers concluded incense can contribute to 'the euphoric feeling produced during religious functions, due to both positive, presumably mild, emotional effects and the sensation of warmth'.[146] A neuroimaging study provided further evidence of the psychoactive nature of incense, finding that it enhances cortical activities.[147] Incense is often reserved for high masses or festivals. The cognitive effect of incense therefore directly communicates the heightened sense of joy associated with these occasions.

3.5.3 Clothing

Formal liturgies typically involve celebrants, servers, and choirs wearing particular vestments commensurate with their roles. At the most basic level, vestments have certain affordances, restricting the kinds of movements which the wearer may perform. Typically heavy garments encourage slower, more deliberate movements, and garments such as cassocks can restrict one's gait and make movements such as running difficult. A study found that altering affordances can change one's perception such that the cost of action is factored into account; for example, wearing a heavy backpack made slopes appear steeper.[148] The constraints imposed by vestments may have subtle effects on perception; that possibility notwithstanding, they certainly encourage measured movements associated with dignified solemnity.

The wearing of clothing also has (other) cognitive effects. One study found that, since scientists and doctors are associated with attentiveness and carefulness, wearing a lab coat increased performance in attention-related tasks.[149] Crucially, the increase in attention only occurred when the participants were actually wearing the coat, and not simply when it was being displayed; this demonstrates that the coat was not merely functioning as a perceptual prime, but the

[144] Ibid., 240.

[145] Arieh Moussaieff et al., 'Incensole Acetate, an Incense Component, Elicits Psychoactivity by Activating TRPV3 Channels in the Brain', *The FASEB Journal* 22, no. 8 (2008).

[146] Ibid., 3033.

[147] M. Iijima et al., 'Effects of Incense on Brain Function: Evaluation Using Electroencephalograms and Event-Related Potentials', *Neuropsychobiology* 59, no. 2 (2009).

[148] Mukul Bhalla and Dennis R. Proffitt, 'Visual-Motor Recalibration in Geographical Slant Perception', *Journal of Experimental Psychology: Human Perception & Performance* 25, no. 4 (1999).

[149] Hajo Adam and Adam D. Galinsky, 'Enclothed Cognition', *Journal of Experimental Social Psychology* 48, no. 4 (2012): 918.

embodied act of wearing it had a direct effect. Participants who were told that the same garment was a painter's smock did not have the same reaction when they wore it. The researchers concluded that both the physical act of wearing the coat and its symbolic pertinence (i.e., the lab coat connoting attentiveness) generated the cognitive effect.

These findings suggest that vestments not only convey the symbolic meanings with which they are associated with to observers, but also influence the cognitive process of those wearing them. The kinds of cognitive effects would then depend on the rich symbolic connotations of vestments and their close association with theologies of priesthood and sacraments. More broadly, wearing vestments may facilitate the activation of a psychological script (a set of behaviours considered appropriate to a given context, such as going to a restaurant), thereby putting its wearer into a liturgical mindset.[150]

3.5.4 Food Consumption

Religious practices often accompany the consumption of food and drink, and such acts of consumption are sometimes embedded in religious practices.[151] As everyday experience attests, being hungry and consuming food modulate emotions.[152] (Conversely, emotional states affect eating practices.)[153] Consistent with the role of emotion in decision making, one study famously raised questions about the impartiality of the justice system when it found that parole judges were far more lenient immediately after their meal breaks than before them.[154] Alcohol consumption also has well known emotional and social effects, such as dampening fear and reducing inhibitions.[155] These effects facilitate social bonding by encouraging self-disclosure.

The Eucharist has its origins in a meal. The physical consumption of the Eucharistic elements adds both tactile and gustatory elements to worship. Although not part of the formal liturgical practices, church communities regularly engage in the ritual practices of sharing meals or consumption of tea and

---

[150] Robert J. Sternberg and Jeffery Scott Mio, *Cognitive Psychology*, 5th ed. (Belmont, CA: Wadsworth, 2009), 309–11.

[151] A lack of consumption, namely fasting, is also an embodied practice in a number of religious traditions. Short-term fasting can affect cognitive function, impairing problem-solving skills; see Ernesto Pollitt et al., 'Fasting and Cognitive Function', *Journal of Psychiatric Research* 17, no. 2 (1982). Theological treatments of fasting typically focus on its ascetic nature. To my knowledge, little has been done to investigate the cognitive effects of long-term fasting in connection with the religious understandings of fasting.

[152] Y. Jiang, J. M. King, and W. Prinyawiwatkul, 'A Review of Measurement and Relationships between Food, Eating Behavior and Emotion', *Trends in Food Science & Technology* 36, no. 1 (2014); Michael Macht and G. Simons, 'Emotions and Eating in Everyday Life', *Appetite* 35, no. 1 (2000).

[153] Michael Macht, 'How Emotions Affect Eating: A Five-Way Model', *Appetite* 50, no. 1 (2008).

[154] Shai Danziger, Jonathan Levav, and Liora Avnaim-Pesso, 'Extraneous Factors in Judicial Decisions', *Proceedings of the National Academy of Sciences* 108, no. 17 (2011).

[155] John J. Curtin et al., 'Alcohol Affects Emotion through Cognition', *Psychological Science* 12, no. 6 (2001).

biscuits. While these practices are easily overlooked, they often play an important function in a community's social life. All of these gustatory practices may be cognitively salient insofar as they generate the effects identified in the aforementioned studies.

3.6 Towards a Cognitive Theory of Ritual

As the preceding survey shows, rituals deploy diverse material artefacts to create multisensory stimuli, and these have numerous cognitive effects, with emotion and memory being recurring themes. Whitehouse has developed an influential cognitive theory of ritual which draws connections between these elements.[156] His theory attempts to account for the diversity of rituals, especially the fact that some rituals are intense and emotion-laden, while others are less so. He categorises rituals according to a cultural-evolutionary framework.[157] For the knowledge of how to execute a ritual to be retained by individuals, and transferred to new initiates, rituals must be memorable. As a package of cultural information, memorability determines a ritual's survival and reproduction (in new participants). Whitehouse proposes two classes of ritual which use different strategies to achieve memorability.

On the one hand, 'doctrinal' rituals primarily rely on repetition to imprint themselves in memory. Hence they are performed frequently, on say a daily or weekly basis. Not all rituals, however, can rely on frequent repetition. Rituals which are performed less frequently—such as annual celebrations or initiations which may be once-in-a-lifetime events—thus require another mechanism to achieve memorability. Whitehouse dubs such rituals 'imagistic'. He argues that imagistic rituals rely on the interaction of emotion and memory to achieve memory.[158] Heightened emotions can lead to the formation of longer-lasting memories. In particular, intense emotional experience can lead to the creation of a special class of memories known as flashbulb memories.[159] McCauley explains, '[f]lashbulb memories are memories for particular episodes that seem startlingly vivid and accurate, such as most older Americans' recollections about how they heard about President Kennedy's assassination'.[160] Thus, '[s]ome religious rituals

---

[156] Harvey Whitehouse, 'Cognitive Evolution and Religion; Cognition and Religious Evolution', *Issues in Ethnology and Anthropology* 3, no. 3 (2008): 41–4.

[157] Harvey Whitehouse, *Modes of Religiosity: A Cognitive Theory of Religious Transmission* (Walnut Creek, CA: Altamira Press, 2004).

[158] However, as McCauley notes, most religious systems emerged among largely illiterate populations for whom this was not an option; see McCauley, 'Ritual', 115.

[159] Ulric Neisser and Eugene Winograd, *Affect and Accuracy in Recall: Studies of 'Flashbulb' Memories* (Cambridge: Cambridge University Press, 1992).

[160] McCauley, 'Ritual', 116.

capitalize on many of the prominent variables that contribute to extraordinary episodic memory that psychological science has uncovered'.[161]

As noted earlier, there are many mechanisms by which a ritual can heighten emotion. McCauley summarises many of these by describing the emotional effect of an assault on the senses: 'Stimulating ritual participants' senses is the most straightforward, sure-fire means available for arousing their emotions. The intuition is that the resulting levels of emotional excitement are often at least roughly proportional to the levels of sensory stimulation a ritual contains. These emotional responses are virtually always involuntary, and with particularly intense sensory stimulation, they are difficult to control.'[162] Thus, in the case of 'imagistic' rituals, causal connections are made from multisensory stimuli to emotion, and from emotion to memory.

Whitehouse's theory cannot account for every aspect of rituals, and focuses only on a handful of variables such as frequency, arousal levels, and memorability. However, it helpfully binds together many cognitive effects found in embodied cognition studies, suggesting an interplay between sensory stimulation, emotion, and memory. One of its limitations, however, is to focus on rituals sustained by biological memory, thus neglecting memory scaffolds such as ritual manuals.

3.7 Conclusion: Material Religion

Embodied cognition studies reveal that religious material culture has a whole host of cognitive effects, and it houses and conveys important theological knowledge and attitudes by virtue of these effects. Although this content may be more subtle and inchoate than the semantic content of texts, it nevertheless shapes religious practitioners.

One important cognitive function of religious material culture is to aid memory. This insight is consistent with the constitution hypothesis, which suggests that memory can be offloaded onto external media. I have surveyed how objects, images, and places can all be used to trigger memory in religious contexts, evoking narratives, ideas, and past experiences. These mechanisms supplement the findings discussed in the previous section, which suggest that body posture and facial expressions also facilitate memory recall. Retrieving such memories is thus context dependent, since when the conditions or cues in the retrieval setting are similar to the original event memory recall is faster. Such findings have led to the development of an encoding specificity theory of memory.[163] Much like the

---

[161] Ibid.   [162] Ibid., 118.
[163] Dijkstra, Kaschak, and Zwaan, 'Body Posture Facilitates Retrieval', 140–1; John H. Riskind, 'Nonverbal Expressions and the Accessibility of Life Experience Memories: A Congruence Hypothesis', *Social Cognition* 2, no. 1 (1983).

modal theory of concepts considered in Part II, this theory proposes that memories are not stored in abstract language-like structures, but consist in sensorimotor states which are simulated upon recall. Findings about memory recall are 'consistent with a view that conceptualizes cognitive processes as an integral part of the sensorimotor environment in which memory for a stimulus or event is stored in the cognitive machinery that processed it'.[164] Situational factors clearly play a role in the cognitive process of memory retrieval.

Memory, however, may be too narrow a category to capture all the effects of material aspects of religion; for memory implies the 'recording' of previously experienced episodes. However, the material aspects of religious practices also provide particular physical constraints which shape the behaviour of participants, even if they are first-time participants (and therefore not simply using material objects to retrieve a memory). Moreover, material objects can trigger emotions, direct attention, give shape to prayers, and evoke behavioural scripts. Given these capacities, material culture *teaches* participants aspects of the faith. The use of 'teach' may seem overly ambitious, since it implies that the objects and places themselves have theological content to convey. However, this is precisely the line I wish to develop in Chapter 7. Material culture, in this view, is not merely a tool which allows individuals to offload their memory, but rather a repository which holds the corporate memory of a tradition.

The material dimension often supports and supplements other aspects of religion. Materiality becomes more prominent, however, when it is at odds with other dimensions. Schaefer cites an example of someone who describes herself as a 'vehement atheist' and yet finds religious objects such as a crucifix meaningful. He observes that '[t]his disjuncture between her declared atheism and her religiosity suggests that the material properties of the object were sitting transversally to the linguistic framework of her religious identity'.[165] To simply take this person's self-report at face value would be to gloss over a co-present religiosity which attaches to material objects.

Similarly, other scholars have pointed to the way in which religious places and objects retain some of their potency even when transferred to a different context. Davison and Milbank observe that 'there is something quite uncompromising about a church building. Even when converted into a nightclub or a bijou residence, it speaks of values that are other. There is no faith anywhere without a concept of sacred places'.[166] Findings from embodied cognition research, such as the capacity for religious buildings to prime religion, provide clues as to why the associations with sacred places persist even when their official function has changed. It is not merely the function of a place which evokes religious associations, but the history and materiality of sacred spaces primes such associations.

---

[164] Dijkstra, Kaschak, and Zwaan, 'Body Posture Facilitates Retrieval', 140.
[165] Schaefer, *Religious Affects*, 110.   [166] Davison and Milbank, *For the Parish*, 156.

Likewise, Berns conducted ethnographic research on visitors to the 'Treasures of Heaven: Saints, Relics and Devotion in Medieval Europe' exhibition at the British Museum, which brought together various manifestations of religious material culture such as reliquaries and icons.[167] She observed that some visitors interacted with the objects as they would in more typical religious settings. For example, one teenage visitor held up a crucifix she was wearing to the cases containing reliquaries, as if to make a contact relic. Another visitor would pay the entrance fee to the exhibition on a weekly basis to come and pray in front of one of the icons. Museum staff reported having to clean the transparent display cases more frequently than usual, on account of the number of visitors who touched or kissed them.[168] Some theorists have proposed that once an object is taken out of its original context and placed in a museum it becomes a 'dead' object; it is only observed at a distance and no longer subject to interaction.[169] Berns' research calls into question the definitiveness of that transition. Even as 'museum pieces' the religious objects retain a residual potency.

These three brief examples demonstrate the salience of religious material culture operating independently of context, function, or explicit belief. They also suggest that the significance of the cognitive effects of religious material culture are easily overlooked when more tractable and explicit textual accounts are available. Embodied cognition studies illuminate the often-subconscious influence of religious material culture and identify its precise effects.

4 Social Engagement

Beyond an individual's movements and interactions with objects and environments, rituals are often *social* activities in which interaction with other agents is crucial. The social dimension of rituals is significant from a cognitive perspective, and cognitive science has much to say about the social nature of cognition.[170] Cognitive scientists have pointed out that the evolutionary development of the human brain and many cognitive functions are shaped by the invariably social nature of almost all human life.[171]

---

[167] Steph Berns, 'Sacred Entanglements: Studying Interactions between Visitors, Objects and Religion in the Museum', (University of Kent, 2015). For an evaluation including visitor responses, see Morris Hargreaves McIntyre, 'Art, Spirituality and Power': An Evaluation of Treasures of Heaven: Saints, Relics and Devotion in Medieval Europe at the British Museum, (British Museum, 2011).

[168] Personal correspondence with James Robinson, *Treasures of Heaven* exhibition curator.

[169] Theodor W. Adorno, 'Valery Proust Museum', in *Prisms* (London: Neville Spearman, 1967).

[170] E.g., see Ziva Kunda, *Social Cognition: Making Sense of People* (Cambridge, MA: MIT Press, 1999).

[171] For an evolutionary account, see Robin I. M. Dunbar, 'The Social Brain Hypothesis', *Evolutionary Anthropology: Issues, News, and Reviews* 6, no. 5 (1998). For a review of neuroscientific evidence, see Ralph Adolphs, 'The Social Brain: Neural Basis of Social Knowledge', *Annual Review of Psychology* 60 (2009).

4.1 Social Emotion

Although emotions can be experienced in solitude, they also have an important social dimension. Emotions are communicated in a number of ways, many of them non-verbal. As Schaefer observes, '[t]he channels of [the transmission of affect] can be olfactory (the wafting of hormones through the air), tactile, sonic (tones of voice, volume, rhythm), or visual (images, bodily postures, facial expressions)'.[172] For instance, a study also found that observers used a slumped posture as a cue for judging that others were depressed or helpless.[173] Emotions can thus be 'read' off particular expressions and postures.

To say that emotion is 'communicated' may, however, give a false impression. It is not necessarily the case that one person, having consciously recognised another's emotional state through various bodily cues, then decides how respond to such emotional information. Rather, emotions are often transmitted beneath the threshold of consciousness. The most notable example of subconscious emotional transmission is the case of 'emotional contagion', in which one person involuntarily mimics the emotion of another. Both crying and laughter can be contagious, transferring automatically without conscious effort. A developmental study, for example, found that infants exposed to the sound of another infant crying manifested distress in both their vocalisations and facial expressions.[174] The finding held for infants aged one, three, six, and nine months, and did not decrease with age. Similar contagion effects have been found in adults.[175]

The unconscious transfer of emotion need not be as obvious as laughter or crying. For example, a study measured peoples' facial responses and emotional self-reports when watching a video of others expressing emotions.[176] Even though this footage contained 'relatively realistic, low intensity, idiosyncratic emotional facial expressions',[177] it nevertheless found evidence that participants mimicked facial expressions for happiness, anger, and sadness and that these emotions exhibited contagion effects. If the facial-feedback hypothesis is correct, and smiling triggers, or at least modulates, happiness, then this would suggest mimicry of facial expressions also influences emotional experience.

In addition to direct mimicry, social settings are sufficient to heighten emotion. One study measured participants' facial reactions to movies in solitary and

---

[172] Schaefer, *Religious Affects*, 65–6.   [173] Riskind and Gotay, 'Physical Posture', 283–5.

[174] E. Geangu et al., 'Contagious Crying Beyond the First Days of Life', *Infant Behavior Development* 33, no. 3 (2010).

[175] Sigal G. Barsade, 'The Ripple Effect: Emotional Contagion and Its Influence on Group Behavior', *Administrative Science Quarterly* 47, no. 4 (2002).

[176] Ursula Hess and Sylvie Blairy, 'Facial Mimicry and Emotional Contagion to Dynamic Emotional Facial Expressions and Their Influence on Decoding Accuracy', *International Journal of Psychophysiology* 40, no. 2 (2001).

[177] Ibid., 138.

social settings.[178] It found that participants had more intense, frequent, and longer facial expressions for positive emotions when they watched films with a friend, as opposed to with a stranger or alone. A similar study found that participants watching a movie smiled more if a friend was in the room watching with them, or even if they believed a friend was watching the same movie in another room, than if they were alone.[179] Emotions, then, are an important part of social interaction; people frequently have the desire to share emotions, and emotional feedback from others influences our own emotional experience.[180]

The social nature of emotion is no doubt operative in communal embodied religious practices. As worshippers come face-to-face they are liable to transmit emotions to one another (see Section 6). As they jointly focus on various aspects of a ritual they are likely to bolster one another's emotions, as was the case with movie-watchers in social emotion studies. Worshippers share in the emotional repertoire of worship, which varies during the mass—for example, contrition during the confession shifting to exuberant praise during the Gloria—and throughout the liturgical year. Emotional contagion facilitates solidarity among gathered worshippers, allowing them to 'rejoice with those who rejoice, weep with those who weep'.[181]

The social dimension of emotion does not require the physical presence of other people. As explored in Section 3.3, religious images convey emotion. This is part of the social nature of emotion. The perceptibility of emotion through facial expression and body posture accounts for our ability to 'read' emotions in images depicting other people. Thus the emotional comportments of figures inscribed in glass, stone, wood, and canvas all have the capacity to transmit emotional content to those who view them.

Emotions can also be conveyed through narratives, whether they are depicted in images or texts. Emotions elicited by narratives have been shown to have physical symptoms and cognitive implications. In particular, a group of researchers found that 'both pain threshold and sense of bondedness to the group increase after watching an emotionally arousing film, but not after watching films that have no emotional content'.[182] They conclude that watching the film activated endorphins, which are known to increase one's pain threshold. Furthermore, the reaction to the movie also had important social implications: 'this increase in pain threshold is associated with a heightened sense of belonging to the group

[178] Ying Jiang, 'Measuring Facial Expression and Emotional Experience under Diverse Social Context in a Negative Emotional Setting' (paper presented at the Measuring Behavior: 9th International Conference on Methods and Techniques in Behavioral Research Wageningen, The Netherlands 2014).

[179] Alan J. Fridlund, 'Sociality of Solitary Smiling: Potentiation by an Implicit Audience', *Journal of Personality & Social Psychology* 60, no. 2 (1991).

[180] Schilbach et al., 'Second-Person Neuroscience', 396–7.   [181] Romans 12:15.

[182] R. I. M. Dunbar et al., 'Emotional Arousal When Watching Drama Increases Pain Threshold and Social Bonding', *Royal Society Open Science* 3, no. 9 (2016): 8.

(group bonding)'.[183] They suggest that, in addition to narratives conveyed by films, these findings extend to all forms of emotional storytelling, 'both to listening to stories as well as watching filmed or staged dramas, whenever doing so arouses a strong emotional response'.[184] The implication for Christian practices is clear. Biblical narratives read in the context of such practices are laden with emotional content; one need only briefly sketch the passion and resurrection narratives at the centre of the gospels to appreciate that they are replete with betrayal, suffering, compassion, sorrow, joy, surprise, shock, fear, amazement, among a much wider emotional repertoire. Moreover, these stories are not merely read out, but are also told and enacted in stained glass windows, altar pieces, nativity and passion plays, the liturgy of the stations of the cross, and, of course, the Eucharist.

4.2 Synchronised Movement and Social Bonding

There is a growing body of literature which shows that synchronous movement increases social bonding.[185] One study found that synchronised movement increased a sense of affiliation, with participants who tapped their fingers in time with an experimenter finding them more likeable.[186] Another study found that participants who performed synchronised activities demonstrated enhanced memory for the utterances and faces of their activity partners, an essential prerequisite for social bonding.[187] Another study found that synchronised movement increased 'embodied rapport' as participants felt greater social closeness.[188] The study's authors suggest that the feelings of oneness created in such moments are an important building block for long-term social relations.

The effect of synchronised movement, however, goes beyond mere feelings of social belonging or interpersonal intimacy; these feelings can translate into prosocial behaviours (i.e., behaviours which benefit others, such as cooperation, generosity, etc.). As evolutionary theorists observe, 'social bonding is not an end in itself; by increasing solidarity, religion facilitates intragroup cooperation'.[189] One study found that strangers who performed synchronised actions were more likely to cooperate.[190] These results held for both synchronised activities involving

---

[183] Ibid., 9.   [184] Ibid., 10.

[185] Baker et al., 'Religion in the Age of Social Distancing', 364.

[186] Michael J. Hove and Jane L. Risen, 'It's All in the Timing: Interpersonal Synchrony Increases Affiliation', *Social Cognition* 27, no. 6 (2009).

[187] C. Neil Macrae et al., 'A Case of Hand Waving: Action Synchrony and Person Perception', *Cognition* 109, no. 1 (2008).

[188] Tanya Vacharkulksemsuk and Barbara L. Fredrickson, 'Strangers in Sync: Achieving Embodied Rapport through Shared Movements', *Journal of Experimental Social Psychology* 48, no. 1 (2012).

[189] Richard Sosis and Candace Alcorta, 'Signaling, Solidarity, and the Sacred: The Evolution of Religious Behavior', *Evolutionary Anthropology: Issues, News, and Reviews* 12, no. 6 (2003): 267.

[190] Scott S. Wiltermuth and Chip Heath, 'Synchrony and Cooperation', *Psychological Science* 20, no. 1 (2009).

gross muscle movements, such as walking in step, as well as those which did not, such as singing. Another study found that synchronised movement, this time rocking in chairs, not only increased participants' motivation to cooperate, but also increased their ability to cooperate on a joint task by improving their ability to coordinate movements with one another.[191] A study extended findings on synchrony by showing that prosocial attitudes also extended to those who had not participated in synchronous movement and even outgroup members who were not present.[192]

Researchers have begun to probe beneath the effects of synchronicity to locate the underlying mechanism. One theory is that synchronised movement leads to 'sensorimotor representational overlap', since one's sensorimotor representations refer to the bodily states and movements of all synchronised participants.[193] Rubber hand experiments demonstrate that people can incorporate extracorporeal body parts, such as a rubber hand which visually appears to be their own, into their own body boundary.[194] Synchrony is one way to achieve this effect: a study found that participants whose cheeks were stroked with a paint brush whilst watching the same thing happening to a face in a video, 'blurred self-other conceptual boundaries'.[195] This blurring, it is hypothesised, facilitates group bonding.

Another potential mechanism is that many synchronised activities are part of a wider suite of activities which all activate endorphins. Researchers who studied responses to emotional narratives (discussed earlier) noted, 'storytelling should be seen as supplementing other social mechanisms (laughter, singing and dancing), all of which seem to have very similar endorphin activating properties and all of which enhance group social bonding'.[196]

Findings on synchronised movement have direct relevance for communal ritual practices, which often involve coordinated movement in time: 'Armies, churches, organizations, and communities often engage in activities—for example, marching, singing, and dancing—that lead group members to act in synchrony with each other'.[197] The ability of ritual to increase prosocial behaviours has been incorporated into evolutionary theories of religion. By fostering cooperation, rituals can avoid the free rider problem, in which some individuals benefit from a community without contributing to it.[198] The ability to reduce free riding makes a group more successful (all other things being equal), giving them

---

[191] Piercarlo Valdesolo, Jennifer Ouyang, and David DeSteno, 'The Rhythm of Joint Action: Synchrony Promotes Cooperative Ability', *Journal of Experimental Social Psychology* 46, no. 4 (2010).
[192] Paul Reddish et al., 'Collective Synchrony Increases Prosociality Towards Non-Performers and Outgroup Members', *British Journal of Social Psychology* 55, no. 4 (2016).
[193] Soliman, Johnson, and Song, 'Understanding Religion', 858.
[194] Matthew Botvinick and Jonathan Cohen, 'Rubber Hands "Feel" Touch That Eyes See', *Nature* 391, no. 6669 (1998).
[195] Maria-Paola Paladino et al., 'Synchronous Multisensory Stimulation Blurs Self-Other Boundaries', *Psychological Science* 21, no. 9 (2010).
[196] Dunbar et al., 'Emotional Arousal', 10.
[197] Wiltermuth and Heath, 'Synchrony and Cooperation', 1.   [198] Ibid., 5.

a group-selection advantage. Cooperation also allows for larger group sizes, which may also increase group fitness.[199]

The findings also have specific relevance to Christian ecclesial practices. One group of researchers observed that many activities which form part of church rituals involve synchrony: 'Group singing, swaying, kneeling, praying, reciting, applauding, and dancing can all require the congregation to synchronize their actions in space and time.'[200] This observation led them to suggest that '[s]tudies in which researchers investigated the effects of synchrony and joint-body schemas might partly explain why a periodic collective activity, such as a pilgrimage to Mecca or attending church on Sunday, is likely to lead to prosocial behaviour.'[201]

Studies have confirmed that church attendance does indeed increase prosociality. One study discovered a 'Sunday effect', which found that religious participants were more likely to donate on Sundays.[202] Another study refined this finding by investigating which aspect of Mass attendance fostered prosociality. It found that the social aspect of mass ('the feelings of cohesion and support developed by attending a collective ritual') correlated with prosociality, rather than positive emotions elicited by the mass or the 'cognitive' function of the mass (here defined as understanding and reflecting upon the meaning of explicit verbal contents, such as readings and sermons).[203] These studies achieve high ecologically validity by measuring the effects of actual church attendance, rather than a ritual or synchronised movement invented for a lab setting. They suggest that general findings about social bonding and prosociality from mechanisms such as synchronised movement are operative within live church settings. As the researchers conclude, this may well explain why 'for centuries, and across various religious traditions and cultures, religious temples are one of the (several but few) places where beggars wait for religious attendees to exit from their collective prayer.'[204] Hence the synchronised movements employed in rituals are about far more than achieving a pleasing aesthetic; they have significant effects on the interpersonal attitudes and behaviours required for a cohesive community.

4.3 Being Watched

Decisions are frequently subject to social influences. We constantly make predictions about how our peers might react to our actions, and make decisions based

---

[199] Robin I. M. Dunbar, 'The Origin of Religion as a Small-Scale Phenomenon', in *Religion, Intolerance, and Conflict: A Scientific and Conceptual Investigation*, ed. Steve Clarke, Russell Powell, and Julian Savulescu (Oxford: Oxford University Press, 2013).

[200] Soliman, Johnson, and Song, 'Understanding Religion', 857.   [201] Ibid., 858.

[202] Deepak Malhorta, '(When) Are Religious People Nicer? Religious Salience and the "Sunday Effect" on Pro-Social Behavior', *Judgment and Decision Making* 5, no. 2 (2010).

[203] Patty van Cappellen, Vassilis Saroglou, and Maria Toth-Gauthier, 'Religiosity and Prosocial Behavior among Churchgoers: Exploring Underlying Mechanisms', *The International Journal for the Psychology of Religion* 26, no. 1 (2016).

[204] Ibid.

on these anticipated responses. Many of these social cues are mediated by embodied behaviours. For example, retailers now routinely place pictures of eyes in their stores to deter shoplifters. This strategy is based on studies which found that placing a picture of eyes can increase cooperation and decrease dishonesty.[205] The effect extends not simply to being watched by another human being but also to representations of eyes.[206] This suggests that the influence of eyes results from a subconscious process rather than rational deliberation, since we know that a static picture of eyes does not constitute another human agent. These findings are consistent with evolutionary models of social interaction which propose that individuals behave so as to maintain their reputation amongst a group or to avoid punishment.[207] These findings again have implications for the effect of religious imagery. Religious figures in images, be they in windows, paintings, sculptures, or other forms, can have cognitive effects even though they are depictions rather than actual agents. Being surrounded by a 'cloud of saints', even if they are only visually depicted, has effects on moral behaviour.

5 Embodying Metaphors

In Chapter 3, I argued that concepts are grounded in sensorimotor states, and abstract concepts are often illuminated by concrete concepts from sensorimotor experience through 'cognitive metaphors'. These findings not only have significance for the nature of theological concepts, as I argued in Chapter 4, but they also have implications for how concepts are activated. For, if concepts consist in part of sensorimotor states, then it follows that engaging various sensorimotor systems is likely to activate or prime related concepts. As Lakoff and Johnson observe, 'not all conceptual metaphors are manifested in the words of a language. Some are manifested in grammar, others in gesture, art, or ritual'.[208]

A number of priming studies supply evidence for links between particular bodily states or actions and *metaphorically* related abstract concepts, such as power, moral purity, importance, affection, and emotional valence. Not only do these studies provide further evidence for the modal nature of concepts, but they also have important implications for embodied religious practices. Namely, by scripting bodily movements and postures, religious rituals can prime related

---

[205] E.g., Max Ernest-Jones, Daniel Nettle, and Melissa Bateson, 'Effects of Eye Images on Everyday Cooperative Behavior: A Field Experiment', *Evolution and Human Behavior* 32, no. 3 (2011).

[206] Kevin J. Haley and Daniel M. T. Fessler, 'Nobody's Watching? Subtle Cues Affect Generosity in an Anonymous Economic Game', *Evolution and Human Behavior* 26, no. 3 (2005).

[207] E.g., Robert Boyd, Herbert Gintis, and Samuel Bowles, 'Coordinated Punishment of Defectors Sustains Cooperation and Can Proliferate When Rare', *Science* 328, no. 5978 (2010); Martin A. Nowak and Karl Sigmund, 'Evolution of Indirect Reciprocity by Image Scoring', *Nature* 393, no. 6685 (1998).

[208] Lakoff and Johnson, *Philosophy in the Flesh*, 57.

abstract concepts. In this section, I survey abstract religious concepts which have associated embodiments.

5.1 Power

Deeply ingrained within the concept of power is a mapping to vertical space. A dominant party '*over*powers' others, while a weaker party is '*under*powered'. This relationship may arise from correlations in our social and physical environments; for example, adults are typically taller and more powerful than children. Aggressive animals usually assert their dominance by making themselves appear larger. The correlation may also arise from human postures related to dominance and submissiveness in social groups. A meta-analysis found that perceivers readily associated a number of non-verbal behaviours with concepts such as higher power, dominance, status, and hierarchy.[209] Additionally, adopting several body states—more facial expressiveness, more bodily openness, and smaller interpersonal distances—all increased dominance behaviour.[210] The same was true for a number of non-semantic aspects of speech: higher power was associated with those who 'spoke with less vocal variability, spoke more loudly, interrupted more, and had more relaxed sounding voices'.[211]

A number of studies have operationalised this metaphor by demonstrating that verticality affects the concept of power. First, a study found that power concepts were, at least in part, represented by verticality, such that judgements about power were related to vertical position.[212] Second, a study found that participants in a taller, more expansive posture reported a greater sense of power than those in a lower, constricted posture.[213] Moreover, this effect was found to be more significant than assigning someone a powerful role such as manager. Third, this association has down-stream effects on decision making; participants in power-related postures were more confident in their decisions and were more likely to prefer information which confirmed their decision.[214] Fourth, participants with a lower position, implying lower power, reacted more aggressively when ostracised.[215]

---

[209] Judith A. Hall, Erik J. Coats, and Lavonia Smith LeBeau, 'Nonverbal Behavior and the Vertical Dimension of Social Relations: A Meta-Analysis', *Psychological Bulletin* 131, no. 6 (2005).

[210] Ibid., 914.   [211] Ibid.

[212] Thomas W. Schubert, 'Your Highness: Vertical Positions as Perceptual Symbols of Power', *Journal of Personality & Social Psychology* 89, no. 1 (2005).

[213] L. Huang et al., 'Powerful Postures Versus Powerful Roles: Which Is the Proximate Correlate of Thought and Behavior?', *Psychological Science* 22, no. 1 (2011). Cf. Lora E. Park et al., 'Stand Tall, but Don't Put Your Feet Up: Universal and Culturally-Specific Effects of Expansive Postures on Power', *Journal of Experimental Social Psychology* 49, no. 6 (2013).

[214] Julia Fischer et al., 'Empower My Decisions: The Effects of Power Gestures on Confirmatory Information Processing', *Journal of Experimental Social Psychology* 47, no. 6 (2011).

[215] Christiane Schoel, Jennifer Eck, and Rainer Greifeneder, 'A Matter of Vertical Position', *Social Psychological and Personality Science* 5, no. 2 (2013).

A mechanism for the effect of posture was proposed by a team which found that those in expansive postures had elevated testosterone levels and decreased cortisol levels.[216] These bodily changes also correlated with increased feelings of power and tolerance for risk.

These findings relate to the way in which religious rituals arrange bodies in vertical space. As Fuller and Montgomery observe, '[m]any forms of Christianity have worshippers kneel and/or divert their gaze downward when supplicating God. Jews, Christians, and Muslims alike are known to bow their heads during prayer or cover heads in sacred settings...For the most part, religions require individuals to adopt postures that render them smaller, lower, or more vulnerable.'[217] They subsequently tested whether submissive postures were associated with religiosity, and found that for participants who identified as religious, being in a low posture induced stronger religious attitudes than a more expansive posture.[218] This is consistent with the findings of another study which observed that religion primed submission-related concepts and made participants more likely to acquiesce to a request to take revenge.[219] Fuller and Montgomery conclude that '[t]he body's physical orientation to its surroundings thus provides important clues to the symbolic or metaphorical nature of religious thought, religious feeling, and religious behavior. People who feel low, pray to a God on high or yearn to be lifted up by the strong hands of their savior. They despair of having fallen from grace, and hope to rise from the dead'.[220] Power can likewise be conveyed by height in religious art and architecture. Commenting on association between verticality and power, Fuller and Montgomery conclude that '[s]uch body-based metaphors fund cultural discourse and cultural symbols, especially our religious discourse and our religious symbols'.[221]

Underlying embodied mechanisms, however, do not *determine* how they are deployed in a particular religious framework. It has been remarked that Christianity did not merely take over secular (or Roman state religious) notions of power, but sought to transform them. For example, commentators have observed that in the Johannine imagination Jesus being *raised* up onto the cross is a sign of his exaltation, as part of a broader descent-and-ascent motif.[222]

---

[216] Dana R. Carney, Amy J. C. Cuddy, and Andy J. Yap, 'Power Posing: Brief Nonverbal Displays Affect Neuroendocrine Levels and Risk Tolerance', *Psychological Science* 21, no. 10 (2010). NB a failure to replicate in Ranehill et al., 'Assessing the Robustness of Power Posing'.

[217] Fuller and Montgomery, 'Body Posture', 228.

[218] Ibid.

[219] Vassilis Saroglou, Olivier Corneille, and Patty Van Cappellen, '"Speak, Lord, Your Servant Is Listening": Religious Priming Activates Submissive Thoughts and Behaviors', *International Journal for the Psychology of Religion* 19, no. 3 (2009).

[220] Fuller and Montgomery, 'Body Posture', 229.   [221] Ibid.

[222] E.g., Wayne A. Meeks, 'The Man from Heaven in Johannine Sectarianism', *Journal of Biblical Literature* 91, no. 1 (1972); Craig R. Koester, *Symbolism in the Fourth Gospel: Meaning, Mystery, Community*, 2nd ed. (Minneapolis: Fortress Press, 2003), 1; Dorothy Ann Lee, *The Symbolic Narratives of the Fourth Gospel: The Interplay of Form and Meaning*, ed. Stanley E. Porter (Sheffield: JSOT Press,

This correlation between vertical height and power relies on a metaphorical embodiment. However, the kind of power being ascribed to Jesus is very different from a notion of dominance or social hierarchy, for in contravention of messianic expectations it is the crucified one who is being exalted. Thus, an entirely conventional association is used to make a decisively novel ascription.[223]

5.2 Purity

Another category relevant to religion is 'purity'. A number of studies have found evidence for a conceptual metaphor relating physical purity with moral purity. One study discovered what researchers coined the 'Macbeth effect': recalling a past unethical deed primed cleaning-related words; participants who copied out a narrative about unethical activity rated cleaning products as more desirable, and using an antiseptic wipe after recalling an unethical deed reduced compensatory behaviour (volunteering) and reduced moral emotions (such as guilt, shame, disgust, regret, embarrassment, and anger).[224] As with other mechanisms, the association between cleanliness and moral purity has downstream implications for decision making: in another study participants who were primed with cleanliness-related concepts, or who physically washed their hands, reduced the severity of moral judgements.[225] A third study even extended these findings to particular motor modalities: participants who conveyed a malevolent lie via voice mail reported that mouthwash was more desirable, while those who conveyed the same message via email preferred hand sanitiser.[226]

The association between cleanliness and moral purity is mirrored on the negative side; disgust has been shown to relate to moral impurity.[227] Researchers suggest that disgust first evolved as a response to potentially dangerous foods, but has subsequently been extended to social and moral categories.[228] This connection is

---

1994), 51; James H. Charlesworth, 'The Symbology of the Serpent in the Gospel of John', in *John, Jesus, and History, Volume 2: Aspects of Historicity in the Fourth Gospel*, ed. Paul N. Anderson, Felix Just, and Tom Thatcher (Atlanta: SBL Press, 2015), 68–9.

[223] See also Masson, *Without Metaphor*, 59.

[224] Chen-Bo Zhong and Katie Liljenquist, 'Washing Away Your Sins: Threatened Morality and Physical Cleansing', *Science* 313, no. 5792 (2006).

[225] Simone Schnall, Jennifer Benton, and Sophie Harvey, 'With a Clean Conscience: Cleanliness Reduces the Severity of Moral Judgments', *Psychological Science* 19, no. 12 (2008). But NB, a direct replication which found a smaller effect size, Johnson, Cheung, and Donnellan, 'Does Cleanliness Influence Moral Judgments?'.

[226] Spike W.S. Lee and Norbert Schwarz, 'Dirty Hands and Dirty Mouths: Embodiment of the Moral-Purity Metaphor Is Specific to the Motor Modality Involved in Moral Transgression', *Psychological Science* 21, no. 10 (2010).

[227] For a review, see Hanah A. Chapman and Adam K. Anderson, 'Things Rank and Gross in Nature: A Review and Synthesis of Moral Disgust', *Psychological Bulletin* 139, no. 2 (2013).

[228] Zhong and Liljenquist, 'Washing Away Your Sins', 1451. Cf. Jonathan Haidt et al., 'Body, Psyche, and Culture: The Relationship between Disgust and Morality', *Psychology and Developing Societies* 9, no. 1 (1997).

evidenced by studies which found that inducing disgust through bad smells, dirty rooms, or disgusting ideas make moral judgements more severe.[229] These findings, it has been argued, have important implications for the way humans make moral judgements.[230] As one group of researchers remark, 'research has established purity as a moral domain and has shown that manipulating physical dirt and pollution through visual or olfactory means can alter moral judgment'.[231]

Insofar as religion is deeply intertwined with moral codes of behaviour, these findings have direct relevance to the ethical dimension of religious systems. Pointing to the relevance of embodied cognition for religion, one group of researchers remark that 'moral intuitions are not simply driven by religious or scriptural moral codes but, instead, may be grounded in human physical experience and natural physiological reactions'.[232] The findings have also been extended directly to religion. One study found that religion strengthened the connection between cleanliness and morality; for example, those with higher God-belief felt cleaner on days when they had performed more prosocial activities.[233] Another study found that religious primes activated cleanliness concepts and made cleaning products seem more desirable, suggesting a similar connection between cleanliness and spiritual purity.[234]

These findings are consistent with the symbolic connection between purity and religious concepts. As Fetterman points out, 'The connection between religiosity and cleanliness is deeply rooted.'[235] For one, numerous religious rituals involve purification: 'ritual washing is often used to bestow symbolic purity, (e.g., baptism, mikvah, ablution), and commonly practised in preparation for contact with sacred objects or activities'.[236] As with power, although Christian texts routinely rely upon the connection between physical cleanliness and moral purity, this metaphor is deployed in distinctive ways.[237]

5.3 Other Embodiments of Metaphors

Although purity and power have direct and obvious links to religious practices, there are many other embodiments which prime metaphorically related abstract

---

[229] Simone Schnall et al., 'Disgust as Embodied Moral Judgment', *Personality and Social Psychology Bulletin* 34, no. 8 (2008).

[230] Haidt, 'The Emotional Dog'.   [231] Zhong and House, 'Dirt, Pollution, and Purity', 123.

[232] Soliman, Johnson, and Song, 'Understanding Religion', 857.

[233] Adam K. Fetterman, 'On God-Belief and Feeling Clean: Daily Experiences Are Related to Feeling Clean, Particularly for Those High in God-Belief', *Social Psychological and Personality Science* 7, no. 6 (2016).

[234] Jesse Lee Preston and Ryan S. Ritter, 'Cleanliness and Godliness: Mutual Association between Two Kinds of Personal Purity', *Journal of Experimental Social Psychology* 48, no. 6 (2012).

[235] Fetterman, 'On God-Belief'.   [236] Preston and Ritter, 'Cleanliness and Godliness', 1365.

[237] E.g., Matthew 23:25–8.

concepts. For example, emotional concepts are again related to verticality. As with power, positive affect was likewise associated with being physically 'up'.[238] The researchers who made this finding point out that religious concepts make use of this connection: 'Objects that are up or high are often considered to be good, whereas objects that are down or low are often considered to be bad. In the Bible, for example, the righteous go "up" to Heaven, whereas sinners go "down" to Hell.'[239]

Similarly, religious language relies upon horizontal bodily orientations. For example, the New Testament repeatedly describes Jesus as sitting at the right hand of God.[240] This is not a purely arbitrary cultural association; a study found the right-handers had positive association with rightward space and negative association with leftward space, while left-handers exhibited the opposite pattern.[241] Researchers have observed that this may underpin religious language: 'Because right-handedness is typically predominant in the population, the religious association between the right side and morality may be grounded in positive affective experience related to right-hand fluency.'[242]

Studies have shown that numerous other embodiments are metaphorically associated with abstract concepts, including physical warmth and interpersonal affection;[243] extending a middle finger and hostility judgements;[244] giving a thumbs-up and favourable evaluations;[245] bearing weight and importance;[246] handling rough surfaces and abrasive social interactions;[247] handling hard or soft materials and making strict or lax judgements respectively;[248] motioning away

---

[238] B. P. Meier and M. D. Robinson, 'Why the Sunny Side Is Up: Association between Affect and Vertical Position', *Psychological Science* 15, no. 4 (2004). For an alternative explanation of this phenomenon, see Dermot Lynott and Kenny Coventry, 'On the Ups and Downs of Emotion: Testing between Conceptual-Metaphor and Polarity Accounts of Emotional Valence-Spatial Location Interactions', *Psychonomic Bulletin & Review* 21, no. 1 (2014).

[239] Meier and Robinson, 'Why the Sunny Side Is Up'.

[240] Matthew 22:44, 26:64; Mark 14:62, 16:19; Luke 20:42, 22:69; Acts 2:33–4, 5:31, 7:55–6; Romans 8:34; Colossians 3:1; Hebrews 1:3, 13, 8:1, 10:12, 12:2; 1 Peter 3:22.

[241] Daniel Casasanto, 'Embodiment of Abstract Concepts: Good and Bad in Right- and Left-Handers', *Journal of Experimental Psychology: General* 138, no. 3 (2009).

[242] Soliman, Johnson, and Song, 'Understanding Religion', 857.

[243] Williams and Bargh, 'Experiencing Physical Warmth'; Hong and Sun, 'Warm It Up'; Storey and Workman, 'The Effects of Temperature'; Ijzerman, Leung, and Ong, 'Perceptual Symbols'; Gockel, Kolb, and Werth, 'Murder or Not?'.

[244] Jesse Chandler and Norbert Schwarz, 'How Extending Your Middle Finger Affects Your Perception of Others: Learned Movements Influence Concept Accessibility', *Journal of Experimental Social Psychology* 45, no. 1 (2009).

[245] Ibid.

[246] Nils B. Jostmann, Daniël Lakens, and Thomas W. Schubert, 'Weight as an Embodiment of Importance', *Psychological Science* 20, no. 9 (2009); Joshua M. Ackerman, Christopher C. Nocera, and John A. Bargh, 'Incidental Haptic Sensations Influence Social Judgments and Decisions', *Science* 328, no. 5986 (2010). However, another study which did not find the same effect with backpacks; see Leah M. Kaufmann and Sarah Allen, 'Adding Weight to Judgments: The Role of Stimulus Focality on Weight-Related Embodied Cognition', *Sensoria: A Journal of Mind, Brain, and Culture* 10, no. 1 (2014).

[247] Ackerman, Nocera, and Bargh, 'Incidental Haptic Sensations'.   [248] Ibid.

from the body and dispelling bad luck;[249] and even bodily and political leanings.[250] All of these metaphorical embodiments should give us pause to consider how religious practices are profoundly cognitive.

5.4 Conclusion

In the previous three sections I surveyed the cognitive effects of bodily movement and material and social interactions. These aspects of ritual were shown to evoke many inchoate effects, such as modulating emotion. This section supplements those findings by demonstrating that embodied practices can also activate more defined conceptual structures, associated with concepts such as power and morality. Again, religious rituals exploit this cognitive mechanism by scripting embodiments which have become associated with particular concepts. These associations are only the building blocks of meaning, however; the overall point depends on how these building blocks are assembled, that is, how metaphors are deployed.

6 Are Some Traditions 'Less Embodied' Than Others?

In the preceding sections, I have frequently drawn examples from ritually elaborate 'high church' traditions, which privilege liturgy at the centre of their religious observance, as well as the tactile piety of the Middle Ages. These traditions, with their rich liturgies and ornate material culture, provide obvious examples of embodied mechanisms at work. Particular traditions emphasise this aspect of religious observance; as Scarlat points out, 'Of the three Christian traditions, Orthodoxy seems to have best understood that knowledge depends on the intelligence of a ritual that takes into account bodily dynamics.'[251]

This observation raises the question of whether embodied cognition is also relevant to traditions which do not emphasise ritual, or even deliberately shun the term. Are some traditions simply 'less embodied' than others? And, subsequently, does embodied cognition have any relevance to less embodied traditions? These are particularly difficult questions to answer exhaustively, given the immense diversity in Christian practices both geographically and temporally; an African Pentecostal service, a North American Quaker meeting, and a medieval Mass have very little in common and, to the casual observer, may appear to be different

---

[249] Yan Zhang, Jane L. Risen, and Christine Hosey, 'Reversing One's Fortune by Pushing Away Bad Luck', *Journal of Experimental Psychology: General* 143, no. 3 (2014).

[250] Katinka Dijkstra et al., 'How Body Balance Influences Political Party Evaluations: A Wii Balance Board Study', *Frontiers in Psychology* 3, no. 536 (2012).

[251] Scarlat, 'Embodied Cognition of Religion', 169.

religions altogether.[252] However, given that it has important implications for the scope of applicability of the current study, I sketch out a response in broad brush terms.

A superficial response to this question would counter that all practices are inexorably embodied; there is no way to escape our embodiment and there are no ecclesial gatherings of disembodied minds. The question, then, is not *whether* a church engages in embodied practices, but rather *which* embodied practices they employ. While this response may go some way to countering the objection, I think that it is not so easily dismissed. It certainly seems to be the case that in some traditions the body and its environment are manipulated far more extensively than in others. Moreover, such manipulations are far more theologically trivial in some cases. While a service involving participants sitting in rows in a plain room and listening to spoken utterances nevertheless requires embodiment, the bodily and environmental factors in such contexts are far more muted than in elaborate ritual contexts. There are fewer interesting insights to be gained from embodied cognition research in the former case.

The distinction between these two classes of ecclesial practices—the minimalist or maximalist participation of the body and its setting—runs along deep theological fault lines. At various points in Christian history there have been concerted attempts to eradicate aspects of religious material culture: notably, the iconoclastic movement in Eastern Christianity and the reformed (as opposed to the Lutheran) branch of the Reformation both sought to remove (or destroy) religious images.

Some traditions have likewise shunned ritual. Debates around the interpretation of the Eucharist provide one prominent example. A whole spectrum of positions has been articulated and argued for, ranging from an affirmation of the real presence of Christ's body and blood in the Eucharistic elements, through to the Eucharist as a memorial which encourages participants to remember Christ's death. Historically those towards the latter end of this spectrum have tended to deemphasise the importance of the Eucharist in Christian worship, sometimes celebrating it less frequently or omitting it altogether in their regular patterns of worship. These patterns persist in contemporary traditions; the very term 'ritual' is considered a pejorative in some branches of Christianity, being associated with 'dead religion' that is characterised by a lack of authenticity and spontaneity. The kinds of rituals in which I have been identifying the mechanism of embodied cognition are thus less central to these traditions.

It seems true, therefore, that some traditions are 'less embodied' than others, if by less embodied one means that they rely less on ritual and material culture. The paucity of embodied action and elaborate environmental interactions, and how

---

[252] Brown and Strawn, *Physical Nature of Christian Life*, 147.

the actions and environment seem incidental to the worship taking place, rather than constitutive of it, means that far fewer mechanisms of embodied cognition can be identified in shaping the theology at work in these practices. However, although these traditions may be 'less embodied', a number of important necessary qualifications secure the relevance of embodied cognition across many divergent traditions.

6.1 The Pervasiveness of Ritual

Ritual is by no means restricted to Eastern Orthodox or 'high church' Western traditions. Even those traditions which would not describe their practices as rituals, nevertheless engage in regular patterns of embodied practices which can be identified as rituals.[253] Given that such traditions do not often explicitly set out their practices, let alone theorise them as rituals, ethnographies are particularly helpful in understanding their pattern of practice (see Section 1.3).

Stanford anthropologist Tanya Luhrmann offers an ethnography of Vineyard churches (a charismatic protestant denomination) in Chicago and Los Angeles.[254] She immediately observed the emotional quality of the communal worship practices.[255] As one of the overall aims of the practices, congregants were encouraged to relate to God as with a friend. To foster such a relationship they would adopt practices in which they engaged with God as they would in an actual human encounter: 'They delighted in the time they spent chatting with God, the time singing with God in the shower.'[256] Sometimes this would include a more elaborate practice: 'The women would set aside the night, and they imagined it romantically: it was a "date". They might pick up dinner or set out a plate at the table, and they imagined their way through the evening talking to God, cuddling with God, and basking in God's attention.'[257] This practice is more than simply an attempt to conceptualise being loved by God, in an abstract or doxastic fashion. The participants use embodied practices to generate the feeling of being loved by a close companion by engaging in the bodily tasks and material culture associated with such an encounter.

Luhrmann offers greater detail on how the feelings that should come from such a relationship are fostered.[258] She notes that '[t]he social life of evangelical churches is rich in specific emotional practices—of behaviour and response performed again and again, the stuff of which culture is made.'[259] Luhrmann

---

[253] Ibid., 150.
[254] T. M. Luhrmann, *When God Talks Back: Understanding the American Evangelical Relationship with God* (New York: Alfred A. Knopf, 2012).
[255] Ibid., 3–6.   [256] Ibid., 80.   [257] Ibid.   [258] Ibid., 101.   [259] Ibid., 111.

describes six 'emotional practices' used to make participants feel loved by God, one of which is 'crying in the presence of God'. She records one such occurrence:

> They cried a lot. People cried when other people prayed out loud over them...And as people cried as others prayed over them, those who were praying aloud were asking God to make them feel safe, loved and protected— wrapped in his arms, soothed by his embrace, washed by his forgiveness. I came to think of these events as prayer 'huddles': one person in the center, usually crying and in distress; the rest of the group crowded around with their hands on the person or (if they could not reach) their hands on the people who were touching the person in the center, as if the physical connection carried a supernatural connection.[260]

Again, it is embodied practices which are being used to generate the desired emotions. Participants are invited to imagine particular bodily interactions (being embraced, being washed). These imagined bodily states, being hugged and washed, might function as primes or associate with emotions. The imagined body states are reinforced by the actual bodily practice: being surrounded in a huddle and having hands laid upon the person at the centre. These comforting bodily gestures were responses to the visceral crying or bawling, as those being prayed for expressed various fears or anxieties about circumstances in their lives. For example, 'the young woman had just learned that she had to move out of her apartment and she needed dental surgery and she had no money for either, she became hysterical, while we prayed that God would hold her in his arms so that she would feel his comfort'.[261] This scenario provides a clear example of emotional contagion.

If we were to ignore the bodily comportments, gestures, and movements in these accounts we would likely miss much of the emotional quality of these religious experiences. Moreover, knowing that bodily states can directly induce emotions, we can see how the practices shape the emotional dynamics at play. Luhrmann's ethnography shows that religious traditions which focus less on explicitly formalised rituals nevertheless engage in particular embodied practice and, as with more formal rituals, these practices deploy mechanisms described by embodied cognition.

A study of churchgoers lends support to the connection between embodiment and emotional experience which Luhrmann observed. The study surveyed congregants, asking them to report the body postures adopted and emotional valence and arousal experienced during a Sunday service.[262] It found that participants

---

[260] Ibid., 112.   [261] Ibid., 113.

[262] Patty van Cappellen, S. Cassidy, and R. Zhang, 'Religion as an Embodied Practice: Organizing the Various Forms and Documenting the Meanings of Christian Prayer Postures', *Psychology of Religion and Spirituality* (in press). And the experimenters note, this study is limited by the fact that it relies on self-report rather than more direct measures.

who attend Catholic churches tended to adopt more downward-oriented and constructive postures, while Baptist or non-denominational congregants tended to adopt more expansive postures. Moreover, those adopting upward-postures reported more positive emotions and higher arousal, whilst the opposite was true for those who had adopted downward-postures. It is noteworthy that the different theological traditions were associated with particular forms of embodiment, and these embodiments modulate emotional experience.

The embodied nature of human cognition is an anthropological constant. It is hardly surprising then that tendencies towards imbuing places and tangible objects with meaning, generating emotive content through patterns of bodily movement, and other such embodied mechanisms can be found in traditions which are less explicitly ritualistic.

Even in traditions which are explicitly and unambiguously liturgical, religious rituals are more pervasive than formal church services. In her ethnographic account of a Greek Orthodox village, Juliet du Boulay offers an immersive description of the way in which the cosmology of Eastern Orthodoxy not only shapes ecclesial practices, but structures almost all facets of village life.[263] Although the Divine Liturgy is at the centre of religious practice, the same cosmology is recapitulated in everyday village life, through the patterns of 'work, marriage, hospitality, kinship, community, death, mourning, and their relationship with the natural and divine worlds'.[264] In a telling passage, she observes that even though the words of liturgical offices are not fully understood, their meaning is readily understood because of the way the liturgy is embedded in the wider patterns of village life:

In the village culture the liturgical tradition finds an authentic voice, and it is this that keeps alive in the people an understanding of their faith so vital that they can absorb the essence of the liturgical offices even when they are not able to understand word for word what is being said. It is the interplay between these two forces, ecclesiastical teaching and village culture, which is the great strength of village life, for the teaching kept intact by the Church and released into anecdote, folk tale, legend, and village custom and practice is transmitted into every area of life and work, feeding into talk and jokes, dreams and visions, prohibitions and prescriptions, and allowing people to keep company with Christ, the saints, and the Mother of God, and to see in rock and stream and mountain the power of the unseen world. The incarnate God of the Gospels becomes a figure so known to them that at times they are not only 'servants of God', but also his friends, mourners, and parents.[265]

---

[263] Juliet du Boulay, *Cosmos, Life, and Liturgy in a Greek Orthodox Village* (Limni: Harvey, 2009).
[264] Ibid., 389–90.   [265] Ibid., 381.

In du Boulay's description liturgy and ritual have porous boundaries. Although distinctive, ecclesial practices are also a microcosm of life as a whole. Hence one need not restrict analysis to formal liturgies; practices beyond the wall of church buildings may equally be theologically pregnant.

Even though embodied practices are more pervasive across Christian traditions and beyond ecclesial settings than one might first imagine, there are nevertheless some traditions which are sparse with respect to embodied practices. As Davison observes:

> Protestantism is no stranger to or enemy of the sacraments, but a certain strain of Protestantism is, with its tendency to exalt the abstract over the concrete: for instance, in a disembodied 'message' of the gospel in isolation from the practices of the Church or in the sacramental theology of Zwingli, who sought to reduce sacraments to the means by which God communicates ideas to us.[266]

There are, of course, always examples of churches where aspects of embodiment or material culture are sparse. Some churches (by necessity or by design) meet in buildings which serve other functions, such as warehouses. No one practice is universally observed. Even for those practices which enjoy widespread engagement, such as baptism and Eucharist, how these practices are embodied varies widely.

Even in such traditions, however, participants nevertheless still have bodies (!) and do things with them during any form of communal worship. As a colleague of mine once remarked, 'sitting on a hard, wooden pew for an extended period of time and listening to a sermon which never seems to end can be a very embodied experience'.[267] Hence, embodiment is not altogether absent in these scenarios. Traditions which emphasise preaching often use embodied mechanisms to encode and convey the value they place on the spoken word; for example, many protestant churches locate (sometimes large and ornate) pulpits centrally and elevate them, for both practical (ensuring that congregants hear the preacher) and symbolic purposes (marking the importance of preaching).

Given the ever-present nature of our embodiment, it is not only the presence of bodily movements and environmental primes which can convey theological meaning, but also their absence. Various traditions deliberately adopt a sparse form of worship. Likewise, in iconoclastic traditions the removal of images was theologically motivated. If we were to enter a medieval cathedral, in which every square centimetre of space was ornamented and brightly coloured, we might well get a sense of sensory overload. That which is highly ornate also risks becoming cacophonous and cluttered, and such embodiments and environments can

---

[266] Davison, *Why Sacraments?*, 8.
[267] I am indebted to Philip Fountain for this insight.

become disorienting or claustrophobic. By reacting against this effect, traditions which adopt particularly sparse and plain worship patterns and environments, aim to provide worship which is characterised by simplicity, spaciousness, and free from (supposed) distractions. The pattern of worship among Quaker communities, where sitting in silence dominates, is one example of a deliberate absence of the 'wordiness' of its parent traditions. These material absences, however, often take on their meaning against the backdrop of a historical presence.

In summary, ritual and embodiment is far more pervasive than the obvious examples suggest. It is certainly true that some traditions shy away for deploying embodied factors more than others; but it is crucial to recognise that 'less embodied' is, by no means, synonymous with disembodied.

7 Conclusion: Scaffolded Religion

Numerous empirical studies have unearthed dozens of bodily mechanisms which suggest that bodily positions and movements, material and social environments all influence cognition in specific ways. The range of these cognitive effects includes emotional arousal, conceptual activation, memory retrieval, social bonding, biasing judgement, and decision making, among others. Although some of the findings cited are subject to further confirmation, the sheer number of studies suggesting that body and environment impinge on cognition makes it difficult to understand cognitive processes independently of their situatedness.

These general mechanisms are doubtless activated in a whole host of human activities, including embodied religious practices: 'inducing a particular embodiment produced a corresponding mental state...The embodiments in rituals may have similar effects on mental states. Indeed the design of rituals may typically attempt to capitalize on such relationships'.[268] Taking this suggestion as a starting point, this chapter has sought to tease out how Christian embodied practices exploit these mechanisms. Drawing upon standard contemporary Eucharistic practices, as well as ethnographic and historical examples of diverse religious practices, it demonstrates that the mechanisms of embodied cognition are directly relevant to numerous practices, even for traditions which identify as less ritualistic.

---

[268] Barsalou et al., 'Embodiment in Religious Knowledge', 43. Cf. Rebecca Sachs Norris, 'Religion, Neuroscience and Emotion: Some Implications of Consumerism and Entertainment Culture', in *Religion and the Body: Modern Science and the Construction of Religious Meaning*, ed. David Cave and Rebecca Sachs Norris (Leiden: Brill, 2012), 105,107; Patty van Cappellen and Megan E. Edwards, 'The Embodiment of Worship: Relations among Postural, Psychological, and Physiological Aspects of Religious Practice', *Journal for the Cognitive Science of Religion* 6, no. 1–2 (2021).

The picture which emerges from this survey is one in which religious cognition is highly scaffolded. The replacement and constitution hypotheses are invaluable conceptual tools with which to analyse religious practices. They explicate the contribution which bodily practices and religious material culture make to religion, through the many and varied cognitive effects they produce. In Chapter 7, I transpose these insights into an explicitly theological register, to consider the meaning and significance of liturgy.

7

Theological Practices

Homo Liturgicus

'Indeed, the genius of [shopping] mall religion is that actually it operates with a more holistic, affective, embodied anthropology (or theory of the human person) than the Christian church tends to assume!'

—James K. A. Smith[1]

In the Christian tradition, liturgy is a far richer concept than the bare ritual described by cognitive science; it is not only a physical performance, but one which is directed towards and in service of God. As I discuss below, embodied acts (such as rituals) are typically enmeshed in larger symbolic systems (such as Christian theology). However, the ritualistic dimension of liturgy, I argue, plays a crucial role in shaping their meaning and significance. For, although liturgy may be more than ritual, it is no less than ritual.

A growing number of theologians have recently turned their attention towards the significance of human embodiment. For example, Fuller observes that '[a]ltered neurochemistry, sexuality, pain, and the so-called social emotions are additional examples of brain-born activities that motivate humans to create, modify, commit to, or reject religious constructions of experience'.[2] Similarly Coakley develops an embodied systematic theology by examining the entanglement between sexual desire and desire for God.[3] These types of projects appeal to embodiment, but do so at a step removed (or a higher level of abstraction) from specific findings in embodied cognition.

A scaffolded view of religion provides a platform for detailed reassessment of the status of liturgy. In this chapter, I argue that the cognitive effects of religious practices suggest that part of the meaning of a liturgy arises from its embodied form (Section 1). Given such embodied meanings, liturgy is itself a bearer of theological content rather than merely an expression of it (Section 2); and since liturgy inculcates theological content it plays a crucial role in forming participants (Section 3).[4] In considering the theological significance of embodied

---

[1] Smith, *Desiring the Kingdom*, 24.   [2] Fuller, *Spirituality in the Flesh*, 19.
[3] Coakley, *God, Sexuality and the Self*.
[4] Accounts of religious experience in liturgical settings can likewise be revised in light of embodied cognition, see Tobias Tan, 'The Corporeality of Religious Experience: Embodied Cognition in Religious Practices', in *Experience or Expression? Religious Experience Revisited*, ed. Thomas Hardke, Ulrich Schmiedel, and Tobias Tan (Leiden: Brill, 2016).

Corporeal Theology: Accommodating Theological Understanding to Embodied Thinkers. Tobias Tanton,
Oxford University Press. © Tobias Tanton 2023. DOI: 10.1093/oso/9780192884589.003.0008

religious practices I once again return to the overarching theological theme of accommodation. Insofar as embodied cognition sheds light on an important facet of what it means to be human, it will be argued that religious practices are uniquely suited to human beings.

1 Embodied versus Symbolic Meaning

Developing a scaffolded account of religion, the Chapter 6 surveyed the mechanisms of embodied cognition at work in ecclesial practices. These findings raise the question of the contribution which the cognitive effects make to the overall *meaning* of these practices. To address this question, I distinguish two contrasting ways in which meaning can attach to embodied practices or material objects, with a view to exploring their interplay.[5]

The *first* meaning-making strategy understands a practice as *symbol*. By symbol, I again mean a sign whose relationship with its referent is *arbitrary* and established by convention.[6] According to this strategy, the meaning of a ritual practice can be 'read' symbolically by decoding the forms of a practice—say a body posture, a processional pattern, or the use of a material object—through the particular symbolic meaning conventionally assigned to it. To study these symbolic meanings, one therefore needs to interrogate the texts and social institutions which establish and propagate the meaning-making conventions. Exploring the cultural deployments of embodiment, Cohen and Leung identify similarly symbolic 'totem embodiments' whose meaning is assigned by the culture, rather than an appropriation of an intrinsic bodily mechanism.[7] For example, they note that 'crossing oneself may evoke a number of complex representations for a Christian, but the cross does not inherently evoke anything and would have little effect on a non-Christian'.[8] Since these associations must be learnt, they hypothesise that they are acquired through frequent repetition in rituals or socialisation.

A *second* strategy understands practices as gaining meaning from their *embodied* form. The cognitive effect of practices gives them an intrinsic embodied meaning. Unlike the symbolic explanation, the meaning of a practice attaches by virtue of the cognitive effects of bodily manipulation or bodily interactions with the environment. Cohen and Leung term this use of embodiments (which I simply call 'embodied meaning') 'pre-wired embodiments'. Such embodiments use evolutionarily prepared mechanisms which are basic and universal to humans

---

[5] For a similar distinction in the context of developmental accounts of communication, see Moritz M. Daum, Jessica A. Sommerville, and Wolfgang Prinz, 'Becoming a Social Agent: Developmental Foundations of an Embodied Social Psychology', *European Journal of Social Psychology* 39, no. 7 (2009).

[6] de Saussure, *Course in General Linguistics*.

[7] Cohen and Leung, 'The Hard Embodiment of Culture'.   [8] Ibid., 1285.

(and other animals).[9] These mechanisms determine the affective and cognitive consequences of particular bodily comportments. Many of the mechanisms surveyed in the previous chapter fall into this category; they track automatic responses to particular bodily or environmental factors which do not rely on cultural conventions.

The distinction between 'embodied' and 'symbolic' meanings is significant because liturgical meaning is often construed in *purely* symbolic terms. Green points out this tendency is found anthropological treatments of embodiment: 'influential studies of religion in Africa have suggested that practices involving the human body are not concerned with the body as such but...with the human body as a symbol of the social order'.[10] Similarly, Fuller observes that '[t]he meaning of altered states of consciousness is not solely derived from the cultural context. Neurochemistry exerts considerable leverage on how we think'.[11] He identifies the same tendency to overlook embodied meanings in religious studies, which 'in recent years become so enamored of the rhetoric emanating from the camp of strong versions of constructivism that most scholars have failed to keep abreast of recent scholarship in the natural and social sciences'.[12] Extreme versions of social constructivism, in which meaning is understood as solely the result of cultural processes, have led to religious practices being understood exclusively in terms of their symbolic meaning.

The assumption—or explicit assertion—that meaning is exclusively symbolic obscures, or totally occludes, the contribution of embodied meanings. By failing to take embodied meaning into account, important aspects of the overall meaning (and formative potential) of practices is neglected. Green responds to fixation with symbolic meaning by showing that practices often have direct physiological effects. Drawing on her field work, she observes that 'Pogoro Catholics [in Southern Tanzania] use medicines to effect the physical and social transformation of their bodies, not to embody representations'.[13]

The remedy to an all-consuming focus on symbolic meaning, however, is not to claim that all meaning derives from underlying embodied factors. Fuller (and many others) rightly decries such responses as reductionist.[14] Brown and Reimer observe that the human brain develops slowly relative to other primates, with the pre-frontal cortex not maturing until after puberty.[15] They conclude that 'human infants and children are remarkably open to formation of their cognitive, emotional, and behavior systems via their interactions with the environment'.[16] Hence biological findings themselves attest the capacity for cultural learning which

[9] Ibid., 1280.
[10] Maia Green, 'Medicines and the Embodiment of Substances among Pogoro Catholics, Southern Tanzania', *The Journal of the Royal Anthropological Institute* 2, no. 3 (1996): 486.
[11] Fuller, *Spirituality in the Flesh*, 96.   [12] Fuller, 'Faith of the Flesh', 138.
[13] Green, 'Medicines', 485.   [14] Fuller, 'Faith of the Flesh', 135.
[15] Brown and Reimer, 'Embodied Cognition', 837.   [16] Ibid., 839.

underpins symbolic conventions. As Fuller explains, 'biological explanations of human behaviour can never be complete since, in humans, genes have given away most of their sovereignty to culture. Human experience is never fully biological'.[17] Hence the biological reductionism of understanding meaning in purely embodied terms is not a viable alternative to the fixation on symbolic meanings. However, if biological reductionism is problematic, so too is 'cultural reductionism' which ignores the underlying biological mechanisms which culture appropriates. There is little merit in substituting one reductionism for another; embodied and symbolic meanings must be considered *together*. Some examples will illustrate how ecclesial practices or material culture take on *both* symbolic *and* embodied meanings.[18]

Consider the meaning of kneeling in prayer. On the symbolic account, kneeling becomes associated with humility and submission through cultural conventions, such as the practice of kneeling before feudal lords. It may be tempting to assume that meaning arises exclusively from such symbolic associations. However, if the meaning of kneeling is exclusively symbolic, then presumably a handstand would be an equally apt prayer posture; it too could be associated with humility by a cultural convention. However, a handstand is clearly not an apt body posture for prayer (as typically understood), suggesting that its meaning is more than purely symbolic.[19] On the embodied account, however, kneeling also derives its meaning from how it configures the human body.[20] Kneeling lowers the body. Vertical height primes power and thus kneeling embodies submission.[21] Similarly, kneeling impairs mobility, removing the possibility of effective flight and thereby rendering one more vulnerable. The bodily form of the practices is therefore consonant with humility.

The usage of incense provides another example of the relationship between embodied and symbolic meanings. Davison and Milbank provide an extended exposition of the meaning of incense in liturgical contexts:

> Incense...is burnt at evening prayer, following the Jewish offering of incense at the evening sacrifice. It is used to prepare people and things for holy use, such as the bread, wine and worshippers at the Eucharistic offertory. It is used to honour holy things, such as the consecrated elements of the Eucharist or the images of the saints. That then allows for an extra-ordinary and moving association: the censing of the body at a funeral, as a holy thing. The web of associations extends further still. This is the incense that was brought, perhaps, by a member of the congregation as a gift for the church at Epiphany. This was in honour of the

---

[17] Fuller, *Spirituality in the Flesh*, 7. See also Edward O. Wilson, *Sociobiology*, Abridged ed. (Cambridge: Belknap Press of Harvard University Press, 1980), 274.

[18] van Cappellen and Edwards, 'The Embodiment of Worship', 68.

[19] Ibid., 61.   [20] Fuller, *Spirituality in the Flesh*, 154.   [21] See Chapter 6, Section 5.1.

incense presented to the infant Christ by the Magi. Incense just like it is pressed into the Paschal candle at Easter Vigil: five grains for the five wounds—'by his holy and glorious wounds may Christ our Lord guard us and keep us'.[22]

This passage provides a rich exploration of multiple layers of the symbolic meaning of incense, which arises from the way incense is situated in a long history of ecclesial practices: its place in regular rituals, its references in sacred texts, its place in the liturgical calendar, its usage in rites of passage, its connection to other symbolic objects and acts, the texts spoken during its usage, and, ultimately, its place in a larger theological narrative pregnant with meaning. However, the description overlooks the embodied meaning of incense, failing to mention the warming and joy-giving effects of incense.[23] Such embodied meanings are easily overlooked.

The embodied meaning of incense may seem vague and insignificant relative to the intricate web of symbolic meanings woven throughout the course of the tradition. Excluding extreme cases (such as hallucinogens), the mechanisms of embodied cognition typically involve relatively small effect sizes. If the empirical evidence shows a link between practices and cognition, this connection can nevertheless be a subtle one. Moreover, embodied meanings are often implicit or affective, which may be difficult to articulate propositionally and susceptible to multiple interpretations.[24] However, given the sheer number of embodied mechanisms identified in the previous chapter the cumulative effect may be profound. Consider, a well 'curated' worship service in which music, architecture, stained-glass windows, movement, gesture, vestments, posture, poise, incense, art, vessels, and other liturgical objects are all 'singing off the same hymn sheet'. In such a context small, individual effects can additively create a compelling and holistic experience, and participating in a ritual is immersive in a way that reading about one is not.

A further advantage of embodied meanings is that they need not be taught. Even regular participants in rituals involving incense may not be aware of the layers of symbolic meaning described by Davison and Milbank. In contrast, participants have the embodied meaning communicated to them automatically. Moreover, the embodied meaning does not require the mental effort of explicit reflection to evoke its web of associations, rather it is simply experienced directly and viscerally. Some of these advantages can also accrue to symbolic meanings

---

[22] Davison and Milbank, *For the Parish*, 110–11. For similar reflections on the material elements of the Eucharist, see Grumett, *Material Eucharist*, 17–70.

[23] See Chapter 5, Section 3.5.

[24] Wynn, *Faith and Place*, 58. Although one might note that textual theologies are not immune from ambiguities and multiple interpretations, as revealed by disagreements in secondary literature, and thus the difference is one of degree rather than kind. Perhaps this explains why theologians often feel on safer ground engaging with explicit linguistic formulations.

once they are firmly attached to particular embodiment. Once a symbolic meaning has been habituated it may likewise become deeply ingrained and automatically prime the symbolic associations. Thus, embodied practices can implicitly evoke a particular meaning without it being explicitly articulated.[25]

Although the embodied and symbolic meanings are compatible in the cases of kneeling or incense, in other cases they come into conflict.[26] For example, in cases of abuse in church contexts, the negative symbolic associations triggered by an ecclesial setting are likely to override any positive affective valence produced by an embodied practice. Furthermore, in some cases one form of meaning predominates. For example, consumption of a strong hallucinogenic or psychoactive substance may lead to bodily effects that are far more prominent than its symbolic meanings.[27] Conversely, in the case of incense the embodied effect is quite a modest relative comparison to the multivalent symbolic meanings. A little warmth and joy could equally be supplied by a sip of port or by reclining next to a fireplace. Even if either embodied or symbolic meaning predominates, both continue to be present; embodied effects with a history of deployment in religious practices quickly accrue cultural layers of meaning, and conversely symbolic associations are usually most effective and most likely to persist when the underlying embodied action or material vehicle is apt for its intended meaning.[28] Embodied and symbolic meanings are inexorably intertwined.[29]

2 Liturgy as Bearer of Theological Content

Liturgical practices can be said to *contain* and *convey* intrinsic theological content by virtue of their cognitive effects. That is to say, if a practice has a relatively stable form that reliably conveys a given embodied meaning whenever it is performed, the practice itself is a *repository of theological content*, in the same way that texts serve as such storehouses. In this section, I argue that the theology-bearing status of liturgical practices inveighs against an oft-assumed way of theorising them as mere expressions of belief and doctrine. The alternative to this model, one which is *consistent with embodied meanings*, recognises the unity of form and content. After setting out these two alternative models, I consider Wainwright's influential

---

[25] See, for example, embodied metaphors described in Chapter 6, Section 5.

[26] E.g., Wolterstorff, 'Knowing God Liturgically', 12–13. Wolterstorff considers the case where implicit knowledge of God found in the way in which God is addressed comes into conflict with explicit theological positions about God.

[27] Fuller, *Spirituality in the Flesh*, 80; Rick Doblin, 'Pahnke's "Good Friday Experiment": A Long-Term Follow-up and Methodological Critique', *The Journal of Transpersonal Psychology* 23, no. 1 (1991).

[28] For example, see Fuller on tobacco smoking practices in North American shamanism in Fuller, *Spirituality in the Flesh*, 83, 86.

[29] Fuller and Montgomery, 'Body Posture', 235.

Doxology as a case study for how these two models play out in contemporary liturgical theology.

2.1 Liturgy as 'Mere Expression'?

The significance of the content-bearing nature of liturgy is clearly seen when contrasted with an alternative model, in which liturgy merely *expresses* belief or doctrine. In such a model 'theology' proper is assumed to be co-terminus with belief or doctrine, and liturgy only comes after theology as an expression of it. This model presupposes that content (i.e., belief or doctrine) is formulated independently of the form in which it is expressed (i.e., liturgy).

The liturgy-as-expression model is present in a number of approaches. For example, Bell classifies religious traditions as either orthodoxic or orthopraxic, depending on whether they emphasise belief or practice respectively.[30] Christianity, Bell contends, falls squarely into the orthodoxic category, and traditions in this category understand rituals as 'expressions of things that should already be in the heart'.[31] Similarly, Wolterstorff observes that coming to know God through liturgical participation has received scant attention in philosophical literature; he speculates that this is because 'writers have assumed that participating in liturgical enactments is not a way of coming to know God but is, rather, a way of expressing and putting into practice knowledge of God already acquired in some other way'.[32] In other words, liturgy simply expresses a pre-existing knowledge, instead of itself being a way in which knowledge is gained.[33]

The liturgy-as-expression model has a number of important implications. First, it sees liturgy as largely insignificant since it is treated as an incidental afterthought. Belief and doctrine are where the 'real action' occurs, and thus determining what constitutes 'right belief' and 'right doctrine' is prioritised; only after these have been determined is liturgy considered.

Second, when particular liturgies are seen as incidental, they also become dispensable. Since the form (liturgy) is largely independent from its content (belief, doctrine), several different expressions may all be compatible with the same set of beliefs. Thus, any particular form of liturgy can be readily replaced by another form, so long as they are seen to express the same content. Hence liturgies-as-expressions are assumed to be malleable, and they can be altered without affecting the underlying theology. Not only can one liturgy be substituted for another,

---

[30] Catherine M. Bell, *Ritual Theory, Ritual Practice* (Oxford: Oxford University Press, 1992), 215.
[31] Ibid.   [32] Wolterstorff, 'Knowing God Liturgically', 2.
[33] Along similar lines, Fiddes critiques the 'application' model, in which liturgy simply applies pre-existing doctrine, see Paul Fiddes, 'Ecclesiology and Ethnography: Two Disciplines, Two Worlds?', in *Perspectives on Ecclesiology and Ethnography*, ed. Pete Ward (Grand Rapids, MI: Eerdmans, 2012), 17–20.

but liturgical expressions can be substituted with other forms of expression. Linguistic expressions, such as the spoken or written word, are then considered as alternative forms of expression which convey the same content. As I observed in the previous chapter, the expressiveness of liturgy is often rather inchoate and multivalent. In contrast, linguistic expressions can be seen to provide far greater clarity and precision (though this is not necessarily the case). Thus linguistic formulations appear to be not only an alternative form of expression, but a superior one. In the case of the 'less embodied' traditions, this can lead to liturgy being marginalised.

A third, related implication is that when liturgy is diminished other aspects of a tradition become privileged. One of these categories is that of belief, as in Bell's classification of Christianity as orthodoxic rather than orthopraxic. Cuneo charts the tendencies in both the philosophy of religion and characterisations of Christianity which have privileged propositional knowledge and belief at the expense of religious practices:

> it is not uncommon to characterize (the core of) Christianity as a set of proposi-tions and the status being a Christian as the property of being such as to accept or believe (some subset of) these propositions. In philosophy, this tendency has been mirrored in contemporary epistemology by an almost exclusive concern with propositional knowledge (and propositional belief). When these two ten-dencies combine in the contemporary discussion of the epistemology of reli-gious belief, the result has been a discussion that focuses almost exclusively on the possibility and character of propositional religious knowledge and meritori-ous propositional religious belief.[34]

If 'theology proper' consists of propositional beliefs and knowledge, then it fol-lows that the best (if not the only) way to convey these beliefs is by way of linguis-tic formulations. Thus, the privileging of propositional beliefs has gone hand-in-hand with a privileging of texts and speech. Vásquez traces the occlusion of the material aspects of religion, arguing that: '[e]merging from Protestant Biblical hermeneutics, religious studies has tended to focus on the great sacred texts, or the theologies of the Niebuhrs, Barths and Tillichs of the world, or the symbolic systems of various self-contained, territorialized cultures.'[35] As a result

---

[34] Cuneo, *Ritualized Faith*, 17–18. Wolterstorff concurs: '[a]nalytic epistemology of religion of the past forty years has followed the lead of analytic epistemology in general in that almost all discussions of knowledge of God have focused on propositional knowledge of God', Wolterstorff, 'Knowing God Liturgically', 3.

[35] Vásquez, *More Than Belief*, 1. For a similar argument on how cognitive science of religion has privileged belief over practice, see Nathaniel F. Barrett, 'Skilful Engagement and the "Effort after Value": An Axiological Theory of the Origins of Religion', in *Evolution, Religion, and Cognitive Science: Critical and Constructive Essays*, ed. Fraser Watts and Léon P. Turner (Oxford: Oxford University Press, 2014).

of this bias towards textuality, Vásquez observes, religious scholars often interpret practices symbolically or hermeneutically.

The privileging of language has also shaped the sub-discipline of liturgical studies. Although this branch of theology expressly examines rituals, it too has historically represented a bias towards the linguistic domain by focusing on the historical development of liturgical *texts*, rather than the theological significance of how the body is deployed beyond linguistic utterances.[36] Even the area of theology which is tasked with understanding ritual has, in many instances, overlooked its embodied nature.

A fourth implication of the liturgy-as-expression model is an implicit anthropology, in which human thought proceeds independently of the body.[37] Humans are primarily characterised as creatures who hold propositional beliefs and knowledge and communicate these in linguistic formulations. Although humans doubtless possess such capacities, to limit humans to them is to distort severely a holistic picture of the embodied human person.

The insights of embodied cognition research are profoundly at odds with each of these four implications of the liturgy-as-expression model. First, if embodied practices cause cognitive effects then the embodied form ought not be understood as an incidental afterthought. Second, given that embodied form (partially) determines a practice's meaning, the form cannot be substituted without altering theological content. Third, an exclusive fixation on beliefs conveyed linguistically neglects embodied meanings. Fourth, embodied cognition suggests an anthropology in which thought is dependent on the particularities of embodiment. In summary, the liturgy-as-expression model is deeply flawed from the perspective of embodied cognition and an alternative is required.

2.2 The Unity of Form and Content

An alternative model of liturgy which is consistent embodied cognition understands liturgy as itself the bearer (rather than merely the 'expresser') of theological content, thereby uniting embodied *form* with its accompanying theological *content*. Insofar as a model which recognises the unity of form and content is the converse of the liturgy-as-expression model, it will have the opposite implications.

2.2.1 Liturgy as Content Laden

A number of scholars recognise the shortcomings of the liturgy-as-expression model, and gesture towards an alternative. Cuneo argues that liturgy, at least in the Eastern tradition, is not a derivative, optional extra: 'for Eastern Christians,

---

[36] An example of this tendency can be seen in the Wainwright case study in Section 2.3.
[37] Smith, *Desiring the Kingdom*, 24.

the liturgy could not be an addendum to the Christian life, something that one does when not performing good works or communicating the teachings of Jesus'.[38] He cites singing as an example of the unity of form and content: 'liturgical singing is particularly fitting and that its fittingness consists (at least in part) in a particular sort of form/content marriage in which singing the liturgical text thereby instantiates important elements of its content'.[39] Given the pervasiveness of ritual (argued for in Chapter 6), Cuneo's insights could be extended, to varying degrees, to many other traditions.

Coakley intuitively discerns the ability of embodied practice to contain cognitive content. She argues that 'if one is resolutely not engaged in the practices of prayer, contemplation, and worship, then there are certain sorts of philosophical insights that are unlikely, if not impossible, to become available to one'.[40] This position recognises the causal path from practices to thought identified in embodied cognition. Elsewhere Coakley more explicitly rejects the liturgy-as-expression model, as she examines 'the idea that liturgy does not merely rehearse, or inculcate, the propositional beliefs of Christian faith that may have already been acknowledged rationally sometime previously, but that liturgy in and of itself purveys a particular kind of "truth" not necessarily limited to the propositional'.[41] This recognition is consistent with Coakley's call for a '*théologie totale*' which 'attends to art, to poetry, to music, and (combining all of these) to liturgy'.[42] She devotes a chapter to an extended discussion of visual representations of the Trinity, in which she explores the relations implied by various representations and how gender is portrayed. The discussion forms a sensitive exploration of how visual depictions can unconsciously inform our theological imaginations. In line with a scaffolded view of religion, this approach recognises that non-linguistic perceptual stimuli participate in our theological thinking.

Turning to environmental factors, Wynn explores the theological significance of embodied knowledge of place. Reflecting on a personal narrative, he observes that 'visits to these places enabled the friends to affirm certain thoughts, and in turn their commitment to certain values, by means of embodied interaction with the places, rather than by way of explicit articulation'.[43] On this account, places cannot be reduced to descriptions or even photographs: one's embodied presence within a space allows for a richer knowledge on account of one's spatial interaction with it.

Moreover, through our bodily knowledge places such as a childhood home can be known intimately. Wynn quotes Bachelard's descriptions of our knowledge of such places: 'the house we were born in is physically inscribed in us. It is a group

---

[38] Cuneo, *Ritualized Faith*, 10.   [39] Ibid., 17.
[40] Coakley, *God, Sexuality and the Self*, 16.   [41] Coakley, 'Beyond "Belief"', 132.
[42] Coakley, *God, Sexuality and the Self*, 91. The fourth volume is projected to be entitled: *Flesh and Blood: Christology, Incarnation, Eucharist*.
[43] Wynn, *Faith and Place*, 28–9.

of organic habits'.[44] The ability to navigate such places in the dark, for example, betrays our familiarities with its spatial dimensions and layouts and how they relate to our bodily dimensions and movements (the distance to a door relative to our gait, the height of a light-switch relative to our hand position). Bachelard goes so far as to suggest that the 'word habit is too worn a word to express this passionate liaison of our bodies, which do not forget, with an unforgettable house'.[45] Against the backdrop of this exploration of place, Wynn argues that place takes on religious significance:

> the religious meaning of a place should not take the quality of human experience there, whether now or in the past, as simply a 'given'—rather, we need to recognize the ways in which places themselves can elicit and structure religiously meaningful experience.[46]

Hence Wynn clearly envisages that physical environments participate in our religious cognition by structuring the experiences.

Davison and Milbank explicitly link the form of the church's practices and the content of its beliefs, applying Wittgenstein's concept of 'forms of life' to the question of ecclesial practices: 'for Wittgenstein, we have a common understanding of what words mean—which is what language is about—because we also share common practices'.[47] Based on this philosophical insight, they reject the liturgy-as-expression model which separates content from form: 'the inextricability of form and content...values, meaning and convictions do not so much lie *beneath* our communal behaviour and "forms of life" as *in* them'.[48] They subsequently express the unity of form and content: 'It is obvious that we can *distinguish* these two ideas; the mistake is to suppose that we can *separate* them. They are bound together: the content is in the form; the meaning is in the practices.'[49]

These thinkers all recognise that liturgical practices inherently contain and convey theological content. Their intuitions or philosophical insights can be fruitfully supplemented by embodied cognition, which identifies the mechanisms by which practice shapes thought and belief. It is not only belief which is determinative, but liturgy also shapes belief. Pascal already intuited this point in *Pensées* when he recommends that one should simply engage in the practice and the belief would come.[50] A scaffolded understanding of cognition lends weight to proposals that liturgy is not secondary or derivative but itself a bearer of content.

---

[44] Ibid., 105.   [45] Ibid.   [46] Ibid., 239.
[47] Davison and Milbank, *For the Parish*, 11.   [48] Ibid., viii. Emphasis original.
[49] Ibid., 2. Emphasis original.
[50] Blaise Pascal, *Pensées and Other Writings*, ed. Anthony Levi and Honor Levi (Oxford: Oxford University Press, 2008), §250–3.

2.2.2 Different Form, Different Content

If form influences content, it follows that a difference in form leads to a difference in content. Davison and Milbank draw out the implications of the content-bearing nature of liturgy: 'Change the form and we change how we understand the content; change the practices and we at least risk changing the meaning.'[51] This insight draws attention to how differences in practices encode different theologies. Davison and Milbank seek to discredit the assumption that one can change the form of an ecclesial practice whilst retaining the same theological content: 'any root and branch "re-expression" of the Church in new practices and forms of life, involves an equally thoroughgoing re-configuration of what the Church believes.'[52] One cannot, therefore, contend that a shift in the form of practice merely constitutes a different expression of the same content, as the liturgy-as-expression model holds.

The same principle applies to differences between traditions. It is not simply the case that common beliefs can be expressed in a variety of liturgical expressions. Rather, liturgical differences underpin real theological differences.[53] The connection between form and content has been recognised at various junctures in history when churches have sought to standardise practices; to take an English example:

> Until the liturgical reforms of the past few decades, the Church of England had a truly universal liturgy in the Book of Common Prayer. This universality spoke eloquently of the fundamental unity of the Church, whether it was celebrated with high-church ceremony or with low-church simplicity. It was the basis of a profound commonality and this was no accident. The Elizabethan settlement insisted upon a common liturgy for the sake of the unity of the English people.[54]

If difference in liturgy had no theological ramifications, insisting on such conformity would be meaningless.

The relationship between form and content is not restricted to how bodies are choreographed in liturgies, but also extends to material culture. The meaning particular objects take on may be determined by how they relate to our bodies; hence the meaning of particular objects is not completely arbitrary. Like embodied meaning, this 'material meaning' differs from a symbolic meaning. Thus, '[i]t is no quirk that we use bread and wine for Holy Communion or that we use water for baptism. The sign used in the sacrament is consistent with what the

---

[51] Davison and Milbank, *For the Parish*, 2. See also, Anna I. Corwin, 'Changing God, Changing Bodies: The Impact of New Prayer Practices on Elderly Catholic Nuns' Embodied Experience', *Ethos* 40, no. 4 (2012).
[52] Davison and Milbank, *For the Parish*, 24.   [53] Ibid.   [54] Ibid., 96–7.

sacrament promises and bestows'.[55] Davison and Milbank reflect on the way in which the use of water in baptism is consonant with baptism's meaning: 'The water of baptism...is primarily an indication of washing, but it also evokes refreshment and sustenance.'[56] In other words, the waters of baptism derive their meaning, in part, from how the physical properties of water *interact with the human body*, serving to wash and to hydrate it. In the terminology of embodied cognition, the meaning depends on the *affordances* that water presents to human bodies given the way they interact with the world.

If the meaning attached to water were purely symbolic, then the relationship between the properties of water and its meaning would be completely arbitrary, and any substance would be equally suitable.[57] Davison counters this view, showing that the material form provides the basis for meaning: 'Sacraments...bear a close material resemblance to the spiritual benefit they promise. Water cleanses; bread and wine sustain and bring joy; reaching out to touch someone is a sign of recognition and support. The material aspect is not arbitrary. The natural meaning is retained but excelled.'[58] 'Natural meaning' here is synonymous with what I have termed 'material meaning'.

One of the implications of a non-arbitrary relationship between the properties of baptismal water and its meaning is that using a different substance would alter the meaning. Davison and Milbank imaginatively engage in such a thought experiment: 'we could not baptize someone in detergent. It would express only one part of what baptism is. Baptism is washing but not only washing. Water, and baptism, has nothing to do with the harshness of soap'.[59] The fact that the relationship between the material and symbolic dimensions of baptismal water is not arbitrary raises difficult questions in examples where there seems to be a dissonance between the material and the symbolic meaning.[60] Davison discusses the historic example of baptism in seawater:

> Baptism in the sea poses an intriguing question about matter...Baptism is primarily about washing and sharing in the death of Christ, and therefore in his resurrection. However, the water of baptism also represents the water that Jesus says will quench every thirst (John 4:13–14; 7:37–39). We cannot drink seawater; it causes thirst rather than relieving it.[61]

What is implicitly invoked here is the notion of affordances (see Chapter 2). The matter-of-fact statement that 'salt water does not quell thirst' is more precisely

---

[55] Ibid., 6.   [56] Ibid.   [57] Ibid.
[58] Davison, *Why Sacraments?*, 56. See also Grumett, *Material Eucharist*.
[59] Davison and Milbank, *For the Parish*, 6.
[60] This is similar to the way in which embodied and symbolic meanings might come in to conflict; see Section 1.
[61] Davison, *Why Sacraments?*, 61–2. See also Grumett, *Material Eucharist*, 25.

formulated as 'salt water does not quell thirst *for human beings on account of the kind of bodies we have*'. The non-thirst-quenching quality of salt water is not a property of the salt water *per se*; rather it is an interactional property which arises on account of *both* the material properties of salt water *and* the particularities of the human body. The meaning salt water has for humans is relative to their bodies, even though the role of our bodies is often overlooked (after all, we have never experienced salt water from a body other than our own). In effective symbols, the material meaning is appropriate for it to bear particular symbolic meaning which is added to it. In summary, embodied cognition explicates how particular bodily and material forms take on non-symbolic meanings for humans; a scaffolded view of religion reveals that altering a bodily or material scaffold—and not only beliefs—alters that content.

2.2.3 Beyond Belief and Texts

Whereas the liturgy-as-expression model identifies theology exclusively with propositional belief conveyed linguistically, a scaffolded account reveals other forms of theological content. In light of embodied and material meanings, theological content can no longer be exclusively restricted to propositional beliefs and texts. A number of theologians and philosophers have criticised accounts which reduce religious knowledge purely to propositions. These thinkers point to aspects of embodiment, or ritual in particular, as offering an alternative source of knowledge to religious belief.[62]

The exclusive fixation on the propositional content in the liturgy-as-expression model comes at the expense of the other forms of knowledge. Wolterstorff identifies practical knowledge (sometimes referred to as knowing-how) and object knowledge (derived from familiarity or acquaintance with an object of one's experience, including persons, substances, etc.) as alternative philosophical categories of knowledge relevant to liturgical practices. He sets out to demonstrate that 'learning to participate in the social practice of acknowledging God liturgically' is a means of gaining 'object knowledge', in this case personal knowledge, of God.[63] He summarises:

A common phenomenon in human affairs is that, by acquiring and employing the know-how of a social practice for engaging things or substances of a certain sort in a certain way, one comes to know those things or substances themselves. So, too, we come to know our fellow human beings by acquiring and exercising the know-how of engaging them in certain ways. Liturgically

---

[62] Coakley, 'Beyond "Belief"'; Cuneo, *Ritualized Faith*; Wolterstorff, 'Knowing God Liturgically'; Wynn, *Faith and Place*.
[63] Wolterstorff, 'Knowing God Liturgically', 3.

acquired knowledge of God is just one instance of this much more general phenomenon.[64]

Following Stump, Wolterstorff argues that object knowledge is not reducible to propositional knowledge.[65] One of the extended examples of object-knowledge, which Wolterstorff takes as paradigmatic, is Elkins' description of painting. A painter-turned-art-historian, Elkins describes how a lifetime of attention to paint can give painters a deep and immersive familiarity (and therefore object-knowledge) of the substance:

> Its materials are worked without [scientific] knowledge of their properties, by blind experiment, by the feel of the paint. A painter knows what to do by the tug of the brush as it pulls through a mixture of oils, and by the look of colored slurries on the palette…Artists become expert in distinguishing between degrees of gloss and wetness—and they do so without knowing how they do it, or how chemicals create their effects.[66]

On Wolterstorff's analysis, this kind of know-how is not reducible to propositional knowledge: 'only a small part of the know-how of the painter consists of beliefs that he holds. Most of it is sub-doxastic, located primarily not in his mind but in his eye and in the muscles of his fingers, wrist, and arm'.[67] Cognitive scientists (and philosophers of cognitive science) may be reticent to grant that this knowledge literally resides in eye, fingers, wrist, and arm, as though if they were severed from the body they would retain such knowledge independently (and Wolterstorff's 'primarily' qualifier is important here). Rather, neural maps for manipulating these body parts to interact with the paint are crucial. Nevertheless, Wolterstorff's point stands; even if this knowledge is not stored in the body, it is nevertheless *about* the body and how it interacts with the environment. Again, the boundaries between perception, action, and cognition are blurred here, and it makes little sense to talk about such knowledge as independent of bodily affordances.

Although Wolterstorff introduces this evocative bodily account of knowledge, when he comes to apply it to the case of liturgy he focuses on the practices of directly addressing God in speech and song in the context of liturgy. He argues that various ways of addressing God tacitly imply things about God: that God is a person who can be addressed, that God listens, that God can be wronged, and so forth.[68] This tacit form of knowledge, Wolterstorff maintains, remains sub-doxastic; it need not be accompanied by a corresponding and explicit propositional knowledge.

---

[64] Ibid., 5.   [65] Ibid., 4.   [66] Cited in ibid., 5–6.
[67] Ibid., 6.   [68] Ibid., 11–13.

While Wolterstorff reaches beyond propositional knowledge, he nevertheless retains a focus on linguistic utterances. Thus, his account largely overlooks the bodily aspects of liturgy (beyond the bodily techniques required for language production). Granted, Wolterstorff readily acknowledges that his narrow focus does not offer a comprehensive account of the kinds of knowledge available through liturgy, and invites a more comprehensive account.[69] The most suggestive part of his argument, with respect to the embodied aspects of liturgy, is found when he gestures beyond his particular focus on linguistic address:

> it is by no means only when addressing God that liturgical participants take God to be a certain way. In kneeling for the prayers and closing their eyes, they take God to be a certain way. In receiving the Eucharistic elements, they take God to be a certain way…Whatever they take God to be like when performing the actions of the liturgy, if God is in fact that way, then by learning to perform those actions and performing them, they come to know God as being that way.[70]

A scaffolded approach extends Wolterstorff's account of the non-propositional, sub-doxastic content of liturgy, by reaching beyond linguistic utterances and exploring embodied and material meanings inherent in liturgical practices.

Coakley offers another critique of exclusively linguistic theological content. She observes that religious epistemology has shown a renewed interest in perception, especially with Alston's work.[71] Although Coakley is sceptical about Alston's assertion that there is direct, unmediated perception of God, she finds his account of 'doxastic practice' more fruitful. This concept proposes that repeated sensory acts offer epistemic justification: 'sensory experience involves both "input" and "output", with a consistency of success in accurate perception that pragmatically "justifies" our reliance on the deliverances of sense experience, all "defeaters" notwithstanding'.[72] Coakley extends the argument to embodied practices: 'What, then, if we were to extend the notion of "doxastic practices" well beyond those of ordinary sense perception…and well beyond such neurotic checkings for initial sensory "reliability", to include such richly coded social undertakings as the bodily performance of liturgy?'[73]

She then draws on insights from feminist epistemology to critique Alston's account of perception. '[S]ecular analytic epistemology', she argues, 'has been inordinately invested in giving an account of the successful perception and re-identification of "medium-sized dry goods" over other forms of epistemic

---

[69]   Ibid., 9, 13.   [70]   Ibid., 13.

[71]   William P. Alston, *Perceiving God: The Epistemology of Religious Experience* (London: Cornell University Press, 1991).

[72]   Coakley, 'Beyond "Belief"', 135.   [73]   Ibid., 137.

negotiation.'[74] As a result, epistemologists have presumed a detached model of perception in which the perceiver inspects an object from a distance. Feminists have rightly critiqued such a model of perception since it neglects the situatedness of the knower and 'the significance of the personal, familial, and communal interactions that enable and sustain such perception in the first place'.[75] As a remedy to this blinkeredness, Coakley appropriates feminist epistemology's account of relational knowledge. Relational knowledge is fundamental to a child's ability to acquire other forms of knowledge, since '[o]ther people are the point of origin of a child's entry into the material/physical environment—in making it—and in fostering entry into the language with which children learn to name'.[76] Relational knowledge, Coakley contends, provides a more suitable analogue for the kind of knowledge acquired in liturgical practice, a knowledge which is irreducible to propositional content. She summarises:

> All the more important, then, is the analogue here with 'knowing God': whereas Alston often slips into talk about 'perceiving God' in individualistic and merely informational terms,...insights about childhood psychology and epistemology suggest how the learned, sensual, and social responses of the liturgy might be parallel, and indispensable, modes of coming to 'know' the divine in some direct sense different from Alston's 'perceiving' of God.[77]

Wynn's exploration of the experience of place likewise explores how embodied meaning exceeds propositional knowledge. The religious significance of place, he suggests, highlights the difficulty of articulating bodily knowledge: '[k]nowledge of place consists, at least in part, in an embodied, practical and, very often, theoretically inarticulate responsiveness to a given region of space'.[78] Thus it is difficult to reduce knowledge of a place to a discursive description.[79] Given one's embodied presence provides access to bodily knowledge, there are some aspects of a place which can only be fully understood by being there.

To correct the bias towards text, Vásquez critiques 'semiotic reductionism', which presumes that practices can be reduced to their symbolic content. To criticise this approach, he argues that symbolic representations cannot 'exhaust the multiple sensorimotor processes associated with experience'.[80] He deploys Merleau-Ponty to emphasise the role of the body in lived experience:

---

[74] Ibid., 138.   [75] Ibid.   [76] Ibid., 139.   [77] Ibid., 140.
[78] Wynn, *Faith and Place*, 8.   [79] Ibid., 30.
[80] Vásquez, *More Than Belief*, 82. For a similar critique in discussions of embodiment in anthropology, see Green, 'Medicines'. Cf. Taylor Carman, *Merleau-Ponty* (London: Routledge, 2008), 18; Maurice Merleau-Ponty, *The Visible and the Invisible*, ed. Claude Lefort, Alphonso Lingis, and Klod Lëfor (Evanston, IL: Northwestern University Press, 1968), 126; Christian Scharen, 'Ecclesiology "from the Body": Ethnographic Notes toward a Carnal Theology', in *Perspectives on Ecclesiology and Ethnography*, ed. Pete Ward (Grand Rapids, MI: Eerdmans, 2012), 66; Lambros Malafouris, *How Things Shape the Mind: A Theory of Material Management* (Cambridge, MA: MIT Press, 2013), 90–4.

By placing carnality as the core of our being-in-the-world, Merleau-Ponty allows us to appreciate the full force of religious phenomena such as healing, glossolalia, conversion, trance, and other ecstatic states that may or may not involve the use of psychoactive components, as well as practices such as fasting, penance, dancing, pilgrimage, rites of passage, and funerary rituals.[81]

These critiques of the ways in which belief and text have been allowed to dominate, open the way for the contribution of practices to be duly recognised. As Davison and Milbank state, 'Nobody contests that the Church expresses her beliefs in words. We need to appreciate that her beliefs are also to be found in her disciplines and how she orders her common life. Our practices are not so much window dressing. They are the arena in which our convictions are learned and held.'[82] Once practices are recognised as bearers of theological content, they can take their rightful place alongside texts and beliefs as constituents of a 'tradition'.

The idea that embodied ecclesial practices are in some way normative for theology is by no means a new one in the Christian tradition. The rubric *Lex Orandi, Lex Credendi* is often taken to mean that the form of worship informs more explicit theological beliefs. Scarlat points out that 'Evagrius of Pontus, a fourth-century Orthodox monastic writer, says that "a theologian is one who prays, and one who prays is a theologian". In other words, the one who wants to understand and know the divine truths must use his body'.[83]

The Eastern Orthodox Church has a particularly rich tradition of reflecting the normative dimension of its liturgy through the notion of 'orthopraxis':

> Christian Orthodoxy is not simply a compendium of firm teachings but it is more an orthopraxis, which means the custodian of an action model. The intention is to preserve and observe some performative acts in its rituals which in fact leads to the idea that the 'right faith' is more of a 'genuine model' to produce faith. The body is also fundamental for both liturgical participation and for theological thinking.[84]

This statement contains a number of points for which I have been arguing on the basis of embodied cognition. First, the concept that theological understanding is not restricted to doctrine, but that practices also form part of the tradition. Second, it is not simply the case that pre-determined beliefs are expressed in the form of a ritual. Rather, in line with Pascal's insight, causation can also operate in the opposite direction, with practices shaping beliefs. Scarlat deploys the findings

---

[81] Vásquez, *More Than Belief*, 84; Kullman and Taylor, 'The Pre-Objective World', 119.

[82] Davison and Milbank, *For the Parish*, 15.

[83] Scarlat, 'Embodied Cognition of Religion', 165.

[84] Ibid. See also Cuneo, *Ritualized Faith*, 8.

of embodied cognition to argue for a 'circularity between the mind and the experience of the body in the Orthodox rituals...the mind is influenced by the experience of the body and the experience of the body becomes the doxological expression of faith'. Third, the body therefore is not merely something which participates in liturgical acts, but in so doing it also participates in theological thinking.

Wolterstorff, Coakley, Vásquez, and Wynn all, in their own ways, reject an exclusively linguistic or doxastic account of religion by highlighting the significance of embodiment, materiality, and liturgy. The way in which embodied meanings exceed linguistic description resonates with an intuitive sense that language is sometimes insufficient to capture embodied experience. However, beyond this vague surplus of meaning, embodied cognition articulates (some of) the non-propositional content in practices and reveals how it arises. It thereby offers a richer understanding of the embodied and material meaning which these scholars strive to articulate.

2.2.4 Homo Liturgicus

If the liturgy-as-expression model was premised on a flawed anthropology, the alternative model recognises that humans are fundamentally embodied creatures. By detailing how humans are embodied, embodied cognition suggests an anthropology in which embodied practices profoundly influence thought. Hence we are creatures for whom liturgy is central. Brown and Strawn note this link between embodied worship and anthropology: 'the aspects of liturgy we want to emphasize as most conducive to embodied worship are those that are most active, participative, and interpersonal. Corporate worship is most clearly about persons as bodies and active agents when we are engaged together in a common activity'.[85] They continue, '[o]ur reason for this emphasis [on participative action] is our view of human nature and the attempt to move away from concepts of non-material inner individualist events as constituting formative worship. What we think and experience during worship, is what our bodies are doing'.[86]

If humans are fundamentally embodied, then accommodation respects embodiment. Davison recognises that sacraments are an accommodation when he observes an uncanny fit between the sacraments and humanity: '[The sacraments] are everything that we are, and purposefully so: physical, material, speaking, cultural'.[87] He also explicitly identifies accommodation with respect to the sacraments, when he states that sacraments are important because 'God thought it fitting to reach human beings in a human way...in his action towards us, God accommodates himself to what we are'.[88] What is true about the sacraments can

---

[85] Brown and Strawn, *Physical Nature of Christian Life*, 150.   [86] Ibid., 152.
[87] Davison, *Why Sacraments?*, 1.   [88] Ibid., 10.

be extended to liturgical practices as a whole: these practices accommodate our embodied way of being in the world.

2.3 Wainwright's Doxology

Even though liturgical theology is tasked with attending to the rituals of the church, it has historically been preoccupied with the historical development of liturgical texts rather than the embodied and material dimensions of the liturgy. It too often operates on the liturgy-as-expression model, failing to recognise the unity of form and content. To demonstrate the utility of these two opposing models as an analytic tool, I examine Wainwright's seminal liturgical theology as a case study.

Wainwright's sizeable systematic theology remains one of the most thorough-going attempts to reunite doctrine and liturgy. He argues that the relationship between doctrine and worship remains under-appreciated: '[m]y conviction is that the relations between doctrine and worship are deeper rooted and further reaching than many theologians and liturgists appeared to recognize in their writings'.[89] He aims to remedy this predicament by writing a systematic theology 'from a liturgical perspective'.[90]

Wainwright's opening paragraph, in which he defines theology and its relation to liturgical practices, is worth quoting at length:

> Theology is an intellectual activity. Yet the sources and resources of theology are richer than the human intellect. Theology is intellectual reflexion on all the dealings between God and humanity. In so far as the theologian is a believer, his [sic] thinking cannot be disengaged from his faith. His faith engages him as a total person, so that even his intellectual reflexion upon his faith is, dialectically and within the unity of his personality, still an activity of faith...His intellect is at the service of his existential vision and commitment.[91]

Wainwright acknowledges the entanglement between theological thought and practice; he rejects a bipolar view of theologians—the theologian who engages in intellectual reflection is the very same person who is caught up in a faith which grips the 'total person'; he recognises that theology itself is a practice, or an 'activity', which finds its place in a broader life of faith. Each of these commitments suggests that theology might be broader than an intellectual exercise.

---

[89] Geoffrey Wainwright, *Doxology: The Praise of God in Worship, Doctrine and Life: A Systematic Theology* (New York: Oxford University Press, 1984), ix.
[90] Ibid.   [91] Ibid., 1.

Beyond this opening statement, Wainwright also discusses the reciprocal relationship between doctrine and liturgy more explicitly. For example, he argues that the theologian 'is aiming at a coherent intellectual expression of the Christian vision. He should examine the liturgy from that angle, both in order to learn from it and in order to propose to the worshipping community any corrections or improvements which he judges necessary'.[92] This statement highlights the bi-directional relationship between liturgy and doctrine. Moreover, it affirms that the practices of liturgy carry theological content: it has something to teach. The reciprocity of doctrine and liturgy is again evident in Wainwright's discussion of the rubric *lex orandi, lex credendi*: '[t]he linguistic ambiguity of the Latin tag corresponds to a material interplay which in fact takes place between worship and doctrine in Christian practice: worship influences doctrine, and doctrine worship'.[93] This suggests that religious practices may constitute theology along-side conceptual formulations.

Despite these intimations that Wainwright might transgress the *status quo*, there are other indications that he is still wedded to the liturgy-as-expression model. First, Wainwright states his position in no uncertain terms in the first sentence: '[t]heology is an intellectual activity'.[94] He thus drives a strict division between the first-order experience and second-order reflection: 'the "architectonic" and "critical" functions of theological reasoning, secondary though that reasoning is in the relation to substantial communion with God, play a proper part in shaping and pruning the continuing primary experience'.[95]

Second, despite Wainwright's renewed emphasis on the importance of liturgy, he often reduces liturgy to its symbolic and linguistic dimensions. Promisingly, he recognises that 'Christian worship uses sacraments and sacramentals, rituals in which *gesture*, and *movement* and *material objects* play a significant part'.[96] However, he then goes on to clarify that '[i]n all these cases, the action is accompanied by verbal interpretation and takes place within a framework of understanding'.[97] Thus his initial focus on the embodied aspect of liturgy quickly retreats back into the realm of the 'intellect' by way of linguistic interpretation.

The privileging of the linguistic is underwritten by a theological anthropology which understands relationship with God as primarily verbal. Again, Wainwright's anthropology seems promising from an embodied perspective when he writes: '[i]t is an embodied humanity endowed with speech that God calls into communion with himself'.[98] Yet, he then goes on to say that '[t]his communion with God, *symbolically* focused in the liturgy, is the primary locus of religious *language* for the Christian'.[99] It is hardly surprising that he devotes chapters to textual sources of scripture, and creeds and hymns, whilst individual sacraments are

---

[92] Ibid.   [93] Ibid., 218.   [94] Ibid., 1.   [95] Ibid., 21.
[96] Ibid., 20. Emphasis original.   [97] Ibid.
[98] Ibid.   [99] Ibid., 20–1. Emphasis added.

treated in one or two pages. The emphasis on liturgy as linguistic carries over into Wainwright's discussion of theology as second-order reflection. He writes, '[t]heological language belongs to the second order: it is the language of reflexion upon the primary experience. The language of worship mediates the substance on which theologians reflect; without that substance, theological talk would have no referent'.[100]

Third, as a result of his bias towards the linguistic, Wainwright often occludes the embodied aspect of liturgy. His discussion of baptism is representative of a broader pattern which analyses liturgy independently of its bodily instantiations. Here Wainwright discusses baptism in terms of its significance, scriptural foundation, symbolic meaning, and doctrinal implications.[101] What are altogether absent from Wainwright's account are the corporeal and material aspects of baptism.

Ironically, perhaps the most compelling description of the material dimensions of liturgy is in Wainwright's discussion of scripture.[102] He opens his chapter on scripture by considering how Bibles are processed, censed, kissed, and housed. He shows that holy books play an important role in liturgy, not simply as a medium for transmitting text, but also as a material object endowed with meaning. Though this focus is absent in the reflections upon other practices, in this instance it provides an example of how the ritual and material aspects could go beyond the abstract and linguistic focus of intellectualist accounts.

In summary, despite Wainwright's recognition of the reciprocal relationship between doctrine and liturgy, he continues to work within a largely linguistic framework. He considers liturgy almost exclusively in its symbolic and textual dimensions at the expense of the role of the body. His failure to discern the significance of the body is a result of his theological anthropology:

> The earthly existence of humanity is embodied existence...Fundamental as the body is, it is the conviction of Christianity that human existence transcends the body and material creation in general. The body and material creation in general have 'spiritual' value as the vehicle and context by and in which human beings may grow in communion with God.[103]

Thus, for Wainwright, the body must ultimately be transcended. Lurking within this statement is a material–spiritual dualism which relegates the body to a secondary concern and encloses theology in an intellectualist paradigm. Wainwright's work provides an example of how even liturgical theology often overlooks bodily and material meanings in favour of symbolic ones.

---

[100] Ibid., 21.   [101] Ibid., 73–4.
[102] Ibid., 149–50.   [103] Ibid., 28.

A scaffolded view of religion provides the necessary resources for a corrective of this one-sided emphasis.

3 Religious Formation

The capacity of liturgies to contain embodied and material meaning suggests that these meanings are conveyed to participants. This affords liturgies the ability to inculcate these meanings, shaping desire and fostering virtues (or vices). Hence the unity of form and content in liturgy calls for a revised account of the formation of the religious subject.

3.1 Bodily Formation

Findings from cognitive science suggest that human behaviour is particularly open to formation from experience. Brown and Reimer observe that the human brain develops slowly relative to other primates; the human pre-frontal cortex does not mature until after puberty whereas the same maturation occurs in chimpanzees at two to three years of age.[104] This long process of maturation, they argue, leaves humans particularly susceptible to formation by their interactions with the world:

> remarkably slow development of the human brain (compared to other primates) means that for nearly two decades brain structure and its functional consequences are particularly open to being shaped by life experiences. Openness to experience allows for greater flexibility and variety in our formation, particularly the formation of important aspects of our most human characteristics: intelligence, personality, and character, as well as assimilation of cultural modes of thought and behavior.[105]

Other findings likewise demonstrate that considerable neuroplasticity persists into adulthood. For example, a famous study on London taxi drivers found that the part of the brain used for spatial reasoning physically expanded in response to habitually having to navigate London's complicated streets over an extended period of time.[106] Given that neural structures have the capacity to significantly

---

[104] Brown and Reimer, 'Embodied Cognition', 837.

[105] Ibid., 839. See also Sarah Lane Ritchie, 'Integrated Physicality and the Absence of God: Spiritual Technologies in Theological Context', *Modern Theology* 37, no. 2 (2021): 297.

[106] Katherine Woollett and Eleanor A. Maguire, 'Acquiring "the Knowledge" of London's Layout Drives Structural Brain Changes', *Current Biology* 21, no. 24 (2011).

reshape themselves in response to the external environment, human thought and behaviour is extremely malleable.[107] Moreover, this makes the human brain particularly adept at appropriating environmental resources as cognitive scaffolds.

Fuller argues that the malleability of the cerebral cortex not only means that it can be shaped by experience, but that the shaping also increases control over behaviour; humans do not simply respond by reflex, but can, in many cases, respond in ways determined by 'higher' cognitive processes: 'what is biologically unique to us is that our proportionately large cerebral cortex makes it possible to override instinctual responses to environmental stimuli and to substitute others instead'.[108]

The openness and malleability of the human mind means that humans are shaped in response to their embodied experience of the outside world. Embodied experience has the capacity to shape various aspects of character. The frequent, repetitive nature of liturgies, often practised over the span of a life-time, makes them ideal vehicles through which to effect formation. As Brown and Reimer explain, '[f]ormation of [personality, character, virtue, wisdom, and even religiousness] is not the accumulation of a rich bank of abstract ideas which one can manipulate off-line to understand the world and act appropriately. Rather, formation occurs in relation to action and feedback, and is preserved in sensorimotor memories that have implications for future actions, most of which exist i[n] the domain of action schemas and habit' (see Conclusion, Section 3.3).[109]

Cuneo envisages a key formative role for liturgy when he argues that among the dominant goals of liturgy is 'that of contributing to the construction of a narrative identity of its participants'.[110] For Cuneo narrative identity is not peripheral to one's self-understanding, but is 'a sequence of events, which has that agent as a subject, to which he or she might refer if he or she were accurately to tell a story of his or her life'.[111]

Embodied cognition contributes towards an explanation of how Cuneo's ambitious vision for liturgy as central to identity formation might be realised. Through their capacity to shape emotions, preferences, judgements, attention, and attitudes, embodied practices can play a powerful role in shaping a person's behaviour. Thus, the bodily and material aspects of religion are significant pedagogical tools, helping to inculcate a religious tradition's values and sentiments. In the remainder of this section I consider how this formative capacity of religious practices might contribute (or fail to contribute) to religious goals such as virtue development and sanctification.

---

[107] Brown and Reimer, 'Embodied Cognition', 838–9.
[108] Fuller, *Spirituality in the Flesh*, 13.
[109] Brown and Reimer, 'Embodied Cognition', 841.
[110] Cuneo, *Ritualized Faith*, 88.   [111] Ibid.

3.2 Virtue

The capacity for habitual practices to inculcate virtues has been recognised since the very inception of virtue ethics.[112] Davison and Milbank echo this Aristotelian insight: 'Character is formed by repetition and routine. This is the way in which things become habitual. By this route, we are formed in good habits.'[113] As a habitual practice, liturgical participation can similarly participate in virtue formation.

Whilst recognising the potential of liturgies to form virtues through habitual action, Herdt argues that mechanical repetition is insufficient on its own to inculcate virtues such as courage.[114] The challenge to act courageously might arise in a completely novel context in which the specific embodied actions have not been rehearsed: 'It is undeniably true that human beings are creatures of habit and that repeated action becomes a kind of second nature to us, performed with ease and without conscious thought. Yet it is also the case that virtuous character requires a capacity to extrapolate from one situation to another.'[115] Therefore the imagination is required for such an extrapolation. However, one way in which liturgies might offer resources for virtue formation beyond habitual action, and train the kind of imaginative leaps which Herdt describes, is through their narrative structure.

Narratives, through their use of concrete language, are particularly embodied (see Chapter 4, Section 3). Brown and Reimer seize on how narratives evoke sensorimotor simulations to argue that they can play a particular role in ethical formation: 'Language used for story telling has a very particular significant formative influence. It allows us to know vicariously the experiences of others, and can open to us new ways of experiencing the world, as well as teaching values and virtues. Stories have this sort of cognitive power because they cause hearers to implicitly simulate the behaviours that are described in the narrative.'[116] By drawing the reader into the story, narratives have a special power to elicit empathy and convey values.

Cuneo notes that liturgies share a deep affinity with narratives: 'The ancient Christian liturgies engage the core narrative in a striking variety of ways: they retell it, interpret it to explore its meaning, re-enact elements of it, celebrate it, and creatively extend it in some surprising ways. It is as if, despite their highly scripted character, these liturgies are restless, determined to explore the core

---

[112] Aristotle, *The Nicomachean Ethics*, trans. William David Ross (London: Oxford University Press, 1954), 1095b.

[113] Davison and Milbank, *For the Parish*, 100.

[114] Jennifer A. Herdt, 'The Virtue of the Liturgy', in *The Blackwell Companion to Christian Ethics*, ed. Stanley Hauerwas and Samuel Wells (Oxford: Wiley-Blackwell, 2011), 536–7.

[115] Ibid., 537.   [116] Brown and Reimer, 'Embodied Cognition', 843.

narrative from as many angles as they feasibly can.'[117] He uses the connection between liturgy and narratives to extend Nussbaum's insights into the significance of literature for the moral life: 'What literature does, Nussbaum suggests, is present us with rich descriptions of characters, their traits, and their often complicated predicaments, allowing us to emotionally engage them and thereby expand our powers of moral judgement, refining our abilities of ethical discernment, deepen our ethical understanding, and have access to alien points of view.'[118] For Cuneo, liturgy too, by immersing us in a narrative world and having us take on the perspective of its characters, fulfils the same role in cultivating moral capacities. Indeed, Cuneo argues that liturgy goes beyond literature in certain aspects of moral formation: 'while reading a novel can be morally transformative, it is not an activity that as such calls for the activity of committing oneself to anything. Liturgical re-enactment...is different since it belongs to the essence of this activity that the assembled commit themselves to ethical and religious ideals.'[119] While the reader of a narrative can take up the perspective of a detached onlooker, practitioners of liturgies find themselves to be participants, enmeshed in the narrative as one of its actors.[120]

Cuneo further specifies the kind of ethics a Christian liturgy ought to inculcate, posing the question 'What does neighbour-love have to do with liturgy?'[121] In his discussion of 'Love and Liturgy', he describes an 'ethic of outwardness' which stands 'in contrast to an *ethic of proximity*, wherein we conform to various ethical directives and ideas—perhaps being open to meeting needs and obligations where we find them—but sparing little effort to expand our attention to the needs and obligations beyond those which we encounter in the various in-groups to which we belong, such as family, friends, church, synagogue, or country.'[122] He argues that such an ethic is central to Jesus' ethical vision. Furthermore, it is precisely this kind of ethical vision which liturgy ought to cultivate through re-enactment.

Although Cuneo intends his account as normative, rather than descriptive, embodied cognition research can shed some light on whether liturgies live up to the role he envisions. A number of the studies surveyed in the previous chapter point to cognitive effects which, if they are not themselves fully-fledged virtues, are at least key ingredients for virtue. Cuneo's connection between liturgy and love suggests that one area of embodied cognition research relevant to virtue formation is work on the emotions. The capacity of embodied practices to train emotions allows them to contribute to what some theologians have termed a

---

[117] Cuneo, *Ritualized Faith*, 66.
[118] Ibid., 95. Cf. Martha Craven Nussbaum, 'Love's Knowledge', in *Love's Knowledge: Essays on Philosophy and Literature* (Oxford: Oxford University Press, 1992).
[119] Cuneo, *Ritualized Faith*, 103.   [120] Ibid., 82.   [121] Ibid., 20.
[122] Ibid., 25.

'pedagogy of desire'.[123] As discussed in Chapter 5, emotions do not simply add a sentimental layer to experiences; they are also implicated in many cognitive processes including decision making. As Izard argues, emotions 'constitute the primary motivational system for human beings'.[124] This affords them a special role in virtue ethics.

Whereas utilitarianism and deontology focus on what constitutes an ethical decision in a given scenario, virtue ethics focuses on the question of capacity: what kind of character formation is required such that an agent can behave ethically when faced with a decision. The focus on habits to inculcate virtues is therefore a process which begins long before the agent is faced with a vexing ethical dilemma. To behave ethically an agent needs not only to know the right course of action, but also possess the will and capacity to pursue it. The shaping of desire is thus crucial to ethical performance; and forming emotional responses to given scenarios is central to this task. If emotions are the primary motivational system, as Izard contends, then they must also be primary to motivating virtuous behaviour. Given that embodied practices often influence and indeed train emotions, they contribute to strengthening ethical capacity.

Embodied cognition findings which show that religious priming, synchronised movement, and awe promote prosociality and social bonding are also particularly relevant to moral formation (see Chapter 6, Section 4). These mechanisms may play an important role in community formation and inculcating virtues such as generosity and charity. However, researchers who conducted a meta-analysis on religious priming and prosociality offer a number of caveats:

> Importantly, we of course do not claim that religion solely encourages prosociality; priming research has also shown religious concepts to encourage uncharitable attitudes, such as racism...Nor is this to say that the prosociality that religion inspires is indiscriminant and universal; religious prosociality is likely preferentially directed toward ingroup members...Nor are we arguing that religion is the only, most effective, or most desirable path to prosociality. For example, priming secular institutions of justice can increase dictator game offers to the same degree as priming religion...None of these caveats, however, refute the evidence that aspects of religious beliefs and rituals motivate people to sacrifice self-interest for others.[125]

These observations caution against a sanguine view of ritual's potential for inculcating virtue; religious practice can also promote vice.

---

[123] Smith, *Desiring the Kingdom*, 94.
[124] Carroll E. Izard, *Human Emotions* (New York: Plenum, 1977), 3.
[125] Shariff et al., 'Religious Priming', 41. See also van Cappellen, Saroglou, and Toth-Gauthier, 'Religiosity and Prosocial Behavior', 20.

Herdt provides a striking example of the liturgical formation of virtue gone wrong.[126] She notes that survey data has shown that US Christians in all major traditions are more likely to find torture often or sometimes justifiable than the religiously unaffiliated. Indeed those who attended services weekly were more likely to countenance torture (54 per cent) than those who seldom or never attend (42 per cent).[127] Herdt is cautious in interpreting these figures; correlation does not demonstrate causation, and other variables such as political affiliation or ideology were better predictors in the study. Hence one cannot conclude from these statistics that Christian liturgies are actively responsible for inculcating these attitudes. Nevertheless, the figures do at least suggest that participation in religious services is insufficient to counteract whatever forces lie at the root of an acceptance of torture. Liturgies alone are not enough, Herdt concludes, to universally instil virtue in this instance.

Another example of potential mal-formation through liturgical participation concerns group identity. Some studies report that religious priming results in negative attitudes towards out-groups.[128] This is precisely the opposite ethic to the one Cuneo associates with the teaching of Jesus and argues that liturgy should nurture. One study nuanced this connection, finding that religion primes increase in-group prosociality while God primes increase out-group prosociality; the researchers suggest that the former is associated with in-group affiliation whereas the latter is related to moral impression management.[129] In contrast to religious priming, findings from synchrony studies found that prosociality extended to out-groups.[130] The complex interaction of potentially competing mechanisms would benefit from further research. Liturgical participation may not be a panacea for all our moral ills, but it can make a significant contribution towards moral formation.

These qualifications notwithstanding, the discovery of virtue-related cognitive effects for religious practices opens new opportunities. In particular, ritual designs could be modified to correspond to particular ethical outcomes.[131] Soliman, Johnson, and Song go as far as to suggest normative implications of embodied mechanisms: 'One intriguing hypothesis is that churches with more synchronous religious rituals...may facilitate the formation of more ethnically diverse congregations in which people whose languages and cultures are different from each other may join together more readily as one. Another possibility in applied research would be to examine whether religious conflicts can be

---

[126]   Herdt, 'The Virtue of the Liturgy', 541–2.   [127]   Ibid., 542.

[128]   LaBouff et al., 'Differences in Attitudes'; Pichon and Saroglou, 'Religion and Helping'.

[129]   Jesse Lee Preston and Ryan S. Ritter, 'Different Effects of Religion and God on Prosociality with the Ingroup and Outgroup', *Personality and Social Psychology Bulletin* 39, no. 11 (2013).

[130]   Reddish et al., 'Collective Synchrony'.

[131]   This is precisely the approach being taken in behavioural economics and public health, see Richard H. Thaler and Cass R. Sunstein, *Nudge: Improving Decisions About Health, Wealth, and Happiness* (New Haven, CT: Yale University Press, 2008).

mitigated via synchronous interfaith activities.'[132] Crucially, it is not merely right belief, but also right practice which contributes to moral formation.

By changing how religion is framed, a scaffolded account of religion also changes the locus of religiously-motivated ethical (or unethical) behaviour. Xygalatas and Lang note that situational factors have often been neglected in surveys and experimental studies on religion; instead research has focused on religious 'disposition', which treated religion as a personality trait.[133] If religion is exclusively in the head one might predict that context is irrelevant to moral performance. However, the research which identified the 'Sunday Effect' suggests that situational factors play an important role in moral performance; as the study notes, the question is less one of whether religious people are more moral but under what conditions they behaviour morally.[134] The need for scaffolding and constant reminders or religious primes reveals the strength of the monastic tradition. The way in which the lives of the consecrated religious are structured provides constant reminders of religiosity, meaning that they are never far (spatially or temporally) from religious scaffolds or the support they provide for moral behaviour.[135]

3.3 Sanctification

The capacity for embodied practices to participate in virtue formation also suggests a role for them in the process of sanctification. 'Be transformed by the renewing of your mind (νοός),' entreats the Pauline imperative.[136] If human minds are inexorably embodied, as embodied cognition suggests, then such renewal cannot solely be achieved by the sheer force of will and does not consist solely in the acquisition and affirmation of right beliefs. Rather, the mind is also renewed by participation in bodily practices which habituate virtues and bring about Christ-likeness.

This position is articulated most explicitly by Tertullian, who argues that the soul is sanctified by means of the body:

the flesh is the very condition on which salvation hinges. And since the soul is, in consequence of its salvation, chosen to the service of God, it is the flesh which actually renders it capable of such service. The flesh, indeed, is washed, in order

---

[132] Soliman, Johnson, and Song, 'Understanding Religion,' 858.
[133] Dimitris Xygalatas and Martin Lang, 'Prosociality and Religion', in *Religion: Mental Religion*, ed. N. Kasumi Clements (London: Macmillan, 2016), 124.
[134] Malhorta, 'Are Religious People Nicer?'.
[135] David A. Snowdon, 'Aging and Alzheimer's Disease: Lessons from the Nun Study', *The Gerontologist* 37, no. 2 (1997).
[136] Romans 12:2.

that the soul may be cleansed; the flesh is anointed, that the soul may be consecrated; the flesh is signed (with the cross), that the soul too may be fortified; the flesh is shadowed with the imposition of hands, that the soul also may be illuminated by the Spirit; the flesh feeds on the body and blood of Christ, that the soul likewise may fatten on its God.[137]

Thus Tertullian argues that embodied religious practices effect sanctification. He envisages that rituals do not merely symbolise certain theological ideas, rather they are performative, bringing about a new reality. As Rivera observes, Tertullian sees corporeal practices not merely as a symbolic expression of sanctification, but the very process by which sanctification is enacted:

The unity of flesh and spirit produces very different challenges than its radical opposition. The soul is saved by means of the flesh, Tertullian argues. This implies not only that humans are saved by the work of Christ, but also that such work has profound implications for Christian corporeal practices. No soul can be saved except in the flesh. It is the flesh that is washed, anointed, signed, 'overshadowed by the imposition of hands,' fed with the body of Christ, and so on— the very means by which the soul becomes closer to God. Asserting the significance of flesh for salvation implies also, for Tertullian, that it is the locus of spiritual discipline and reform.[138]

Tertullian's claim may sound overblown: can merely showing up to church and going through the motions constitute one's sanctification? However, from the perspective of embodied cognition this claim sounds less extravagant, since religious practices have concrete cognitive effects with transformative potential. Davison and Milbank echo Tertullian's view on the significance of corporeal practices for effecting salvation: 'Salvation is no abstract, rarefied, or purely spiritual matter. In two related ways it is concrete and worked out in flesh and blood: it meets us in corporeal and social ways and then it reorders our patterns of life and relations in the world.'[139]

In Chapter 4, Section 5.2 I noted that re-narrating the story of the incarnation is one of the ways in which it is mediated. This account is extended in the present chapter: the incarnation is also mediated by its explicit liturgical re-enactment. Davison and Milbank identify the bodily nature of mediation:

It has been probed and elucidated by human thought, a flame passed from mind to mind, from life to life. Our encounter is a mediated encounter. The revelation

---

[137] Tertullian, *On the Resurrection of the Flesh* (New York: Charles Schribner's Sons, 1896), 551.
[138] Rivera, *Poetics of the Flesh*, 58.
[139] Davison and Milbank, *For the Parish*, 59.

of God comes to us through human links stretching back to the coming of Christ. In fact, even to talk of the passage from 'mind to mind' underplays mediation. That transition is itself mediated by physical things: by objects and the body, but book and pen, by mouth and ear, by drama and liturgy, by imitating our parents and grandparents.[140]

In light of embodied cognition, we might well say that the material and bodily mediation of the incarnation is itself a passing from 'mind to mind'; it is simply the case the mind is far wider a phenomenon than we previously imagined. Thus, the incarnation not only accommodates human comprehension, it also accommodates the bodily nature of human formation by establishing embodied practices.

3.4 Different Practices, Different Formation

In Chapter 6, I argued that all Christian traditions are at least minimally embodied, while recognising that some traditions rely more heavily on embodiment than others; and in Section 2 I argued that given the presence of embodied meanings in practices, variations in practice also result in variations in theology. These two insights can be extended to argue that differences in practice can also lead to variation in formation.

Even if all worship practices are, at the very least, minimally embodied, the question of whether the embodiments deployed are theologically salient remains. Although we may not be able to escape our bodies, how particular traditions choreograph ecclesial practices may not encode any significant theological content. In this sense 'less embodied' traditions miss an opportunity with respect to pedagogy. Practices which are not theologically salient fail to contribute towards formation; or, even worse, practices which work against the theology being explicitly espoused undermine it and create a cognitive dissonance.[141]

Garrigan provides a poignant example of how practices can work against the theology being explicitly espoused at the linguistic level.[142] She analyses various practices of passing the peace in the conflict-riven context of Ireland. Garrigan notes that although the official line promotes peace in accordance with biblical teaching and church doctrine, the actual practices involved in ecclesial practices often undermine the agenda of peace. Participants in these congregations, Garrigan argues, are implicitly being formed in ways which fail to promote peace.

---

[140] Ibid., 35.

[141] Helen Cameron, *Talking About God in Practice: Theological Action Research and Practical Theology* (London: SCM Press, 2010).

[142] Siobhan Garrigan, *The Real Peace Process: Worship, Politics and the End of Sectarianism* (London: Routledge, 2010).

As embodied creatures, humans are shaped by whichever embodied practices they undertake. Again, this underlines the point that 'less embodied' traditions risk neglecting a potential source of formation; moreover, they risk leaving a vacuum which allows other embodied practices to shape their congregants in ways which may diverge from their theological and ethical imperatives.

Smith vividly illustrates this point with an extended description of a liturgy which can profoundly shape our desires. 'I would like to invite you for a tour of one of the most important religious sites in our metropolitan area,'[143] he begins. The liturgy he describes, however, does not take place in an ecclesial setting, but is the 'liturgy' of the shopping mall. With rich ethnographic detail, he sketches the scene in terms of its popularity ('the sheer popularity of the site...throbbing with pilgrims every day of the week');[144] architecture ('a dazzling array of glass and concrete with recognizable ornamentation...the architecture of the building has a recognizable code that makes us feel at home in any city. The large glass atriums at the entrances are framed by banners and flags; familiar texts and symbols on the exterior walls help foreign faithful to quickly and easily identify what's inside; and the sprawling layout of the building is anchored by larger pavilions or sanctuaries akin to the vestibules of medieval cathedrals'); calendar ('the worship space is very much governed by a kind of liturgical, festal calendar, variously draped in the colors, symbols, and images of an unending litany of holidays and festival');[145] iconography ('these same icons of the good life are found in such temples across the country and around the world');[146] material culture ('We don't leave this transformative experience with just good feelings or pious generalities, but rather with something concrete and tangible, with newly minted relics');[147] and rituals ('after time spent focused and searching in what the faithful call 'the racks,' with our newfound holy object in hand, we proceed to the altar, which is the consummation of worship...behind the altar is the priest who presides over the consummating transaction. And this is a religion of transaction, of exchange and communion').[148] In summary, the shopping mall, Smith argues, enacts a liturgy which strives to shape our desires in accordance with its particular ethic (that of consumer capitalism): 'This is a gospel whose power is *beauty*, which speaks to our deepest desires and compels us to come not with dire moralisms but rather with a winsome invitation to share in this envisioned good life.'[149]

Smith charges that the typical way in which we conceptualise worldviews, in terms of beliefs and ideas, leads to the pedagogical function of embodied practices being overlooked. '[T]he genius of mall religion', he contends, 'is that actually it operates with a more holistic, affective, embodied anthropology...than

---

[143] Smith, *Desiring the Kingdom*, 2.   [144] Ibid.   [145] Ibid.
[146] Ibid.   [147] Ibid.   [148] Ibid.
[149] Ibid.

the Christian church tends to assume!'[150] Considering the shopping mall from the perspective of a more accurate embodied anthropology allows one to locate its potency with respect to formation: 'An idea-centric or belief-centric approach will fail to see the pedagogy at work in the mall, and thus will also fail to articulate a critique and counter-pedagogy.'[151] 'Less embodied' traditions fail to form their practitioners through embodied practices, thereby leaving a vacuum which is readily filled by other practices attempting to shape our desires; to Smith's shopping mall, with its rituals of consumer capitalism, one might add the rituals of the nation state and its civil religion, cultural rites-of-passage, national trust tourism, military scripted practices, and many others. While some of these practices may, arguably, at times shape us in positive or at least benign ways, they may also be starkly at odds with a rightly ordered Christian desire.[152]

Michael Burdett applies these insights to contrast Christian incarnational practices with posthumanism.[153] He argues that the difference between posthuman ideologies and an incarnational Christian account is not merely a difference in belief systems, but also a difference in practices. Posthuman visions of practice and Christian practices such as the Eucharist are largely incommensurate bodily performances since they habituate very different kinds of affections and dispositions. He concludes that 'the Christian performance of embodied life has Christ as template and...the Eucharist...provides a counter-practice or corrective to the detrimental performance of posthuman existence'.[154] This argument again exemplifies that divergent practices will result in contrasting kinds of formation.

4 Conclusion

Embodied cognition contributes to a more holistic picture of what it means to be human. It rejects an overly cerebral vision focused exclusively on beliefs, in favour of a rich account of how our bodily nature permeates our idiosyncratic way of thinking. This insight helps us to see that we do not simply have bodies, we are bodies. The resulting picture is one in which human experience and virtue are shaped by bodily practices. An embodied anthropology calls for a re-evaluation of liturgy: it is no longer simply a footnote to ecclesiology—something that happens in church—but a central aspect of theological anthropology.

---

[150] Ibid.   [151] Ibid., 24.

[152] For a critique of Smith's strong dichotomy between Christian and secular practices, see Herdt, 'The Virtue of the Liturgy'.

[153] Michael S. Burdett, 'Incarnation, Posthumanism and Performative Anthropology: The Body of Technology and the Body of Christ', *Christian bioethics: Non-Ecumenical Studies in Medical Morality* (2021): 2, https://doi.org/10.1093/cb/cbab009.

[154] Ibid., 13.

Insofar as embodied cognition enriches anthropology, it also again illuminates aspects of human nature which are accommodated. Hence liturgical practices can be understood as an accommodation to our embodiment. They convey theological meaning to us and contribute to our sanctification as embodied creatures.

Conclusion: Theology for Humans

In the Introduction, I proposed an illustrative foil for this project—*angelic theology*: the kind of theology that might be done by angels given their incorporeal nature. Whatever angelic theology might look like (as embodied creatures, it may simply be beyond our comprehension), I suggest that it would be decidedly different from *human* theology because the latter relies upon human cognitive capacities; and these capacities—embodied cognition posits—are profoundly dependent on our corporeality.[1]

Embodied cognition goes beyond merely asserting *that* our minds are embodiedby providing rich details on precisely *how* they are embodied. The details give us new insights into how our concepts are grounded in embodied experience (Part II). They also show us how our cognition extends to bodily states and is scaffolded by environmental resources; as a result, embodied practices are inherently cognitive (Part III). These insights provide us with a richer account of what it means to be an embodied creature.

Embodied cognition thus makes important contributions to a holistic theological anthropology and, as has been repeatedly stressed throughout my argument, that anthropology articulates epistemological constraints which are relevant to accommodation. Part of the burden of this study, then, has been to conduct a wide-ranging exploration of *how* theological understanding is accommodated to embodied creatures, rather than simply asserting *that* it is accommodated. This task requires delving into the intricacies of human theological understanding to probe that *to which* theological knowledge is accommodated, namely human cognitive capacities. Here, cognitive science proves to be an indispensable dialogue partner.

Developing accommodation in light of embodied cognition has time and time again led the argument back to the incarnation—the supreme exemplar of accommodation, and the font of other sources of accommodation. In taking on human form, God meets us as embodied cognisors. On the receptive side of revelation, human understanding of God is thus grounded in embodied cognition and bodily practices are suited to our formation. Our theology, unlike angelic theology, cannot be conducted independently of our embodiment. A theology for humans is a corporeal theology.

---

[1] Kidd, 'The Embodied Mind and How to Pray with One', 19.

Corporeal Theology: Accommodating Theological Understanding to Embodied Thinkers. Tobias Tanton, Oxford University Press. © Tobias Tanton 2023. DOI: 10.1093/oso/9780192884589.003.0009

In the remainder of this chapter I observe that previous definitions of the theology and articulations of theological method typically keep the body at arm's length (Section 1). In contrast to these approaches, I propose corporeal theology in response to the insights of embodied cognition (Section 2). Such a methodology is not entirely new as 'contextual' theologies have been at the forefront of attending to the body. I consider three examples of contextual theologies (feminist theology; black/womanist theologies; and theologies of disability) in which embodiment features (Section 3). These examples demonstrate a fundamental compatibility with the embodied theological methodology I outline, but they also pose challenges by raising the issues of symbolic meanings ascribed to the body and bodily diversity (Section 4).

1 Beyond 'Intellectualist' Theologies

If theological understanding is inexorably embodied, then what are the implications for theological methodology? Theology is often construed as a purely intellectual exercise, involving abstract reflective thinking which is thought to be independent of embodied practices. As de Cruz observes, the activities associated with academic theology do not typically involve elaborate bodily practices: 'Theology...is relatively sparse in its practices: it primarily involves reading, writing and reflection, and is only performed by specialists, such as monks and scholars.'[2] This observation may lead us to conclude that embodiment is largely irrelevant to the task of theology.[3]

This assumption is codified in the common distinction between 'first-order' religious practices such as prayer and rituals and 'second-order' theological reflection. The former is the purview of ordinary practitioners, whilst the latter is restricted to specialists who analyse the former in an abstract and detached fashion. For example, in a survey of the history of the term theology, Whaling concludes that 'theologia has usually been a second-order activity arising out of faith or spirituality rather than being equated with faith or spirituality'.[4] In his influential *The Nature of Doctrine*, Lindbeck clarifies the relationship between these two orders, suggesting that the first provides the raw 'data' for the second: 'theology is understood as the scholarly activity of second-order reflection on the data of religion (including doctrinal data) and of formulating arguments for or against material positions (including doctrinal ones)'.[5] A corollary of this view is that theology proceeds in exclusively linguistic terms, without recourse to bodily

---

[2] de Cruz, 'Cognitive Science of Religion', 491.
[3] Watts, 'Embodied Cognition and Religion', 751.
[4] Frank Whaling, 'The Development of the Word 'Theology'', *Scottish Journal of Theology* 34, no. 4 (1981): 312.
[5] Lindbeck, *The Nature of Doctrine*, 10.

practices.[6] What is striking about traditional definitions of theology is that they often define theology in explicit contrast to the practices of faith.

A similar division is supposed in McCauley's discussion of the cognitive status of academic theology. McCauley argues for a distinction between two kinds of cognition. On the one hand, he describes 'maturationally natural' cognitive systems as those which are easily acquired in the normal course of human development without any special intervention. On the other hand, the mastery of other cognitive tasks requires harder work; their acquisition requires special institutional support. Hearing and speaking one's mother tongue would fall into the former category, whilst reading and writing fall into the latter category.

McCauley, in line with many other cognitive scientists of religion, argues that many of the cognitive capacities employed in 'popular religion' are 'maturationally natural'; that is, they develop naturally during the course of development without any special training. He contrasts this with academic theology, which involves theoretical work requiring less intuitive forms of analytic thinking. He understands '[c]arefully crafted theological formulations' such as 'classical Christological doctrine' as being 'on a par cognitively with science'.[7] He summarises:

> Theology, like sciences, is done most readily, most thoroughly, and most memorably when it is a literate endeavour. We, quite literally, have few, if any, traces of any theology in nonliterate cultures. The literature theologians produce, like the literature of sciences, is theoretical, polemical, analytical, and synthetic.[8]

McCauley thus differentiates theology from the maturationally natural dimension of popular religion, including its religious rituals.[9] Indeed, he sees theology as an optional extra to 'religion'; it is a rarefied addendum to religious practices across the globe and requires both economies of scale and institutional support. For McCauley, smaller-scale religious manifestations and those in illiterate cultures thus lack theology altogether. As with theologians who maintain that theology is second-order reflection, McCauley identifies theology with an academic, intellectual task performed exclusively in the domain of language.

Embodied cognition, however, poses some challenges for this kind of circumscription of theology. Recall that many concepts evoked in the absence of things which they represent nevertheless rely on sensorimotor simulations and are thus shaped by embodiment. Hence even offline cognition is shaped by embodiment

---

[6] E.g., Barth, *Church Dogmatics 1/1*, 3–4; Karl Barth, *Church Dogmatics*, ed. Geoffrey William Bromiley, Thomas F. Torrance, and G. T. Thomson (Edinburgh: T&T Clark, 1936–1977), vol. 1/1, 3–4. John Macquarrie, *Principles of Christian Theology* (London: SCM, 1966), 1.

[7] Robert N. McCauley, *Why Religion Is Natural and Science Is Not* (Oxford: Oxford University Press, 2011), 11.

[8] Ibid., 212.   [9] Ibid., 211.

and the theological concepts deployed by theologians are grounded in embodied experience (Part II).[10] Similarly, embodied practices shape participants' thinking (Part III). Academic theologians who sit at a desk and write theology are the same theologians who engage in other embodied religious (and non-religious) practices.[11] Short of living a bi-polar existence, these two practices are likely to influence each other. Even if the act of penning a theological tome is only trivially an embodied practice, it is the act of a theologian who engages in—and is formed by—any number of non-trivially embodied practices.[12]

Embodied cognition theorists point to how abstract domains of thought are embodied and scaffolded. For example, Clark observes 'advanced cognition depends crucially on our abilities to dissipate reasoning: to diffuse achieved knowledge and practical wisdom through complex social structures, and to reduce loads on individual brains by locating those brains in complex webs of linguistic, social, political, and institutional constraints'.[13] This observation might equally extend to the task of academic theology. If theology is corporeal, then academic theological methodology ought to embrace embodied practices.

2 Towards a Corporeal Theology

The critique of an 'intellectualist' theological methodology suggests that embodied practices ought to be considered as part and parcel of theological method. Contra Lindbeck, religious practices do not simply provide the 'raw data' which the academic theologian then systematises to reveal their meaning (as the first-/second-order distinction suggests).[14] The practices are themselves meaningful and they, like a volume in systematics, have a theology; the practices already participate in the task of theological thinking.

The consequence of this is that the theologian cannot be content styling themself on the social scientist, the literary critic, or the armchair philosopher (though each of those disciplines may indeed furnish her with useful tools); rather they must also see themselves as part ethnographer. That is to say, their task is not merely to be shaped by and to critique texts but also to be shaped by and critique practices. Moreover, the nature of engagement ought not be merely reading about or even observing practices. Instead, the embodied nature of cognition means that there is a level of engagement that can only be achieved *through bodily participation*.[15] As I have noted (Chapter 6, Section 1.3), anthropologists rely on 'participant observation', which includes embodied presence and shared participation

---

[10] Hostetter and Alibali, 'Visible Embodiment', 497. Brown and Reimer, 'Embodied Cognition', 838.
[11] Wainwright, *Doxology*, 1.   [12] Smith, *Desiring the Kingdom*, 25.
[13] Clark and Toribio, 'Doing without Representing?', 180.
[14] Lindbeck, *The Nature of Doctrine*, 10.   [15] Scharen, 'Ecclesiology "from the Body"', 66.

in practices. This methodology provides a depth of understanding that allows for a 'thick description' which could not be achieved at a distance.[16] Embodied cognition research provides a raft of empirical evidence to support this intuition. It also provides an impetus for theologians to employ an ethnographic-like methodology of embodied presence and participation in practices.

Theologians have only recently begun to embrace such a methodology. Coakley argues that non-reductive sociology can reconnect doctrines with the world of lived experience: 'doctrine can be made newly alive by reference to its earthed manifestations, as well as ways in which doctrine is abused in its earthed distortions'.[17] Wynn uses an autobiographical narrative to convey the significance of bodily presence in certain places.[18] He argues for the importance and irreducibility of first-hand experience over second-hand information:

> first-hand experience will be action-guiding not when it takes the form of simple observation, but when it is constituted by salient perception of some environment, and is caught up therefore in a correlative emotional feeling and predisposition to act.[19]

Others have similarly called for the use of ethnographic methodologies, especially in the context of ecclesiology.[20] Scharen, for example, uses Merleau-Ponty's thought to argue for a 'theology *from* the body', in which theologians use the bodily knowledge gained from participation in practices.[21] The alternative to intellectualist theologies, which attempt to keep the body at arm's length, is a theological method that embraces religious practices and the bodily knowledge they bring.

3 Embodiment in Contextual Theologies

Although embodied cognition provides one powerful impetus for adopting a corporeal theology, aspects of an embodied methodology have been pioneered by 'contextual' theologies.[22] These theological movements often draw inspiration from Latin American liberation theology, which critiqued the inherited theological tradition as being inadequate for responding to the concrete conditions of poverty and oppression, and at times being complicit in perpetuating these

---

[16] Ward, 'Introduction', 6–7.   [17] Coakley, *God, Sexuality and the Self*, 85.
[18] Wynn, *Faith and Place*, 18–29.   [19] Ibid., 229.
[20] Ward, ed., *Perspectives on Ecclesiology and Ethnography*.
[21] Scharen, 'Ecclesiology "from the Body"', 65–70.
[22] Though the term itself can be problematic, especially if it is defined over and against systematic theology; many contextual theologies are rigorous and systematic in their approach, whilst classical systematic theologies are interestingly products of their own historical moments and geographical locations, making them also contextual in that sense.

dehumanising social, political, and economic conditions. The flipside of this negative critique is the positive task of articulating a theology which arises from and is accountable to church communities working for social and political change.

Subsequent contextual theologies have likewise sought to further liberative movements in other contexts of oppression and marginalisation: feminist theology responds to patriarchal contexts; black theology addresses the cultures of white supremacy; queer theology challenges norms of gender and sexuality; disability theology critiques ableism; to name but a few. These theological movements have increasingly appreciated that the form of oppression they seek to dismantle readily overlaps with other forms of oppression, resulting in an emphasis on intersectional identities and movements such as womanist theology, which speaks from the vantage point of black African-American women.

Insofar as these theological movements have eschewed abstract and universalising theologies, in favour of theologies which speak to particular concrete contexts, they have often also been at the forefront of theological considerations of embodiment. In this section I briefly consider some of the ways in which contextual theologies have analysed the body. As a mere conversation starter, this engagement will only be able to scratch the surface of the rich and varied accounts of embodiment offered in a handful of contextual theologies. Rather than offering a comprehensive survey of all possible contextual theologies, or an exhaustive account of embodiment in any particular contextual theology, the focus here will be on identifying a few examples of where the insights of embodied cognition can be productively brought into conversation with contextual theologies.

3.1 Feminist Theology

Embodiment has been a central theme in feminist theology. However, feminist theologians have pursued a wide variety of projects with respect to embodiment; taking stock of feminist treatments of embodiment, Ross identifies five features:

> (1) A suspicion of views that see women as being more 'naturally' embodied than are men; (2) a rejection of a dualist framework (e.g. body-soul) for conceptualizing embodiment; (3) a concern to place embodiment in a historical and social context; (4) an extension of embodiment as a value to wider issues, such as the nature of the person, norms for moral action, and the human relationship to the earth; (5) a celebration of embodiment in new forms of ritual and liturgy.[23]

---

[23] Susan A. Ross and Mary Catherine Hilkert, 'Feminist Theology: A Review of Literature', *Theological Studies* 56, no. 2 (1995): 331.

Feminist theologies have thus been concerned with critiquing the way in which binaries such as mind–body, spiritual–material, reason–emotion, and culture–nature have been gendered to marginalise women.[24] Although women have been associated with bodily and physical terms in these binaries, the feminist response has not typically been to pivot attention to the other term in the binary. Rather the binaries themselves have been deconstructed and subsequently attempts have been made to recover embodiment in a non-dualistic framework.

In her classic essay 'The Human Situation: A Feminine View', Valerie Saiving (Goldstein) argues that theology has been largely written from the perspective of male experience and does not adequately interpret women's experience.[25] Saiving articulates the differences in male and female experience by drawing upon a range of scholarship from anthropology, psychoanalysis, and sociology. She argues that differences arise from *bodily* differences and the way in which these differences play out in parental interactions during childhood and later development. Saiving thus adopts an essentialist position, positing that bodily differences result in essential differences between female and male experiences (though she also acknowledges that culture is superimposed on these differences and therefore allows for social constructivist explanations for many examples of gender roles).

Saiving's early example of feminist theology is likely to attract criticism from those who see her biological or psychoanalytic essentialism as outdated, particularly her conclusions that women are associated with passivity or are more closely bound to nature than men.[26] Moreover, others may be sceptical about any form of gender essentialism, preferring constructivist accounts such as Judith Butler's construal of gender as a kind of performance.[27] Such constructivist accounts avoid the notion that gender characteristics or traits are inscribed into the natural order, and therefore beyond contestation or change. However, strong versions of constructivism have been subject to critiques of their own, including the charge that they obscure bodily particularity. Serene Jones summarises:

> Seeing culture as the origin of sex and gender is troubling because it seems to imply that women do not exist apart from one's cultural proclivity to identify them as such. This suggests, further, that the people we confront each day are only cultural constructs and, hence, that bodies as 'matter' do not really matter. If strong feminist constructivism were to lead to such conclusions, it would

---

[24] Serene Jones, *Feminist Theory and Christian Theology: Cartographies of Grace* (Minneapolis: Fortress Press, 2000), 28–9.

[25] Valerie Saiving Goldstein, 'The Human Situation: A Feminine View', *The Journal of Religion* 40, no. 2 (1960): 101.

[26] Ibid., 104–5.

[27] Judith Butler, *Gender Trouble: Feminism and the Subversion of Identity* (London: Routledge, 1990).

seem to undermine the possibility of talking about the material realities of women's lives.[28]

This concern notwithstanding, constructivism has not always proven to be an obstacle for attending to the body. Take, for example, political philosopher Iris Marion Young's famous essay 'Throwing Like a Girl: A Phenomenology of Feminine Body Comportment Motility and Spatiality'.[29] In this paper Young considers a feminine style of bodily comportment which is common (though by no means universal) among women in advanced industrial societies. For example, Young observes:

> Women generally are not as open with their bodies as are men in their gait and stride...Though we now wear pants more than we used to and consequently do not have to restrict our sitting postures because of dress, women still tend to sit with their legs relatively close together and their arms across their bodies. When simply standing or leaning, men tend to keep their feet farther apart than do women, and we also tend more to keep our hands and arms touching or shielding our bodies. A final indicative difference is the way each carries books or parcels; girls and women most often carry books embraced to their chests, while boys and men swing them along their sides.[30]

Young is primarily a constructivist with respect to this feminine style of bodily comportment: she ascribes it to socialisation rather than differences in anatomy or physiology.[31] Furthermore, she critiques cultural norms which police this kind of bodily comportment as oppressive: 'Women in sexist society are physically handicapped. Insofar as we learn to live out our existence in accordance with the definition that patriarchal culture assigns to us, we are physically inhibited, confined, positioned, and objectified.'[32]

For Young, however, the distinctive feminine bodily comportment is not merely an *expression* of oppressive cultural codes. Instead, drawing on the phenomenology of Merleau-Ponty (and thereby sharing a common intellectual ancestor with embodied cognition), she suggests that 'it is the ordinary purposive orientation of the body as a whole toward things and its environment that initially defines the relation of a subject to its world'.[33] Hence the differences in bodily comportment can themselves produce a different kind of subjectivity and experience of the world (Chapter 7, Section 3).

---

[28] Jones, *Feminist Theory*, 36.
[29] Iris Marion Young, 'Throwing Like a Girl: A Phenomenology of Feminine Body Comportment Motility and Spatiality', *Human Studies* 3, no. 2 (1980).
[30] Ibid., 142.   [31] Ibid., 152.   [32] Ibid.   [33] Ibid., 140.

Insofar as embodied cognition extends Merleau-Ponty's project, it could equally develop Young's thought. For the paradigm of embodied cognition, one might hypothesise that the kinds of comportments which Young describes are likely to have particular cognitive effects. (Perhaps new studies could be designed to measure them.) Furthermore, given Young's observation that these comportments are malformative, one could use the tools of embodied cognition to propose alternative forms of embodiment. Although Young is not writing as a theologian, the close analysis of how gendered embodiment shapes experience could readily update and enrich Saiving's account of feminine experience which theology has often neglected.

No attempt has been made here to adjudicate the complex debate between various versions of gender essentialism and constructivism.[34] However, we have observed that essentialists and constructivists alike have attended to the body and found it a productive site for analysis. Whether bodily differences are ascribed to biology, psychology, or socialisation, feminist theorists have argued that they shape women's experience. These bodily experiences form both a neglected source for theological reflection and a context which doctrines may or may not adequately address (to return to Saiving's foundational insights). A corporeal theology likewise advocates for attention to embodied experiences and practices.

3.2 Womanist and Black Theologies

In attending to African-Americans' experience in the United States, black theology offers another example of an embodied theological methodology. Womanist theologian Kelly Brown Douglas provides a particularly developed account of black bodies.[35] Responding to examples of the violent killings of African-Americans such as Trayvon Martin, Douglas seeks to uncover the reasons why black people in the United States are unable to 'stand their ground' (a legal argument for self-defence in some states, sometimes appealed to justify killings) and why black murder victims often posthumously face trial by media.

Moving beyond the details of individual cases, Douglas probes the deeper causes of these cultural conditions by providing a genealogical account of meanings ascribed to black bodies in the United States by the dominant white culture.[36]

---

[34] Jones, *Feminist Theory*, 22–48.

[35] Kelly Brown Douglas, *Stand Your Ground: Black Bodies and the Justice of God* (Maryknoll, New York: Orbis Books, 2015). See also Douglas' rich description of Blues women in Kelly Brown Douglas, *Black Bodies and the Black Church: A Blues Slant* (New York: Palgrave Macmillan, 2012), 31–59. M. Shawn Copeland, *Enfleshing Freedom: Body, Race, and Being* (Fortress Press, 2010), 7–22.

[36] For other genealogical accounts of the role of theology in conceptions of race, see Copeland, *Enfleshing Freedom*; Willie James Jennings, *The Christian Imagination: Theology and the Origins of Race* (New Haven: Yale University Press, 2010); J. Kameron Carter, *Race: A Theological Account* (Oxford: Oxford University Press, 2008).

Tracing the confluence of a mythology of Anglo-Saxon exceptionalism with a natural law theory, she carefully documents the construal of black bodies as possessing essentialised racial characteristics. These essentialisms—which commodify and dehumanise black people as chattels, cast them as dangerously hypersexualised and violent, and thereby assign guilt—seek to identify racial characteristics and ultimately white supremacy as part of the natural order. (Here Douglas' argument echoes the feminist critique of the way in which gender essentials are deployed to legitimise sexism.) The appeal to natural law theory, and later (pseudo-)scientific racial theories, adds a theological dimension to these racial essentialisms; they are inscribed into the created order and thus to question them would be to second-guess the creator. Thus, these 'theo-ideologies', as Douglas calls them, authorise the subjugation and oppression of African-Americans. She summarises:

> the social-cultural conceptions that coalesce to deem the black body—especially the black male body—as not just inferior to the white body but as a threat to it. These conceptions depict the black body as chattel, hypersexual, and dangerous. Validated with a sacred canopy, these conceptualisations interact to inscribe indelible guilt upon black bodies.[37]

These theo-ideologies readily create an environment in which black bodies are seen as threats and attacked. Douglas identifies the resulting culture of violence against black people through prominent media examples as well as her own powerful witness of encounters she has faced raising a black son. She also cites a psychological study in which participants were tasked with shooting armed suspects in a video game; the study found that African American targets were more likely to be mistakenly shot. The experimenters summarise: 'in the case of the African American targets, participants simply set a lower threshold for the decision to shoot, being willing to shoot targets who seemed less threatening'.[38] A number of other studies have produced similar findings.[39]

Douglas' account focuses on meanings which are imposed upon the body by larger cultural narratives and mythologies, rather than ones arise from embodied practices (see Chapter 7, Section 1). However, these narratives are internalised and shape experience. Hence, in addition to analysing discourses *about* black

---

[37] Douglas, *Stand Your Ground*, 50.

[38] Joshua Correll et al., 'The Police Officer's Dilemma: Using Ethnicity to Disambiguate Potentially Threatening Individuals', *Journal of Personality and Social Psychology* 83 (2003): 1319.

[39] E.g., Jennifer T. Kubota and Tiffany A. Ito, 'The Role of Expression and Race in Weapons Identification', *Emotion (Washington, D.C.)* 14, no. 6 (2014); Yara Mekawi and Konrad Bresin, 'Is the Evidence from Racial Bias Shooting Task Studies a Smoking Gun? Results from a Meta-Analysis', *Journal of Experimental Social Psychology* 61 (2015).

bodies, black theologians (including Douglas) draw upon phenomenology for articulations of the experience of black bodies which are constantly perceived as threatening and presumed guilty. M. Shawn Copeland similarly appeals to an embodied phenomenology: 'The body is our perspective in this world.'[40] She observes that '[i]n a white, racially bias-induced horizon, blackness is aberration and defilement, a source of dread and intimidation; thus, the black body must be hidden, concealed, spatially segregated.'[41] This cultural 'horizon' leads to a 'crushing objectification' and a particular experience which Copeland captures in the question 'how does it feel to be a problem?'[42]

In addition to an embodied phenomenology, the narratives which Douglas and Copeland identify are also no doubt codified in bodily practices and bodily responses. Embodied mechanisms are clearly in play for those whose black bodies are constantly surveyed and judged, and who therefore live with an anxiety generated by the lack of security their cultural environment offers. Conversely, those whose cultural narratives have inculcated racial prejudices experience visceral fear or disgust responses. Moreover, the cultural mythologies which Douglas identifies are not merely transmitted in some kind of pure, intellectual ether; rather they are encoded in the bodily interactions which her son encounters and visual depictions such as *Time* magazine's digital alternation to darken O. J. Simpson's face implicitly suggesting a link between blackness and criminality.[43]

As well as inculcating the problem, embodied practices are drawn upon to formulate a liberating response. Copeland, for example, explores the way in which the Eucharist offers not only a memorial of a first-century lynching, but also anticipates an 'enfleshment of freedom' through its resurrection hope.[44] By attending to the formative (and malformative) potency of embodied practices, these womanist theologians again prefigure a corporeal theology.

3.3 Theologies of Disability

Embodiment again plays a crucial role in the work of theologians writing about disability. However, as with feminist debates around essentialism and constructivism, the significance of the physical body is understood differently in particular models of disability. The medical model tends to conflate an impairment (a loss of form or function such as damage to the optic nerve) with disability (the inability

---

[40] Copeland, *Enfleshing Freedom*, 16, quoting Lewis Gordon.   [41] Ibid.
[42] Ibid.   [43] Douglas, *Stand Your Ground*, 82.
[44] Copeland, *Enfleshing Freedom*, 107–29.Cf. James H. Cone, *The Cross and the Lynching Tree* (Maryknoll, N.Y.: Orbis Books, 2011); William Cavanaugh, 'Torture and Eucharist: Theology, Politics, and the Body of Christ', *Landas: Journal of Loyola School of Theology* 26, no. 2 (2012).

to perform a task).[45] In this model, 'the body is a biological machine that functions to a greater or lesser extent'.[46] Impairments are hence seen as intrinsically problematic and disability can be overcome through medical interventions which 'fix' impairments.

Critics of the medical model argue it locates the problem in disabled people themselves, rather than social structures and attitudes which preclude their full participation.[47] In response, they propose the alternative social model which construes disability as a sociopolitical phenomenon. This model distinguishes between impairments and disability, arguing that an impairment (e.g., damage to the optical nerve) need not lead to a disability (e.g., an inability to read) if one removes unjust social structures which exclude (e.g., making available audio or braille books).[48] There is a compatibility here with a scaffolded view of cognition (see Chapter 5): a cognitive or perceptual task can still be accomplished in spite of an impairment if one provides adequate environmental resources. Hence, for the social model, the problem lies with prejudiced social structures which fail to provide equal access by accommodating impairments rather than the impairment itself.[49] Moreover, it identifies people with disabilities as a minority group who face discrimination in the form of 'ableism', which is akin to other forms of discrimination such as sexism and racism.[50] This shared identity empowers the marginalised group to advocate for social and political change.

Although Creamer readily acknowledges the shortcomings of the medical model, she also argues that it has strengths which the social model lacks. In particular she contends that, by locating the problem in social structures and attitudes that disable, the bodily experience of impairment is ignored: 'By focusing primarily on ableism and experiences of discrimination, the minority [or social] model fails to take into account the physical and emotional reality of impairment.'[51] This neglect of the bodily experience of impairments, Creamer argues, is likely to exclude those who find it difficult to celebrate their impairments as an essential part of their embodiment and identity: 'When the experience of impairment is deproblematized, there is little room for people with disabilities to have a negative or even ambivalent relationship to their impairment.'[52] The inclusion of critical reflection on embodied experience subsequently becomes one of Creamer's desiderata when she develops her own limits model of disability.[53]

---

[45] Deborah Beth Creamer, *Disability and Christian Theology: Embodied Limits and Constructive Possibilities* (Oxford: Oxford University Press, 2009), 23.
[46] Ibid., 24.   [47] Ibid.   [48] Ibid., 3–14.
[49] Nancy L. Eiesland, *The Disabled God: Toward a Liberatory Theology of Disability* (Nashville: Abingdon Press, 1994), 62.
[50] Creamer, *Disability and Christian Theology*, 25.
[51] Ibid., 27 (there are resonances here with critiques of gender constructivists, see Section 2.1).
[52] Ibid.   [53] Ibid., 31.

As with the complex debates around gender essentialism and constructivism, my purpose here is not adjudicate between models of disability, but merely to observe that embodiment features in all of the positions (albeit in different guises). For the medical model, the embodied experience of an impairment is acknowledged. The social model, by contrast, critiques cultural construals of impairments as 'defects' or deviations from an ideal, normative form of embodiment, and seeks to change social structures (be they attitudes, laws, architectural designs, etc.) which present obstacles to full participation in society by those with impairments. (Creamer's limits model arguably does both.) Hence when theologians engage with questions of disability, they inevitably encounter profound questions of embodiment.

Nancy Eiesland's classic *The Disabled God* identifies the body as a locus for theological reflection.[54] Strongly echoing a corporeal theology advocated for at the beginning of this chapter, she articulates her own methodological priorities in the following terms: 'An accessible theological method necessitates that the body be represented as flesh and blood, bones and braces, and not simply the rationalized realm of activity.'[55]

In applying this methodology, Eiesland draws on her own experience and the stories of others with disabilities as they reflect on encounters within the church.[56] Similarly to Douglas' observation that theology played an active role in promoting racial ideologies, Eiesland observes that various theologies are applied to disabled bodies. These can (paradoxically) range from an assumption that physical disability is a consequence of sin and requires healing, through to theologies which cast disability as a form of virtuous suffering that should be seen as a character-building gift.[57]

Eiesland finds these theologies denigrating, patronising, or simply unrealistic: 'disability becomes a fate to be avoided, a tragedy to be explained, or a cause to be championed rather than an ordinary life to be lived.'[58] In keeping with the social model of disability, she labels them 'disabling theologies' (it is the theology, rather than underlying impairments, which disables). Moreover, whether these theologies condemn impaired bodies (through association with sin) or valorise them (as examples of virtuous suffering), their ultimate effect is to explain away disability without requiring any social change to achieve equality and justice.

The pastoral theology of John Swinton provides a particularly poignant exploration of embodiment and disability. He observes that at a certain point in the diminishment of capabilities, dementia patients lose the capacity to articulate faith in a linguistic form. Despite this impairment, such patients often retain their habitual, embodied knowledge and have the ability to sing hymns or to

---

[54] Eiesland, *The Disabled God*, 22.   [55] Ibid., 22.   [56] Ibid., 31–48.
[57] Ibid., 70–5.   [58] Ibid., 75.

participate in the embodied aspects of ritual practices such as kneeling and receiving the Eucharist elements. Swinton's work echoes the way in which Clark points to Alzheimer's patients as an example of our reliance on our environments:

> Many of these patients live surprisingly normal lives in the community, despite the fact that standard assessments of their capabilities suggest that many such patients should be incapable of surviving outside of special-care institutions. The key to such surprising success, it seems, lies in the extent to which the individuals rely on highly structured environments which they create and then inhabit.[59]

Swinton elaborates Merleau-Ponty's concept of habit memory to argue that dementia patients draw upon a bodily form of memory to preform ritual acts:

> their frail movements, the taking of the bread and the wine, their fragile embrace, the apparently unknowing share in the words of the ritual are reflective not of loss but of enduring love. They represent the habits of a lifetime inscribed by Jesus on the bodies of those who love...They know and remember Jesus in their bodies. Unless we choose to yield to the apparently inevitable thrust of dualism here, we can do nothing other than recognise that *the memory of the body is a real and profound conduit that leads people into the presence of Jesus.*[60]

Swinton's work is a fine example of how theology can engage with bodily knowledge in a scaffolded account of religion. This is a particularly crucial task in contexts where linguistic capacities are no longer available, but it also reveals the significance of scaffolding even for those without memory loss. Language can be rather loud and distract from subtler yet pervasive expressions and inculcations of faith.

In the course of the Barth-Brunner debate (see Chapter 1, Section 4), Brunner argues that the ability to use language gave humans the capacity to receive revelation. Although I broadly agreed with Brunner's position that human capacities constitute a (passive) point of contact of divine revelation, I argued that Brunner's circumscription of the relevant capacities to linguistic capacities alone was too narrow. Swinton's work demonstrates that other embodied capacities are also salient to possessing and expressing faith. By broadening theological concerns

---

[59] Clark, *Being There*, 66.

[60] John Swinton, 'On Being a Disciple When You've Forgotten Who God Is: Dementia as Time for Learning', in *Society for the Study of Theology Annual Conference* (Nottingham: 2013), 11. Emphasis original. Cf. John Swinton, 'What the Body Remembers: Theological Reflections on Dementia', *Journal of Religion, Spirituality & Aging* 26, no. 2–3 (2014).

beyond texts and beliefs, the impetus given by a corporeal theology allows the embodiment of faith to be recognised.

3.4 Conclusions: Opportunities and Challenges

This all-too-brief foray into three contextual theologies reveals that to theologise about and from particular human bodies is not a novel innovation (although insights from embodied cognition offer a new impetus for such a methodology). Rather, contextual theologians have long been attending to the concrete conditions of a wide range of bodies. Although each of the dialogue partners (and there could be many more) offers its own insights drawn for a particular set of bodily experiences, there are some general lessons for a corporeal theology.

First, contextual theologies demonstrate the fruitfulness of attending to the body. Such attention to bodies negatively highlights theologies which create oppressive judgements towards bodies (patriarchal theologies in feminist thought, racial theo-ideology in Douglas, disabling theology in Eiesland, etc.) and positively identifies alternative theologies which endeavour to adequately address aspects of the wide gamut of 'the human situation'. Each of these theologies is not restricted to beliefs or symbols, but also takes the form of particular embodiments.

Second, a number of our interlocutors draw on embodied phenomenological accounts, tracing the ways in which embodiment shapes lived experience in the world. For Young and Swinton, the insights of Merleau-Ponty are crucial. In a passage reminiscent of Merleau-Ponty's phenomenology, Copeland writes 'The body incarnates and points beyond to what is "the most immediate and proximate object of our experience" and mediates our engagement with others, with the world, with the Other.'[61] Hence these thinkers share a common intellectual ancestor with embodied cognition and insofar as Merleau-Ponty provides a fruitful framework, so too the further elaborations of his core ideas by the embodied cognition paradigm promise to be equally productive.

Third, and more critically, contextual theologies provide a reminder that bodies are, for better or for worse, inscribed in larger cultural matrices of meaning. Embodied cognition emphasises that thinking occurs *from* the environmentally situated body. Contextual theologies often move in the opposite direction, considering how bodies are thought *about* through larger cultural narratives, symbols, and ideologies. Hence they tend to place less emphasis on how bodies perceive and cognise, in favour of how they *are* perceived and cognised in particular contexts.

---

[61] Copeland, *Enfleshing Freedom*, 7.

Following Mary Douglas, Copeland captures this dynamic by distinguishing between the physical body and the social body 'which constrains the way the physical body is perceived'.[62] However, rather than choosing between these two loci of analysis, Copeland interrogates the relation between the two, as this approach 'avoids the trap of detaching the embodied subject from historical or social or religious contexts, which would render the subject eternal, universal, absolute'.[63] In Chapter 7, I argued that meaning was not *exclusively* symbolic but, in light of embodied cognition, should also be understood as embodied. The intent in this suggestion was to bring an often-neglected site of meaning into focus, rather than to substitute a symbolic myopia with an embodied one. Contextual theologies, including the social constructivist positions around gender, race, and disability, forcefully remind us that embodiment in an ecclesial setting does not occur in an historical, ideological, or political vacuum; congregants do not miraculously shed the meanings inscribed by cultures on their bodies when they cross the threshold of a church building. Hence, following Copeland, one promising route to further develop an embodied theological methodology would be to attend to the interplay between physical and social bodies, between the perceiving and the perceived body.

4 Bodily Diversity

Another aspect of embodiment which comes to the fore in contextual theologies is its sheer diversity. Human bodies vary widely along all of the dimensions which intersectional theologies explore (and more). A longstanding critique raised by contextual theologies and the critical discourses they deploy with is to observe that particular kinds of experiences or bodies (typically young, white, male, heterosexual, able-bodied ones) have been problematically assumed to represent human universals.[64] The positing of false universals can easily lead to the neglect of certain kinds of bodies by rendering them invisible. Alternatively, privileged forms of embodiment are set up as normative or ideal bodies, with any divergence from the 'norm' being judged as a 'deficiency'. Does the portrait of the body sketched by the literature on embodied cognition unwittingly fall into the trap of positing a false universal form of human embodiment, or establishing a normative kind of embodiment?

First, internal critiques within the psychological guild have pointed out that samples have often been unrepresentative. As discussed in Chapter 6, Section 1.2, the practice of recruiting undergraduates from a researcher's own institution

---

[62] Ibid., 8.   [63] Ibid.   [64] E.g., Eiesland, *The Disabled God*, 28.

has resulted in study participants being predominantly from western, educated, industrialised, rich, and democratic (or 'WEIRD') societies, and evidence suggests that samples from this group do not generalise well to the human population in many domains.[65] Many experimental psychologists have registered this critique and responded by attempting to replicate results in cross-cultural settings as a mark of best practice. However, given that this critique is a relatively recent development and cross-cultural studies require additional time and resources, many of the studies quoted in this work may rely on WEIRD samples.

Second, even if more representative samples can be recruited, a concern may remain about whether embodied cognition focuses too heavily on a universal portrait of human cognition. It is certainly true that many studies in embodied cognition aim to identify mechanisms common to large segments of the human population. This would represent a bias in the research questions which are pursued and those which are neglected, rather than a problem with the underlying data which is used (as is the case for WEIRD samples).

The search for common or widely shared implications of human embodiment is not problematic in itself; only when this pursuit comes at the expense of investigating bodily differences will the overall picture likely become skewed. Young's work on bodily comportment offers a model for bringing the general and the particular into conversation. Reflecting on her use of Merleau-Ponty, she writes:

> I assume that at the most basic descriptive level, Merleau-Ponty's account of the relation of the lived body to its world, as developed in the Phenomenology of Perception (1962), applies to any human existence in a general way. At a more specific level, however, there is a particular style of bodily comportment which is typical of feminine existence[66]

A similar methodology could be deployed when engaging with embodied cognition, with embodied cognition providing an account of general mechanism (e.g., the interaction between body posture and memory), but further elaboration being required about how these mechanisms interact with subsets of bodies and the cultural meanings ascribed them.

Additionally, embodied cognition could investigate the effects of bodily differences or the way in which mechanisms function in particular contexts. Some empirical and theoretical work has already emerged in this area, especially in relationship to the 'bodily relativity hypothesis'.

---

[65] Henrich, Heine, and Norenzayan, 'The Weirdest People'.
[66] Young, 'Throwing Like a Girl', 141.

4.1 Bodily Relativity Hypothesis

Given that, arguably, all concepts ultimately relate back to sensorimotor experience, the body (which determines sensorimotor capacities) shapes an organism's conceptual repertoire (see Chapter 3). This relationship between bodies and concepts is elucidated by the 'bodily relativity hypothesis', which proposes that an organism's concepts are relative to the kind of body it has.[67] One interesting prediction of this hypothesis is that organisms with different physiologies will have different concepts (the 'body-specificity hypothesis'). Casasanto explains this prediction as follows: 'to the extent that the content of minds depends on our interactions with our environment, people with different kinds of bodies—who interact with the environment in systematically different ways—should tend to form correspondingly different neural and cognitive representations'.[68] Hence if the body underwrites our perceptual experience and our concepts are thereby contingent upon it, then bodily variation should result in conceptual variation.

This hypothesis is not a particularly new idea. The notion of bodily relativity has been broached, at least implicitly, by some of the great thinkers of the twentieth century. Wittgenstein once wrote, in his characteristically aphoristic manner, that 'if a lion could talk, we could not understand him'.[69] On one reading, this aphorism suggests that lions and humans would have a markedly different experience of the world by virtue of the differences between their physiologies; and therefore, following the hypothesis that concepts are grounded in experience, the concepts and words used by a speaking lion might well be incomprehensible to humans.

Bodily relativity is also implicitly present in Nagel's famous argument that first-person phenomenological experience is fundamentally irreducible to third-person descriptions; even if one were to dissect a bat and to compile an exhaustive understanding of its anatomy, Nagel argues, one would not gain knowledge of what it is like to be—or to experience the world as—a bat.[70] Hence humans can never know the first-person perspective of a bat. In the course of his argument Nagel relies on the fact that humans and bats have very different physiology. In particular bats use echolocation, a mode of perception which involves emitting sounds and perceiving the distances of objects based on the time taken for the sound to echo back. Nagel's argument is premised on the intuition that difference in physiology (and especially perceptual capacities) correlates with differences in phenomenology, a different way of experiencing the world. If one grants the

---

[67] Daniel Casasanto, 'Bodily Relativity', in *The Routledge Handbook of Embodied Cognition*, ed. Lawrence E. Shapiro (New York: Routledge, 2014), 108–9.

[68] Ibid., 108.

[69] Ludwig Wittgenstein, *Philosophical Investigations: The German Text, with a Revised English Translation*, trans. G. E. M. Anscombe (Wiley, 1991), 190.

[70] Thomas Nagel, 'What Is It Like to Be a Bat?', *The Philosophical Review* 83, no. 4 (1974).

additional insight that concepts are grounded in experience, then Nagel's account suggests that a bodily difference results in conceptual difference.

Even if bodily relativity seems to be intuitively appealing, the body specificity hypothesis is a difficult prediction to test across different species; lions, after all, cannot speak. There is, however, some degree of physiological variation among the human population. Even though intra-species physiological variation is relatively small in comparison to inter-species variation, differences between humans may prove sufficiently significant to have a detectable effect on human conceptions.

Casasanto proposes one common variation, left- and right-handedness, as a test case for whether bodily difference correlates with difference in thought.[71] In a series of studies both left- and right-handers were asked to imagine actions usually performed by their dominant hand or simply to read verbs denoting such actions. Brain scans reveal that when right-handers perform these tasks, pre-motor regions in their left-hemispheres activate (consistent with a hemisphere controlling the motor movement for the opposite side of the body), whereas for left-handers, pre-motor regions in their right-hemispheres activate. Moreover, interfering in these pre-motor areas in the hemisphere that controls the dominant hand (using transcranial magnetic stimulation) affects the processing of manual action verbs but no other verbs. He concludes that '[p]eople tend to understand verbs as referring to actions they would perform with their particular bodies— not to a Platonic ideal of the action, or to the action as it is performed by the majority of language users. In this sense, people with different bodies understand the same verbs to mean something different.'[72]

Glenberg and Kaschack explain that if meaning 'derives from the biomedical nature of bodies and perceptual systems,'[73] then it will be species-specific. Drawing upon Gibson's notion of 'affordances', they note that organisms with different body morphologies will encounter different affordances in the same environment: 'a chair affords sitting for adult humans, but not for mice or elephants, who have the wrong sorts of bodies to sit in an ordinary chair'.[74] Given that affordances both derive from the body and play a role in conceptualisation, this lends further credence to the bodily relativity hypothesis.

Barsalou likewise recognises that his theory of perceptual symbols implies bodily relativity.[75] Since amodal symbols only refer by virtue of conventions, transformations in the symbol (e.g., enlarging or shrinking it, rotating it, etc.) have no bearing on its meaning (or reference, so long as it is recognisable). Modal symbols, on the other hand, are analogical: their structure is isomorphic to that

---

[71] Casasanto, 'Bodily Relativity', 108–10.
[72] Ibid., 110. Cf. Sanders, *Theology in the Flesh*, 24.
[73] Glenberg and Kaschak, 'Grounding Language in Action', 558.
[74] Ibid., 558–9.   [75] Barsalou, 'Perceptual Symbol Systems', 598–9. See Chapter 3.

which they represent. Hence a structural change in the representation implies a change in the referent. Barsalou points out that this makes the physical realisation of a symbol critical, since different perceptual systems imply a different conceptual system.[76] Echoing Wittgenstein's intuition, Barsalou observes that '[t]o the extent that different animals have different perceptual and bodily systems, they should have different conceptual systems'.[77]

Does this mean that humans with different bodies will have different concepts? This is certainly a possibility, *if* the bodily difference is salient to the particular concept, as Casasanto's work suggests. However, Barsalou notes that human bodies typically have a great deal in common: 'Although perceptual systems produce variable embodiment across different individuals, they also produce shared embodiment at a more general level. Because most humans have roughly the same mechanisms for perceiving color, they have roughly the same conceptual representations of it.'[78] However, he also recognises the presence of variation: 'Because humans vary on all phenotypic traits to some extent, they are likely to vary on all the perceptual discriminations that could be extracted to form perceptual symbols'.[79]

In summary, the bodily relativity hypothesis highlights the fact that a modal theory of concepts makes concepts contingent on the particularities of embodiment. Although concepts may intuitively seem universal—they are, after all, all we have ever known—a modal theory of concepts suggests that they are in fact species-specific, and perhaps subject to intra-species variation.

4.2 Accommodating Bodily Diversity

In suggesting that bodily differences result in different (but overlapping) conceptual repertoires, the bodily relativity hypothesis raises poignant questions in relation to theological language concepts: are theological concepts equally intelligible to all humans, regardless of the particularities of their embodiment?

It would be difficult to argue that all theological concepts and language are equally accommodating to all people. Even Casasanto's study on right- and left-handedness has implications for theological language as the New Testament frequently describes Jesus as sitting 'at the right hand' of God.[80] It is clearly possible for a left-handed person to comprehend this phrase by decoding it through familiarity with linguistic conventions (one might classify it as a 'dead' metaphor). However, Casasanto's study suggests that left-handers will conceptualise this phrase differently from a right-hander.

---

[76] Ibid., 598.   [77] Ibid., 607.   [78] Ibid., 599.   [79] Ibid.
[80] E.g., Mark 16:19. Aquinas grapples with this anthropomorphism in Aquinas, *Summa Theologica*, p. 3, q. 58.

Differences in conceptualisation can easily be extended to less trivial cases. Referencing his own experience of becoming blind, theologian John Hull notes that blind and sighted people have very different forms of lived experience: 'Only when you become blind do you realise that you were living in a sighted world. So it is that most sighted people, who have perhaps never experienced disability or had occasion to empathise with a disabled loved one, do not acknowledge a plurality of genuine human worlds.'[81] Many biblical images assume sighted experience, such as blindness metaphors which understand blindness as a deficit.[82] Articulating a view akin to the bodily relativity hypothesis, Hull argues that these differences in bodily structure result in different epistemologies. Theologies of disability must therefore engage with different images of God:

> In seeking to understand the human image of God as a contribution to a theology of disability, we must commence not with the formal belief structure of Christian theology, which exists as ideas, beliefs and concepts in the form of sentences but with an epistemology rooted in bodily structures. To be disabled is to have a different physical or mental structure. It is these structures themselves which must be the starting point for a theology of disability[83]

One might easily extend these insights to speculations about other theological concepts. Perhaps biological females, males, and intersex people have some divergences in their conceptual repertoires by virtue of bodily differences and experiences.[84] Do those who have given birth have a deeper understanding of Jesus' saying that to enter the Kingdom of God is to be born from above (John 3)? Do those who have experienced the anxiety, ostracization, and constant bodily fear responses associated with living in violent and oppressive regimes have a richer notion of Jesus' own persecution narrated in the passion narratives? What of those whose economic circumstances render then vulnerable to hunger, thirst, exposure to the elements, or prolonged illness without medical care; do they read the concept of 'the poor' in the gospels differently by virtue of their acquaintance with the related bodily experiences?

To accommodate this diversity, Hull argues for a 'poly-anthropomorphic rather than uniform' image of God.[85] This raises a broader question about the nature of accommodation: is there a one-size-fits-all accommodation to some generic human condition? Or does the diversity of human embodiment require more tailored forms of accommodation? Glen Sunshine notes that images of

---

[81] John M. Hull, 'Blindness and the Face of God: Toward a Theology of Disability', in *The Human Image of God* ed. Hans-Georg Ziebertz (Leiden: Brill, 2000).

[82] Louise J. Lawrence, 'Disease and Disability Metaphors in Gospel Worlds', *Interpretation* 73, no. 4 (2019).

[83] Hull, 'Blindness'.   [84] Ibid.   [85] Ibid., 215.

accommodation in patristic writings often imply the latter. For example, he observes that Origen individualises his notion of accommodation; revelation 'was not accommodated simply to the culture in which it was first given, but rather is accommodated in a dynamic fashion to each reader according to [their] ability'.[86] Such an individualised account of accommodation might be extended beyond various degrees of progress in the Christian life (the purpose for which Origen proposes it), but also to accommodate a diversity of embodiments.

4.3 Incarnational Breadth

In the preceding discussion of the bodily nature of theological concepts (Chapter 4), the incarnation played a key role: as a bodily route to knowledge of God it accommodated human conceptual capacities whilst avoiding idolatry. Even if some theological concepts (such as sitting at God's right hand) do not appear to accommodate diverse embodiments, can the incarnation still be identi-fied as the ultimate accommodation to human understanding in light of human bodily diversity? This is by no means a new question; many contextual theologies have sought to articulate Christ's solidarity with their own 'context'.

In feminist theology, for example, Rosemary Radford Ruether classically articulated the question 'Can a male savior save women?'[87] O'Neil forcefully expresses the bind this question creates for feminist theologians: on the one hand, emphasising an incarnation into male form respects the particularities of Jesus' embodied existence but excludes the bodies of women from the incarnation (especially given the patristic saying that 'what has not been assumed has not been healed'); on the other hand, emphasising incarnation into a general human nature risks a form of Docetism or Gnosticism which attenuates Jesus' embodi-ment.[88] O'Neil (and others) attempts to forge a middle path between the horns of this dilemma, by recognising that maleness was one of the historical particular-ities of Jesus embodiment but arguing that it ought not be functionalised theo-logically; that is, Jesus' masculinity was not essential for his Christic function and identity. This nuanced position seeks to both respect Jesus' concrete embodiment whilst including the embodiment of women within the incarnation.

Many contextual theologies have sought to emphasise ways in which Christ's solidarity with their own contexts of oppression can be symbolically expressed. One of the reoccurring motifs to convey Christ's solidarity with these contexts is an emphasis on shared marginalisation: the historical Jesus' own particular

---

[86] Sunshine, 'Accommodation Historically Considered', 240.

[87] Rosemary Radford Ruether, *To Change the World: Christology and Cultural Criticism* (London: SCM, 1981), 51–62.

[88] Mary O'Neill, 'Female Embodiment and the Incarnation', in *Themes in Feminist Theology for the New Millennium (I)*, ed. F. Eigo (Villanova, PA: Villanova University Press, 2002), 39.

concern for and ministry to those on the margins, as well as his own ultimate status as a marginalised victim—a Palestinian peasant crucified outside the city walls. However, this solidarity with the margins is anything but an abstract and disembodied notion; many of those whom Christ encounters are marginalised precisely on account of their embodiment, and Christ's own marginalisation is enacted in a profoundly embodied and spatial way in the passion narratives. It is also telling that many contextual theologies capture the notion of solidarity most succinctly in visual depictions or linguistic descriptions of Christ's body transposed into various forms of embodiment.

Theologians of disability, for example, have appealed to various images of Christ to express the incarnation's solidarity with people with disabilities. Eiesland classically points to the resurrected Christ, who still bears impairments in his hands, feet, and side, as an image of the disabled God.[89] However, Eiesland's account (by her own circumscription) only deals with physical disabilities; and, given the internal complexity of the category of disability, this image may have its own limitations.[90] Considering blindness, Hull identifies the blindfolded Christ as a Christ who enters into the experience of blind people.[91] Reflecting on developmental disabilities, Swinton recalls encountering the suggestion that Jesus had Down's syndrome and finding that this suggestion 'opened up new vistas of hope, reconciliation, and revelation'.[92]

In a similar expression of solidarity, James Cone introduces the symbol of the Black Christ,[93] and forcefully notes the parallels between the cross and the lynching tree.[94] Countless artists have depicted Christ bearing certain ethnic characteristics or in the idioms of various indigenous art forms, such as Robert Campbell's indigenous Australian Christological images. Feminist theologians have reflected on Christa images, such as the sculpture by Edwina Sandys.[95] Elisabeth Ohlson Wallin's *Ecce Homo* photographic exhibition depicted Christological scenes with LGBTQ people and those suffering from AIDS. These images all lay claim to Christ's incarnation and use imagery of shared embodiment to express Christ's solidarity with various forms of suffering or marginalisation. Artists and contextual theologians alike have become heralds of the incarnation, proclaiming 'God took on your flesh too.'

---

[89] Eiesland, *The Disabled God*.   [90] Creamer, *Disability and Christian Theology*, 17–18.

[91] Hull, 'Blindness', 228.

[92] John Swinton, 'The Body of Christ Has Down's Syndrome: Theological Reflections on Vulnerability, Disability, and Graceful Communities', *Journal of Pastoral Theology* 13, no. 2 (2003): 76.

[93] James H. Cone, *A Black Theology of Liberation*, fortieth anniversary ed. (New York: Orbis Books, 2010), 125–30; Kelly Brown Douglas, *The Black Christ*, 25th Anniversary ed. (Maryknoll, New York: Orbis Books, 2019).

[94] Cone, *The Cross and the Lynching Tree*.

[95] Michele Schumacher, 'Feminist Christologies', in *The Oxford Handbook of Christology*, ed. Francesca Murphy (Oxford University Press, 2015).

Contextual theologians have observed that Jesus' embodiment has often been presumed to correspond to 'normative' conceptions of embodiment (white, able-bodied, male, heterosexual, affluent and therefore well looked after, etc.). However, on closer inspection Jesus does not easily fit into these categories as a Palestinian peasant who arguably performed gender and sexuality differently from the norms of his day. Although contextual theologies have been at the forefront of considering the breadth of the incarnation, to identify this question as a specific problem for 'contextual' theologies risks reinforcing problematic norms about embodiment. The question of whether the incarnation accommodates historically privileged forms of embodiment (a category which itself varies depending on context) must equally be posed. (Indeed this question poses particular difficulties since one cannot appeal to shared marginalisation as a basis of Christological solidarity.) Common Western depictions of a 'blond-haired blue-eyed' Jesus can themselves be recognised as attempts to contextualise the incarnation and convey solidarity, even as one questions the failure to recognise them as contextualisations, their excluding effect when they become the ubiquitous style of visual depiction, and their imbrication in ideologies and power dynamics.

The incarnation involves the taking on of a specific form of embodiment in a 'scandal of particularity'. However, the way in which a broad range of contextual theologies have managed to lay claim to the incarnation suggests that it can be a successful accommodation to a wide range of human embodiments. This conclusion seems to vindicate Barsalou's intuition that humans have sufficiently similar embodiment to share a common conceptual repertoire (see Section 4.1), as the incarnation speaks to this shared human understanding.[96]

4.4 Moving Beyond the Human?

Even if one can maintain that the incarnation plausibly serves as an accommodation to the whole gamut of human embodiment, one might still ponder exactly how broad the incarnation's accommodation is: how much could human embodiment change whilst still being accommodated by the particular incarnation in Jesus of Nazareth? There are several different kinds of alternative embodiment one could consider in pondering this question.

First, one might consider the status of the incarnation vis-à-vis non-human animals. Niels Gregerson proposes that, read against the backdrop of evolutionary history and deep ecology, the assertion that the Word became flesh might be

---

[96] To clarify, the kind of accommodation in play here is an epistemological one, that is, an accommodation to human understanding, rather than a soteriological accommodation to the human need for redemption. One could hold that the incarnation does not accommodation all humans in the former sense but does so in the latter sense.

understood as an incarnation into the flesh of all creatures on Earth.[97] Whilst this proposal articulates a kind of ontological participation in the incarnation by virtue of shared flesh, it does not address the epistemological question posed by the bodily relativity hypothesis. Namely, if bats and lions have significantly different conceptual repertoires from humans, does an incarnation into human form still accommodate them?

Second, although we have discussed human bodily diversity in a synchronic perspective, considering it in a diachronic perspective introduces the potential for even greater variety. How far back in human evolutionary history does the incarnation accommodate?[98] Given that transhumanists advocate for an embrace of human technological enhancements, how dramatic would these changes have to be before post-humans are no longer accommodated? Again the bodily relativity hypothesis raises the prospect that post-humans with vastly different forms of embodiment will no longer be accommodated by the incarnation.

Third, the recent discovery of exoplanets has led some to speculate that the probability of intelligent life elsewhere in the universe is significant. Extraterrestrial life forms may have radically different forms of embodiment from our own. Would this life be accommodated by the human incarnation? If not, is it possible that God is also incarnated into other life forms in order to accommodate them? Speculation about multiple incarnations has a long theological pedigree and, for example, was already present in Aquinas' thought.[99] The question of accommodation and the bodily relativity hypothesis provides a perspective on this question.

As Crisp observes, the question of multiple incarnations is tied up with the reasons or motivations for the incarnation.[100] Even if one grants that multiple incarnations are metaphysically possible (a point of debate in the literature), if a single incarnation fulfils the reasons for God becoming incarnate, this would seem 'to render any further incarnations otiose'.[101] This line of thinking is often applied with respect to the soteriological reason for the incarnation. If Christ's salvific work has cosmic significance, as Colossians 1:15–20 suggests (' through him God was pleased to reconcile to himself all things, whether on earth or in heaven'), there is no need for other incarnations on salvific grounds. Indeed, Crisp tentatively pursues this line of argument by following Anselm and Calvin in

---

[97] Gregersen, 'Deep Incarnation'.

[98] On the difficulties of aligning scientific and theological definitions of human, see Jonathan Jong, 'What Are Human Beings (That You Are Mindful of Them)? Notes from Neo-Darwinism and Neo-Aristotelianism', in *Issues in Science and Theology: Are We Special? Human Uniqueness in Science and Theology*, ed. Michael Fuller, et al. (Cham: Springer, 2017).

[99] Olli-Pekka Vainio, *Cosmology in Theological Perspective: Understanding Our Place in the Universe* (Ada, MI: Baker Publishing Group, 2018), 85–105, 157–69.

[100] Oliver D. Crisp, 'Multiple Incarnations', in *Reason, Faith and History: Philosophical Essays for Paul Helm*, ed. M. W. F. Stone and Paul Helm (Aldershot: Routledge, 2008), 234.

[101] Ibid., 233.

supposing that reconciliation is the primary motivation of the incarnation.[102] Likewise, Clough argues the *human* particularity of the incarnation is no more soteriologically significant than other particularities of the incarnation, such as the maleness or the historical or geographical location of Jesus of Nazareth.[103]

However, this line of thinking restricts itself to considering the soteriological reason for the incarnation. Our investigation, however, has brought the epistemic reason for the incarnation to the fore; and it may provide a separate motivation for multiple incarnations.[104] (This would be especially salient if the one disagrees with the Anselmian position that the incarnation was strictly necessary to achieve reconciliation; according to the alternative view it is within God's power to achieve forgiveness by other means, and hence reconciliation no longer seems to be a motivation for the incarnation.[105]) As we have seen, a human incarnation seems to neatly accommodate human understanding; and the understanding of other intelligent life may require a different form of accommodation, which could motivate other incarnations.

Engagement with cognitive science may further clarify the epistemological impetus for multiple incarnations. Namely, one might distinguish between what I shall call 'logistical' restrictions to epistemic access and 'corporeal' restrictions. By the former, I mean that intelligent life elsewhere in the universe may not hear of our incarnation due to factors such as inter-planetary distances, the possible speed of communications, and the heat death of the universe ('logistical factors'), and this may prevent them from accessing the knowledge of the divine available from our incarnation (perhaps motivating a different incarnation). However, there may also be 'corporeal' epistemic restrictions associated with our incarnation. Namely, if the human conceptual repertoire is shaped by human embodiment, as the cognitive science we have explored suggests, then creatures with significantly different bodily configurations and sensory modalities may have a very different and potentially incommensurable conceptual repertoire (so the 'bodily relatively hypothesis', see Section 4.1).[106] Hence the other creatures may require a different incarnation if our incarnation is not sufficiently accommodated to their cognitive profiles.

As many others working on this question readily acknowledge, thinking in the area of multiple incarnations is highly speculative. My goal here has not been to provide a fully developed position on the topic. Rather, I hope to have shown that motivations for the incarnation play into debates around multiple incarnations. Providing a more comprehensive account of the epistemological reasons for the

[102] Ibid., 234–5.
[103] David L. Clough, *On Animals: Systematic Theology* (London: Bloomsbury, 2014), 83–4.
[104] Vainio, *Cosmology in Theological Perspective: Understanding Our Place in the Universe*, 166.
[105] Aquinas, *Summa Theologica*, 3.1.2; Richard Swinburne, *The Christian God* (Oxford: Oxford University Press, 1994), 216–17.
[106] Casasanto, 'Bodily Relativity'.

incarnation through an engagement with cognitive science and within the framework of accommodation brings new insights to bear on such debates.

4.5 Practicing with Diverse Bodies

The preceding sections have primarily engaged with the question of whether the diverse range of human embodiment pose a challenge for the argument developed in Part II that the incarnation accommodates human concepts. Part III of this volume extended the application of accommodation to suggest that liturgical practices are an accommodation to human bodily nature. Bodily diversity again poses a critical challenge for this second application; are liturgical practices accommodated to the diversity of human embodiment?

Again, contextual theologians have been at the forefront of grappling with this question. Considering liturgies from a feminist perspective, Marjorie Procter-Smith asks the question 'are they for us?'—a question that implicitly evokes accommodation.[107] As is true of liturgical theology more general, much of this work has focused on liturgical texts and symbolic meanings in the liturgy, particularly the way in which language and images for God are gendered.[108] Ruether, however, crafts rites that address aspects of (some) women's bodily experience, such as liturgies which address feelings of loss around miscarriage and termination.[109] Moreover, she includes rubrics which guide participants to move their bodies in particular ways.[110] These ritual movements encode theological meanings not only in the words uttered but also in gesture and movement. Likewise she references liturgies which capture embodied meaning by manipulating material objects and she considers the architectural spaces in which the liturgies take place.[111] This attentiveness to the embodied and material aspects of liturgy resonates with the bodily and scaffolded vision of liturgical practices outlined in Chapter 6, Sections 2 and 3. Furthermore, it addresses bodily diversity by capturing and articulating bodily experiences which are often neglected.

Disability theologians have also questioned whether liturgies accommodate bodies with impairments. Alongside Swinton's insightful observation that the embodied dimensions of liturgies allow for an expression of faith for those who have lost linguistic capacity, such as those with dementia (see Section 2.3), there is the painful reality that these embodied dimensions are unavailable to many others. For all of the embodied dimensions of religious practice surveyed in

---

[107] Marjorie Procter-Smith, *In Her Own Rite: Constructing Feminist Liturgical Tradition* (Nashville: Abingdon Press, 1990), 13.

[108] See Chapter 7, Section 2.2.

[109] Rosemary Radford Ruether, *Women-Church: Theology and Practice of Feminist Liturgical Communities* (San Francisco: Harper & Row, 1985), 121–2, 173–5.

[110] E.g., ibid., 184.   [111] Ibid., 175–8.

Chapter 6, one can readily imagine forms of human embodiment which are excluded from them by virtue of impaired mobility, limited bodily movement, sensory impairments, gluten or alcohol intolerance, impaired social cognition, and so on.

Given the variety of impairments and the internal complexity of the category of disability there is no one-size-fits-all response to obstacles to liturgical participation.[112] The sheer variety of embodied mechanisms in liturgies may be helpful here: if some forms of bodily participation are not possible they can be substituted for others which have similar cognitive or affective effects. Embodied cognition provides a rich tool for adapting liturgies, linking embodied mechanisms to particular cognitive effects so that alternatives can be identified.

Drawing on the social model of disability, theologians such as Eiesland point out that impairments need not lead to disabling liturgies if equal access is provided through means such as accessible architectural spaces. She argues that this is particularly crucial for the Eucharist:

> The Eucharist as a central and constitutive practices of the church is a ritual of membership. Someone who can take or serve communion is a real Christian subject. Hence inclusion of people with disabilities in the ordinary practice of receiving and administering the Eucharist is a matter of bodily mediation of justice and an incorporation of hope.[113]

She goes even further by questioning the theological status of a Eucharistic which does not provide such access: 'a body practice of eucharist that excludes or segregates people with disabilities is not a celebration of the real body of Christ'.[114] A similar point has been made by John Zizioulas with respects to all kinds of bodily diversity; for Zizioulas, universal accessibility is an essential and constitutive aspect of Eucharistic celebration:

> A eucharist which discriminates between races, sexes, ages, professions, social classes etc. violates not certain ethical principles but its eschatological nature. For that reason such a eucharist is not a 'bad'—i.e. morally deficient—eucharist but no eucharist at all. It cannot be said to be the body of the One who sums up all into Himself.[115]

Eiesland and Zizioulas thereby turn the question on its head; instead of asking 'Can the embodied practice be made to accommodate bodily diversity?', they ask

---

[112] Creamer, *Disability and Christian Theology*, 17–18.
[113] Eiesland, *The Disabled God*, 112.   [114] Ibid., 114.
[115] Jean Zizioulas, *Being as Communion: Studies in Personhood and the Church* (Crestwood, NY: St. Vladimir's Seminary Press, 1985), 255.

'Can it be said to be a Eucharist if it fails to accommodate?' Hence the Eucharist accommodates bodily (and other forms) of diversity by definition since failures to accommodate call into question the theological propriety of the embodied practice.

5 Conclusion: Accommodation as a Gift and Ongoing Task

This concluding chapter has advocated for a corporeal theology in light of the engagement with embodied cognition staged in the preceding chapters. I have argued that many contextual theologies already exemplify such an embodied theological methodology. There are opportunities for synergies here, with embodied cognition offering a detailed portrait of the embodied human subject. Theologies which oppress and theologies which foster flourishing are equally imbricated in embodied practices and concepts, and therefore directing attention to the level of embodiment offers one avenue for incisive theological analysis.

The engagement with contextual theologies has also posed some constructive challenges which have refined an embodied theological method. First, they demonstrate that alongside meanings which arise from the body, meanings are also ascribed to the body. Hence physical and social embodiment need to be considered in relation to one another. Second, they highlight the fact of bodily diversity, raising the critical question: whose embodiment is being accommodated?

In grappling with this poignant question, we have seen that important theological work is required to ensure that diverse embodiments are accommodated by theological concepts, by embodied ecclesial practices, and are included in the solidarity of the incarnation. This crucial theological task provides a challenge to church communities and leaders, and academic theologians alike: are all bodies accommodated in your theology and in your worship?

A twofold understanding of accommodation thus emerges. On the one hand, accommodation is a sheer gift of grace; it is God transcending the boundary between creator and creature to meet us in our own materiality and flesh. However, as contemporary theologians have stressed, divine agency need not be seen in competition with human agency.[116] Hence, on the other hand, accommodation is an ongoing task of theology and ecclesial communities which are called to remove any obstacles to the accommodation of any body.

---

[116] E.g., Kathryn Tanner, *Jesus, Humanity and the Trinity: A Brief Systematic Theology* (Minneapolis, MN: Fortress Press, 2001), 2–3.

Bibliography

Abril, José M. 'Evidence of Churches Aligned to the Sun on the Patron Saint's Day in Southern Spain after the Twelfth Century'. *Journal of Skyscape Archaeology* 3, no. 1 (2017): 29–48.

Ackerman, Joshua M., Christopher C. Nocera, and John A. Bargh. 'Incidental Haptic Sensations Influence Social Judgments and Decisions'. *Science* 328, no. 5986 (2010): 1712–15.

Adam, Hajo, and Adam D. Galinsky. 'Enclothed Cognition'. *Journal of Experimental Social Psychology* 48, no. 4 (2012): 918–25.

Adams, Fred, and Ken Aizawa. 'The Bounds of Cognition'. *Philosophical Psychology* 14, no. 1 (2001): 43–64.

Adams, Frederick, and Kenneth Aizawa. 'The Value of Cognitivism in Thinking About Extended Cognition'. *Phenomenology and the Cognitive Sciences* 9, no. 4 (2010): 579–603.

Adolphs, Ralph. 'The Social Brain: Neural Basis of Social Knowledge'. *Annual Review of Psychology* 60 (2009): 693–716.

Adorno, Theodor W. 'Valery Proust Museum'. In *Prisms*, 175–85. London: Neville Spearman, 1967.

Adydede, Murat. *The Language of Thought Hypothesis* 2010 [cited 28 August 2016]. Available from https://plato.stanford.edu/archives/fall2015/entries/language-thought/.

Ahmed, Ali, and Osvaldo Salas. 'Religious Context and Prosociality: An Experimental Study from Valparaíso, Chile'. *Journal for the Scientific Study of Religion* 52, no. 3 (2013): 627–37.

Alston, William P. *Perceiving God: The Epistemology of Religious Experience*. London: Cornell University Press, 1991.

Andresen, Jensine. 'Introduction: Towards a Cognitive Science of Religion'. In *Religion in Mind: Cognitive Perspectives on Religious Belief, Ritual and Experience*, edited by Jensine Andresen, 1–44. Cambridge: Cambridge University Press, 2001.

Andrews, Stephen. 'The Ambiguity of Capacity: A Rejoinder to Trevor Hart'. *Tyndale Bulletin* 45, no. 1 (1994): 169–79.

Aquinas, Thomas. *Scriptum Super Libros Sententiarum Magistri Petri Lombardi Episcopi Parisiensis*. Vol. 1. Paris: P. Lethielleux, 1929.

Aquinas, Thomas. *Quaestiones Disputatae De Veritate*. Roma: Editori di san Tommaso, 1972.

Aquinas, Thomas. *Summa Theologica*. Complete English ed. Westminster MD: Christian Classics, 1981.

Aquinas, Thomas. *Summa Contra Gentiles, Library of Latin Texts. Series A*. Turnhout, Belgium: Brepols Publishers, 2010.

Aristotle. *The Nicomachean Ethics*. Translated by William David Ross. London: Oxford University Press, 1954.

Aristotle. *De Anima*. Edited by W. D. Ross. Oxford: Clarendon Press, 1961.

Arnau, Eric, Anna Estany, Rafael González del Solar, and Thomas Sturm. 'The Extended Cognition Thesis: Its Significance for the Philosophy of (Cognitive) Science'. *Philosophical Psychology* 27, no. 1 (2014): 1–18.

Asratian, Ēzras Asratovich. *I.P. Pavlov: His Life and Work*. Moscow: Foreign Languages Publishing House, 1953.

Athanasius. *On the Incarnation*. Translated by John Behr. Yonkers, NY: St Vladimir's Seminary Press, 2011.

Atkinson, P., and M. Hammersley. 'Ethnography and Participant Observation'. In *Handbook of Qualitative Research*, edited by N. K. Denzin and Y. S. Lincoln, 248–61. Thousand Oaks, CA: Sage Publications, 1994.

Augustine. *The Trinity*. Washington, DC: Catholic University of America Press, 1963.

Augustine. *De Trinitate, Library of Latin Texts*. Series A. Turnhout, Belgium: Brepols Publishers, 2010.

Augustine. *Epistulae, Library of Latin Texts*. Series A. Turnhout, Belgium: Brepols Publishers, 2010.

Aveyard, Mark E. 'A Call to Honesty: Extending Religious Priming of Moral Behavior to Middle Eastern Muslims'. *PLOS ONE* 9, no. 7 (2014): e99447.

Bailenson, Jeremy N. 'Nonverbal Overload: A Theoretical Argument for the Causes of Zoom Fatigue'. *Technology, Mind, and Behavior* 2, no. 1 (2021).

Baker, Joseph O., Gerardo Martí, Ruth Braunstein, Andrew L. Whitehead, and Grace Yukich. 'Religion in the Age of Social Distancing: How Covid-19 Presents New Directions for Research'. *Sociology of religion* 81, no. 4 (2020): 357–70.

Bangert, Marc, and Eckart O. Altenmüller. 'Mapping Perception to Action in Piano Practice: A Longitudinal DC-EEG Study'. *BMC Neuroscience* 4, no. 1 (2003): 26.

Banner, Michael. *The Ethics of Everyday Life: Moral Theology, Social Anthropology, and the Imagination of the Human*. Oxford: Oxford University Press, 2014.

Barbalet, J. M. 'William James' Theory of Emotions: Filling in the Picture'. *Journal for the Theory of Social Behaviour* 29, no. 3 (1999): 251–66.

Barrett, Justin L., and Frank C. Keil. 'Conceptualizing a Nonnatural Entity: Anthropomorphism in God Concepts'. *Cognitive Psychology* 31, no. 3 (1996): 219–47.

Barrett, Nathaniel F. 'Skilful Engagement and the "Effort after Value": An Axiological Theory of the Origins of Religion'. In *Evolution, Religion, and Cognitive Science: Critical and Constructive Essays*, edited by Fraser Watts and Léon P. Turner, 92–108. Oxford: Oxford University Press, 2014.

Barsade, Sigal G. 'The Ripple Effect: Emotional Contagion and Its Influence on Group Behavior'. *Administrative Science Quarterly* 47, no. 4 (2002): 644–75.

Barsalou, Lawrence W. 'Perceptions of Perceptual Symbols'. *Behavioral and Brain Sciences* 22, no. 04 (1999): 637–60.

Barsalou, Lawrence W. 'Perceptual Symbol Systems'. *Behavioral and Brain Sciences* 22, no. 4 (1999): 577–609.

Barsalou, Lawrence W. 'Grounded Cognition'. *Annual Review of Psychology* 59 (2008): 617–45.

Barsalou, Lawrence W., Aron K. Barbey, W. Kyle Simmons, and Ava Santos. 'Embodiment in Religious Knowledge'. *Journal of Cognition and Culture* 5, no. 1–2 (2005): 14–57.

Barth, Karl. *The Word of God and the Word of Man*. London: Hodder and Stoughton, 1928.

Barth, Karl. *Church Dogmatics*. Edited by Geoffrey William Bromiley, Thomas F. Torrance and G. T. Thomson. Edinburgh: T&T Clark, 1936–1977.

Barth, Karl. 'No! Answer to Emil Brunner'. In *Natural Theology*, 65–128. London: Centenary Press, 1946.

Barth, Karl. *The Epistle to the Romans*. Translated by Edwyn Clement Hoskyns. Oxford: Oxford University Press, 1968.

Barth, Karl. *Church Dogmatics: The Doctrine of the Word of God*. Translated by G. T. Thomson. Vol. 1/1. Edinburgh: T&T Clark, 1969.

Barth, Karl. *Church Dogmatics: The Doctrine of God*. Translated by G. T. Thomson. Vol. 2/1. Edinburgh: T&T Clark, 1980.

Bayle, Peter. 'Rimini (Gergory of)'. In *The Dictionary Historical and Critical of Mr Peter Bayle*, 874–8. London: J.J. Knapton and P. Knapton, 1737.

Beauregard, Mario, and Vincent Paquette. 'Neural Correlates of a Mystical Experience in Carmelite Nuns'. *Neuroscience Letters* 405, no. 3 (2006): 186–90.

Beilock, S. L., and S. Goldin-Meadow. 'Gesture Changes Thought by Grounding It in Action'. *Psychological Science* 21, no. 11 (2010): 1605–10.

Beilock, Sian L., and Sara Gonso. 'Putting in the Mind Versus Putting on the Green: Expertise, Performance Time, and the Linking of Imagery and Action'. *The Quarterly Journal of Experimental Psychology* 61, no. 6 (2008): 920–32.

Beilock, Sian L., Ian M. Lyons, Andrew Mattarella-Micke, Howard C. Nusbaum, and Steven L. Small. 'Sports Experience Changes the Neural Processing of Action Language'. *Proceedings of the National Academy of Sciences* 105, no. 36 (2008): 13269–73.

Bell, Catherine M. *Ritual Theory, Ritual Practice*. Oxford: Oxford University Press, 1992.

Benin, Stephen D. *The Footprints of God: Divine Accommodation in Jewish and Christian Thought, Suny Series in Judaica*. Albany, NY: State University of New York Press, 1993.

Berns, Steph. 'Sacred Entanglements: Studying Interactions between Visitors, Objects and Religion in the Museum'. University of Kent, 2015.

Bhalla, Mukul, and Dennis R. Proffitt. 'Visual-Motor Recalibration in Geographical Slant Perception'. *Journal of Experimental Psychology: Human Perception & Performance* 25, no. 4 (1999): 1076–96.

Boethius. *The Consolation of Philosophy*. Translated by David R. Slavitt. Cambridge, MA: Harvard University Press, 2008.

Boff, Leonardo. 'The Need for Political Saints: From a Spirituality of Liberation to the Practice of Liberation'. *Cross Currents* 30, no. 4 (1980): 369.

Bonaventure. *Breviloquium, Library of Latin Texts. Series A*. Turnhout, Belgium: Brepols Publishers, 2010.

Borghi, Anna M., and Felice Cimatti. 'Words Are Not Just Words: The Social Acquisition of Abstract Words'. *Rivista Italiana di Filosofia del Linguaggio* 5 (2012): 22–37.

Borghi, Anna M., and Diane Pecher. 'Introduction to the Special Topic Embodied and Grounded Cognition'. *Frontiers in Psychology* 2 (2011): 187.

Boroditsky, Lera, and Michael Ramscar. 'The Roles of Body and Mind in Abstract Thought'. *Psychological Science* 13, no. 2 (2002): 185–9.

Botvinick, Matthew, and Jonathan Cohen. 'Rubber Hands "Feel" Touch That Eyes See'. *Nature* 391, no. 6669 (1998): 756–6.

Boyd, Robert, Herbert Gintis, and Samuel Bowles. 'Coordinated Punishment of Defectors Sustains Cooperation and Can Proliferate When Rare'. *Science* 328, no. 5978 (2010): 617–20.

Bridgeman, Bruce, and Merrit Hoover. 'Processing Spatial Layout by Perception and Sensorimotor Interaction'. *The Quarterly Journal of Experimental Psychology* 61, no. 6 (2008): 851–9.

Brooks, Rodney A. 'Elephants Don't Play Chess'. *Robotics and Autonomous Systems* 6, no. 1–2 (1990): 3–15.

Brooks, Rodney A. 'Intelligence without Representation'. *Artificial Intelligence* 47 (1991): 139–59.

Brooks, Rodney A. 'New Approaches to Robotics'. *Science* 253, no. 5025 (1991): 1227–32.

Brown, Warren S., and Kevin S. Reimer. 'Embodied Cognition, Character Formation, and Virtue'. *Zygon* 48, no. 3 (2013): 832–45.

Brown, Warren S., and Brad D. Strawn. *The Physical Nature of Christian Life: Neuroscience, Psychology, and the Church*. Cambridge: Cambridge University Press, 2012.

Brunner, Emil. 'Nature and Grace: A Contribution to the Discussion with Karl Barth'. In *Natural Theology*, 15–64. London: Centenary Press, 1946.

Buccino, G., F. Binkofski, G. R. Fink, L. Fadiga, L. Fogassi, V. Gallese, R. J. Seitz, K. Zilles, G. Rizzolatti, and H. J. Freund. 'Action Observation Activates Premotor and Parietal Areas in a Somatotopic Manner: An FMRI Study'. *European Journal of Neuroscience* 13, no. 2 (2001): 400–4.

Buccino, G., L. Riggio, G. Melli, F. Binkofski, V. Gallese, and G. Rizzolatti. 'Listening to Action-Related Sentences Modulates the Activity of the Motor System: A Combined TMS and Behavioral Study'. *Cognitive Brain Research* 24, no. 3 (2005): 355–63.

Bultmann, Rudolf Karl. 'Neues Testament Und Mythologie: Das Problem Der Entmythologisierung Der Neutestamentlichen Verkündigung'. *Kerygma und Mythos: Ein Theologisches Gespräch* 1 (1960): 15–48.

Bultmann, Rudolf Karl. 'New Testament and Mythology'. In *Kerygma and Myth: A Theological Debate*, edited by Hans Werner Bartsch, 1–44. New York: Harper & Row, 1961.

Bultmann, Rudolf Karl. 'New Testament and Mythology (1941)'. In *New Testament and Mythology and Other Basic Writings*, edited by Schubert M. Ogden, 1–44. Philadelphia: Fortress Press, 1984.

Burdett, Michael S. 'Incarnation, Posthumanism and Performative Anthropology: The Body of Technology and the Body of Christ'. *Christian Bioethics: Non-Ecumenical Studies in Medical Morality* (2021).

Butler, Judith. *Gender Trouble: Feminism and the Subversion of Identity*. London: Routledge, 1990.

Cacioppo, John T., Joseph R. Priester, and Gary G. Berntson. 'Rudimentary Determinants of Attitudes. Ii: Arm Flexion and Extension Have Differential Effects on Attitudes'. *Journal of Personality & Social Psychology* 65, no. 1 (1993): 5–17.

Calvin, Jean. *The Commentaries of John Calvin on the Old Testament*. 30 vols. Vol. 15. Edinburgh: Calvin Translation Society, 1843.

Calvin, Jean. *A Commentary on the Twelve Minor Prophets*. Vol. 1. Carlisle, PA: Banner of Truth Trust, 1986.

Calvin, Jean. *Institutes of the Christian Religion*. Translated by Henry Beveridge. Grand Rapids MI: Eerdmans, 1989.

Calvo-Merino, B., D. E. Glaser, J. Grèzes, R. E. Passingham, and P. Haggard. 'Action Observation and Acquired Motor Skills: An FMRI Study with Expert Dancers'. *Cerebral Cortex* 15, no. 8 (2005): 1243–9.

Cameron, Helen. *Talking About God in Practice: Theological Action Research and Practical Theology*. London: SCM Press, 2010.

Carman, Taylor. *Merleau-Ponty, Routledge Philosophers*. London: Routledge, 2008.

Carney, Dana R., Amy J. C. Cuddy, and Andy J. Yap. 'Power Posing: Brief Nonverbal Displays Affect Neuroendocrine Levels and Risk Tolerance'. *Psychological Science* 21, no. 10 (2010): 1363–8.

Carter, J. Kameron. *Race: A Theological Account*. Oxford: Oxford University Press, 2008.

Casasanto, Daniel. 'Embodiment of Abstract Concepts: Good and Bad in Right- and Left-Handers'. *Journal of Experimental Psychology: General* 138, no. 3 (2009): 351–67.

Casasanto, Daniel. 'Bodily Relativity'. In *The Routledge Handbook of Embodied Cognition*, edited by Lawrence E. Shapiro, 108–17. New York: Routledge, 2014.

Cavanaugh, William. 'Torture and Eucharist: Theology, Politics, and the Body of Christ'. *Landas: Journal of Loyola School of Theology* 26, no. 2 (2012): 1–15. https://doi.org/10.13185/LA2012.26202.

Chambers, Craig G., Michael K. Tanenhaus, Kathleen M. Eberhard, Hana Filip, and Greg N. Carlson. 'Circumscribing Referential Domains During Real-Time Language

Comprehension'. *Journal of Memory and Language* 47, no. 1 (2002): 30–49. https://doi. org/10.1006/jmla.2001.2832.

Chambers, Craig G., Michael K. Tanenhaus, and James S. Magnuson. 'Actions and Affordances in Syntactic Ambiguity Resolution'. *Journal of Experimental Psychology: Learning, Memory, & Cognition* 30, no. 3 (2004): 687–96.

Chandler, Jesse, and Norbert Schwarz. 'How Extending Your Middle Finger Affects Your Perception of Others: Learned Movements Influence Concept Accessibility'. *Journal of Experimental Social Psychology* 45, no. 1 (2009): 123–8.

Chapman, Hanah A., and Adam K. Anderson. 'Things Rank and Gross in Nature: A Review and Synthesis of Moral Disgust'. *Psychological Bulletin* 139, no. 2 (2013): 300–27.

Charlesworth, James H. 'The Symbology of the Serpent in the Gospel of John'. In *John, Jesus, and History, Volume 2: Aspects of Historicity in the Fourth Gospel*, edited by Paul N. Anderson, Felix Just, and Tom Thatcher, 63–72. Atlanta: SBL Press, 2015.

Charry, Ellen T. 'Experience'. In *The Oxford Handbook of Systematic Theology* edited by Kathryn Tanner, John Webster, and Iain Torrance, 413–30. Oxford: Oxford University Press, 2007.

Chemero, Anthony. 'An Outline of a Theory of Affordances'. *Ecological Psychology* 15, no. 2 (2003): 181–95. https://doi.org/10.1207/S15326969ECO1502_5.

Chemero, Anthony. *Radical Embodied Cognitive Science*. Cambridge, MA: MIT Press, 2009.

Cicero, Marcus Tullius. *De Oratore*. Translated by E. W. Sutton. Cambridge, MA: Harvard University Press, 1948.

Clark, Andy. *Being There: Putting Brain, Body, and World Together Again*. Cambridge, MA: MIT Press, 1997.

Clark, Andy. 'Coupling, Constitution, and the Cognitive Kind: A Reply to Adams and Aizawa'. In *The Extended Mind*, 81–100. Cambridge MA: MIT Press, 2010.

Clark, Andy, and David Chalmers. 'The Extended Mind'. *Analysis* 58, no. 1 (1998): 7–19.

Clark, Andy, and Josefa Toribio. 'Doing without Representing?' *Synthese* 101, no. 3 (1994): 401–31. https://doi.org/10.2307/20117968.

Clough, David L. *On Animals: Systematic Theology*. London, UK: Bloomsbury, 2014.

Coakley, Sarah. 'Beyond 'Belief': Liturgy and the Cognitive Apprehension of God'. In *The Vocation of Theology Today: A Festschrift for David Ford*, edited by Tom Greggs, Rachel Muers, and Simeon Zahl, 131–45. Eugene OR: Wipf and Stock, 2013.

Coakley, Sarah. *God, Sexuality and the Self: An Essay 'on the Trinity'*. Cambridge: Cambridge University Press, 2013.

Coakley, Sarah, ed. *Faith, Rationality and the Passions*. Oxford: Wiley-Blackwell, 2012.

Cohen, Dov, and Angela K. Y. Leung. 'The Hard Embodiment of Culture'. *European Journal of Social Psychology* 39, no. 7 (2009): 1278–89. https://doi.org/10.1002/ejsp.671.

ComRes. 'Hope: Perceptions of Jesus Research'. London: ComRes, 2017.

Cone, James H. *A Black Theology of Liberation*. Fortieth anniversary ed. New York: Orbis Books, 2010.

Cone, James H. *The Cross and the Lynching Tree*. Maryknoll, NY: Orbis Books, 2011.

Copeland, M. Shawn *Enfleshing Freedom: Body, Race, and Being*: Fortress Press, 2010.

Correll, Joshua, Bernadette Park, Charles Judd, and Bernd Wittenbrink. 'The Police Officer's Dilemma: Using Ethnicity to Disambiguate Potentially Threatening Individuals'. *Journal of personality and social psychology* 83 (2003): 1314–29. https://doi.org/10.1037//0022-3514.83.6.1314.

Corwin, Anna I. 'Changing God, Changing Bodies: The Impact of New Prayer Practices on Elderly Catholic Nuns' Embodied Experience'. *Ethos* 40, no. 4 (2012): 390–410. https://doi.org/10.1111/j.1548-1352.2012.01267.x.

Creamer, Deborah Beth. *Disability and Christian Theology: Embodied Limits and Constructive Possibilities, American Academy of Religion Academy Series.* Oxford: Oxford University Press, 2009.

Crippen, Matthew. 'Preface'. *Contemporary Pragmatism* 14, no. 1 (2017): 1–3. https://doi.org/10.1163/18758185-01401001.

Crisp, Oliver D. 'Multiple Incarnations'. In *Reason, Faith and History: Philosophical Essays for Paul Helm,* edited by M. W. F. Stone and Paul Helm. Aldershot: Routledge, 2008.

Cuneo, Terence. *Ritualized Faith: Essays on the Philosophy of Liturgy, Oxford Studies in Analytic Theology.* Oxford: Oxford University Press, 2016.

Curtin, John J., Christopher J. Patrick, Alan R. Lang, John T. Cacioppo, and Niels Birbaumer. 'Alcohol Affects Emotion through Cognition'. *Psychological Science* 12, no. 6 (2001): 527–31. https://doi.org/10.1111/1467-9280.00397.

Damasio, Antonio R. 'Concepts in the Brain'. *Mind & Language* 4, no. 1–2 (1989): 24–8. https://doi.org/10.1111/j.1468-0017.1989.tb00236.x.

Damasio, Antonio R. *Descartes' Error: Emotion, Reason and the Human Brain.* London: Vintage, 1994.

Damasio, Antonio R. *Looking for Spinoza: Joy, Sorrow, and the Feeling Brain.* London: Vintage, 2004.

Damasio, Antonio R., and Hanna Damasio. 'Brain and Language'. *Scientific American* 267, no. 3 (1992): 89–95.

Danziger, Shai, Jonathan Levav, and Liora Avnaim-Pesso. 'Extraneous Factors in Judicial Decisions'. *Proceedings of the National Academy of Sciences* 108, no. 17 (2011): 6889–92. https://doi.org/10.1073/pnas.1018033108.

Daugman, John G. 'Brain Metaphor and Brain Theory'. In *Philosophy and the Neurosciences: A Reader,* edited by William Bechtel, Pete Mandik, and Jennifer Mundale, 23–36. Oxford: Blackwell Publishers, 2001.

Daum, Moritz M., Jessica A. Sommerville, and Wolfgang Prinz. 'Becoming a Social Agent: Developmental Foundations of an Embodied Social Psychology'. *European Journal of Social Psychology* 39, no. 7 (2009): 1196–206. https://doi.org/10.1002/ejsp.672.

Davis, Joshua Ian, Ann Senghas, Fredric Brandt, and Kevin N. Ochsner. 'The Effects of Botox Injections on Emotional Experience'. *Emotion* 10, no. 3 (2010): 433–40.

Davison, Andrew. *Why Sacraments?* London: SPCK, 2013.

Davison, Andrew, and Alison Milbank. *For the Parish: A Critique of Fresh Expressions.* London: SCM Press, 2010.

Day, Matthew. 'Religion, Off-Line Cognition and the Extended Mind'. *Journal of Cognition and Culture* 4, no. 1 (2004): 101–21. https://doi.org/10.1163/156853704323074778.

de Bruyn, Theodore S. *Making Amulets Christian: Artefacts, Scribes, and Contexts.* Oxford: Oxford University Press, 2017.

de Bruyn, Theodore S., and Jitse H. F. Dijkstra. 'Greek Amulets and Formularies from Egypt Containing Christian Elements: A Checklist of Papyri, Parchments, Ostraka, and Tablets'. *The Bulletin of the American Society of Papyrologists* 48 (2011): 163–216. http://www.jstor.org/stable/24519990.

de Cruz, Helen. 'Cognitive Science of Religion and the Study of Theological Concepts'. *Topoi* 33, no. 2 (2014): 487–97. https://doi.org/10.1007/s11245-013-9168-9.

de Saussure, Ferdinand. *Course in General Lingustics.* Translated by A. Riedlinger. Edited by C. Bally and A. Sechehaye. New York: McGraw-Hill, 1966. http://doi.org/10.1007/s11245-013-9168-9.

Deacon, Terrence William. *The Symbolic Species: The Co-Evolution of Language and the Brain.* New York: W.W. Norton, 1997.

Deigh, John. 'Cognitivism in the Theory of Emotions'. *Ethics* 104, no. 4 (1994): 824–54. https://doi.org/10.2307/2382220.

DesCamp, Mary Therese, and Eve E. Sweetser. 'Metaphors for God: Why and How Do Our Choices Matter for Humans? The Application of Contemporary Cognitive Linguistics Research to the Debate on God and Metaphor'. *Pastoral Psychology* 53, no. 3 (2005): 207–38. https://doi.org/10.1007/s11089-004-0554-5.

Descartes, René. *Meditations on First Philosophy: With Selections from the Objections and Replies*. Translated by Michael Moriarty, *Oxford World's Classics*. Oxford: Oxford University Press, 2008 [1641].

Devonshire Jones, Tom, Linda Murray, and Peter Murray. 'Baptistry'. In *The Oxford Dictionary of Christian Art and Architecture*, 51–2. Oxford: Oxford University Press, 2013.

di Luca, Samuel, Alessia Granà, Carlo Semenza, Xavier Seron, and Mauro Pesenti. 'Finger–Digit Compatibility in Arabic Numeral Processing'. *The Quarterly Journal of Experimental Psychology* 59, no. 9 (2006): 1648–63. https://doi.org/10.1080/17470210500256839.

Dijkstra, Katinka, Anita Eerland, Josjan Zijlmans, and Lysanne Post. 'How Body Balance Influences Political Party Evaluations: A Wii Balance Board Study'. *Frontiers in Psychology* 3, no. 536 (2012). https://doi.org/10.3389/fpsyg.2012.00536.

Dijkstra, Katinka, Michael P. Kaschak, and Rolf A. Zwaan. 'Body Posture Facilitates Retrieval of Autobiographical Memories'. *Cognition* 102, no. 1 (2007): 139–49. https://doi.org/10.1016/j.cognition.2005.12.009.

Doblin, Rick. 'Pahnke's "Good Friday Experiment": A Long-Term Follow-up and Methodological Critique'. *The Journal of Transpersonal Psychology* 23, no. 1 (1991): 1–28.

Douglas, Kelly Brown. *Black Bodies and the Black Church: A Blues Slant, Black Religion/ Womanist Thought/Social Justice*. New York: Palgrave Macmillan, 2012.

Douglas, Kelly Brown. *Stand Your Ground: Black Bodies and the Justice of God*. Maryknoll, New York: Orbis Books, 2015.

Douglas, Kelly Brown. *The Black Christ*. 25th Anniversary ed. Maryknoll, New York: Orbis Books, 2019.

Dove, Guy. 'How to Go Beyond the Body: An Introduction'. *Frontiers in Psychology* 6 (2015): 1–3. https://doi.org/10.3389/fpsyg.2015.00660.

Dove, Guy. 'Three Symbol Ungrounding Problems: Abstract Concepts and the Future of Embodied Cognition'. *Psychonomic Bulletin and Review* 23, no. 4 (2016): 1109–21. https://doi.org/10.3758/s13423-015-0825-4.

Doyen, Stéphane, Olivier Klein, Cora-Lise Pichon, and Axel Cleeremans. 'Behavioral Priming: It's All in the Mind, but Whose Mind?' *PLOS ONE* 7, no. 1 (2012): e29081. https://doi.org/10.1371/journal.pone.0029081.

du Boulay, Juliet. *Cosmos, Life, and Liturgy in a Greek Orthodox Village*. Limni: Harvey, 2009.

du Sautoy, Marcus. *What We Cannot Know: Explorations at the Edge of Knowledge*. London: 4th Estate, 2016.

Duhaime, Erik P. 'Is the Call to Prayer a Call to Cooperate? A Field Experiment on the Impact of Religious Salience on Prosocial Behavior'. *Judgment and Decision Making* 10, no. 6 (2015): 593–6.

Dunbar, R. I. M., Ben Teasdale, Jackie Thompson, Felix Budelmann, Sophie Duncan, Evert van Emde Boas, and Laurie Maguire. 'Emotional Arousal When Watching Drama Increases Pain Threshold and Social Bonding'. *Royal Society Open Science* 3, no. 9 (2016). https://doi.org/10.1098/rsos.160288.

Dunbar, Robin I. M. 'The Social Brain Hypothesis'. *Evolutionary Anthropology: Issues, News, and Reviews* 6, no. 5 (1998): 178–90.

Dunbar, Robin I. M. 'The Origin of Religion as a Small-Scale Phenomenon.' In *Religion, Intolerance, and Conflict: A Scientific and Conceptual Investigation*, edited by Steve Clarke, Russell Powell, and Julian Savulescu, 48–66. Oxford: Oxford University Press, 2013.

Earp, Brian D., Jim A. C. Everett, Elizabeth N. Madva, and J. Kiley Hamlin. 'Out, Damned Spot: Can the "Macbeth Effect" Be Replicated?' *Basic and Applied Social Psychology* 36, no. 1 (2014): 91–8. https://doi.org/10.1080/01973533.2013.856792.

Earp, Brian D., and David Trafimow. 'Replication, Falsification, and the Crisis of Confidence in Social Psychology.' *Frontiers in Psychology* 6 (2015): 621. https://doi.org/10.3389/fpsyg.2015.00621.

Edelman, Gerald M. *Bright Air, Brilliant Fire: On the Matter of the Mind*. London: Allen Lane, 1992.

Eiesland, Nancy L. *The Disabled God: Toward a Liberatory Theology of Disability*. Nashville: Abingdon Press, 1994.

Eilan, Naomi. 'Joint Attention, Communication, and Mind.' In *Joint Attention: Communication and Other Minds*, edited by Naomi Eilan, Christoph Hoerl, Teresa McCormack and Johannes Roessler, 1–33. Oxford: Oxford University Press, 2005.

Einstein, Albert. *Albert Einstein: Philosopher-Scientist*. Translated by Paul Arthur Schilpp, *Library of Living Philosophers*. New York: MJF Books, 1949.

Ernest-Jones, Max, Daniel Nettle, and Melissa Bateson. 'Effects of Eye Images on Everyday Cooperative Behavior: A Field Experiment.' *Evolution and Human Behavior* 32, no. 3 (2010): 172–8. https://doi.org/10.1016/j.evolhumbehav.2010.10.006.

Eusebius of Caesarea. *Proof of the Gospel*. Translated by W. J. Ferrar. 2 vols. London, 1920.

Fetterman, Adam K. 'On God-Belief and Feeling Clean: Daily Experiences Are Related to Feeling Clean, Particularly for Those High in God-Belief.' *Social Psychological and Personality Science* 7, no. 6 (2016): 552–9. https://doi.org/10.1177/1948550616641474.

Fiddes, Paul. 'Ecclesiology and Ethnography: Two Disciplines, Two Worlds?' In *Perspectives on Ecclesiology and Ethnography*, edited by Pete Ward, 13–35. Grand Rapids MI: Eerdmans, 2012.

Fischer, Julia, Peter Fischer, Birte Englich, Nilüfer Aydin, and Dieter Frey. 'Empower My Decisions: The Effects of Power Gestures on Confirmatory Information Processing.' *Journal of Experimental Social Psychology* 47, no. 6 (2011): 1146–54. https://doi.org/10.1016/j.jesp.2011.06.008.

Fischer, Martin H., and Rolf A. Zwaan. 'Embodied Language: A Review of the Role of the Motor System in Language Comprehension.' *The Quarterly Journal of Experimental Psychology* 61, no. 6 (2008): 825–50. https://doi.org/10.1080/17470210701623605.

Fisher, Matthew, Mariel K. Goddu, and Frank C. Keil. 'Searching for Explanations: How the Internet Inflates Estimates of Internal Knowledge.' *Journal of Experimental Psychology: General* 144, no. 3 (2015): 674–87. https://doi.org/10.1037/xge0000070.

Fisher, Matthew, and Daniel M. Oppenheimer. 'Who Knows What? Knowledge Misattribution in the Division of Cognitive Labor.' *Journal of Experimental Psychology: Applied* 27, no. 2 (2021): 292–306. https://doi.org/10.1037/xap0000310.

Flexas, Albert, Jaume Rosselló, Julia F. Christensen, Marcos Nadal, Antonio Olivera La Rosa, and Enric Munar. 'Affective Priming Using Facial Expressions Modulates Liking for Abstract Art.' *PLOS ONE* 8, no. 11 (2013): e80154. https://doi.org/10.1371/journal.pone.0080154.

Fodor, Jerry A. *The Language of Thought, Language and Thought Series*. Cambridge, MA: Harvard University Press, 1975.

Fodor, Jerry A. *The Language of Thought*. Cambridge, MA: Harvard University Press, 1975.

Frey, William H., and Muriel Langseth. *Crying: The Mystery of Tears*. Minneapolis MN: Winston Press, 1985.

Fridlund, Alan J. 'Sociality of Solitary Smiling: Potentiation by an Implicit Audience'. *Journal of Personality & Social Psychology* 60, no. 2 (1991): 229–40.

Fuller, Robert C. 'Faith of the Flesh: Bodily Sources of Spirituality'. *Religious Studies Review* 31, no. 3–4 (2005): 135–9. https://doi.org/10.1111/j.1748-0922.2005.00009.x.

Fuller, Robert C. *Spirituality in the Flesh: Bodily Sources of Religious Experience.* Oxford: Oxford University Press, 2008.

Fuller, Robert C., and Derek E. Montgomery. 'Body Posture and Religious Attitudes'. *Archive for the Psychology of Religion* 37, no. 3 (2015): 227–39. https://doi.org/ 10.1163/15736121-12341310.

Funkenstein, Amos. *Theology and the Scientific Imagination: From the Middle Ages to the Seventeenth Century.* Princeton: Princeton University Press, 1986.

Gainotti, Guido. 'The Role of Body-Related and Environmental Sources of Knowledge in the Construction of Different Conceptual Categories'. *Frontiers in Psychology* 3, no. 430 (2012): 1–8. https://doi.org/10.3389/fpsyg.2012.00430.

Gallese, Vittorio, and George Lakoff. 'The Brain's Concepts: The Role of the Sensory-Motor System in Conceptual Knowledge'. *Cognitive Neuropsychology* 22, no. 3–4 (2005): 455–79. https://doi.org/10.1080/02643290442000310.

Garfinkel, Sarah N., and Hugo D. Critchley. 'Threat and the Body: How the Heart Supports Fear Processing'. *Trends in Cognitive Sciences* 20, no. 1(2015).

Garrigan, Siobhan. *The Real Peace Process: Worship, Politics and the End of Sectarianism.* London: Routledge, 2010.

Geangu, E., O. Benga, D. Stahl, and T. Striano. 'Contagious Crying Beyond the First Days of Life'. *Infant Behavior Development* 33, no. 3 (2010): 279–88. https://doi.org/10.1016/j. infbeh.2010.03.004.

Gentilucci, M., F. Benuzzi, L. Bertolani, E. Daprati, and M. Gangitano. 'Language and Motor Control'. *Experimental Brain Research* 133, no. 4 (2000): 468–90. https://doi. org/10.1007/s002210000431.

Gervais, Will M., and Joseph Henrich. 'The Zeus Problem: Why Representational Content Biases Cannot Explain Faith in Gods'. *Journal of Cognition and Culture* 10, no. 3 (2010): 383–9. https://doi.org/10.1163/156853710X531249.

Gibbs, Raymond W. *Embodiment and Cognitive Science.* Cambridge: Cambridge University Press, 2006.

Gibson, James J. *The Ecological Approach to Visual Perception, Psychology Press Classic Editions.* New York: Pyschology Press, 1979.

Glenberg, Arthur M., Manuel de Vega, and Arthur C. Graesser. 'Framing the Debate'. In *Symbols and Embodiment: Debates on Meaning and Cognition,* edited by Manuel De Vega, Arthur M. Glenberg, and Arthur C. Graesser, 1–8. Oxford: Oxford University Press, 2008.

Glenberg, Arthur M., and Michael P. Kaschak. 'Grounding Language in Action'. *Psychonomic Bulletin & Review* 9, no. 3 (2002): 558–65. https://doi.org/10.3758/bf03196313.

Glenberg, Arthur M., and Sarita Mehta. 'The Limits of Covariation'. In *Symbols and Embodiment: Debates on Meaning and Cognition,* edited by Manuel De Vega, Arthur M. Glenberg, and Arthur C. Graesser, 11–32. Oxford: Oxford University Press, 2008.

Glover, Scott, David A. Rosenbaum, Jeremy Graham, and Peter Dixon. 'Grasping the Meaning of Words'. *Experimental Brain Research* 154, no. 1 (2004): 103–8. https://doi. org/10.1007/s00221-003-1659-2.

Gockel, Christine, Peter M. Kolb, and Lioba Werth. 'Murder or Not? Cold Temperature Makes Criminals Appear to Be Cold-Blooded and Warm Temperature to Be Hot-Headed'. *PLOS ONE* 9, no. 4 (2014): e96231. https://doi.org/10.1371/journal.pone.0096231.

Godden, D. R., and A. D. Baddeley. 'Context-Dependent Memory in Two Natural Environments: On Land and Underwater'. *British Journal of Psychology* 66, no. 3 (1975): 325.

Goldin-Meadow, Susan, and Sian L. Beilock. 'Action's Influence on Thought: The Case of Gesture'. *Perspectives on Psychological Science* 5, no. 6 (2010): 664–74. https://doi.org/10.1177/1745691610388764.

Goldin-Meadow, Susan, and Susan M. Wagner. 'How Our Hands Help Us Learn'. *Trends in Cognitive Sciences* 9, no. 5 (2005): 234–41. https://doi.org/10.1016/j.tics.2005.03.006.

Goldstein, Valerie Saiving. 'The Human Situation: A Feminine View'. *The Journal of Religion* 40, no. 2 (1960): 100–12.

Gould, Stephen Jay. 'Exaptation: A Crucial Tool for an Evolutionary Psychology'. *Journal of Social Issues* 47, no. 3 (1991): 43–65. https://doi.org/10.1111/j.1540-4560.1991.tb01822.x.

Granito, Carmen. 'Where Are Abstract Concepts From? Embodiment Beyond the Body'. *Rivista Italiana di Filosofia del Linguaggio* 5 (2012): 84–98.

Green, Maia. 'Medicines and the Embodiment of Substances among Pogoro Catholics, Southern Tanzania'. *The Journal of the Royal Anthropological Institute* 2, no. 3 (1996): 485–98. https://doi.org/10.2307/3034899.

Gregersen, Niels Henrik. 'Deep Incarnation: Why Evolutionary Continuity Matters in Christology'. *Toronto Journal of Theology* 26, no. 2 (2010): 173–88. https://doi.org/10.3138/tjt.26.2.173.

Gregersen, Niels Henrik, ed. *Incarnation: On the Scope and Depth of Christology*. Minneapolis: Fortress Press, 2015.

Gregory of Nazianzus. *Orationes*. Edited by Jacques Paul Migne. Vols. 35–36, *Patrologiae Cursus Completus Series Graeca*. Paris: Imprimerie Catholique, 1857–1912.

Gregory of Nyssa. *Adversus Eunomium*. Edited by Jacques Paul Migne. Vol. 45, *Patrologiae Cursus Completus Series Graeca*. Paris: Imprimerie Catholique, 1857–1912.

Grumett, David. *Material Eucharist*. Oxford: Oxford University Press, 2016.

Guite, Malcolm. *Waiting on the Word: A Poem a Day for Advent, Christmas and Epiphany*. Norwich: Canterbury Press, 2015.

Guthrie, Stewart. 'Why Gods? A Cognitive Theory'. In *Religion in Mind: Cognitive Perspectives on Religious Belief, Ritual and Experience*, edited by Jensine Andresen, 94–112. Cambridge: Cambridge University Press, 2001.

Haidt, Jonathan. 'The Emotional Dog and Its Rational Tail: A Social Intuitionist Approach to Moral Judgment'. *Psychological Review* 108, no. 4 (2001): 814–34. https://doi.org/10.1037/0033-295X.108.4.814.

Haidt, Jonathan, Paul Rozin, Clark McCauley, and Sumio Imada. 'Body, Psyche, and Culture: The Relationship between Disgust and Morality'. *Psychology and Developing Societies* 9, no. 1 (1997): 107–31.

Halbertal, Moshe, and Avishai Margalit. *Idolatry*. Translated by Naomi Goldblum. Cambridge MA: Harvard University Press, 1992.

Haley, Kevin J., and Daniel M. T. Fessler. 'Nobody's Watching? Subtle Cues Affect Generosity in an Anonymous Economic Game'. *Evolution and Human Behavior* 26, no. 3 (2005): 245–56. https://doi.org/10.1016/j.evolhumbehav.2005.01.002.

Hall, Judith A., Erik J. Coats, and Lavonia Smith LeBeau. 'Nonverbal Behavior and the Vertical Dimension of Social Relations: A Meta-Analysis'. *Psychological Bulletin* 131, no. 6 (2005): 898–924.

Hamilton, Maryellen, and Suparna Rajaram. 'The Concreteness Effect in Implicit and Explicit Memory Tests'. *Journal of Memory and Language* 44, no. 1 (2001): 96–117.

Harnad, Stevan. 'The Symbol Grounding Problem'. *Physica D: Nonlinear Phenomena* 42, no. 1–3 (1990): 335–46.

Harper, R. I. 'The Kalendarium Regine of Guillaume De St. Cloud'. Emory University, 1966.

Hart, Trevor A. 'A Capacity for Ambiguity: The Barth-Brunner Debate Revisited'. *Tyndale Bulletin* 44, no. 2 (1993): 289–305.

Haueisen, Jens, and Thomas R. Knösche. 'Involuntary Motor Activity in Pianists Evoked by Music Perception'. *Journal of Cognitive Neuroscience* 13, no. 6 (2001): 786–92. https://doi.org/10.1162/08989290152541449.

Hauk, Olaf, Matthew H. Davis, Ferath Kherif, and Friedemann Pulvermüller. 'Imagery or Meaning? Evidence for a Semantic Origin of Category-Specific Brain Activity in Metabolic Imaging'. *European Journal of Neuroscience* 27, no. 7 (2008): 1856–66. https://doi.org/10.1111/j.1460-9568.2008.06143.x.

Hauk, Olaf, and Friedemann Pulvermüller. 'Somatotopic Representation of Action Words in Human Motor and Premotor Cortex'. *Neuron* 41, no. 2 (2004): 301–7.

Havas, David A., Arthur M. Glenberg, Karol A. Gutowski, Mark J. Lucarelli, and Richard J. Davidson. 'Cosmetic Use of Botulinum Toxin-a Affects Processing of Emotional Language'. *Psychological Science* 21, no. 7 (2010): 895–900. https://doi.org/10.1177/0956797610374742.

Hecht, Heiko, Stefan Vogt, and Wolfgang Prinz. 'Motor Learning Enhances Perceptual Judgment: A Case for Action-Perception Transfer'. *Psychological Research* 65, no. 1 (2001): 3.

Henrich, Joseph, Steven J. Heine, and Ara Norenzayan. 'The Weirdest People in the World?' *Behavioral and Brain Sciences* 33, no. 2–3 (2010): 61–83. https://doi.org/10.1017/S0140525X0999152X.

Herdt, Jennifer A. 'The Virtue of the Liturgy'. In *The Blackwell Companion to Christian Ethics*, edited by Stanley Hauerwas and Samuel Wells. Oxford: Wiley-Blackwell, 2011.

Herrmann, Patricia A., Cristine H. Legare, Paul L. Harris, and Harvey Whitehouse. 'Stick to the Script: The Effect of Witnessing Multiple Actors on Children's Imitation'. *Cognition* 129, no. 3 (2013): 536–43.

Hess, Ursula, and Sylvie Blairy. 'Facial Mimicry and Emotional Contagion to Dynamic Emotional Facial Expressions and Their Influence on Decoding Accuracy'. *International Journal of Psychophysiology* 40, no. 2 (2001): 129–41.

Hinton, Ian. 'Church Alignment and Patronal Saint's Days'. *The Antiquaries Journal* 86 (2008): 206–26. https://doi.org/10.1017/S0003581500000111.

Hoare, Peter G. 'Orientation of English Medieval Parish Churches'. In *Handbook of Archaeoastronomy and Ethnoastronomy*, edited by Clive L. N. Ruggles, 1711–18. New York: Springer, 2015.

Hong, Jiewen, and Yacheng Sun. 'Warm It up with Love: The Effect of Physical Coldness on Liking of Romance Movies'. *Journal of Consumer Research* 39, no. 2 (2012): 293–306. https://doi.org/10.1086/662613.

Hostetter, Autumn B., and Martha W. Alibali. 'Visible Embodiment: Gestures as Simulated Action'. *Psychonomic Bulletin & Review* 15, no. 3 (2008): 495–514.

Hostetter, Autumn B., and William D. Hopkins. 'The Effect of Thought Structure on the Production of Lexical Movements'. *Brain and Language* 82, no. 1 (2002): 22–9. https://doi.org/10.1016/S0093-934X(02)00009-3.

Hove, Michael J., and Jane L. Risen. 'It's All in the Timing: Interpersonal Synchrony Increases Affiliation'. *Social Cognition* 27, no. 6 (2009): 949–60. https://doi.org/10.1521/soco.2009.27.6.949.

Huang, L., A. D. Galinsky, D. H. Gruenfeld, and L. E. Guillory. 'Powerful Postures Versus Powerful Roles: Which Is the Proximate Correlate of Thought and Behavior?' *Psychological Science* 22, no. 1 (2011): 95–102. https://doi.org/10.1177/0956797610391912.

Hull, John M. 'Blindness and the Face of God: Toward a Theology of Disability'. In *The Human Image of God* edited by Hans-Georg Ziebertz, 215–29. Leiden: Brill, 2000.

Hurley, Susan L. *Consciousness in Action*. Cambridge MA: Harvard University Press, 1998.

Hutto, Daniel D. *Folk Psychological Narratives: The Sociocultural Basis of Understanding Reasons*. Cambridge MA: MIT Press, 2008.

Iijima, M., M. Osawa, N. Nishitani, and M. Iwata. 'Effects of Incense on Brain Function: Evaluation Using Electroencephalograms and Event-Related Potentials'. *Neuropsychobiology* 59, no. 2 (2009): 80–6.

Ijzerman, Hans, Angela K.-y. Leung, and Lay See Ong. 'Perceptual Symbols of Creativity: Coldness Elicits Referential, Warmth Elicits Relational Creativity'. *Acta Psychologica* 148 (2014): 136–47. https://doi.org/10.1016/j.actpsy.2014.01.013.

Irenaeus of Lyon. *Sancti Irenaei Episcopi Lugdunensis, Libros Quinque Adversus Haereses.*, 1857.

Izard, Carroll E. *Human Emotions, Emotions, Personality, and Psychotherapy*. New York: Plenum, 1977.

James, William. 'What Is an Emotion?' *Mind* 9, no. 34 (1884): 188–205. https://doi.org/10.2307/2246769.

Jennings, Willie James. *The Christian Imagination: Theology and the Origins of Race*. New Haven: Yale University Press, 2010.

Jenson, Robert W. *Systematic Theology: The Triune God*. Vol. 1. New York: Oxford University Press, 1997.

Jiang, Y., J. M. King, and W. Prinyawiwatkul. 'A Review of Measurement and Relationships between Food, Eating Behavior and Emotion'. *Trends in Food Science & Technology* 36, no. 1 (2014): 15–28.

Jiang, Ying. 'Measuring Facial Expression and Emotional Experience under Diverse Social Context in a Negative Emotional Setting'. Paper presented at the Measuring Behavior: 9th International Conference on Methods and Techniques in Behavioral Research Wageningen, The Netherlands 2014.

John Chrysostom. *On the Incomprehensible Nature of God*. Translated by Paul W. Harkins, edited by R. J. Deferrari. Vol. 3, *The Fathers of the Church*. Washington DC: Catholic University of America Press, 1979.

Johnson, David J., Felix Cheung, and M. Brent Donnellan. 'Does Cleanliness Influence Moral Judgments? A Direct Replication of Schnall, Benton, and Harvey (2008)'. *Social Psychology* 45, no. 3 (2014): 209–15. https://doi.org/10.1027/1864-9335/a000186.

Johnson, Elizabeth A. *She Who Is: The Mystery of God in Feminist Theological Discourse*: Crossroad, 1993.

Johnson, Mark. *The Meaning of the Body: Aesthetics of Human Understanding*. Chicago: University of Chicago Press, 2007.

Johnstone, Brick, Angela Bodling, Dan Cohen, Shawn E. Christ, and Andrew Wegrzyn. 'Right Parietal Lobe-Related "Selflessness" as the Neuropsychological Basis of Spiritual Transcendence'. *The International Journal for the Psychology of Religion* 22, no. 4 (2012): 267–84. https://doi.org/10.1080/10508619.2012.657524.

Jolij, Jacob, and Maaike Meurs. 'Music Alters Visual Perception'. *PLOS ONE* 6, no. 4 (2011): e18861. https://doi.org/10.1371/journal.pone.0018861.

Jones, James W. *Living Religion: Embodiment, Theology, and the Possibility of a Spiritual Sense*. New York: Oxford University Press, 2019.

Jones, Serene. *Feminist Theory and Christian Theology: Cartographies of Grace, Guides to Theological Inquiry*. Minneapolis: Fortress Press, 2000.

Jong, Jonathan. 'What Are Human Beings (That You Are Mindful of Them)? Notes from Neo-Darwinsim and Neo-Aristotelianism'. In *Issues in Science and Theology: Are We Special? Human Uniqueness in Science and Theology*, edited by Michael Fuller, Dirk Evers, Anne Runehov, and Knut-Willy Sæther, 79–97. New York: Springer, 2017.

Jong, Jonathan, Christopher Kavanagh, and Aku Visala. 'Born Idolaters: The Limits of the Philosophical Implications of the Cognitive Science of Religion'. *Neue Zeitschrift für Systematische Theologie und Religionsphilosophie* 20, no. 2 (2015): 244–66.

Jostmann, Nils B., Daniël Lakens, and Thomas W. Schubert. 'Weight as an Embodiment of Importance'. *Psychological Science* 20, no. 9 (2009): 1169–74. https://doi.org/10.1111/j.1467-9280.2009.02426.x.

Jüngel, Eberhard. *God as the Mystery of the World: On the Foundation of the Theology of the Crucified One in the Dispute between Theism and Atheism.* Translated by Darrell L. Guder. London: Bloomsbury, 2014.

Just, Marcel Adam. 'What Brain Imaging Can Tell Us About Embodied Meaning'. In *Symbols and Embodiment: Debates on Meaning and Cognition*, edited by Manuel De Vega, Arthur M. Glenberg, and Arthur C. Graesser, 75–84. Oxford: Oxford University Press, 2008.

Justin Martyr. 'Dialogues Cure Trephine Judo'. In *Patrologiae Cursus Completus Series Graeca*, edited by Jacques Paul Migne, 461–800. Paris: Imprimerie Catholique, 1857–1912.

Kahneman, Daniel. *Thinking, Fast and Slow.* London: Allen Lane, 2011.

Kaschak, Michael P., John L. Jones, Julie Carranza, and Melissa R. Fox. 'Embodiment and Language Comprehension'. In *The Routledge Handbook of Embodied Cognition*, edited by Lawrence A. Shapiro, 118–26. London: Routledge, 2014.

Kaufman, Gordon D. *In Face of Mystery: A Constructive Theology.* Cambridge, MA: Harvard University Press, 1993.

Kaufmann, Leah M., and Sarah Allen. 'Adding Weight to Judgments: The Role of Stimulus Focality on Weight-Related Embodied Cognition'. *Sensoria: A Journal of Mind, Brain, and Culture* 10, no. 1 (2014): 41–8.

Keltner, Dacher, and Jonathan Haidt. 'Approaching Awe, a Moral, Spiritual, and Aesthetic Emotion'. *Cognition and Emotion* 17, no. 2 (2003): 297–314. https://doi.org/10.1080/02699930302297.

Kidd, Erin. 'The Embodied Mind and How to Pray with One'. In *Putting God on the Map: Theology and Conceptual Mapping*, edited by Erin Kidd and Jakob Karl Rinderknecht, 19–42. Lanham: Fortress Academic, 2018.

Kidd, Erin, and Jakob Karl Rinderknecht. 'An Introduction to Conceptual Mapping'. In *Putting God on the Map: Theology and Conceptual Mapping*, edited by Erin Kidd and Jakob Karl Rinderknecht, 1–18. Lanham: Fortress Academic, 2018.

Kidd, Erin, and Jakob Karl Rinderknecht. *Putting God on the Map: Theology and Conceptual Mapping.* Lanham: Fortress Academic, 2018.

Kierkegaard, Søren. *Training in Christianity, and the Edifying Discourse Which 'Accompanied' It.* London: Oxford University Press, 1941.

Kintsch, Walter. 'Symbol Systems and Perceptual Representations'. In *Symbols and Embodiment: Debates on Meaning and Cognition*, edited by Manuel De Vega, Arthur M. Glenberg, and Arthur C. Graesser, 145–62. Oxford: Oxford University Press, 2008.

Kirchhoff, Michael D. 'Extended Cognition & the Causal-Constitutive Fallacy: In Search for a Diachronic and Dynamical Conception of Constitution'. *Philosophy and Phenomenological Research* 90, no. 2 (2015): 320–60. https://doi.org/10.1111/phpr.12039.

Klatzky, Roberta L., James W. Pellegrino, Brian P. McCloskey, and Sally Doherty. 'Can You Squeeze a Tomato? The Role of Motor Representations in Semantic Sensibility Judgments'. *Journal of Memory and Language* 28, no. 1 (1989): 56–77. https://doi.org/10.1016/0749-596X(89)90028-4.

Knoblauch, Andreas. 'Symbols and Embodiment from the Perspective of a Neural Modeller'. In *Symbols and Embodiment: Debates on Meaning and Cognition*, edited by Manuel De Vega, Arthur M. Glenberg, and Arthur C. Graesser, 117–43. Oxford: Oxford University Press, 2008.

Koester, Craig R. *Symbolism in the Fourth Gospel: Meaning, Mystery, Community.* 2nd ed. Minneapolis: Fortress Press, 2003.

Kousta, Stavroula-Thaleia, Gabriella Vigliocco, David P. Vinson, Mark Andrews, and Elena Del Campo. 'The Representation of Abstract Words: Why Emotion Matters'. *Journal of Experimental Psychology: General* 140, no. 1 (2011): 14–34.

Krause, Florian, Harold Bekkering, and Oliver Lindemann. 'A Feeling for Numbers: Shared Metric for Symbolic and Tactile Numerosities'. *Frontiers in Psychology* 4, no. 7 (2013): 1–8. https://doi.org/10.3389/fpsyg.2013.00007.

Kristiansson, Mattias, Richard Wiik, and Erik Prytz. 'Bodily Orientations and Actions as Constituent Parts of Remembering Objects and Intentions before Leaving Home'. *Sensoria: A Journal of Mind, Brain, and Culture* 10, no. 1 (2014): 21–7. https://doi.org/10.7790/sa.v10i1.385.

Krueger, Joel. 'Extended Mind and Religious Cognition'. In *Mental Religion: The Brain, Cognition, and Culture*, edited by N. Kasumi Clements, 237–54. New York: Macmillan, 2016.

Kubota, Jennifer T., and Tiffany A. Ito. 'The Role of Expression and Race in Weapons Identification'. *Emotion (Washington, D.C.)* 14, no. 6 (2014): 1115–24. https://doi.org/10.1037/a0038214.

Kullman, Michael, and Charles Taylor. 'The Pre-Objective World'. *The Review of Metaphysics* 12, no. 1 (1958): 108–32. https://doi.org/10.2307/20123686.

Kunda, Ziva. *Social Cognition: Making Sense of People*. Cambridge MA: MIT Press, 1999.

LaBouff, Jordan P., Wade C. Rowatt, Megan K. Johnson, and Callie Finkle. 'Differences in Attitudes toward Outgroups in Religious and Nonreligious Contexts in a Multinational Sample: A Situational Context Priming Study'. *The International Journal for the Psychology of Religion* 22, no. 1 (2012): 1–9. https://doi.org/10.1080/10508619.2012.634778.

LaFleur, William R. 'Body'. In *Critical Terms for Religious Studies*, edited by Mark C. Taylor, 36–54. Chicago: University of Chicago Press, 1998.

Lakoff, George, and Mark Johnson. *Metaphors We Live By*. Chicago: Chicago University Press, 1980.

Lakoff, George, and Mark Johnson. *Philosophy in the Flesh: The Embodied Mind and Its Challenge to Western Thought*. New York: Basic Books, 1999.

Lakoff, George, and Rafael E. Núñez. *Where Mathematics Comes From: How the Embodied Mind Brings Mathematics into Being*. New York: Basic Books, 2000.

Lamm, Julia A. *The Living God: Schleiermacher's Theological Appropriation of Spinoza*. University Park, PA: Pennsylvania State University, 1996.

Landauer, Thomas K. 'Latent Semantic Analysis (LSA), a Disembodied Learning Machine, Acquires Human Word Meaning Vicariously from Language Alone'. *Behavioral and Brain Sciences* 22, no. 4 (1999): 624–5. https://doi.org/10.1017/S0140525X99002149.

Landauer, Thomas K., and Susan T. Dumais. 'A Solution to Plato's Problem: The Latent Semantic Analysis Theory of Acquisition, Induction, and Representation of Knowledge'. *Psychological Review* 104, no. 2 (1997): 211–40.

Lang, Martin, Panagiotis Mitkidis, Radek Kundt, Aaron Nichols, Lenka Krajčíková, and Dimitris Xygalatas. 'Music as a Sacred Cue? Effects of Religious Music on Moral Behavior'. *Frontiers in Psychology* 7, no. 814 (2016).

Lawrence, Louise J. 'Disease and Disability Metaphors in Gospel Worlds'. *Interpretation* 73, no. 4 (2019): 377–85. https://doi.org/10.1177/0020964319857608.

Lee, Dorothy Ann. *The Symbolic Narratives of the Fourth Gospel: The Interplay of Form and Meaning*. Edited by Stanley E. Porter, *Journal for the Study of the New Testament: Supplement Series*. Sheffield: JSOT Press, 1994.

Lee, Spike W. S., and Norbert Schwarz. 'Dirty Hands and Dirty Mouths: Embodiment of the Moral-Purity Metaphor Is Specific to the Motor Modality Involved in Moral Transgression'. *Psychological Science* 21, no. 10 (2010): 1423–5. https://doi.org/10.1177/0956797610382788.

Lindbeck, George A. *The Nature of Doctrine: Religion and Theology in a Postliberal Age*. London: SPCK, 1984.

Lindemann, Oliver, Prisca Stenneken, Hein T. van Schie, and Harold Bekkering. 'Semantic Activation in Action Planning'. *Journal of Experimental Psychology: Human Perception & Performance* 32, no. 3 (2006): 633–43.

Lois-González, Rubén C., and Xosé M. Santos. 'Tourists and Pilgrims on Their Way to Santiago. Motives, Caminos and Final Destinations'. *Journal of Tourism and Cultural Change* 13, no. 2 (2015): 149–64. https://doi.org/10.1080/14766825.2014.918985.

Longfellow, Erica, and Elisabeth Dutton. 'Paradise Lost: A Staged Reading in the Chapel of New College, Oxford'. *Milton Quarterly* 49, no. 3 (2015): 208–14. https://doi.org/10.1111/milt.12138.

Lorenzen, Thorwald. 'The Meaning of the Death of Jesus'. *American Baptist Quarterly* 4, no. 1 (1985): 3–34.

Luhrmann, T. M. *When God Talks Back: Understanding the American Evangelical Relationship with God*. New York: Alfred A. Knopf, 2012.

Lynott, Dermot, Katherine S. Corker, Jessica Wortman, Louise Connell, M. Brent Donnellan, Richard E. Lucas, and Kerry O'Brien. 'Replication of "Experiencing Physical Warmth Promotes Interpersonal Warmth" by Williams and Bargh (2008)'. *Social Psychology* 45, no. 3 (2014): 216–22. https://doi.org/10.1027/1864-9335/a000187.

Lynott, Dermot, and Kenny Coventry. 'On the Ups and Downs of Emotion: Testing between Conceptual-Metaphor and Polarity Accounts of Emotional Valence-Spatial Location Interactions'. *Psychonomic Bulletin & Review* 21, no. 1 (2014): 218–26. https://doi.org/10.3758/s13423-013-0481-5.

Macht, Michael. 'How Emotions Affect Eating: A Five-Way Model'. *Appetite* 50, no. 1 (2008): 1–11. https://doi.org/10.1016/j.appet.2007.07.002.

Macht, Michael, and G. Simons. 'Emotions and Eating in Everyday Life'. *Appetite* 35, no. 1 (2000): 65–71. https://doi.org/10.1006/appe.2000.0325.

Macquarrie, John. *Principles of Christian Theology, Library of Philosophy and Theology*. London: SCM, 1966.

Macrae, C. Neil, Oonagh K. Duffy, Lynden K. Miles, and Julie Lawrence. 'A Case of Hand Waving: Action Synchrony and Person Perception'. *Cognition* 109, no. 1 (2008): 152–6. https://doi.org/10.1016/j.cognition.2008.07.007.

Madsen, William G. 'Earth the Shadow of Heaven: Typological Symbolism in Paradise Lost'. *PMLA* 75, no. 5 (1960): 519–26. https://doi.org/10.2307/460663.

Maimonides, Moses. *The Guide for the Perplexed*. Translated by M. Friedländer. Skokie, IL: Varda, 2002.

Malafouris, Lambros. *How Things Shape the Mind: A Theory of Material Management*. Cambridge, MA: MIT Press, 2013.

Malhorta, Deepak. '(When) Are Religious People Nicer? Religious Salience and the "Sunday Effect" on Pro-Social Behavior'. *Judgment and Decision Making* 5, no. 2 (2010): 138–43.

Marsh, Kerry L., Michael J. Richardson, and R. C. Schmidt. 'Social Connection through Joint Action and Interpersonal Coordination'. *Topics in Cognitive Science* 1, no. 2 (2009): 320–39. https://doi.org/10.1111/j.1756-8765.2009.01022.x.

Martin, Alex, Cheri L. Wiggs, Leslie G. Ungerleider, and James V. Haxby. 'Neural Correlates of Category-Specific Knowledge'. *Nature* 379, no. 6566 (1996): 649–52. https://doi.org/10.1038/379649a0.

Masson, Robert. *Without Metaphor, No Saving God: Theology after Cognitive Linguistics, Studies in Philosophical Theology*. Leuven, Belgium: Peeters, 2014.

McCabe, Herbert, and Brian Davies. 'God and Creation'. *New Blackfriars* 94, no. 1052 (2013): 385–95. https://doi.org/10.1111/j.1741-2005.2012.01486.x.

McCauley, Robert N. 'Ritual, Memory, and Emotion: Comparing Two Cognitive Hypotheses'. In *Religion in Mind: Cognitive Perspectives on Religious Belief, Ritual and Experience*, edited by Jensine Andresen, 115–40. Cambridge: Cambridge University Press, 2001.

McCauley, Robert N. *Why Religion Is Natural and Science Is Not*. Oxford: Oxford University Press, 2011.

McCluskey, Stephen C. 'Orientation of Christian Churches'. In *Handbook of Archaeoastronomy and Ethnoastronomy*, edited by Clive L. N. Ruggles, 1703–10. New York: Springer, 2015.

McFague, Sallie. *Metaphorical Theology: Models of God in Religious Language*. Philadelphia: Fortress Press, 1982.

McFarland, Ian A. 'Accommodation'. In *The Cambridge dictionary of Christian theology*, edited by Ian A. McFarland, Iain R. Torrance, and Karen Kilby, 2. Cambridge: Cambridge University Press, 2011.

McGilchrist, Iain. *The Master and His Emissary: The Divided Brain and the Making of the Western World*. New Haven, CT: Yale University Press, 2009.

McGrath, Alister E. *Science and Religion: An Introduction*. Oxford: Blackwell Publishers, 1999.

McGrath, Alister E. *Historical Theology: An Introduction to the History of Christian Thought*. Second ed. Hoboken: John Wiley & Sons, 2012.

McKinney, Mark E., Robert J. Gatchel, Donald Brantley, and Rick Harrington. 'The Impact of Biofeedback-Manipulated Physiological Change on Emotional State'. *Basic & Applied Social Psychology* 1, no. 1 (1980): 15–21.

McKinsey, Michael. *Skepticism and Content Externalism* 2018 [cited 10 October 2021]. Available from https://plato.stanford.edu/archives/win2021/entries/embodied-cognition/.

Meeks, Wayne A. 'The Man from Heaven in Johannine Sectarianism'. *Journal of Biblical Literature* 91, no. 1 (1972): 44–72. https://doi.org/10.2307/3262920.

Meier, B. P., and M. D. Robinson. 'Why the Sunny Side Is Up: Association between Affect and Vertical Position'. *Psychological Science* 15, no. 4 (2004): 243–7. https://doi.org/10.1111/j.0956-7976.2004.00659.x.

Meier, Brian P., David J. Hauser, Michael D. Robinson, Chris Kelland Friesen, and Katie Schjeldahl. 'What's "Up" with God? Vertical Space as a Representation of the Divine'. *Journal of Personality & Social Psychology* 93, no. 5 (2007): 699–710.

Mekawi, Yara, and Konrad Bresin. 'Is the Evidence from Racial Bias Shooting Task Studies a Smoking Gun? Results from a Meta-Analysis'. *Journal of Experimental Social Psychology* 61 (2015): 120–30.

Menary, Richard. 'Introduction to the Special Issue on 4e Cognition'. *Phenomenology and the Cognitive Sciences* 9, no. 4 (2010): 459–63. https://doi.org/10.1007/s11097-010-9187-6.

Merleau-Ponty, Maurice. *Phenomenology of Perception*. Edited by Colin Smith, *International Library of Philosophy and Scientific Method*. London: Routledge, 1962.

Merleau-Ponty, Maurice. *The Visible and the Invisible*. Edited by Claude Lefort, Alphonso Lingis and Klod Lëfor, *Northwestern University Studies in Phenomenology & Existential Philosophy*. Evanston IL: Northwestern University Press, 1968.

Milton, John. *Paradise Lost*. Edited by Stephen Orgel, Jonathan Goldberg, and Philip Pullman. Oxford: Oxford University Press, 2005.

Morris Hargreaves McIntyre. ' "Art, Spirituality and Power": An Evaluation of Treasures of Heaven: Saints, Relics and Devotion in Medieval Europe at the British Museum'. British Museum, 2011. http://www.britishmuseum.org/pdf/British_Museum_treasures-of-heaven-exhibitionevaluation_2011.pdf.

Moussaieff, Arieh, Neta Rimmerman, Tatiana Bregman, Alex Straiker, Christian C. Felder, Shai Shoham, Yoel Kashman, Susan M. Huang, Hyosang Lee, Esther Shohami, Ken Mackie, Michael J. Caterina, J. Michael Walker, Ester Fride, and Raphael Mechoulam.

'Incensole Acetate, an Incense Component, Elicits Psychoactivity by Activating TRPV3 Channels in the Brain'. *The FASEB Journal* 22, no. 8 (2008): 3024–34. https://doi.org/10.1096/fj.07-101865.

Muis, Jan. 'Can Christian Talk About God Be Literal?' *Modern Theology* 27, no. 4 (2011): 582–607. https://doi.org/10.1111/j.1468-0025.2011.01704.x.

Murphy, Nancey C. *Bodies and Souls, or Spirited Bodies?, Current Issues in Theology.* Cambridge: Cambridge University Press, 2006.

Myung, Jong-yoon, Sheila E. Blumstein, and Julie C. Sedivy. 'Playing on the Typewriter, Typing on the Piano: Manipulation Knowledge of Objects'. *Cognition* 98, no. 3 (2006): 223–43. https://doi.org/10.1016/j.cognition.2004.11.010.

Nagel, Thomas. 'What Is It Like to Be a Bat?' *The Philosophical Review* 83, no. 4 (1974): 435–50. https://doi.org/10.2307/2183914.

Neisser, Ulric, and Eugene Winograd. *Affect and Accuracy in Recall: Studies of "Flashbulb" Memories, Emory Symposia in Cognition.* Cambridge: Cambridge University Press, 1992.

Norris, Rebecca Sachs. 'Religion, Neuroscience and Emotion: Some Implications of Consumerism and Entertainment Culture'. In *Religion and the Body: Modern Science and the Construction of Religious Meaning*, edited by David Cave and Rebecca Sachs Norris, 105–28. Leiden: Brill, 2012.

Norton, Michael I., and Francesca Gino. 'Rituals Alleviate Grieving for Loved Ones, Lovers, and Lotteries'. *Journal of Experimental Psychology: General* 143, no. 1 (2014): 266–72.

Nowak, Martin A., and Karl Sigmund. 'Evolution of Indirect Reciprocity by Image Scoring'. *Nature* 393, no. 6685 (1998): 573–7. https://doi.org/10.1038/31225.

Nussbaum, Martha Craven. 'Love's Knowledge'. In *Love's Knowledge: Essays on Philosophy and Literature*, 261–85. Oxford: Oxford University Press, 1992.

Nussbaum, Martha Craven. *Upheavals of Thought: The Intelligence of Emotions.* Cambridge: Cambridge University Press, 2001.

Nussbaum, Martha Craven. *Hiding from Humanity: Disgust, Shame, and the Law.* Princeton, NJ: Princeton University Press, 2004.

O'Neill, Mary. 'Female Embodiment and the Incarnation'. In *Themes in Feminist Theology for the New Millennium (I)*, edited by F. Eigo, 35–66. Villanova, PA: Villanova University Press, 2002.

Origen. *Homilies Sur Jérémie.* Translated by P. Husson. Edited by Henri de Lubac and J. Daniélou. Vol. 238, *Sources Chrétiennes.* Paris, 1977.

Orsi, Robert A. 'Roundtable on Ethnography and Religion: Doing Religious Studies with Your Whole Body'. *Practical Matters* 2 (2013): 1–6.

Paladino, Maria-Paola, Mara Mazzurega, Francesco Pavani, and Thomas W. Schubert. 'Synchronous Multisensory Stimulation Blurs Self-Other Boundaries'. *Psychological Science* 21, no. 9 (2010): 1202–7. https://doi.org/10.1177/0956797610379234.

Park, Lora E., Lindsey Streamer, Li Huang, and Adam D. Galinsky. 'Stand Tall, but Don't Put Your Feet Up: Universal and Culturally-Specific Effects of Expansive Postures on Power'. *Journal of Experimental Social Psychology* 49, no. 6 (2013): 965–71. https://doi.org/10.1016/j.jesp.2013.06.001.

Pascal, Blaise. *Pensées and Other Writings.* Edited by Anthony Levi and Honor Levi, *Oxford World's Classics.* Oxford: Oxford University Press, 2008.

Peirce, Charles S. *The Writings of Charles S. Peirce: A Chronological Edition.* Edited by Edward C. Moore. Vol. 2. Bloomington IA: Indiana University Press, 1984.

Pellegrino, G., L. Fadiga, L. Fogassi, V. Gallese, and G. Rizzolatti. 'Understanding Motor Events: A Neurophysiological Study'. *Experimental Brain Research* 91, no. 1 (1992): 176–80. https://doi.org/10.1007/bf00230027.

Penfield, Wilder, and Edwin Boldrey. 'Somatic Motor and Sensory Representation in the Cerebral Cortex of Man as Studied by Electrical Stimulation'. *Brain* 60, no. 4 (1937): 389–443. https://doi.org/10.1093/brain/60.4.389.

Percy, Martyn. 'Adventure and Atrophy in a Charismatic Movement: Returning to the "Toronto Blessing"'. *Journal of Contemporary Religion* 20, no. 1 (2005): 71–90. https://doi.org/10.1080/135379000313918.

Pettersen, Alvyn. *Athanasius*. London: Geoffrey Chapman, 1995.

Pichon, Isabelle, and Vassilis Saroglou. 'Religion and Helping: Impact of Target Thinking Styles and Just-World Beliefs'. *Archive for the Psychology of Religion* 31, no. 2 (2009): 215–36.

Pickard, Stephen. *Seeking the Church: An Introduction to Ecclesiology*. London: SCM, 2012.

Piff, Paul K., Pia Dietze, Matthew Feinberg, Daniel M. Stancato, and Dacher Keltner. 'Awe, the Small Self, and Prosocial Behavior'. *Journal of Personality & Social Psychology* 108, no. 6 (2015): 883–99. https://doi.org/10.1037/pspi0000018.

Pollitt, Ernesto, Nita L. Lewis, Cutberto Garza, and Robert J. Shulman. 'Fasting and Cognitive Function'. *Journal of Psychiatric Research* 17, no. 2 (1982): 169–74. https://doi.org/10.1016/0022-3956(82)90018-8.

Pope Francis. 'Encyclical Letter Laudato Si' of the Holy Father Francis on the Care for Our Common Home'. Vatican, Rome: The Holy See, 2015.

Pope Paul VI. 'Dogmatic Constitution on the Church: Lumen Gentium'. Vatican, Rome: The Holy See, 1964. http://www.vatican.va/archive/hist_councils/ii_vatican_council/documents/vatii_const_19641121_lumen-gentium_en.html#.

Preissl, Hubert, Friedemann Pulvermüller, Werner Lutzenberger, and Niels Birbaumer. 'Evoked Potentials Distinguish between Nouns and Verbs'. *Neuroscience Letters* 197, no. 1 (1995): 81–3. https://doi.org/10.1016/0304-3940(95)11892-Z.

Prenter, Regin. 'Dietrich Bonhoeffer and Karl Barth's Positivism of Revelation'. In *World Come of Age*, edited by Ronald Gregor Smith, 93–130. Philadephia: Fortress Press, 1967.

Preston, Jesse Lee, and Ryan S. Ritter. 'Cleanliness and Godliness: Mutual Association between Two Kinds of Personal Purity'. *Journal of Experimental Social Psychology* 48, no. 6 (2012): 1365–8. https://doi.org/10.1016/j.jesp.2012.05.015.

Preston, Jesse Lee, and Ryan S. Ritter. 'Different Effects of Religion and God on Prosociality with the Ingroup and Outgroup'. *Personality and Social Psychology Bulletin* 39, no. 11 (2013): 1471–83.

Prinz, Jesse J. *Furnishing the Mind: Concepts and Their Perceptual Basis*. Cambridge, MA: MIT Press, 2002.

Prinz, Jesse J. *Gut Reactions: A Perceptual Theory of Emotion*. Oxford: Oxford University Press, 2004.

Procter-Smith, Marjorie. *In Her Own Rite: Constructing Feminist Liturgical Tradition*. Nashville: Abingdon Press, 1990.

Pulvermüller, Friedemann. 'Brain Mechanisms Linking Language and Action'. *Nature Reviews Neuroscience* 6, no. 7 (2005): 576–82. http://dx.doi.org/10.1038/nrn1706.

Pulvermüller, Friedemann. 'Grounding Language in the Brain'. In *Symbols and Embodiment: Debates on Meaning and Cognition*, edited by Manuel De Vega, Arthur M. Glenberg, and Arthur C. Graesser, 85–116. Oxford: Oxford University Press, 2008.

Pulvermüller, Friedemann, Olaf Hauk, Vadim V. Nikulin, and Risto J. Ilmoniemi. 'Functional Links between Motor and Language Systems'. *European Journal of Neuroscience* 21, no. 3 (2005): 793–7. https://doi.org/10.1111/j.1460-9568.2005.03900.x.

Pulvermüller, Friedemann, Werner Lutzenberger, and Hubert Preissl. 'Nouns and Verbs in the Intact Brain: Evidence from Event-Related Potentials and High-Frequency Cortical Responses'. *Cerebral Cortex* 9, no. 5 (1999): 497–506. https://doi.org/10.1093/cercor/9.5.497.

Pulvermüller, Friedemann, Yury Shtyrov, and Risto Ilmoniemi. 'Brain Signatures of Meaning Access in Action Word Recognition'. *Journal of Cognitive Neuroscience* 17, no. 6 (2005): 884–92. https://doi.org/10.1162/0898929054021111.

Putnam, Hilary. 'Brains in a Vat'. In *Reason, Truth and History*, 1–21. Cambridge: Cambridge University Press, 1981.

Pyysiäinen, Ilkka. 'Introduction: Cognition and Culture in the Construction of Religion'. In *Current Approaches in the Cognitive Science of Religion*, edited by Ilkka Pyysiäinen and Veikko Anttonen, 1–13. London: Continuum, 2002.

Rahner, Karl. 'The "Spiritual Senses" According to Origen'. In *Theological Investigations*, 81–103. London: Darton, Longman and Todd, 1979.

Rahner, Karl. 'The Body in the Order of Salvation'. In *Theological Investigations*, 71–89. London: Darton, Longman and Todd, 1981.

Rahner, Karl. *God and Revelation*. Vol. 18, *Theological Investigations*. London: Darton, Longman and Todd, 1983.

Rahner, Karl. *Foundations of Christian Faith: An Introduction to the Idea of Christianity*. Edited by William V. Dych. New York: Crossroad, 1997.

Ranehill, Eva, Anna Dreber, Magnus Johannesson, Susanne Leiberg, Sunhae Sul, and Roberto A. Weber. 'Assessing the Robustness of Power Posing'. *Psychological Science* 26, no. 5 (2015): 653–6. https://doi.org/10.1177/0956797614553946.

Ransom, Michael R., and Mark D. Alicke. 'On Bended Knee: Embodiment and Religious Judgements'. *Current Research in Social Psychology* 21, no. 9 (2013).

Reddish, Paul, Eddie M. W. Tong, Jonathan Jong, Jonathan A. Lanman, and Harvey Whitehouse. 'Collective Synchrony Increases Prosociality Towards Non-Performers and Outgroup Members'. *British Journal of Social Psychology* 55, no. 4 (2016): 1–17. https://doi.org/10.1111/bjso.12165.

Rescorla, Michael. *The Computational Theory of Mind* 2015 [cited 2 April 2016]. Available from https://plato.stanford.edu/archives/spr2017/entries/computational-mind/.

Rikhof, Herwi. *The Concept of Church: A Methodological Inquiry into the Use of Metaphors in Ecclesiology*. London: Sheed and Ward, 1981.

Riskind, John H. 'Nonverbal Expressions and the Accessibility of Life Experience Memories: A Congruence Hypothesis'. *Social Cognition* 2, no. 1 (1983): 62–86. https://doi.org/10.1521/soco.1983.2.1.62.

Riskind, John H., and Carolyn C. Gotay. 'Physical Posture: Could It Have Regulatory or Feedback Effects on Motivation and Emotion?' *Motivation and Emotion* 6, no. 3 (1982): 273–98. https://doi.org/10.1007/bf00992249.

Ritchie, Sarah Lane. 'Integrated Physicality and the Absence of God: Spiritual Technologies in Theological Context'. *Modern Theology* 37, no. 2 (2021): 296–315. https://doi.org/10.1111/moth.12684.

Rivera, Mayra. *Poetics of the Flesh*. Durham, NC: Duke University Press, 2015.

Rizzolatti, Giacomo, and Laila Craighero. 'The Mirror-Neuron System'. *Annual Review of Neuroscience* 27, no. 1 (2004): 169–92. https://doi.org/10.1146/annurev.neuro.27.070203.144230.

Robbins, Philip, and Murat Aydede, eds. *The Cambridge Handbook of Situated Cognition*, *Handbook of Situated Cognition*. Cambridge: Cambridge University Press, 2009.

Rosch, Eleanor H. 'Natural Categories'. *Cognitive Psychology* 4, no. 3 (1973): 328–50. https://doi.org/10.1016/0010-0285(73)90017-0.

Rosch, Eleanor, Carolyn B. Mervis, Wayne D. Gray, David M. Johnson, and Penny Boyes-Braem. 'Basic Objects in Natural Categories'. *Cognitive Psychology* 8, no. 3 (1976): 382–439. https://doi.org/10.1016/0010-0285(76)90013-X.

Ross, Susan A. 'God's Embodiment and Women'. In *Freeing Theology: The Essentials of Theology in Feminist Perspective*, edited by Catherine Mowry LaCugna, 185–210. San Francisco: Harper, 1993.

Ross, Susan A., and Mary Catherine Hilkert. 'Feminist Theology: A Review of Literature'. *Theological Studies* 56, no. 2 (1995): 327–52. https://doi.org/10.1177/004056399505600206.

Roy, Deb. 'A Mechanistic Model of Three Facets of Meaning'. In *Symbols and Embodiment: Debates on Meaning and Cognition*, edited by Manuel De Vega, Arthur M. Glenberg, and Arthur C. Graesser, 195–222. Oxford: Oxford University Press, 2008.

Rudd, Melanie, Kathleen D. Vohs, and Jennifer Aaker. 'Awe Expands People's Perception of Time, Alters Decision Making, and Enhances Well-Being'. *Psychological Science* 23, no. 10 (2012): 1130–6. https://doi.org/10.1177/0956797612438731.

Rudy, Kathryn M. 'Dirty Books: Quantifying Patterns of Use in Medieval Manuscripts Using a Densitometer'. *Journal of Historians of Netherlandish Art* 2, no. 1–2 (2010). https://doi.org/10.5092/jhna.2010.2.1.1.

Rudy, Kathryn M. 'Kissing Images, Unfurling Rolls, Measuring Wounds, Sewing Badges and Carrying Talismans: Considering Some Harley Manuscripts through the Physical Rituals They Reveal'. *Electronic British Library Journal* (2011): 1–56. https://doi.org/10.23636/979.

Rudy, Kathryn M. 'Virtual Pilgrimage through the Jerusalem Cityscape'. In *Visual Constructs of Jerusalem*, edited by Bianca Kühnel, Galit Noga-Banai, and Hanna Vorholt, 381–93. Turnhout, Belgium: Brepols, 2014.

Rudy, Kathryn M. 'Sewing the Body of Christ: Eucharist Wafer Souvenirs Stitched into Fifteenth-Century Manuscripts, Primarily in the Netherlands'. *Journal of Historians of Netherlandish Art* 8, no. 1 (2016): 1–47. https://doi.org/10.5092/jhna.2016.8.1.1.

Ruether, Rosemary Radford. *To Change the World: Christology and Cultural Criticism.* London: SCM, 1981.

Ruether, Rosemary Radford. *Women-Church: Theology and Practice of Feminist Liturgical Communities.* San Francisco: Harper & Row, 1985.

Rutchick, Abraham M. 'Deus Ex Machina: The Influence of Polling Place on Voting Behavior'. *Political Psychology* 31, no. 2 (2010): 209–25. https://doi.org/10.1111/j.1467-9221.2009.00749.x.

Rybanska, Veronika, Ryan McKay, Jonathan Jong, and Harvey Whitehouse. 'Rituals Improve Children's Ability to Delay Gratification'. *Child Development* 89, no. 1 (2017). https://doi.org/10.1111/cdev.12762.

Sacchett, Carol, and Glyn W. Humphreys. 'Calling a Squirrel a Squirrel but a Canoe a Wigwam: A Category-Specific Deficit for Artefactual Objects and Body Parts'. *Cognitive Neuropsychology* 9, no. 1 (1992): 73–86. https://doi.org/10.1080/02643299208252053.

Sanders, John. *Theology in the Flesh: How Embodiment and Culture Shape the Way We Think About Truth, Morality and God.* Minneapolis: Fortress Press, 2016.

Saroglou, Vassilis, Olivier Corneille, and Patty Van Cappellen. ' "Speak, Lord, Your Servant Is Listening": Religious Priming Activates Submissive Thoughts and Behaviors'. *International Journal for the Psychology of Religion* 19, no. 3 (2009): 143–54. https://doi.org/10.1080/10508610902880063.

Sassin Allen, Anne. 'Church Orientation in the Landscape: A Perspective from Medieval Wales'. *Archaeological Journal* 173, no. 1 (2016): 154–87. https://doi.org/10.1080/00665983.2016.1110781.

Scarlat, Paul. 'Embodied Cognition of Religion and Christian Orthodox Tradition'. *Ortodoxia* 3 (2016): 156–76.

Schab, Frank R. 'Odor Memory: Taking Stock'. *Psychological Bulletin* 109, no. 2 (1991): 242–51.

Schaefer, Donovan O. *Religious Affects: Animality, Evolution, and Power.* Durham: Duke University Press, 2015.

Scharen, Christian. 'Ecclesiology "from the Body": Ethnographic Notes toward a Carnal Theology'. In *Perspectives on Ecclesiology and Ethnography*, edited by Pete Ward, 50–70. Grand Rapids MI: Eerdmans, 2012.

Schilbach, Leonhard, Bert Timmermans, Vasudevi Reddy, Alan Costall, Gary Bente, Tobias Schlicht, and Kai Vogeley. 'Toward a Second-Person Neuroscience'. *Behavioral and Brain Sciences* 36, no. 4 (2013): 393–414. https://doi.org/10.1017/S0140525X12000660.

Schleiermacher, Friedrich. *The Christian Faith.* Edited by H. R. Mackintosh and J. S. Stewart. Edinburgh: T&T Clark, 1928.

Schleiermacher, Friedrich. 'Selections from the First Edition of F. D. E. Schleiermacher's Christian Belief'. In *Hegel, Hinrichs, and Schleiermacher on Feeling and Reason in Religion*, edited by Eric von der Luft. Lewiston: Edwin Mellen Press, 1987.

Schleiermacher, Friedrich. *On Religion: Speeches to Its Cultured Despisers.* Translated by Richard Crouter. Edited by Karl Ameriks and Desmond M. Clarke, *Cambridge Texts in the History of Philosophy*. Cambridge: Cambridge University Press, 1996.

Schnall, Simone, Jennifer Benton, and Sophie Harvey. 'With a Clean Conscience: Cleanliness Reduces the Severity of Moral Judgments'. *Psychological Science* 19, no. 12 (2008): 1219–22. https://doi.org/10.1111/j.1467-9280.2008.02227.x.

Schnall, Simone, Jonathan Haidt, Gerald L. Clore, and Alexander H. Jordan. 'Disgust as Embodied Moral Judgment'. *Personality and Social Psychology Bulletin* 34, no. 8 (2008): 1096–109. https://doi.org/10.1177/0146167208317771.

Schoel, Christiane, Jennifer Eck, and Rainer Greifeneder. 'A Matter of Vertical Position'. *Social Psychological and Personality Science* 5, no. 2 (2013): 149–57. https://doi.org/10.1177/1948550613488953.

Schubert, Thomas W. 'Your Highness: Vertical Positions as Perceptual Symbols of Power'. *Journal of Personality & Social Psychology* 89, no. 1 (2005): 1–21.

Schubert, Thomas W., and Gün R. Semin. 'Embodiment as a Unifying Perspective for Psychology'. *European Journal of Social Psychology* 39, no. 7 (2009): 1135–41. https://doi.org/10.1002/ejsp.670.

Schumacher, Michele 'Feminist Christologies'. In *The Oxford Handbook of Christology*, edited by Francesca Murphy: Oxford University Press, 2015.

Scorolli, Claudia. 'Action, Perception and Language'. *Rivista Italiana di Filosofia del Linguaggio* 5 (2012): 1–6.

Searle, John. 'Minds, Brains and Programs'. *Behavioral and Brain Sciences* 3 (1980): 417–57. https://doi.org/10.1017/S0140525X00005781.

Sereno, Sara C., Keith Rayner, and Michael I. Posner. 'Establishing a Time-Line of Word Recognition: Evidence from Eye Movements and Event-Related Potentials'. *Neuroreport* 9, no. 10 (1998): 2195–200.

Shapiro, Lawrence A. 'The Embodied Cognition Research Programme'. *Philosophy Compass* 2, no. 2 (2007): 338–46. https://doi.org/10.1111/j.1747-9991.2007.00064.x.

Shapiro, Lawrence A. 'Symbolism, Embodied Cognition, and the Broader Debate'. In *Symbols and Embodiment: Debates on Meaning and Cogntion*, edited by Manuel De Vega, Arthur M. Glenberg, and Arthur C. Graesser, 57–74. Oxford: Oxford University Press, 2008.

Shapiro, Lawrence A. *Embodied Cognition, New Problems of Philosophy.* New York: Routledge, 2011.

Shapiro, Lawrence A, ed. *The Routledge Handbook of Embodied Cognition.* London: Routledge, 2014.

Shapiro, Lawrence A., and Shannon Spaulding. *Embodied Cognition* 2021 [cited 20 October 2021]. Available from https://plato.stanford.edu/archives/win2021/entries/embodied-cognition/.

Shariff, Azim F., Aiyana K. Willard, Teresa Andersen, and Ara Norenzayan. 'Religious Priming: A Meta-Analysis with a Focus on Prosociality'. *Personality and Social Psychology Review* 20, no. 1 (2016): 27–48. https://doi.org/10.1177/1088868314568811.

Sheldrake, Philip F. 'A Spiritual City? Place, Memory, and City Making'. In *Architecture, Ethics, and the Personhood of Place*, edited by Gregory Caicco, 50–68. London: University Press of New England, 2007.

Sheridan, Jenny, and Glyn W. Humphreys. 'A Verbal-Semantic Category-Specific Recognition Impairment'. *Cognitive Neuropsychology* 10, no. 2 (1993): 143–84. https://doi.org/10.1080/02643299308253459.

Shiota, Michelle N., Dacher Keltner, and Amanda Mossman. 'The Nature of Awe: Elicitors, Appraisals, and Effects on Self-Concept'. *Cognition and Emotion* 21, no. 5 (2007): 944–63. https://doi.org/10.1080/02699930600923668.

Silveri, M. Caterina, and G. Gainotti. 'Interaction between Vision and Language in Category-Specific Semantic Impairment'. *Cognitive Neuropsychology* 5, no. 6 (1988): 677–709. https://doi.org/10.1080/02643298808253278.

Skinner, Burrhus Frederic. *Verbal Behavior, Century Psychology Series*. New York: Appleton-Century-Crofts, 1957.

Sloboda, John A. *Exploring the Musical Mind: Cognition, Emotion, Ability, Function*. Oxford: Oxford University Press, 2005.

Slone, D Jason. *Theological Incorrectness: Why Religious People Believe What They Shouldn't*. Oxford: Oxford University Press, 2004.

Smith, James K. A. *Desiring the Kingdom: Worship, Worldview, and Cultural Formation, Cultural Liturgies*. Grand Rapids, MI: Baker Academic, 2009.

Smith, James K. A. *Imagining the Kingdom: How Worship Works, Cultural Liturgies*. Grand Rapids, MI: Baker Academic, 2013.

Snowdon, David A. 'Aging and Alzheimer's Disease: Lessons from the Nun Study'. *The Gerontologist* 37, no. 2 (1997): 150–6. https://doi.org/10.1093/geront/37.2.150.

Sokolowski, Robert. *The God of Faith and Reason: Foundations of Christian Theology*. Washington, DC: Catholic University of America Press, 1995.

Soliman, Tamer M., Kathryn A. Johnson, and Hyunjin Song. 'It's Not "All in Your Head": Understanding Religion from an Embodied Cognition Perspective'. *Perspectives on Psychological Science* 10, no. 6 (2015): 852–64. https://doi.org/10.1177/1745691615606373.

Sorrentino, Sergio. 'Feeling as a Key Notion in a Transcendental Conception of Religion'. In *Schleiermacher, the Study of Religion, and the Future of Theology: A Transatlantic Dialogue*, edited by Brent W. Sockness and Wilhelm Gräb, 97–108. Berlin: Walter De Gruyter, 2010.

Sosis, Richard, and Candace Alcorta. 'Signaling, Solidarity, and the Sacred: The Evolution of Religious Behavior'. *Evolutionary Anthropology: Issues, News, and Reviews* 12, no. 6 (2003): 264–74. https://doi.org/10.1002/evan.10120.

Sosis, Richard, and Jordan Kiper. 'Religion Is More Than Belief: What Evolutionary Theories of Religion Tell Us About Religious Commitments'. In *Challenges to Moral and Religious Belief: Disagreement and Evolution*, edited by Michael Bergmann and Patrick Kain, 256–76. Oxford: Oxford University Press, 2014.

Soskice, Janet Martin. 'Can a Feminist Call God "Father"?' In *Women's Voices: Essays in Contemporary Feminist Theology*, edited by Teresa Elwes, 15–29. New York: Marshall Pickering, 1992.

Spinazzè, Eva. 'The Alignment of Medieval Churches in Northern-Central Italy and in the Alps and the Path of Light inside the Church on the Patron Saint's Day'. *Mediterranean Archaeology and Archaeometry* 16, no. 4 (2016): 455–63. https://doi.org/10.5281/zenodo.220970.

Steels, Luc. 'The Symbol Grounding Problem Has Been Solved, So What's Next?' In *Symbols and Embodiment: Debates on Meaning and Cognition*, edited by Manuel De Vega, Arthur M. Glenberg, and Arthur C. Graesser, 223–44. Oxford: Oxford University Press, 2008.

Stepper, Sabine, and Fritz Strack. 'Proprioceptive Determinants of Emotional and Nonemotional Feelings'. *Journal of Personality and Social Psychology* 64, no. 2 (1993): 211–20. https://doi.org/10.1037/0022-3514.64.2.211.

Sterelny, Kim. 'Minds: Extended or Scaffolded?' *Phenomenology and the Cognitive Sciences* 9, no. 4 (2010): 465–81. https://doi.org/10.1007/s11097-010-9174-y.

Sternberg, Robert J., and Jeffery Scott Mio. *Cognitive Psychology*. Fifth ed. Belmont, CA: Wadsworth, 2009.

Stevenson, Andrew. 'We Came Here to Remember: Using Participatory Sensory Ethnography to Explore Memory as Emplaced, Embodied Practice'. *Qualitative Research in Psychology* 11, no. 4 (2014): 335–49. https://doi.org/10.1080/14780887.2014.908990.

Storey, Simon, and Lance Workman. 'The Effects of Temperature Priming on Cooperation in the Iterated Prisoner's Dilemma'. *Evolutionary Psychology* 11, no. 1 (2013). https://doi.org/10.1177/147470491301100106.

Strack, Fritz. 'Reflection on the Smiling Registered Replication Report'. *Perspectives on Psychological Science* 11, no. 6 (2016): 929–30. https://doi.org/10.1177/1745691616674460.

Strack, Fritz, Leonard Martin, and Sabine Stepper. 'Inhibiting and Facilitating Conditions of the Human Smile: A Nonobtrusive Test of the Facial Feedback Hypothesis'. *Journal of Personality and Social Psychology* 54, no. 5 (1988): 768–77.

Sunshine, Glenn S. 'Accommodation Historically Considered'. In *The Enduring Authority of the Christian Scriptures*, edited by D.A. Carson, 238–65. Grand Rapids MI: Eerdmans, 2016.

Swinburne, Richard. *The Christian God*. Oxford: Oxford University Press, 1994.

Swinton, John. 'The Body of Christ Has Down's Syndrome: Theological Reflections on Vulnerability, Disability, and Graceful Communities'. *Journal of Pastoral Theology* 13, no. 2 (2003): 66–78. https://doi.org/10.1179/jpt.2003.13.2.006.

Swinton, John. 'On Being a Disciple When You've Forgotten Who God Is: Dementia as Time for Learning'. In *Society for the Study of Theology Annual Conference*. Nottingham, UK, 2013.

Swinton, John. 'What the Body Remembers: Theological Reflections on Dementia'. *Journal of Religion, Spirituality & Aging* 26, no. 2–3 (2014): 160–72. https://doi.org/10.1080/15528030.2013.855966.

Tan, Tobias. 'The Corporeality of Religious Experience: Embodied Cognition in Religious Practices'. In *Experience or Expression? Religious Experience Revisited*, edited by Thomas Hardke, Ulrich Schmiedel, and Tobias Tan, 207–26. Leiden: Brill, 2016.

Tanton, Tobias. 'Accommodating Embodied Thinkers'. *Modern Theology*, no. 37 (2021): 316–35.

Tanner, Kathryn. *Jesus, Humanity and the Trinity: A Brief Systematic Theology*. Minneapolis, MN: Fortress Press, 2001.

Tertullian. *On the Resurrection of the Flesh, Ante-Nicene Fatrthers*. New York: Charles Schriner's Sons, 1896.

TeSelle, Sallie McFague. 'Parable, Metaphor, and Theology'. *Journal of the American Academy of Religion* 42, no. 4 (1974): 630–45.

Tettamanti, Marco, Giovanni Buccino, Maria Cristina Saccuman, Vittorio Gallese, Massimo Danna, Paola Scifo, Ferruccio Fazio, Giacomo Rizzolatti, Stefano F. Cappa, and Daniela Perani. 'Listening to Action-Related Sentences Activates Fronto-Parietal Motor Circuits'. *Journal of Cognitive Neuroscience* 17, no. 2 (2005): 273–81. https://doi.org/10.1162/0898929053124965.

Thaler, Richard H., and Cass R. Sunstein. *Nudge: Improving Decisions About Health, Wealth, and Happiness*. New Haven CT: Yale University Press, 2008.

The Open Science Collaboration. 'Estimating the Reproducibility of Psychological Science'. *Science* 349, no. 6251 (2015). https://doi.org/10.1126/science.aac4716.

Tillich, Paul. *Dynamics of Faith*. New York: Harper & Row, 1957.

Tucker, Mike, and Rob Ellis. 'The Potentiation of Grasp Types During Visual Object Categorization'. *Visual Cognition* 8, no. 6 (2001): 769–800. https://doi.org/10.1080/13506280042000144.

Vacharkulksemsuk, Tanya, and Barbara L. Fredrickson. 'Strangers in Sync: Achieving Embodied Rapport through Shared Movements'. *Journal of Experimental Social Psychology* 48, no. 1 (2012): 399–402. https://doi.org/10.1016/j.jesp.2011.07.015.

Vainio, Olli-Pekka. *Cosmology in Theological Perspective: Understanding Our Place in the Universe*: Baker Publishing Group, 2018.

Valdesolo, Piercarlo, Jennifer Ouyang, and David DeSteno. 'The Rhythm of Joint Action: Synchrony Promotes Cooperative Ability'. *Journal of Experimental Social Psychology* 46, no. 4 (2010): 693–5. https://doi.org/10.1016/j.jesp.2010.03.004.

van Cappellen, Patty, S. Cassidy, and R. Zhang. 'Religion as an Embodied Practice: Organizing the Various Forms and Documenting the Meanings of Christian Prayer Postures'. *Psychology of Religion and Spirituality* (in press).

van Cappellen, Patty, and Megan Edwards. 'Emotion Expression in Context: Full Body Postures of Christian Prayer Orientations Compared to Specific Emotions'. *Journal of Nonverbal Behavior* 45, no. 4 (2021): 545–65. https://doi.org/10.1007/s10919-021-00370-6.

van Cappellen, Patty, and Megan E. Edwards. 'The Embodiment of Worship: Relations among Postural, Psychological, and Physiological Aspects of Religious Practice'. *Journal for the Cognitive Science of Religion* 6, no. 1–2 (2021): 56–79. https://doi.org/10.1558/jcsr.38683.

van Cappellen, Patty, Vassilis Saroglou, and Maria Toth-Gauthier. 'Religiosity and Prosocial Behavior among Churchgoers: Exploring Underlying Mechanisms'. *The International Journal for the Psychology of Religion* 26, no. 1 (2016): 19–30. https://doi.org/10.1080/10508619.2014.958004.

van Elk, Michiel, Annika Karinen, Eva Specker, Eftychia Stamkou, and Matthijs Baas. '"Standing in Awe": The Effects of Awe on Body Perception and the Relation with Absorption'. *Collabra* 2, no. 1 (2016): 1–16. https://doi.org/10.1525/collabra.36.

Varela, Francisco J., Eleanor Rosch, and Evan Thompson. *The Embodied Mind: Cognitive Science and Human Experience*. Cambridge, MA: MIT Press, 1991.

Vásquez, Manuel A. *More Than Belief: A Materialist Theory of Religion*. Oxford: Oxford University Press, 2011.

Vial, Theodore. 'Anschauung and Intuition, Again (or "We Remain Bound to the Earth")'. In *Schleiermacher, the Study of Religion, and the Future of Theology: A Transatlantic Dialogue*, edited by Brent W. Sockness and Wilhelm Gräb, 39–50. Berlin: Walter De Gruyter, 2010.

Vigliocco, Gabriella, Stavroula-Thaleia Kousta, Pasquale Anthony Della Rosa, David P. Vinson, Marco Tettamanti, Joseph T. Devlin, and Stefano F. Cappa. 'The Neural Representation of Abstract Words: The Role of Emotion'. *Cerebral Cortex* 24, no. 7 (2014): 1767–77. https://doi.org/10.1093/cercor/bht025.

Vohs, Kathleen D., Yajin Wang, Francesca Gino, and Michael I. Norton. 'Rituals Enhance Consumption'. *Psychological Science* 24, no. 9 (2013): 1714–21. https://doi.org/10.1177/0956797613478949.

von Neumann, J. *The Computer and the Brain*. New Haven: Yale University Press, 1958.

Wagenmakers, E. J., Titia Beek, Laura Dijkhoff, and Quentin F. Gronau. 'Registered Replication Report: Strack, Martin, & Stepper (1988)'. *Perspectives on Psychological Science* 11, no. 6 (2016): 917–28. https://doi.org/10.1177/1745691616674458.

Wainwright, Geoffrey. *Doxology: The Praise of God in Worship, Doctrine and Life: A Systematic Theology*. New York: Oxford University Press, 1984.

Ward, Graham. 'Bodies: The Displaced Body of Jesus Christ'. In *Radical Orthodoxy: A New Theology*, edited by John Milbank, Catherine Pickstock, and Graham Ward, 163–81. London: Routledge, 1999.

Ward, Graham. *Christ and Culture, Challenges in Contemporary Theology*. Malden, MA: Blackwell, 2005.

Ward, Graham. *How the Light Gets In: Ethical Life I*. Oxford: Oxford University Press, 2016.

Ward, Pete. 'Introduction'. In *Perspectives on Ecclesiology and Ethnography*, edited by Pete Ward. Grand Rapids: Eerdmans, 2012.

Ward, Pete, ed. *Perspectives on Ecclesiology and Ethnography, Studies in Ecclesiology and Ethnography*. Grand Rapids, MI: Eerdmans, 2012.

Warrington, Elizabeth K., and Rosaleen McCarthy. 'Category Specific Access Dysphasia'. *Brain* 106, no. 4 (1983): 859–78. https://doi.org/10.1093/brain/106.4.859.

Warrington, Elizabeth K., and Rosaleen McCarthy. 'Categories of Knowledge: Further Fractionations and an Attempted Integration'. *Brain* 110, no. 5 (1987): 1273–96.

Warrington, Elizabeth K., and T. Shallice. 'Category Specific Semantic Impairments'. *Brain* 107 (1984): 829–54. https://doi.org/10.1093/brain/107.3.829.

Watts, Fraser. 'Embodied Cognition and Religion'. *Zygon* 48, no. 3 (2013): 745–58. https://doi.org/10.1111/zygo.12026.

Watts, Fraser. *A Plea for Embodied Spirituality: The Role of the Body in Religion*. London: SCM, 2021.

Webster, Gregory D., and Catherine G. Weir. 'Emotional Responses to Music: Interactive Effects of Mode, Texture, and Tempo'. *Motivation and Emotion* 29, no. 1 (2005): 19–39. https://doi.org/10.1007/s11031-005-4414-0.

Webster, John. *Barth*. 2nd ed. London: Continuum, 2004.

Wells, Gary L., and Richard E. Petty. 'The Effects of Overt Head Movements on Persuasion: Compatibility and Incompatibility of Responses'. *Basic & Applied Social Psychology* 1, no. 3 (1980): 219–30. https://doi.org/10.1207/s15324834basp0103_2.

Whaling, Frank. 'The Development of the Word "Theology"'. *Scottish Journal of Theology* 34, no. 4 (1981): 289–312.

Whitehouse, Harvey. *Modes of Religiosity: A Cognitive Theory of Religious Transmission, Cognitive Science of Religion Series*. Walnut Creek, CA: Altamira Press, 2004.

Whitehouse, Harvey. 'Cognitive Evolution and Religion; Cognition and Religious Evolution'. *Issues in Ethnology and Anthropology* 3, no. 3 (2008): 35–47. https://doi.org/10.21301/eap.v3i3.2. Wilder, Amos N. 'Mythology and the New Testament: A Review of Kerygma Und Mythos'. *Journal of Biblical Literature* 69, no. 2 (1950): 113–27. https://doi.org/10.2307/3262079.

Willander, Johan, and Maria Larsson. 'Smell Your Way Back to Childhood: Autobiographical Odor Memory'. *Psychonomic Bulletin & Review* 13, no. 2 (2006): 240–4. https://doi.org/10.3758/bf03193837.

Williams, Lawrence E., and John A. Bargh. 'Experiencing Physical Warmth Promotes Interpersonal Warmth'. *Science* 322, no. 5901 (2008): 606–7. https://doi.org/10.1126/science.1162548.

Williams, Rowan. *Silence and Honey Cakes: The Wisdom of the Desert*. Oxford: Lion, 2003.

Williams, Rowan. 'Barth on the Triune God'. In *Wrestling with Angels: Conversations in Modern Theology*, edited by Mike Higton, 106–49. London: SCM Press, 2007.

Williams, Rowan. 'The Church as Sacrament'. *International Journal for the Study of the Christian Church* 10, no. 1 (2010): 6–12. https://doi.org/10.1080/14742251003643825.

Williams, Rowan. *The Edge of Words: God and the Habits of Language*. London: Bloomsbury, 2014.

Wilson, Andrew D., and Sabrina Golonka. 'Embodied Cognition Is Not What You Think It Is'. *Frontiers in Psychology* 4, no. 58 (2013): 1–13. https://doi.org/10.3389/fpsyg.2013.00058.

Wilson, Edward O. *Sociobiology*. Abridged ed. Cambridge: Belknap Press of Harvard University Press, 1980.

Wilson, Robert A., and Lucia Foglia. *Embodied Cognition* 2011 [cited 14 January 2014]. Available from http://plato.stanford.edu/archives/fall2011/entries/embodied-cognition/.

Wilson, Robert A., and Lucia Foglia. *Embodied Cognition* 2015 [cited 9 December 2015]. Available from http://plato.stanford.edu/archives/win2015/entries/embodied-cognition/.

Wiltermuth, Scott S., and Chip Heath. 'Synchrony and Cooperation'. *Psychological Science* 20, no. 1 (2009): 1–5. https://doi.org/10.1111/j.1467-9280.2008.02253.x.

Wittgenstein, Ludwig. *Philosophical Investigations: The German Text, with a Revised English Translation*. Translated by G. E. M. Anscombe: John Wiley & Sons, 1991.

Wittgenstein, Ludwig. *Tractatus Logico-Philosophicus*. Translated by David Pears and Brian McGuinness, *Routledge Classics*. New York: Routledge, 2003.

Wolterstorff, Nicholas. 'Knowing God Liturgically'. *Journal of Analytic Theology* 4 (2016): 1–16. https://doi.org/10.12978/jat.2016-4.130818221405b.

Woollett, Katherine, and Eleanor A Maguire. 'Acquiring "the Knowledge" of London's Layout Drives Structural Brain Changes'. *Current Biology* 21, no. 24 (2011): 2109–14. https://doi.org/10.1016/j.cub.2011.11.018.

Wu, Ling-ling, and Lawrence W. Barsalou. 'Perceptual Simulation in Conceptual Combination: Evidence from Property Generation'. *Acta Psychologica* 132, no. 2 (2009): 173–89. https://doi.org/10.1016/j.actpsy.2009.02.002.

Wynn, Mark. *Emotional Experience and Religious Understanding: Integrating Perception, Conception and Feeling*. Cambridge: Cambridge University Press, 2005.

Wynn, Mark. *Faith and Place: An Essay in Embodied Religious Epistemology*. Oxford: Oxford University Press, 2009.

Xygalatas, Dimitris. 'Effects of Religious Setting on Cooperative Behavior: A Case Study from Mauritius'. *Religion, Brain & Behavior* 3, no. 2 (2013): 91–102. https://doi.org/10.1080/2153599X.2012.724547.

Xygalatas, Dimitris, and Martin Lang. 'Prosociality and Religion'. In *Religion: Mental Religion*, edited by N. Kasumi Clements, 119–33. London: Macmillan, 2016.

Young, Iris Marion. 'Throwing Like a Girl: A Phenomenology of Feminine Body Comportment Motility and Spatiality'. *Human Studies* 3, no. 2 (1980): 137–56. https://doi.org/10.2307/20008753.

Yu, Chen. 'Linking Words to World: An Embodied Perspective'. In *The Routledge Handbook of Embodied Cognition*, edited by Lawrence A. Shapiro, 139–49. London: Routledge, 2014.

Zajonc, R. B., Sheila T. Murphy, and Marita Inglehart. 'Feeling and Facial Efference: Implications of the Vascular Theory of Emotion'. *Psychological Review* 96, no. 3 (1989): 395–416.

Zhang, Yan, Jane L. Risen, and Christine Hosey. 'Reversing One's Fortune by Pushing Away Bad Luck'. *Journal of Experimental Psychology: General* 143, no. 3 (2014): 1171–84.

Zhong, Chen-Bo, and Julian House. 'Dirt, Pollution, and Purity: A Metaphoric Perspective on Morality'. In *The Power of Metaphor: Examining Its Influence on Social Life*, edited by Mark J. Landau and Michael D. Robinson, 109–31. Washington, DC: American Psychological Association, 2014.

Zhong, Chen-Bo, and Katie Liljenquist. 'Washing Away Your Sins: Threatened Morality and Physical Cleansing'. *Science* 313, no. 5792 (2006): 1451–2. https://doi.org/10.1126/science.1130726.

Zizioulas, Jean. *Being as Communion: Studies in Personhood and the Church, Contemporary Greek Theologians*. Crestwood, NY: St. Vladimir's Seminary Press, 1985.

Zwaan, Rolf A. 'Experiential Traces and Mental Simulations in Language Comprehension'. In *Symbols and Embodiment: Debates on Meaning and Cognition*, edited by Manuel De Vega, Arthur M. Glenberg and Arthur C. Graesser, 181–94. Oxford: Oxford University Press, 2008.

Zwaan, Rolf A., and Lawrence J. Taylor. 'Seeing, Acting, Understanding: Motor Resonance in Language Comprehension'. *Journal of Experimental Psychology: General* 135, no. 1 (2006): 1–11.

Index